FICTION UPDATED:
THEORIES OF FICTIONALITY, NARRATOLOGY, AND POETICS

Novels, movies, and lies – these are all fictions that provoke with their *as ifs* and *what ifs*. In response to the idea that fiction has somehow become an unfashionable topic in contemporary criticism, this volume argues that the question of fiction needs to be updated in the absence of a widely accepted theory of truth. This collection, dedicated to the noted scholar and literary critic Lubomír Doležel, covers an extensive number of theoretical and historical issues relevant to our understanding of the status of fictions – literary or not.

Fiction Updated offers approaches to fiction and poetics that, in an imaginary topography of contemporary humanities, dwell at a distance from both the mimetic theory of literature and deconstruction. The contributors introduce new perspectives to the problem of fictionality, or broaden the scope of its applications, by examining the works of such authors as Homer, Casanova, Aristotle, Woolf, Vaihinger, Borges, Kundera, Coetzee, and Bakhtin.

The collection is divided into six thematic sections. The first includes papers that attempt to approach the issue of fictionality from a philosophical perspective. The second section is also theoretical and concentrates on models. The third emphasizes the more concrete problems of fictional worlds, such as character, genre, and gender. The fourth section deals with fiction and history, while the fifth treats poetics. The last section focuses on the contribution of Lubomír Doležel to the theory of fictionality and fictional semantics.

Calin-Andrei Mihailescu is an associate professor of Spanish and Comparative Literature in the Modern Languages Department, University of Western Ontario.

Walid Hamarneh is an assistant professor in the Arabic and Comparative Literature departments, University of Texas, Austin

THEORY/CULTURE

Editors:
Linda Hutcheon, Gary Leonard, Jill Matus,
Janet Paterson, and Paul Perron

EDITED BY CALIN-ANDREI MIHAILESCU
AND WALID HAMARNEH

Fiction Updated:
Theories of Fictionality,
Narratology, and Poetics

UNIVERSITY OF TORONTO PRESS
Toronto and Buffalo

© University of Toronto Press Incorporated 1996
Toronto Buffalo London
Printed in Canada

ISBN 0-8020-0576-4 (cloth)
ISBN 0-8020-6995-9 (paper)

∞

Printed on acid-free paper

Canadian Cataloguing in Publication Data

Main entry under title:

Fiction updated: theories of fictionality, narratology, and poetics

(Theory/culture)
Some essays are rev. versions of papers presented at a
conference entitled Fictions and worlds, held at the
University of Toronto, spring, 1990.
Includes bibliographical references.
ISBN 0-8020-0576-4 (bound)   ISBN 0-8020-6995-9 (pbk.)

1. Fictions, Theory of. 2. Literature – Philosophy.
3. Literature – History and criticism – Theory, etc.
I Hamarneh, Walid, 1952–   . II. Mihailescu, Calin
Andrei, 1956–   . III. Series

PN49.F53 1996   801'.9   C95-933272-3

University of Toronto Press acknowledges the financial assistance to its publishing
program of the Canada Council and the Ontario Arts Council.

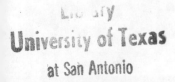

Contents

ACKNOWLEDGMENTS   vii

CONTRIBUTORS   ix

INTRODUCTION: UNDER THE JEALOUS GAZE OF TRUTH   Calin-Andrei Mihailescu and Walid Hamarneh   3

Part 1: Fictions and Philosophies   19

1 Are Fictional Worlds Possible? RUTH RONEN   21

2 Questions About the Nature of Fiction NICHOLAS RESCHER   30

3 Fortress Fiction JOHN WOODS   39

4 Literary Fictions and Philosophical Theories: The Possible-Worlds Story PETER McCORMICK   48

Part 2: Models   63

5 On Fictional Discourse FÉLIX MARTÍNEZ-BONATI   65

6 The Perception of Fictional Worlds PIERRE OUELLET   76

7 Beyond Reality and Fiction? The Fate of Dualism in the Age of (Mass) Media SIEGFRIED J. SCHMIDT   91

8 Models, Madness, and the Hereafter CESARE SEGRE   105

Part 3: Names, Genre, Gender   111

9 Characters and Their Versions URI MARGOLIN   113

10 Naming Names in Telling Tales PETER W. NESSELROTH   133

11 Fictionality, Narration, and the Question of Genres FRANCESCO LORIGGIO   144

12 Narratology, Narratological Criticism, and Gender GERALD PRINCE   159
13 The Renaissance Dialogue and Its Zero-Degree Fictionality EVA KUSHNER
    165

Part 4: Fictions and Histories   173
14 Signposts in Oral Epic: Metapragmatic and Metasemantic Signals NANCY
    FELSON-RUBIN   175
15 Of Worlds and Nutshells: On Casanova's *Icosameron* DIDIER COSTE
    187
16 Ironies of History: *The Joke* of Milan Kundera PETER STEINER   197
17 The Politics of Impossible Worlds LINDA HUTCHEON   213

Part 5: Poetics   227
18 Thoughts on Aristotle's *Poetics* UMBERTO ECO   229
19 Chronotopes in Diegesis MICHAEL RIFFATERRE   244
20 Deconstructing Bakhtin LADISLAV MATEJKA   257
21 Scratching the Bronze Mirror: Looking for Traces of Fictionality in
    Chinese Poetics DOUWE W. FOKKEMA   267
22 Formalist and Structuralist Activity in Poland: Tradition and Progress
    EDWARD MOŻEJKO   274

Part 6: Doležel and His Worlds   291
23 An Improbable Side by Side: Doležel and Borges in Prague HANS-GEORGE
    RUPRECHT   293
24 Lubomír Doležel's Contribution to Contemporary Literary Studies
    THOMAS G. PAVEL   303

    BIBLIOGRAPHY   311

Acknowledgments

This volume is dedicated to Lubomír Doležel. Most of the twenty-four essays collected here are contributions to the contemporary debates in the theory of fictionality. Others examine issues in narratology and the history of poetics (Eco, Możejko). Finally, the two papers by Pavel and Ruprecht are devoted to Lubomír Doležel's scholarship. It goes almost without saying that all the papers are linked to Doležel's intellectual interests and contributions to the development of criticism.

The project, initiated by the editors, was preceded by a conference, 'Fictions and Worlds,' devoted to Doležel and held at the University of Toronto in the spring of 1990. Most of the contributions to the volume are revised versions of the papers presented at that conference. Umberto Eco, Nancy Felson-Rubin, Douwe W. Fokkema, Félix Martínez-Bonati, Edward Możejko, Nicholas Rescher, and Cesare Segre have gracefully agreed to have their contributions added to the volume.

The theories of fictionality constitute a wide field of research rather than a discipline. The names of most of the scholars who have significantly contributed to this field appear in the table of contents of this volume. *Fiction Updated* is the document of an influential academic community whose frontiers are neither national nor political nor philosophical.

In editing this collection, we incurred some notable debts. We first of all thank Peter W. Nesselroth for his essential help and constant interest in the volume. We also thank Eva Kushner, Linda Hutcheon, and Paul Perron for their personal involvement in the process of editing and publication. Substantial financial aid to the publication of the volume has been provided by the Centre for Comparative Literature, University of Toronto, the Smallman Fund, University of Western Ontario, and also by the Department of Slavic Studies, University of Toronto. For their help in the editorial process, we thank

Christine Gosselin, Russell Kilbourn, François Lachance, Karim Mamdani, Larry Marks, and Robert Olsen.

CALIN-ANDREI MIHAILESCU
WALID HAMARNEH

LUBOMÍR DOLEŽEL

A Fellow of the Royal Society of Canada and Professor Emeritus at the University of Toronto, Dolezel received degrees from the Prague Charles University and the Czechoslovak Academy of Sciences. He has taught at the University of Toronto and the University of Prague, and has been a visiting professor at the University of Amsterdam and the University of Michigan. He is widely regarded as one of the main adherents of the Prague School and as one of the best-known proponents of statistical stylistics, narratology, poetics, and the theory of fictionality. He received the Book Prize of the Czechoslovak Academy of Sciences in 1960. In 1990 the Centre for Comparative Literature, University of Toronto, organized an international conference devoted to his work.

Contributors

DIDIER COSTE has taught French literature and Literary Theory in Paris, San Diego, Montreal, Pau, and Calaceite.

UMBERTO ECO is Professor of Semiotics at the University of Bologna.

NANCY FELSON-RUBIN is Professor of Classics at the University of Georgia.

DOUWE W. FOKKEMA is Professor of Comparative Literature at Utrecht University.

WALID HAMARNEH is Assistant Professor of Arabic and Comparative Literature at the University of Texas, Austin.

LINDA HUTCHEON is Professor of English and Comparative Literature at the University of Toronto.

EVA KUSHNER has taught French and Comparative Literature at Carleton University, McGill, University of Toronto, and Victoria College.

FRANCESCO LORIGGIO is Associate Professor of Italian and Comparative Literature at Carleton University.

URI MARGOLIN is Professor of Comparative Literature at the University of Edmonton.

LADISLAV MATEJKA is Professor Emeritus of Slavic Languages and Literatures at Indiana University, Bloomington.

FÉLIX MARTÍNEZ-BONATI teaches Spanish and Comparative Literature at Columbia University.

PETER McCORMICK is Professor of Philosophy at the University of Ottawa.

CALIN-ANDREI MIHAILESCU is Associate Professor of Spanish and Comparative Literature at the University of Western Ontario.

EDWARD MOŻEJKO is Professor of Slavic and Comparative Literature at the University of Alberta.

PETER W. NESSELROTH is Professor of French and Comparative Literature at the University of Toronto.

PIERRE OUELLET teaches in the Department of Literary Studies and in the doctoral program in semiology at the University of Quebec.

THOMAS G. PAVEL is Professor of French and Comparative Literature at Princeton University.

GERALD PRINCE is Magnin Family Term Professor of Romance Languages and co-director of the Center for Cultural Studies at the University of Pennsylvania.

NICHOLAS RESCHER is University Professor of Philosophy at the University of Pittsburgh.

MICHAEL RIFFATERRE is University Professor at Columbia University and director of the School of Criticism and Theory at Dartmouth.

RUTH RONEN is Senior Lecturer in Poetics and Comparative Literature at Tel Aviv University.

HANS-GEORGE RUPRECHT is Professor of Comparative Literature and Linguistics at Carleton University.

SIEGFRIED J. SCHMIDT is Professor of Linguistics, Literary Studies, and Media Studies at the University of Siegen.

CESARE SEGRE is Professor of Romance Philology at the University of Pavia.

PETER STEINER is Professor of Slavic Literatures at the University of Pennsylvania.

JOHN WOODS is Professor of Philosophy at Lethbridge University.

FICTION UPDATED

Introduction:
Under the Jealous Gaze of Truth

CALIN-ANDREI MIHAILESCU
AND WALID HAMARNEH

'Nobody, so far as I know, has ever tried to relate the theory of literary fictions to the theory of fictions in general, though, I think something of the sort might have been in Ogden's mind when he assembled Bentham's *Theory of Fictions*.'[1] Frank Kermode's statement, made more than a quarter of a century ago in *The Sense of an Ending* (1967, 36), has been unquestionably outdated by an impressive number of attempts to situate the fictionality of literature within the framework of the theory of fictions in general. Today one can safely talk about established, rich, and ramified contemporary research traditions dealing with the theory of literary fictions. There exists even the suspicion, voiced in this volume by Fokkema and Hutcheon, that the interest in a 'general theory of fiction' may be considered as *déjà passé*.[2]

In the present context of literary theoretical debates, one is tempted to see in Sidney's much celebrated '[y]e Poett nothing affirmes and therefore never lyeth' a re-inauguration of the fiction of literary truth, rather than a solution to its problem. For the contemporary readers of various persuasions, for whom the literary appears to hover either inside or outside the vast land once bordered by truth and falseness, the question arises whether literature should be understood outside of an empirical conception of truth, or of truth altogether.

If one feels that the relationship between truth and literature belongs to an *ancien régime* of critical discourse, one ought to remind oneself that the concept of fiction cannot be elaborated upon outside of its incipient relation to truth. The restoration of the discourse on 'literary truth' in the context of the theory of fictionality need not be seen as reactionary; rather, it should be viewed as both an unavoidable and a preliminary procedure to set the theoretical discussion in coherent terms.

The work of Lubomír Doležel, to whom the present volume is dedicated, offers an exemplary attempt to reach a high level of coherence in the discourse on the fictional status of literature. A historical contextualization of his work on fiction is needed, one that, though it may be incomplete, places it in a new light.[3]

Doležel's project to utilize possible-worlds semantics was part of a general trend that he shared with a number of other literary scholars, such as Marie-Laure Ryan and Thomas G. Pavel. Yet Doležel's approach bears a number of characteristics that differ from the others. The introduction of this 'semanticist' perspective was prompted by a considerable shift in literary studies, which occurred as the structuralist assumptions and procedures were losing their foothold.

Following an intellectually productive period, structuralism increasingly began to face challenges resulting from its inability to provide adequate answers to a number of issues and problems. This moment of crisis came at a time when most of the achievements of structuralism were being subsumed into the cores of different sciences and disciplines. The preservation of these achievements was, therefore, the signpost for structuralism's becoming an integral part of the accepted paradigm and, at the same time, for its being surpassed.

Propp's pioneering hypothesis that narrative structures are reducible to a one-dimensional succession of functions was found to be, in many ways, a useless demolition. Later developments by Barthes (1977),[4] Todorov (1969), and Bremond (1973) refined the Proppian model and were characteristically successful in dealing with the analysis of oral and premodern narratives.

The 'universal models of the narrative' (for instance, Bremond's) echo the formalized shape of oral narratives. The self-tailored 'objective character' of structuralist research was ensured by a fundamental and hidden homology between the model and the texts approached: their narrative mobility and internal dynamics are predicated on a structure that resembles a dictionary entry. Some basic and fundamental relationships within narrative can only be accounted for when action and development take place in a multidimensional space, that is, when the narrative structure is considered from the outset as a logical, semantical, and pragmatical complex.[5]

Soon it became clear that such an approach could not be as satisfactorily used in dealing with the works of Thomases like Mann and Pynchon. For modern and postmodern narratives challenge the explanatory abilities of formalist models in different ways than premodern narratives do.

'Classical' narratology[6] emerged as the attempt to supplement the model of functions with refined details eventually meant to address more properly the question of modern narrative, and of narrative altogether. Since the 'ancestral' *Don Quixote*, this narrative disengaged itself from the bonds of the established genres and established itself as both an archi-genre and an anti-genre (Bakhtin, Jameson).

In line with many inherent tendencies in structuralism,[7] attempts to face the central problem of meaning in literary texts were focusing more and more on recent developments of analytical philosophy. Within this large tradition, theories of possible-worlds semantics, as developed by philosophers like Kripke, Hintikka, Rescher, von Wright, Plantinga, and Lewis, were thought to provide answers to the problem of meaning in literary texts, without compromising their autonomy and without the need to resort to any 'extratextual' entity, like the reader. This approach also provided a way to face these issues without having to resort to strategies, like those of deconstruction, which deny the stability of the narrative or textual structure.[8]

The theories and concepts developed within possible-worlds semantics were not readily transferable to the analysis of literary texts, not only because of problems of terminology, but also because the analysis of linguistic products has been predicated, in classical analytical philosophy, on a process of oversimplification of the object taken into consideration.

The central target of Doležel's theoretical construct is the mimetic approach to literary texts. Within his model, fictional worlds are characterized as (a) 'sets of possible states of affairs' (1988, 482; 1989a, 230); (b) 'unlimited and maximally varied' (1988, 483; 1989a, 231) – compossibility is the only restriction applied to limit the maximality as 'only such possible entities are admitted into the world as comply with its general order' (1988, 484; 1989a, 231–2); (c) 'accessible from the actual world' (1988, 484; 1989a, 232). This accessibility is possible only through semiotic channels (semiotic textual mediation) and by means of information processing.

It is readily clear that these three characteristics not only are based on the framework of possible-worlds semantics, but are also in line with the fundamental philosophical tenets of Doležel's model which essentially comply with a realistic attitude.

Turning to fictional worlds of literature, Doležel points out three additional features that are specific to them: (d) '[f]ictional worlds of literature are incomplete' (1988, 486; 1989a, 233) – this logical deficiency is, according to Doležel, an 'important factor' of the 'aesthetic efficiency' of literary fictional worlds; (e) '[m]any fictional worlds of literature are not semantically homogeneous' (1988, 487; 1989a, 234); (f) '[f]ictional worlds of literature are constructs of textual activity' (1988, 488; 1989a, 235).

The sum total of these features indicates that this is not merely a constructive model of literary fictional worlds; it is also a model with teeth that has a number of targets. The first is the mimetic theory of literature with its different variants. This includes Aristotle, Lukács, Auerbach, Marxist reflection theory, and almost all sociological theories of literature. The second is the deconstructionist trend, which questions the stability of literary meaning and the possibility of the literary fact. The third is the hermeneutical (including the *Rezeptionsästhetik*) trend, which conceives of the meaning as being produced by the reader of the text, rather than by the text itself. Thus Doležel emphasizes the following points. The non-mimetic nature of fictional worlds is the result of them being constructed worlds. This is based on the work of Kripke, for whom 'possible worlds are stipulated, not discovered by powerful telescopes' (Kripke 1980, 44). Constructed worlds are the result of constructional texts, and have no prior existence to these texts, while descriptive texts are representations of the actual world to which they refer and according to which their truth value is determined. Doležel contends that descriptive texts are dependent upon the actual world, while literary fictional worlds are dependent upon literary texts. In this context, he criticizes Nelson Goodman and the radical constructivism adopted by some literary scholars, like Siegfried Schmidt, who maintain that all texts are world-constructing and all worlds are dependent on texts.

Doležel subsequently concludes that fictional worlds, because they are textually determined constructs, 'cannot be altered or cancelled.' A question, not addressed by Doležel, arises here: To what extent is any text eternally fixed? A stable text would render all interest in different versions of works irrelevant, unless one considers each version as a completely different text that constructs its own independent world, a view which would then raise more difficulties and problems. In addition to this, such a concept of text is essentially one based on written rather than oral discourse. Many studies of oral literature have shown that oral texts are not fixed entities, nor can their different oral versions be considered independent entities. In the case of written texts, one should bear in mind that for many centuries manuscripts were copied, and errors, or even direct interventions by copiers, occurred. Such a rigid conception of the text essentially leads to the cutting back of the fictional world, since the latter is reducible to the constructive text. Doležel constantly reproaches deconstructionists for their ontological reduction of literary worlds to texts, and he dubs this an idealistic stand.

For Doležel, then, there is a clear-cut ontological separation between the actual and the possible (fictional), which leads to such statements as 'the identity of fictional individuals is protected by the boundary between the actual and the possible worlds' (1988, 483; 1989a, 230). He does not allow for the theoretical intrusion of one into the other, in order to preserve the autonomy of the fictional world without necessarily cutting the umbilical cord between the fictional and the actual. It is only from the actual world that the fictional can be accessed, or, in Doležel's words, 'fictional worlds are accessible from the actual

world only through semiotic channels by means of information processing'
(1988, 485; 1989a, 232). This formulation raises a number of problems, the
most obvious being the possibility of semiotic channelling through the bringing
of the fictional into the real world.

Doležel emphasizes that possible-worlds semantics makes us aware that the
material from the actual world that goes into the making of the fictional world
has to 'undergo a substantial transformation at the world boundary: it has to
be converted into non-actual possibles, with all the ontological, logical and
semantical consequences' (1988, 485; 1989a, 232–3). One of the problems
here is that semiotic mediation is used again as a magic formula to resolve
extremely complex and variable processes. This forces Doležel to resort to what
might be termed a subjectivist aesthetics when he attempts to account for the
processes of constructing fictional worlds. He contends that literary fictions
'are constructed in the creative act of the poetic imagination, in the activity
of poesis. The literary text is the medium of this activity; with the semiotic
potentials of the literary text, the poet brings into fictional existence a possible
world which does not exist prior to this poetic act' (1988, 489).

Around such a subjectivist aesthetics a number of issues gather. First, Doležel's
belief in the completeness of the actual as opposed to the incompleteness of the
fictional prompts him to criticize some versions of reader-response aesthetics,
especially that of W. Iser, who postulates that the reader's main activity is
filling in the gaps of incompleteness in literary texts, thereby consummating
their aesthetic value. Doležel then highlights the importance of incompleteness
because this very fact contributes greatly to the richness of the texts and because
it allows, among other elements, for a variety of interpretations.

But the most ambitious, and probably the more interesting and original,
part of Doležel's work is his attempt to provide a general typology of fictional
worlds. Basing his argument on the extensional/intensional dichotomy, he
develops an extremely ambitious typology (which deserves a longer discussion),
a number of analytical concepts which are of great value to literary scholars,
and new venues for a further development of similar concepts. After dividing
fictional worlds into primary (sets of compossible narrative agents [1979a, 196])
and secondary narrative worlds, he introduces two typologies, an extensional
and an intensional one. Within the first, he develops two subtypes, a categorical
typology and a modal one, based upon the types of macroconstraints that can
be identified.

The categorical macroconstraints 'control the admission of the constituent
semiotic categories into the structure of the fictional world' (1985c, 265). The
first type is the static world into which unchangeable objects are admitted. The
second is a world into which the force of nature causes 'nature events.' The

third is a world into which one agent is admitted, and the last is one in which two or more agents are present with the resultant interactions.

The modal typology utilizes the work done by philosophers like von Wright, Hintikka, and Rescher, and is based on global extensional restrictions that determine the narrative potentials of fictional worlds. These universal modalities are the alethic, deontic, axiological, and epistemic. The alethic world is constructed under the constraints of possibility, impossibility, and necessity (1985c, 266); the deontic, under the constraints of permission, prohibition, and obligation (266); the axiological, by the imposition of the operators of goodness, badness, and indifference; and the epistemic, by those of knowledge, ignorance, and belief (267). Each one of these classes can be divided into subtypes that are homogeneous, non-homogeneous, or hybrid (267).

The intensional typology is based on the two basic functions: the authentication function and the explicitness/implicitness function. These intensional functions transform extensional macrostructures into intensional macrostructures. It is exactly here that the typology becomes most productive and most problematic, as it offers greater potentialities for developing more rigorous literary critical terms and comes closer to attacking, head on, some of the old-new problems in the approach to the constitution of narrative, such as genre, point of view, etc. Doležel's typology is put to work, with noticeable results, in his analyses of Defoe, Flaubert, Gogol, Faulkner, and especially Kafka, his favourite writer, to whom he has devoted several papers.

To appreciate Doležel's contribution to fictionality, it is essential to remember that his work is a part of a larger trend that attempts to instil more rigour in the study of literature and to benefit from developments in philosophy and aesthetics. But it wants to do this while insisting on the autonomy of the literary work. This obsession with, and great reverence for, literature has led to a 'mild isolationism,' a phenomenon that is critically invoked in this volume.

To contextualize more properly Doležel's work, one needs to take a step back and reconsider the concept of fiction. A first distinction should be made between *fiction making*, a process of making up of imaginary happenings, feigning, and *fiction*, a product, something made up or imagined (a lie, a legal fiction, or a novel).[9] Some fictions (e.g., a novel) preserve, to various extents, the trace of their production; others (e.g., a lie) present themselves as truth.

One may further distinguish between products that are fictitious (lies such as 'the previous sentence is written in Chinese') and those that are fictional (stories such as Hemingway's 'The Killers').[10] Fictitious propositions, which are false with respect to accepted truth, contrast with the fictional propositions, which do not correspond to truth judgment. It is both reasonable and widely accepted to state that, among propositions or statements, those fictitious are false, while those fictional are neither true nor false. Yet this should not entail, as it did in the standardized approaches of Russell or Stalnaker, the autism of truth and of what does not fall under truth judgments, their mutual muteness. One finds no longer compulsory reasons to restrict the free travel and smuggling of entities, propositions, and statements to and from the lands of truth and of non-truth.

If a lie can project a fictional entity, that is, an entity that cannot be judged according to truth,[11] it means that the grip of truth has slackened to the extent that it can account only for the propositional form, not for the propositional content. One should not take this limitation pessimistically; truth undermines the conventional understanding of the concept of truth as it goes beyond it. To forbid the sentences of fiction a truth value in the first place, like John Woods's 'gapper,' turns out to be not only a restrictive act but one that borders on meaninglessness. In the order of critical discourse, truth without fiction is a fiction.

In a restricted sense, the making of fictional sentences and texts is to be defined as the set of discursive procedures that leads to escaping the limitations of truth judgment. Fictional products are arrived at through these procedures, the traces of which they keep: rather than being static, fictional products are to be viewed as being in tension with their alleged nonfictional counterparts. Both a fictitious sentence ('Napoleon died in 1970') and a factually true one ('Napoleon died in 1821') may be treated as fictional once they appear in contexts that help relativize their truth value.[12] Fictional sentences and texts, on the other hand, are most commonly reduced to the realm of truth by way of assent because of sheer or controlled ignorance.

Factual sentences cannot become analytically true (or false), that is, true (or false) in all possible worlds. Logical possible worlds are not prepared to deal with fictional sentences, indeed, are not meant to. Logical possible worlds are extensions and testers of a concept of truth against which fictional sentences are born. As Ouellet points out in his paper, the logicians' concept of possible worlds does not help understand the world of fiction; the former disguises a theology and forces the latter to wander around it. 'In effect,' writes Ouellet, 'does the World – as we call it in our modern ontological debates – not play the role that God previously assumed in those theological dramas that opposed (with arguments still in use) iconoclasts and icon worshippers? Doesn't the meaning of fiction, like that of images, find itself reduced, by our modern Byzantines, to the simple function of truth or non-truth, with respect to the World?'

The historical changes that took place in the symbolic economy of the West, which led to the substitution of the dominant pair '(sublunar) world/transcendent realm' with 'fictional world/actual world,' follow the general lines of secularization processes. These changes preserved, however, the formal aspect of the double-world structure as the framework for the investment of symbolic energy. The unquestionable ultimate value perseveres in the new arrangement by way of transference from God to an irrefutable rational Truth.[13] And, to continue Ouellet's observation, as long as the 'truth of the world' will be taken for granted, our theoretical interest in fiction will amount to statements about local correspondences between fiction and the world. This narrowly focused attitude of the discourse on fiction reinforces the flat belief in 'truth of the world,' that is, a terminal truth obtained by avoiding criticism, rather than by making the effort to overcome it from the inside.[14]

The opposition to such a view of the world does not necessarily translate into a revolutionary outcry to reverse the order of world and fiction. Rather, it calls for a reconsideration of the static view arrived at in the form of a hierarchy.[15]

Since something fictional exists but is not the case, the belief in flying horses or in Stephen Dedalus's ability to fax back relegates the believer to the realm of the naive or the pathological. However, the belief in the innocence of fiction is more dangerous. This volume, in its entirety, bears witness to the fact that it is fiction rather than truth that constitutes the major point of interest in contemporary criticism.

In a second move, the meditation on fiction leads the 'search for truth,' whatever this may mean, to new paths. To quote Rescher quoting Lord Byron, '"truth is stranger than fiction"; but strangeness isn't everything.' Truth is strange because it is accessible via fictions. Fictions are irreplaceable mediators, and however exotic some of them may appear, they are more familiar than truth. The undisputable Truth of our age of *Weltanschauungen* lies in the universality of fictional mediation.[16]

It follows that the definition according to which literature is fictional could turn either into an *a priori* or into a demand. The *a priori* reduces the function of aesthetic experience to a mere reassertion of the analytic truth, that 'literature is fictional.' The demand is to enrich the very notion of fiction to the point that the sense of adventure involved in aesthetic experience becomes one of its dimensions. While the former appears to fit the program of theoretical meditation on literature into the schedule of Enlightenment and post-Enlightenment reason, the latter offers wider avenues to the contemporary debates concerning the status of aesthetic fictions. From the perspective of the latter, truth appears to be helpful at the initial stage of inquiry, but it becomes extraneous at a later stage, and utterly out of place at the end. A displacement has taken place in the theoretical discourse on aesthetic fictions: truth has been repositioned. From being placed at the peak, conclusion, or 'exemplary horizon' of the aesthetic, truth has become an auxiliary concept to be dealt with in the introductory part of the theoretical discourses on literature. In this sense, those theories of fictionality that deal with truth perform a historically relevant introductory work. Looked at in a wider historical framework, this particular displacement of truth follows a pattern inscribed in the very constitution of Enlightenment reason.

The contemporary discourse on the aesthetic diminishes the room once so generously allotted to truth. The aesthetic is no longer caught up in a hierarchy where it has to pay tribute to science (the realm of truth) and, in so doing, to reinforce the unity of that hierarchy and aesthetics' own inferiority. This displacement, which at first may be regarded as 'the revenge of the aesthetic,' gains a less shallow meaning once it becomes apparent that the exclusion of the aesthetic from the Enlightenment project is one of the main causes that led to the autonomization of the aesthetic.[17]

Instead of defending the right to recognition of aesthetic fictions, and thus perpetuating the idiosyncrasies of an old epistemology, we suggest marking at the other end of the spectrum the limit that oversees our theoretical approach and that relativizes its assumptions. This limit is expressed by Nietzsche's dictum '[o]nly as an *aesthetic phenomenon* is existence and the world forever *justified*.'[18]

It is within these limits that the theories of fictionality, which recently and decidedly claimed Leibniz as their distant forefather, need to specify procedures for freeing aesthetic fictions from what these theories conceive of as superstitious conceptions of truth. Thinkers like Nietzsche act as still distant 'others' who might be expected to justify, even if in surprising forms, the project of the theories of fictionality.

In a shorter historical perspective, the theories of fictionality appear to be an attempt to crop the heritage of structuralism, and to partly rescue it from the multiple attacks it had to endure in the last quarter of a century, especially from poststructuralisms and hermeneutics. Theories of fictionality – research traditions rather than a defined discipline – have been contributed by such literary scholars and philosophers as Lubomír Doležel, Umberto Eco, Zoltan Kanyo, Hans-Heinrich Lieb, Félix Martínez-Bonati, Thomas G. Pavel, Jerzy Pelc, Gisa Rauh, Nicholas Rescher, Michael Riffaterre, Ruth Ronen, Richard Routley (Sylvan), Marie-Laure Ryan, Siegfried Schmidt, Cesare Segre, John Woods, Nicholas Wolterstorff, etc.

Characteristic of the theories of fictionality is the attempt to overcome the analytical concept of truth, whose value was not doubted by Russell, the early Wittgenstein, Carnap, Schlick, and Ayer. Wolterstorff, Pavel, and Ronen, among others, offer sound reasons for resisting the analytical procedures that clean house by eliminating shadowy areas from the scope, and in the name, of analytical truth. In fact, logical positivism is interested in avoiding *la chose littéraire* and, even more, the propositions of classical metaphysics, or those found in the writings of Nietzsche and Heidegger. All these, Carnap pointed out on one unfortunate occasion, are to be considered 'literary' as a means of excluding them from the scope of the research of analytical philosophy (1931, 69–71). The analytic notion of truth operates in the absence of fictions, of 'ill-formed' sentences, of 'meaningless' propositions like the Nietzschean 'truth is the longest-lived lie.' This procedure is not able to veil the fact that the universality of the truth of analytical philosophy obtains at the price of eliminating a great deal of phenomena. These phenomena are declared irrelevant, although they may happen to be, in many cases, the most interesting ones, not only to other philosophers, but also to literary scholars. It comes as no surprise that the Carnapian procedure reveals its own belief in the non-negotiable Truth that everything can be semantically decided (provided that what cannot be decided is excluded beforehand). Good semantics becomes good (tautological) logic, and the possibility of creating meaning is cautiously ousted.

If Viennese positivism had no place whatsoever for the aesthetic, it appears that the desire to formalize literary semantics denotes certain masochistic characteristics on the part of literary scholars who let themselves be inspired by it. It was left to some illustrious representatives of speech-act theory[19] to rule out the genuine relevance of literary utterances and to consider them 'fictional.' In turn, it is becoming apparent that the feigned speech-act theory of fictionality has been overcome by recent theories of fictionality. The Searlian concept of fictionality as an act of 'pretending' has been discredited, as have been Ohmann's 'quasi-speech acts' and Ingarden's 'quasi statements,' as characteristics of the literary texts. Martínez-Bonati is right to invoke experience in his criticism of Austin (and Herrnstein-Smith, Ohmann, and Searle) when he says: 'there is nothing in our common experience of literature to support the idea … that language and action in poetry or fiction are *intrinsically* less language and less action than in ordinary experience. The deprivation affecting literary language is a radical one, but it is not in the field of describable attributes, it is the lack of the attribute of proper existence[20] – that is, the fact of its being purely imaginary' (1981, 158).

That fictional discourse is a parasite feeding on serious discourse is, at least since Austin's rigorous attempt, a belief that contemporary theories of fictionality seek to challenge, because they understand literature as an irreducible and self-sustaining act. Ronen's article in this volume provides valuable arguments in this respect. She differentiates between literary fictions and counterfactuals, or Kripke-fictions, that is, 'total "ways the world might have been," or states or histories of the entire world' (Kripke 1980, 18), or, as Ronen puts it, 'non-actualized states of the world or possible situations that did not take place.' Literary fictions are set aside from the course of the Kripkean world. They are not reducible to the condition of counterfactuality. They are not unaccomplished prophecies.

Once on their own, the theories of fictionality choose a conservative ontology of their object. Doležel, Routley, Howell, and others hold that, unlike actuality, fiction is incomplete.[21] The belief that actuality is in some way complete is complemented and reinforced by the belief that the data contained in fiction do not lend themelves to completion as actuality does. Fiction is ontologically incomplete only if it is thought of in isolation. But this isolation helps a great deal in sustaining the comforting belief in the completeness of actuality.

The dignity of fiction seems to lie not in its acknowledged incompleteness or completeness,[22] but in its ability to impress itself on the reader in such a way that the distance between the actual and the fictional becomes irrelevant. Nothing is complete, except ideology and nothingness. The articles of McCormick, Hutcheon, and Coste offer different views on this issue.

Taking experience into account, we realize that the reading process should not be degraded to a mere filling in of the blanks more or less marked in the literary texts. Reading is, rather, a change of mind that allows for an actualization of the fictional contents. By 'actualization' we do understand the opposite of 'possibilization,' for this would reduce fiction to the interplay of a simplified Hegelian logic. Rather, *actual*-ization (or *real*-ization) denotes the operation on the part of the reader of suspending disbelief in the existence of such objects as blue flying horses and their pedigree. One surmises that the distance that separates the actual from the fictional is reduced in the process of reading so that one may 'believe,' under the circumstances of fiction, what one reads. The absurdity of such a belief represents the main point of resistance against the re-universalization of truth.[23]

Although in general the 'fictionalists' strongly oppose deconstruction, it is not devoid of irony to find that the anti-deconstructive assault of such 'anti-theorists' like Walter Benn Michaels and Steven Knapp[24] can be devised against some central procedures used by the mostly constructivist 'fictionalists.'[25] In his paper, Douwe W. Fokkema writes: 'The problem of fictionality is less popular than it used to be. Various authors, in the last two or three decades, have emphasized that the world we know consists of texts, thus undoing the oppositional relationship between linguistic sign and extralinguistic world ... The notion of correspondence to reality (or non-correspondence to reality) can no longer serve as a criterion, since knowledge of reality is not directly accessible and always tainted by the vehicle of language. It is clear that this ends the discussion of fictionality, in which, at least in the occidental tradition, the notion of non-correspondence to reality plays a crucial part.'

Yet the 'death of fiction' appears to be nothing other than a side effect of the 'death of Truth.' Therefore, this 'death of fiction' would arguably be the death of fiction as *ancilla veritatis*, of that understanding of fiction as dependent on a humanistic or positivistic concept of truth. It appears that Fiction has forced Truth out. This process, which began in Nietzsche's work and is developed now on a popular scale, appears to have an ironic outcome: Fiction has forced itself out, and what we are left with is an open field of, and for, fictions. As Fokkema points out, and as Loriggio attempts to dismiss, deconstruction has played a decisive role in forcing out Fiction as an inheritor to, and hypostasis of, Truth.

From a slightly different angle, Hutcheon's question challenges the 'fortress of the universal,' as she understands possible-world semantics, one of the strongholds of the theories of fictionality: '[C]ould it be, by analogy, that semiotic urge to universalize rules and descriptions of narrative systems might also prove to be based on a "*homogeneous* cultural imperative" that in fact works to normalize the heterogeneous and different?'

In this light, the interest in a general theory of fictions appears to be an outdated mixture of logical analysis turned against logical positivism, which does not dare to tackle more politically sensitive issues like marginality, subjectivity, and the emergence of media as a (first-)world power. The old truth, implies Hutcheon, is discarded but a new one does not emerge. Segre and Prince provide points of resistance against Hutcheon's contention, even if their approaches make limited theoretical claims.

On the other hand, it is significant to see why the concept of the subject is an issue addressed indirectly in this volume. There is a widespread, Benvenistean belief that, as Martínez-Bonati puts it, 'all narrative is implicitly or potentially first-person narrative, because all speech is the speech of an *I*, of a subject that always can refer to himself.' Like many fictionalists, Martínez-Bonati considers that the 'I' represents a 'primitive,' or a basic notion which goes undefined. The subject of the enunciation is not problematized; rather, its presence is taken for granted.

Historically speaking, a displacement took place in modernity, from the awareness that the Truth cannot be attained to the understanding of the fact that the subject cannot be properly touched by fictions. In this sense, the subject-formation in modernity amounts to a changing of places: the subject comes to occupy the old place of Truth, while fiction comes to fill the void left by the subject. Fictions try to reach us but they are unable to, for the modern (Cartesian) subject is to be defended from, and not invaded by, fictions. This subject is to be defended from itself, from its own destabilizing potential. By occupying the inscrutable place of the old Truth, the modern subject, from Descartes to Kant to Hegel to Husserl, is done away with in the formal approaches to literature. From Propp to Bremond, the subject of narratology is an object in the sense that it is objectified and set to a securing distance from itself. The 'objective, science-like' approach to literature has always been based on the existence of a subject treated with antibiotics. In this anti-Bakhtinian context alluded to by Matejka, it is all too apparent that fiction separates the subject from itself and reduces the 'self' to a semiotic index. To establish its claim to universality, this understanding of fiction needs to return to the Hegelian notion of the 'abstract possible,' and to state that fiction is the possibilization of everything, including the actual.[26]

In this established framework, Felson-Rubin, Nesselroth, Margolin, and Kushner provide arguments to flesh out the subject of fiction seen either as *énonciateur* or referent for names or as a partner in a dialogue. Coste's article, as well as his previous work on narratology, evidences the need to challenge this framework.

As defenders of modern subjectivity, poetics and narratology appear to remain on the conservative side of the theories of fictionality. For Segre and Matejka and, to a lesser extent, for Eco and Możejko, fictionality can still give poetics and narratology shelter and meaning, and can still constitute at least a way station for the future. Riffaterre presents a different approach to the way in which poetics, taking a Bakhtinian turn, can avoid becoming dependent on a general theory of fictionality.

The variety of theoretical perspectives displayed in this volume may stimulate debates for years to come. The relations among poetics, narratology, and the theories of fictionality addressed by the papers here are far from a settled issue.

NOTES

1 Jeremy Bentham, whose treatise foreshadows Vaihinger's philosophy of the 'as if,' is not listed among the forerunners of recent theories of fictionality. As Costa Lima notes, Bentham's theory 'anticipates the central role that language will command in the neopositivist circle, [but] it offers nothing anticipatory of a theory of poetic fictionality' (1988, 38). Since Foucault's *Surveiller et punir* (1977, 195–228), it has been fashionable to acknowledge Bentham's *panopticon* as his sole significant

contribution. One may add that an exception that passes unnoticed by Kermode is O. Barfield's 'Poetic Diction and Legal Fiction' (1947).

2 The suspicion is based on two observations: the theories of fictionality would be too much interested in the general conditions of (literary) fictions to be discriminative at a concrete level; and they are too obviously rooted in the tradition of verbal texts, appearing to be out of touch with developments in media theory, virtual reality experiments, etc. See also the excellent overview of the problem provided by Ryan (1991).

3 The following summary tries to stick as closely as possible to Doležel's own words, and to the order he himself provided for the discussion in his more recent contributions to the study of fictional worlds. The discussion follows a different path from that of Pavel in his essay dedicated to Doležel in the present volume.

4 Roland Barthes (1975). Barthes's influential article was originally published in a much talked about issue of *Communications* (8 [1966]) along with articles by Claude Bremond, Umberto Eco, A.J. Greimas, Violette Morin, and Tzvetan Todorov.

5 The concepts of 'narrative text' and 'narrative structure' are both suspect abstractions, in the sense that texts that are empirically available for study can rarely be explained through a comprehensive system of narrative rules. Narrative texts can be explained by means of the conventions that are valid within a cultural community at a specific time and in relationship to a specific literary communication form (a genre).

6 The term 'narratology' was first used by Todorov (1969).

7 According to Pavel (1986, 4), the main tendencies of structuralism are 'mythocentrism, semantic fundamentalism, and the doctrine of the centrality of text, with its corollaries, an antiexpressive stand and an immanentist approach to culture.'

8 Doležel describes possible-worlds semantics as 'able to free literary theory from the sterile view that fictional texts lack reference, as well as from the embarrassing concept of self-reference. Secondly, and more importantly, possible-world semantics leads us to postulate a more dynamic relationship between fictional text and its world: fictional worlds do not preexist texts' (1985b, 189).

9 The two meanings of 'fiction' correspond to the opposition suggested by Julia Kristeva (1968, 88) between a linguistics of production (enunciation, von Humboldt's *energeia*) and one of representation (*énoncé*, von Humboldt's *ergon*). See also Jameson (1987, 79–81).

10 In a different terminology (Pelc 1986), the term 'fictitious' defines entities and objects, while 'fictional' defines statements about those entities and objects.

11 In general, the contemporary theories of fictionality have no use for the Platonic commitment to truth that leads to the eventual exile of literary fictions from

the *polis* in the tenth book of the *Republic*. Even a less radical resistance to the destabilizing powers of fiction is hardly of interest in this context; one could think, for instance, of the non-Platonic Hellenistic and Roman tradition that is eclipsed in the twentieth-century Leibnizian revival. For the concept of fiction seen as a mingling of truth and falsehood, where truth is either philosophical or historical, see Horace's *Ars poetica*, 151 (Brink 1971, 60) and Plutarch's *Moralia*, 16b–c, 25b–c (1956, 1: 83, 133). For the widespread view (Cicero's, *Ad Herennium*'s, etc.) that fiction is a narration midway between the truth of *historia* and the falsehood of *mythos*, see Sextus Empiricus's *Against the Grammarians*, 263–4 (1949, 149).

12 Anti-systemic modern thinking is particularly keen on pointing to such contexts which are either avoided or reduced in logical positivism and in the late writings of Heidegger.

13 Truth-with-a-capital-T denotes a transcendental entity that is presented as non-negotiable and changeless.

14 'The fundamental event of the modern age is the conquest of the world as picture ... As soon as the world becomes picture, the position of man is conceived as a world view ... It is no wonder that humanism first arises where the world becomes picture ... [S]ince the end of the eighteenth century *Weltanschauung* has become the expression of the fundamental stance of man in relation to what is, in its entirety, defined as a world view' (Heidegger 1977, 133–4).

15 Or, rather, of 'higher-archy,' as the investment of the sacred is reduced to a mere measurement of the respective positions of 'real world' and 'fictional world.'

16 In a different vein, Baudrillard presents the simulacrum in the light of the history of the modern concept of truth as a critical disclosure of an alien falseness, handed out by Marx, Nietzsche, and Freud. For Baudrillard, '[t]he simulacrum is never that which conceals the truth – it is the truth which conceals that there is none. The simulacrum is true' (1984, 253). This well-known formula does not take into account that it is the very reproducibility of 'truth' at a 'metatheoretical' level that allows the simulacrum to be specified as true. The untimely enthusiasm occasioned by the discovery of the negativity of truth helps Baudrillard overlook the participation of the simulacrum in the cunning reproduction of 'truth.'

17 What to Snow's 'scientist' should appear as development alien to 'science' may be seen as a development of science, in the form of the rise of the neglected (i.e., the aesthetic) to an autonomous status.

18 Nietzsche 1967, 22, 52, 141. The first occurrence is in the 'Attempt at a Self-Criticism' which introduces the second edition published in 1878. 'The famous quotation, twice repeated in the *Birth of Tragedy*, should not be taken too serenely, for it is an indictment of existence rather than a panegyric of art. It accounts, however, for the protective nature of the Apollonian moment' (de Man 1979, 93).

19 The opposition between the Wittgenstein of *Tractatus* (and its remarkable success in Vienna and, until today, in most departments of philosophy in the Anglo-Saxon world) and the Wittgenstein of *Philosophical Investigations* expresses in its purest form the reaction of an emerging speech-acts theory against the excesses of logical positivism.

20 To consider that 'existence' – imaginary or not – is an attribute is a choice that entails metaphysical contradictions and theological quarrels. 'Attributing' existence grounds the optimistic belief in, and the common procedure of, a universal semantics. However, this choice hardly affects the limited scope of Martínez-Bonati's criticism.

21 See Howell 1979, 134–7; Routley 1979, 8–9; Wolterstorff 1980, 136–40; Doležel, 1985b, 195; Pavel 1986, 104–8; Ronen 1988, 497–9.

22 McCormick, commenting on Doležel's claim that fictional worlds are incomplete, restates that 'the incompleteness of fictional worlds distinguishes them from the usual Carnapian construal of a possible worlds framework as complete.'

23 Kendall Walton considers that 'what is true is to be believed; what is fictional is to be imagined' (1990, 41), although 'it would be mistaken to identify the fictional with what is imagined' (37). This argument is based on the belief that it represents a truth, while the presentation of the truth has a typical flaw: it hypostasizes 'belief' in such a way that the subject of belief agrees to the pre-established objectivity of truth. In this homogeneous, compact view, the subject turns out to be expendable, the 'belief' turns out to be nurtured by something like a 'machine of beliefs,' and truth turns out to be universal.

24 1982, 723–42. See also Godzich's rejection of some of their main arguments (Godzich 1987).

25 For two different 'constructivist' approaches in this volume, see Schmidt's and Margolin's articles.

26 Such approaches as those represented by Stalnaker or McCormick's essay in the present volume allow for a precise and limited scope of the possibilization of the actual.

PART 1
FICTIONS AND PHILOSOPHIES

1

Are Fictional Worlds Possible?[1]

RUTH RONEN

Fictionality poses an intricate problem for literary theory because it indicates the duality inherent in the fictional universe: it is a world ontologically and epistemically separated from what is external to it, while at the same time being a world modelled in certain ways after reality. That is, fictionality stresses the autonomy and dependence of the literary system relative to other world systems.

The concept of possible worlds has become a productive and popular source for theorizing on literary fiction in recent years. A possible world is the name for a model constituted of a set of objects, related in certain ways and maintaining some relationship with the actual state of the world. Such a partial autonomy of alternative and parallel worlds, which the concept of possible worlds tries to formally define, appears as an attractive solution to the problem of fictionality. The conceptual framework connected with the notion of possible worlds thus seems at first glance to offer a new outlook on some of the pressing problems with which literary theory concerns itself: fictionality, the ontology of fictional worlds and of fictional objects, generic problems such as realism, and even the semantics of fictional narrative. My intention in this paper is to look into some aspects of possible-worlds thinking and to explore their relevance to the problem of fictionality, exposing in this way the presuppositions of theories nourished by possible-worlds concepts.

In exploring the interaction between possible worlds and fictionality, the question that poses itself is the following: To what extent is the analogy between possible and fictional worlds true to the original meaning of the concept of possible worlds? How is the concept of possible worlds actually interpreted, and what are the modifications it undergoes when transferred and adopted by the theoretical discourse on literature? My aim in this essay is to characterize the type of use that an accurate and literal understanding of possible worlds imposes on literary theory.

The first problem that arises when fictionality is defined in terms of possible worlds concerns the concept of actuality. The belief in possible worlds is based on the assumption that things might have been different and that one can describe alternative courses things might have taken. In other words, possible worlds ascribe a concrete ontological content to non-actual modalities by presenting non-actual states of affairs and alternative parallel worlds. It is a way of characterizing non-actual but concrete situations.

Fictional worlds are such non-actual states of affairs, yet assets of related objects; they are, unlike possible worlds, not 'total ways the world might have been, or states or histories of the entire world' (Kripke 1972, 18). It seems counter-intuitive to treat fictional worlds as non-actualized states of the world or as possible situations that did not take place. Although to treat non-actual worlds in terms of concrete ontologies can offer a productive solution for the problem of fictionality, fictional worlds are not non-actual in the same sense that possible worlds are, that is, they are not alternative ways the world might have been.

A literary theory of fictionality making use of possible-worlds concepts consequently seems to require a considerable modification of the concept of actuality. Fictional worlds are, in this respect, less directly linked to the actual world than possible worlds. If we look more closely at specific versions of possible-worlds models, we discover three views on the actuality of possible states of affairs.

According to one radical view, possible worlds are as actual as the real world. Thus, according to Lewis (1973), who is the major proponent of such an actualism, 'actual' is an indexical term and the inhabitants of each world see their universe as the actual one. To grasp this ontological extravagance of Lewis, it should be noted that for Lewis possible worlds are parallel worlds, autonomous 'foreign countries' with their own laws and with an actuality of their own. Such worlds do not exist in a way that differs from the mode of existence of the actual world.

A second view is the one commonly termed 'moderate realism.' Possible worlds are perceived as actual worlds, but only in a restricted sense: they are components of the actual world. The actual world is a complex structure that includes both its actualized facts and also ways things might have been. The ways things might have been are composite elements of reality. If possible worlds are part of an actual-world model, one has to face the lingering question of what differentiates possible worlds from the actual state of things. Kripke and Putnam, as well as other philosophers, approach the question of the mode of existence of possible worlds by claiming that possible worlds are abstract entities, hypothetical situations, not real 'parallel worlds' (Putnam 1983, 60;

Kripke 1972, 16ff.). They thus differentiate between the ontology of the actual world and the ontology of hypothetical possible constructs which form the non-actualized part of the world.

The third view is the one that denies possible worlds any kind of heuristic or explanatory power, and therefore any kind of actuality. The most common ground for rejecting this notion is the argument that a belief in possible worlds assumes the existence, or at least the accessibility, of an actual world, a belief that is basically unacceptable. The myth of actuality as a constant background behind non-actual possibilities is not only part of a metaphysical stand that accepts the actual world as the best, inevitable, and only world that could have been actualized, but also part of a moderate stand that chooses to see the actual world only as a contingency. Actuality is a relative notion, and is therefore indistinguishable from non-actual states of the world. This may seem to be another version of the Lewis approach, but whereas Lewis attributes absolute realism to all worlds, a philosopher like Goodman attributes existence to none. Lewis sees all worlds as equally real and concrete; Goodman sees all worlds as versions subject to radical relativism.

These three views on the heuristic significance of possible worlds, their degree of actuality, and their position in relation to the actual world, already indicate the main problem in adopting this concept in the description of fictional worlds. Whereas a view of possibilism in the way Lewis proposes leads to ontological extravagance which most philosophers disagree with, the more common conception of possible worlds as abstract entities or hypothetical states describing the ways the world might have been will not do for fiction. An absolute relativism of the kind that Goodman promotes contradicts a cultural intuitive sense of division between fiction and reality, although in certain contexts this dividing line can prove to be rather fuzzy.

Possible worlds can be conceived of as abstract constructs forming alternative world-models. As such they can allow the possibility of having a world-model empty of entities. The only restriction on constructing hypothetical world-models is their logical possibility, and it is thus logically possible to discuss in concrete terms an empty world. It is not only, as will be shown below, that logical possibility is not necessarily a valid criterion in the construction of fictional worlds, but also that the abstract-hypothetical nature of possible worlds, which defines their alternativeness to actuality and which allows the possibility of emptiness, contradicts the very nature of fictionality. Fictional worlds are, by definition, 'pregnant' worlds, concrete constellations of objects, and not abstract constructs (see Eco 1979, 218).

The 'pregnancy' of fictional worlds implies that fictional ontologies depend on the presence of concrete fictional entities; fictional worlds are worlds possessing some kind of concrete reality. Thus, if one is not to use possible worlds as a metaphor, the view of possible worlds as hypothetical abstract sets does not make sense and cannot be operative in describing fictional worlds. In other words, it seems that the concept of world is used differently in each framework. Whereas in a philosophical framework, a world has the status of a conceptual construct, in literary theory, worlds are literally understood as constellations of concrete constructs.

Possible worlds are alternative worlds that allow trans-identification with actual object sets. It is possible to identify the same entity across separate worlds, although that entity can be characterized, located, or even named differently in each world. The notion of transworld identity is another aspect of possible-world framework that welcomes, and at the same time problematizes, an analogy with the notion of fictionality.

Lewis describes alternative worlds as parallel worlds or as distant planets which are necessarily autonomous. He consequently rejects transworld identifications as inconceivable and contradictory to the nature of beings. Kripke, on the other hand, claims that possible worlds are kinds of mini-worlds describing the total ways things might have been. Kripke proposes the example of a play in probabilities where two dice are thrown. The thirty-six possible states of the dice are thirty-six possible worlds. Although it is obvious that Kripke's possible mini-worlds simplify accessibility and transworld identity, it is clear already in this example why such a concept of possibilism cannot be adopted as a model for fictionality. Fictional worlds are parallel worlds and not total states of the world, and as such they are likely to raise problems that the case of the dice easily satisfies. We are more likely to identify the dice in the actual world with each of their appearances in alternative states of the world than we are to identify a Napoleon from history with his (possibly deviating) incarnation in fiction.

The main incompatibility between possible worlds and fictional worlds is revealed in the concept of possibility. Whereas the notion of possible worlds, or of non-actual states of the world, is tied to the logic and probabilities of actuality, a model for fictional worlds should be able to accommodate a logic that deviates from standard logic. Possible worlds are possible, whereas fictional worlds might be impossible. This point can be even more radically phrased. The notion of possible worlds is destined to distinguish non-actual, but possible, states of affairs from impossible ones. In a theoretical framework that should account for the fictionality of worlds, it is not only that impossibility is allowed, but that the standard of possibility is not at issue. I refer here not to the fact that fictional worlds can include supernatural elements, but to the fact that contradictions do not collapse the coherence and internal truth-value of fictional worlds. A fictional character can be born on two contradicting dates, the same event can take place in two different locations simultaneously, etc. No sensible reader of postmodern texts rejects the worlds of these texts as impossible or incomprehensible on such grounds. Fictional worlds thus require an alternative principle, of compatibility or the like, to distinguish between 'possible' and 'impossible' fictional worlds.

Moreover, fictional worlds have logico-semantic properties for which standard logic cannot account. To elucidate this point, it can be instructive if we look at the problem of counterfactuals and the principle of similarity with which counterfactuals are handled. Lewis's work on counterfactuals is an attempt to explain a counterfactual situation away as a possible world more or less similar, or more or less close, to actuality. The truth of a counterfactual cannot be determined from knowledge of the truth-values of the antecedent or the consequent of a counterfactual ('if I drop the glass, it will break'). Rather, a counterfactual is true at a world just in case the consequent is true at all the nearest possible worlds in which the antecedent is true. Without going any further into this philosophical analysis, I would like to point out the way problems of inference in non-actual situations are solved by Lewis, as by other possible-worlds theorists. Lewis's treatment of counterfactuals, like Kripke's example of dice-throwing, shows that we can infer or determine the truth of propositions about possible worlds by relying on their similarity or closeness to the state of affairs realized in the world. In other words, if the dice had fallen differently, no change in the laws of probability or the logic of the world would have ensued. Likewise, the notion of similarity in the case of counterfactuals guarantees that, in the worlds closest to the actual worlds, when a glass is thrown on the floor there are no fairies to catch it before it reaches the floor, that there is a standard 'terrestrial' gravity force, and that a glass cannot at the same time be safely situated on a table and in pieces on the floor.

This notion of similarity is fully manifested in the definition of possible worlds as possible worlds as maximal sets. When philosophers assume the occurrence of an alternative possible world, in which a different set of state-propositions obtains (in which, for instance, the dice fell differently), all other domains of the actual world that were not contradicted by the occurrence of that possible world continue to obtain. The philosophical definition of possible worlds assumes that each world is a complete set of propositions and not a partial world consisting of those propositions explicitly asserted. This maximality of worlds is not unproblematic in itself: it implies that we can make a hypothetical local change in a world (in which the glass was situated safely elsewhere) and maximize an overall similarity to the actual world, that is, we 'tinker' with the actual world at one point, and then let the laws of nature operate without further interference (Putnam 1983, 60ff.).

It is, however, the case that fictional worlds require a logic that is not the regular metalogic of nonfictional propositions, a logic including different laws of inference and of reference. Thus we cannot assume in the context of fictional worlds a maximization of sets. Reading maximal sets into fictional worlds would produce a counter-intuitive conception of fictional worlds. Fiction prevents us from reading into it a content that is not explicitly or implicitly stated by the statements of the text and that derives from what is, in this context, our irrelevant knowledge of the world. Fictional worlds thus require different laws of inference than those obtaining in our accounts of other possible worlds.

A fictional world requires a model accounting for its distinctive laws of inference and identification, distinctive both in relation to laws of the actual world and in relation to laws of non-actual and possible states of affairs. In a fictional world such as that of Père Goriot, we are faced with what might have happened if a character such as Rastignac was to walk the streets of Paris in the nineteenth century. The fictional world certainly clings to, and depends on, frames of actuality. Yet, at the same time, a model for fiction should account for its indispensable degree of autonomy. Fictional worlds are not part of the total histories of the world. They are not abstract hypothetical constructs but something else. Fictional worlds are related to the actual world, but they are not necessarily possible alternatives to this world. They can include impossible situations, impossible entities, and be subject to different laws of probability. Thus, Paris inhabited by fictional characters, and hypothetically furnished with impossible states, cannot be straightforwardly connected to actual Paris. The law of minimal departure (Ryan 1980) is extremely problematic in fiction.

The ontic nature of possible worlds is defined relative to the actual world. One of the advantages of possible worlds is that they give concrete content to the modal distinction between necessity and possibility. Thus, a necessary assertion is true in all possible worlds, whereas a possible assertion is true in at least one world. The concreteness of possibilities is achieved because we assume that the world incorporates alternative ways things might have happened. This implies that, at least hypothetically, we can situate ourselves outside the actual world, and examine all the possibilities that have not been actualized and determine which proposition is true in which world. Possibility is therefore a matter of comparing the states of affairs holding in different worlds, and this is one of the motivations for developing the notion of possible worlds. Yet such a notion of possibility may lead to a metaphysical Platonism of a suspicious kind, where one can be situated at an extraterrestrial standpoint, contemplating the modal structure of the universe.

Putnam, who tries to tackle this problem while retaining the concept of possible worlds, claims that the notion of 'all possible worlds' raises many problems 'notably, how we are supposed to have epistemic access to this Platonic heaven of sets we pretend to be describing' (1983, 67). Putnam's solution is not to try to explain possibility with possible worlds, but to define the latter as relative to a fixed language. Possible worlds defined as language-independent hypothetical situations are bound to lead to Platonic or metaphysical view of possibilities. Another solution is, again, that of Lewis, who claims that 'actual' is just the property people in each possible world attach to their world. In this way, the difficulty of accounting for a privileged overview of all possible worlds is evaded. Lewis's view makes sense when we come to deal with fictional worlds. In fiction, although readers are aware of the world's being fictional, they are willing to grant this world a certain autonomy vis-à-vis reality, to commit themselves epistemically to the laws of fiction, to suspend their disbelief. Moreover, modern literary theory regards the mimetic view, namely, that literature is a mode for directly representing or even reflecting the real world, as obsolete. In a non-mimetic framework, fiction is granted a position in relation to which the real world has no privileged position. It is recognized that modes and degrees of reliance of fictional worlds on the real world reflect different representational conventions and not a fixed similarity. The autonomy of fictional worlds, an autonomy that literary theory strives to secure, in a way works against the attempt to describe these worlds in terms of specific similarities and degrees of accessibility among worlds. Moreover, this autonomy disarms the notion of possibility in the context of fictional worlds.

Here, as in previous contexts, literary theory appears to benefit from a radical philosophical view of possible worlds rather than from more moderate views. Only when possible worlds are grasped as, to some extent, hermetic worlds in relation to which the actual world has no privilege are they likely to add explanatory power to literary theory in its dealing with worlds of fiction.

In view of the above, it seems that a fictional world can be considered a possible world only in a radically modified way. The analogy between fictional worlds and possible worlds must obey severe restrictions. Consequently, 'a possible world' can only be considered a metaphor for fictional existence. In examining the conceptual components that build the notion of possible worlds (the components of actuality, possibilism, concrete and abstract modes of existence, accessibility, and transworld identity), one recognizes that these are understood and interpreted differently when applied to the case of fictional worlds. One might conclude that the interdisciplinary move of possible worlds from philosophy to literary theory necessarily entails a considerable loss of original meaning.

If this is the case, the question obviously is: Why do literary theorists make use at all of possible-worlds concepts, if such concepts are at the most metaphorically adequate, or at the least very restrictedly relevant to the problem of fictionality? Which are the conceptual gains of appropriating possible worlds into discussions of fictionality? To answer this query, we should look into the nature of the larger philosophical context in which the notion of possible worlds has been developed. The possible-worlds framework reflects and is part of a broader philosophical attempt to relax the meaning of certain philosophical concepts and to propose a largely non-positivist and non-metaphysical framework for ubiquitous philosophical problems such as reference, truth-values, modalities, possible and non-actual existence, etc. This philosophical orientation suits the literary discipline engaged in an attempt to grasp the essence of fictionality.

Without going very much into the nature of this relaxation of concepts exemplified in the philosophical talk about possible worlds, I will illustrate briefly the way the notion of truth is interpreted within the possible-worlds framework. The point is that the development of logical models for possible worlds and for counterfactual situations, the attempt to examine the standard of truth in modal contexts, imposed a relaxation of truth standards. The concept of truth has undergone radical change in modern philosophy, as reflected in the move from a 'correspondence theory of truth' to a 'pragmatic theory of truth.' This move is marked by the replacement of truth as an absolute logical standard establishing the relation between language and world with what can be described as a semiotic-oriented principle in terms of which one can describe truth relative to the way a universe of discourse is constructed and is operated. Current philosophy allows us to make valid references to objects and truthful assertions based on weaker standards of belief or of warranted assertability. Truth is not a fixed overall standard, but is, rather, a changing and tentative one. It is the practical uses to which we put a statement which determines its truth-value. In our linguistic usages, we can decide whether a proposition is true or assertible even when the mode of existence of the objects to which that proposition refers is doubtful or indeterminate. Such developments open the way for considering standards of truth as internal to a universe of discourse, be it fictional or nonfictional. The strong semantic relation between words and reality is then replaced by the weaker semantic relation Rorty terms the relation of 'talking about.' The truth of a reference is hence determined by the very laws of discourse. The philosophical attempts to approach the truth of fiction are understandable in this context. Fiction, like possible worlds and counterfactuals, is a discourse uncommitted to actual states of affairs, and it hence requires a truth standard that will account for one's ability to refer to non-existent objects and states. In short, truth, being one of the logical principles questioned by fiction, is already well relativized in philosophical discussions of possible worlds. The less metaphysical and rigid, the more relativized and semiotic the concept of truth has become, the more appropriate it proves to be for a definition of truth in fiction. Introducing standards of validation defined relative to a universe of discourse is one case that explains the conceptual affinity between current discussions in literary theory and the possible-worlds framework. This affinity is significant because the framework of possible worlds enables us to see worlds as semiotic models, as language-dependent constructs. If we think of possible worlds as simply possible states of affairs relative to some fixed language, and not as abstractions independent of the linguistic frame we use to talk about them, it becomes possible to identify them with semiotic conventions of world construction. At this point, the analogy between possible worlds and fictional worlds becomes apparent and productive.

Note, however, that, although this is the key to understanding and to promoting the talk on possible worlds in the context of a literary theory of fiction, the place of possible worlds in literary theory is a more complicated one. Possible worlds do not only attest to the feasibility of a semiotic view of worlds; if this were the case, possible worlds might have become a new version of anti-referential propensities in literary theorizing. Rather, possible-worlds talk in literary theory marks what Pavel has called the end of the moratorium on referential considerations. Current debates in philosophy confirm this tendency, being concentrated on the question of whether 'possible worlds' is a language-dependent epistemology or a language-dependent ontology. Such debates, phrased in various ways, demonstrate why the analogy between possible worlds and fictional worlds can generate research that is true to the intricate nature of both.

NOTE

1 A later, expanded version of this essay appears as chapter 2 in the author's *Possible Worlds in Literary Theory* (Cambridge: Cambridge University Press, 1994). Reprinted with the permission of Cambridge University Press.

2

Questions About the Nature of Fiction

NICHOLAS RESCHER

I propose to raise a number of somewhat bizarre-sounding questions about fiction, questions so far out of the ordinary way of viewing things that perhaps only a philosopher would find them intriguing, though others might find them sufficiently curious for wry amusement.

WHO INVENTED FICTION?

Who invented fiction? What is the first work of fiction, chronologically speaking, among all the various books that populate our libraries?

This is a question that must be answerable if we are to stake a successful claim to knowing what we are talking about in this domain. We must be in a position to say just what fiction actually is. And if a work of fiction is one that exhibits all or most of the features of some specifiable list, F_1, F_2, ... F_n, then we can simply work our way through a chronologically ordered file of the extant *opera omnia* of the race, checking off, one by one, their possession of these various features. The first time we come up with a sufficiently solid row of yesses, we are home free.

But what is fiction? What are those several properties or characteristics that mark a work of fiction as such. Fiction is an invented account of the imaginary doings of imaginary persons. This sort of thing, at any rate, is what a dictionary will tell us. But here, as elsewhere, the concept of persons must be construed more widely than that of people. People are human beings, members of *homo sapiens*; persons, however, include rational animals (as in *Watership Down*) or even intelligent robots (as in various sorts of science fiction). In the end, it seems that only rational agency matters. *Webster's Third New International Dictionary* is skating on very thin ice in characterizing fiction as 'invented prose narrative ... that deals imaginatively with human experience.' For we surely need not be so parochial about it. There is no reason of fundamental principle why the alien inhabitants of other planets cannot have fiction.

Moreover, exactly what happens if we do away with an insistence on the 'imaginatively' invented in the preceding formula? What if real actions by imaginary people are at issue? For example, consider a work that introduces an imagined attorney from eighteenth-century Williamsburg who gradually slides into doing all the things done by George Washington; ultimately, Congress appoints him to lead the army; he crosses the Delaware to surprise the Hessians, commands at Yorktown, is elected as the first U.S. president, etc. One would, I think, have to suppose that this work remains fictional even though the actions of its fictional people are almost entirely real.

What of imaginary actions by real people? What if we imagine an account, accurate to some point, in which George Washington at one stage begins systematically to do various fictional things that the real Washington did not. Again, I suppose that, as long as imaginary actions play a sufficiently prominent role, we are still dealing with a work of fiction. (We need not now discuss the implications of this principle for careless historiography.)

The situation becomes even murkier if neither of the people knows the acts are imaginary. What if a story takes the Borges-like turn of the fancy that, after Washington and Jefferson left the fourth session of the Continental Congress, Washington did all of the things that we now believe Jefferson historically did, and vice versa, that is, if they simply reversed roles? Now neither the agents nor the acts are fictional. What is imaginary is simply that one great act of role-reversal. But one would have to suppose that so massive a lapse from the fact would qualify the work as one of fiction.

So it seems that the best we can do is to require that a work of fiction is one that presents a substantial narrative account or story in which imaginary persons and/or imaginary actions or events play a prominent role. And the weight of whatever looseness that this definition has must be carried by that weasel-word 'prominent.' One thing seems clear: the boundary that separates fiction from nonfiction cannot be neat and simple.

Another delicate issue is the considerable length which that previous definition envisions. We can surely have a story that satisfies the requirement of being about imaginary persons and imaginary events, and yet be too short to count as a work of fiction. Presumably one would not call the fables of Aesop or the parables of the New Testament fiction. A work of fiction must be more substantial than that. The dictionaries equate fiction with the novel, and give the French and German *roman* as equivalents. Fiction in the book review section of the *New York Times* might as well be called novels. It does indeed seem that a work of fiction must also be substantial or of considerable length, so that a short story, though in all other regards perfectly fictional, does not really qualify as such.

Then, too, a work of fiction must have a certain unity, a certain integrity and closure. A series of stories strung together like narrative beads on a rope, *Thousand and One Nights,* for example, would not qualify as a true work of fiction, a novel. Nor would a series of volumes produced – again in Borges fashion – by a literary Methuselah who produces an otherwise fictional account of the doings of a group of imaginary characters in a multi-value story stretching it beyond the limits of all the works in the Library of Congress, the British Library, and the Bibliothèque Nationale combined. So vast a fictional *oeuvre* hardly qualifies as a single work; whatever it is, it is not a novel. A work of fiction must have a substantial degree of comprehensiveness combined with a limitation of scope and integrity of treatment.

On this basis we find three salient features that are characteristic of fiction: a prominent role for the activities of imaginary persons and/or imaginary actions or events; substantial length and comprehensiveness; significant limitation of scope and unified integrity of treatment as represented in an interconnectedness of events and episodes within a narrative space of moderate scope. This seems to be about the best we can do to specify just what a work of fiction is.

With this crucial preliminary aside, we can now return to our problem of determining the first work of fiction. In carrying out this exercise, it appears doubtful that one can come up with a promising candidate earlier than Aristides of Miletos, the Greek author whose *Milesian Tales* date from around 100 B.C. But, of course, getting the details right will not be easy, or uncontroversial.

One more quick preliminary. Must a work of fiction be written? Presumably not. The characters in *Fahrenheit 451* memorize books, but they could perfectly well have learned them by heart, episode by episode, as their author produces them. Again, must it be in prose? I venture to think not. Had Voltaire written *Candide* in verse, or Johnson *Rasselas,* we would presumably be perfectly happy to see those characterized as fiction. (Those original medieval romances – from which the French *roman* gets its use – were written in verse for two hundred years before prose gained the upper hand.) But the point is debatable.

WHO INVENTED THE IDEA OF FICTION?

Even as people were speaking prose before the idea of prose had been invented as such, so they were writing fiction before anybody thought of this idea. But who originally thought of it? Who first presented us not with a work of fiction, but with some explicit account of the concept of fiction as we now understand it? This is a question on which, to my very great regret, I can really shed no light. All I do know is that etymological dictionaries are of little help in resolving the problem because all of the words at issue (fiction, novel, *roman*) had other cognate uses long before their specific employment in one context.

CAN ONE PRODUCE A WORK OF FICTION BY MISTAKE?

Consider the following situation. Smith sees a series of films on a certain subject (e.g., Rambo I to XII). Mistakenly (and rather foolishly), he thinks these are documentaries, that is, more or less accurate re-creations of the actual doings of actual people. (In fact, they are complete fantasies.) Now Smith sets out to write a history based on these sources. He strings together an account that puts together the data that come his way in the most coherent, plausible, and systematic fashion he can. The whole thing, of course, is a tissue of imaginary unrealities. But can we say he has produced a work of fiction? Or does intent have to come into it? Is intent perhaps decisive? Think of the following Borges-reminiscent episode. Jones writes a work of fiction about a month in the life of a contemporary Chinese family. Even as he writes, episode by episode, event by event, his story is in fact being actualized; unbeknown to him, reality is actually enacting his scenario. From the first word to the final period, what he has produced is indistinguishable from a most painstakingly accurate history. Has he nevertheless not produced a work of fiction? And yet when both works are printed, the history and the fiction, one cannot tell which is which. Perhaps this question can be settled by tracing back along causal chains to an author and his or her intentions and sources. But it is not easy to say. It does seem, however, that intent – or, at any rate, purported intent – is a significant part of what distinguishes a work as fiction. Being an inventive product of the imagination is not enough. Think of the man who, having decided to become a spy for a foreign power, drops out of the usual course of his life at home for a year of training in an espionage school in the land of his newly adopted loyalty. He returns home with an elaborate cover story of his own invention (so let us assume), a fanciful fiction populated with all sorts of imaginary people and episodes. But this story, though filled with fictional material, is not a work of fiction in the accepted sense. For its author intends and expects his story to be accepted as fact. In the production of a work of fiction, the issue of intent is crucial; presumably, its author must indeed want his or her brain-child to be received as a strictly literary production.

DOES GOD READ FICTION?

Does God read fiction? The issue of atheism is irrelevant here. The question is not Does God exist and read fiction? Belief in God's existence has nothing to do with it. The question is a hypothetical one: *If* a God as conceived of along the lines of the Judeo-Christian tradition were to exist, *then* would he read fiction? Of course, not read. But know?

God is omniscient. He knows everything people do. Ergo he knows everything that Cervantes did when he wrote *Don Quixote*, that Ignazio Ferolina did when he set it in type, that Miguel de Unamuno did when he read it. He knows every section, every word, every comma on every page of every edition. Perhaps he does not read it – his knowledge is a *totum simul*. But he certainly knows what is says, has it by heart, so to speak.

Does he enjoy it? Does its humour get to him? Does God have a sense of humour? Or is he – like Queen Victoria – not amused? Does God have fun? Difficult questions. But doubtless when the element of suspense is altogether lost, the fun goes out of fiction.

Presumably, God does not know stories and fictions as such. Perhaps he only has what the medieval philosophers called middle knowledge of them, knowledge mediated by his knowledge of how people react to certain things. He may be part of the author's audience, but not of the readership.

IS IT TRUE THAT TRUTH IS STRANGER THAN FICTION?

The saying that truth is stranger than fiction has already been mentioned, but we should pause for a moment to ask ourselves? Is it really true?

The truth of things goes on into endlessly proliferating detail. No matter how much is told to us, we can ask for more and expect to get a sensible and informative answer. But with fiction the course of meaningful questioning soon comes to a stop. We come to an end with the line of further detail we can meaningfully ask for. Fiction has finite cognitive depth. The world of a fiction has a closure of sorts. Did Sancho Panza trim his mustache short? How much of it has turned grey?

It is a crucial facet of our epistemic stance towards the real world to recognize that every part and parcel of it has features lying beyond our present cognitive reach, at any present whatsoever. But in this regard real things differ in an interesting and important way from their fictional counterparts. To make this difference plain, it is useful to distinguish between two types of information about a thing, namely, that which is generic and that which is not. Generic information tells about those features of the thing which it has in common with everything else of its kind or type. For example, a particular snowflake will share with all others certain facts about its structure, its chemical composition, its melting point, etc. On the other hand, it will also have various properties that it does not share with other members of its own infimum species – its particular shape, for example, or the angular momentum of its descent. These are its non-generic features.

A key fact about fictional particulars is that they are of finite cognitive depth. A point will always be reached when one cannot say anything characteristically new about them presenting non-generic information that is not inferentially implicit in what has already been said. (New generic information can, of course, always be forthcoming through the progress of science. When we learn more about coal in general we learn more about the coal in Sherlock Holmes's grate.) The finiteness of the cognitive depth means that the presentation of ampliatively novel non-generic information must in the very nature of the case come to a stop where fictional things are at issue. With real things, on the other hand, there is no reason of principle why this process need ever terminate. *Au contraire*, we have every reason to presume them to be cognitively inexhaustible. And any adequate metaphysico-epistemological world-view must recognize that the ongoing process of science is a process of conceptual innovation that always leaves some facts about things wholly outside the cognitive range of the inquirers of any particular period. Fact is not only stranger than fiction, it is more complex.

The cognitive depth of fiction is always finite: fiction, unlike reality, is the finite product of a finite mind. It presents a world whose constituent detail is the limited creation of a limited intellect. Unlike the real world, it is a realm bounded within the limits of thought and language. Because of this, one is bound to reach the end of its road with a finite number of steps. Reality just isn't like that. It is like an unendingly layered onion; you can always peel off further layers of microscopic and sub-microscopic detail without ever reaching an end. Thus reality has more complications, more twists and turns that cannot be anticipated than fiction ever can have. It can surprise us in ways fiction never can. Reality is to fiction as chess is to tic-tac-toe. In sum, truth is stranger than fiction. But, of course, strangeness isn't everything.

WHAT CAN FICTION TEACH US THAT REALITY CANNOT?

The ancient Egyptians, the early Hebrews, the Mayas and Aztecs – among others – presumably lacked fiction. Just what did they forego? How serious a loss does a person/society/culture sustain when fiction is missing? How serious an impoverishment does its absence represent? Is there any lesson about life that we cannot learn without fiction?

A case of some sort can surely be made for saying that the loss is not a major one. There is much truth to the saying that truth is stranger than fiction. It is not easy to think of any lessons about human nature or about the conduct of life that cannot be learned as well, or almost as well, without fiction. Even the staunchest devotee of fiction would, I think, find it difficult to meet the challenge of coming up with an example of some useful insight into the human condition that would not be acquired without the mediation of fiction. Does this consideration render fiction useless? I think not.

Reality may be infinitely complex, but it is also totally unfocused. It does not involve a directing of attention. Nature presents many things together: its favoured connective is 'and' rather than 'and so.' It has no point of view, but is all at once. It conjoins, but does not prioritize. Unlike the human eye or the human mind, reality has no focus.

The manifold of occurrences in the real world accordingly has three features that fiction abrogates. First, it is unfocused: it is not like a stage with some things centred and others peripheral; it speaks in a monotone, without stress or emphasis; nothing is more central, more significant; things may differ in size or frequency, but not in importance. Secondly, it is value neutral: nature and history are impartial; they do not take sides; they do not differentiate between the good guys and the bad, equipping the one with white hats and the other with black. Thirdly, it is ateleological: its changes do not select with a view to some evaluatively significant objective. There is no purposive connection.

The overall point is that in the real of objective reality of nature and of history there is no selection: not by importance, not by merit, not by purpose. Reality's world is an evaluatively unstructured agglomeration. It is amorphous to an extent that fiction neither can nor should be.

In this regard, then, reality as such is totally different from human reality, reality as we human beings experience it. The dimension of meaning of centrality, purposive order, and evaluative assessment is something co-ordinate with mind. Only minds can provide a point of view in terms of a structure of significance, value, and purposive connection. The reality of our experience is focused; the human mind, like the human eye, attends to things in a directed way. Even as our visual field has a centre, so does our attentive field: we tend to focus on things one at a time. In this regard, human language, with its sequential now this, now that, epitomizes the sequentially focused flow of human thought.

Accordingly, the linear flow of narrative fiction with its one-thing-at-a-time focus of attention is singularly well fitted for this portrayal of human reality. It may not afford an optimal instrument for depicting reality as nature encompasses it, but it is well attuned to the portrayal of reality as we experience it. Accordingly, the great strength of fiction resides not so much in its utility in providing information, but rather in its effectiveness in providing insight – its service as an instrumentality for gaining a grasp on life as we people experience it.

The world of fiction, unlike that of natural reality, is not axiologically neutral: it can present us with a through-and-through humanistic domain, teaching us lessons for the conduct of human life in a way that other more factually oriented disciplines cannot. (Note that we can only learn from history insofar as history is made to emulate fiction.) Fiction gives insight into a human world of values in the way that the dispassionate (value-free) study of objective reality in standard science never actually can.

Its being somehow poorer than reality is thus an advantage to the world of fiction. For it enables us to achieve a clarity of focus on issues of value and morality that the shaded complexities of life and the notorious opacity of the hearts and minds of our fellows renders it near impossible to achieve in the domain of the real.

The crucial thing about fiction is that it confronts us with a way of looking at the world that is different from our own personal one. This largely serves to explain why we cannot easily imagine an author reading her own novel with real interest. It's not just that she knows what happens next; if that were the crux, then people would never enjoy rereading the same novel, and that's just not so. Rather, it cannot carry her out of her own way of seeing things, cannot broaden the range of her experiences, by opening a window on a different vista on the conduct of life. The reading of biography is the closest approximation (albeit one that always involves the clutter of superfluous detail exactly because it deals with reality).

HOW SERIOUS A MATTER WOULD THE LOSS OF FICTION BE?

Fiction is not only an exercise in, but also a testing ground for, the imagination. Role-playing, thought experimentation, and all the other imaginative processes of though are too important and too fertile a human resource to be sacrificed without loss. *Homo sapiens* is an amphibian who lives in the realm of reality and in the realm of possibility as well. The loss of the second realm diminishes our very nature. And none of our resources is a more efficient and effective entry into this realm than is fiction.

And there is, of course, another less utilitarian aspect of the matter. No doubt a culture could exist and thrive despite the loss of a major art form like music, or sculpture, or poetry, or fiction. But it would undoubtedly sustain a major loss thereby: an impoverishment of the imagination and the stunting of a significant sector of the creative spirit.

CONCLUSION

These ruminations have an end in view and are designed to point towards a particular conclusion. It is this: there is a substantially uncultivated field of inquiry out there just waiting to be developed, a field which might be called the theory of fiction.

Most of the time when academics concern themselves with fiction, they deal with what might be called its natural history. They go out into the field, so to speak, collecting samples in order to study them and arrange them into illuminating configurations. But they seldom probe beneath the works of fiction to get at the underlying theoretical principles that are at issue with this interesting genre of intellectual creativity. And this state of affairs is to some extent regrettable. For over and above the scholarly descriptive issues that works of fiction themselves exhibit, there lies a whole section of challenging, and by no means uninstructive, theoretical questions that their very existence poses for us.

3

Fortress Fiction

JOHN WOODS

It has been well said that 'literary phenomena rather convincingly show the inadequacy of most going formal semantics' (Routley 1979, 3). I once made the mistake of suggesting, in the preface to *The Logic of Fiction* (Woods 1974), that a satisfactory literary semantics would not be all that difficult to produce, and then proceeded to write a book that demonstrated the opposite. The demonstration, moreover, was exemplary rather than discursive. If that book did a reasonably good job of specifying the problems, it did considerably less in solving them (Routley 1979, 3). Wiser heads have known longer than I the startling and intractable nastiness that literature throws in the face of the would-be semanticist. Our friend Doležel has prudently inveighed against over-simple theoretical devices in the service of the fell swoop (Doležel 1979a). Possible worlds won't do, as he has shown us. Greater complexity is required than is afforded by maximal consistent sets of propositions. While the idiom of worlds is still useful, multiplicity is needed and at least some degree of incommensurability. In any event, if casual intercourse is allowed to obtain between the worlds of fiction and our own, nothing good will come of it. A certain restraint is called for.

Back in the 1960s, with an even sunnier optimism than that of the preface to *The Logic of Fiction*, I tried to make good on what I called a naive theory of (the semantics of) fiction. Although I saw it less clearly then than now, there is a certain similarity between a naive literary semantics and the pre-paradoxical state of affairs with naive set theory and naive truth theory. The great appeal of these accounts lay in their intuitiveness. In doing set theory the old way, one had fair confidence that one was getting at how sets really are. The confidence was shattered by Russell's paradox which demonstrated the existence of a set that is a member of itself if and only if it is not. The naive theory of truth suffered a similar set-back. For all its origins in Pauline scripture, history has chosen the name of Tarski for reference to a paradox that demonstrates the existence of a statement that is true if and only if it is not.

The Russell set and the Tarski sentence are each arresting in two ways. They are a logical disaster since the negation inconsistency that each yields up pullulates alarmingly, and absolute inconsistency comes in its wake. Everything is now provable. They are saddening in another way; they demonstrate that our intentions were faulty, and they forced the theorist to build his accounts in the dark, detached from his antecedent and persisting convictions about how sets and natural languages really are.

Modern set theory and modern semantics conspicuously portray the shock of this loss of intuitive innocence. Sets are not got via the cumulative hierarchy and truth, too, is given hierarchical display. Though paradox is averted in either case, one has to work hard to believe that the theories are true, that sets and languages really are that way. Of course, in the early days, the process of post-paradox theory construction was one guided by the methodological principle to keep the reformation as intuitive as possible. It is a demonstration of the depth of the damage done by the paradoxes that this principle has been honoured more in the breach than in the observance.

In my first writings about fiction, I yielded to a natural confidence in the role of intuitions. A semantics for literary phenomena should honour as much as possible what we already know of them, and defections, if required, should be modest and circumspect. In particular, I knew that there would be a problem with mingle, with sentences such as 'Sherlock Holmes lived in London' and 'Sherlock Holmes had tea with Gladstone.' And I was aware that story-endorsed contradictions such as the Keith contradiction in Bradbury's tale called for a certain gingerliness about closure properties. But unlike set theory and truth theory, adjustments could be made with minimal violence to the intuitive axioms. It has taken me a long time to realize the futility of that hope. Literary semantics are in comparably worse shape, and have incomparably worse prospects, than post-paradoxical set theory and truth theory ever did on their darkest days. Let us see why this is so.

The distinctive feature of a strongly paraconsistent or dialethic logic is that some inconsistencies are there held true. This gives negation inconsistency, but absolute inconsistency does not trail after. And a good thing, too, otherwise the world would be trivial – everything would be true. For those interested in personal identity, when thinking of paraconsistency in this dialethic way, I tend to invoke the names of Sylvan (né Routley), Myer, Priest, and Brady (Routley and Meyer 1975; Priest and Routley 1984; Priest 1987; Brady 1989).

Dialethists have attracted the attention of Professor Quine. He says that they don't know what they are talking about. The brusqueness of the rebuke is perhaps diminished by its predictability and, in any event, Antipodean fervour has not noticeably slackened. Still, Quine asks a reasonable question, paraphrasable as 'What do they think that they are doing?' So what are they doing?

Dialethists are doing several interesting things at once. They are exploiting Quine's own holism, especially the doctrine that not even a principle of logic is immune from overthrow, and they are also responding to a challenge – as it happens it is Quine's challenge – to see to it that the ways of deviancy are not too costly to bear. (Quine's admonition has something of the gravamen of Pascal's entreaties to the Christian sceptic. His warnings – Quine's – are meant to be dire.)

The dialethic program is philosophically at its most interesting in the effort it makes to advance itself by way of cost-benefit considerations. (Very Pascalian, by turn.) To date, the best developed of these centre around set theory and truth theory. The received wisdom is that the Russell paradox, which demonstrates the existence of a set that is a member of itself if and only if it isn't, demolished naive (that is, intuitive) set theory. The dialethist is not so sure. He notices with disapproval that all going post-Russellian set theory is transacted via the cumulative hierarchy (CH). The CH, depending as it does on a prior notion of the ordinals, either takes ordinality as primitive or analyses it in the set theory itself once it is up and running. Either way, there are problems. In the first instance, specification of the CH is severely understated; in the other, it is circular.

The received wisdom also has it that the Tarski paradox, which demonstrates the existence of a statement that is true if and only if it is not, put paid to naive (that is, intuitive) semantics. But, says the dialethist, post-paradox semantics is unsatisfactory. For one thing, in Tarski's own version of it we are commanded to the view that the truth predicate is infinite-wise ambiguous, and this makes for deep empirical inadequacy when such theories are applied to natural languages. There are alternatives to Tarski's account, to be sure – those of Gupta and Herzberger, for example – but they too offend in kindred ways.

A further dialectic complaint is about the classical logic that undergirds modern theories of sets and of truth. It fails, they say, to characterize paradox properly. We have all been raised to think that the sting of paradox lies in its contradiction. A paradox, then, is a sentence false under every admissible valuation. Not so: Paradoxes are sentences that are true and false simultaneously. Yes, if Excluded Middle is available for service, we will always get a contradiction from a paradox. But it will be a contradiction discernible in syntax only. False for all valuations and true for all valuations, too, it will not quite fit the anterior semantic specification of contradiction. It will over-fit it.

It becomes apparent that the dialethist is reckoning up costs and benefits. Post-Russellian set theory is bad mathematics. Post-paradox semantics is an empirical disgrace. And classical logic doesn't know what paradox is. They impose unacceptable costs. They should be replaced.

It is now proposed that we reject some further advice from Quine. Quine says that when set theory or semantics get into trouble it is best, because least disruptive, to try to fix set theory and semantics, and we should 'not lay fairer fields to waste.' That is, we should leave logic alone. As good as this advice may be in general, the paraconsistentist refuses it in the cases at hand. He wants it to go the other way round. He proposes to leave set theory alone and semantics alone (inconsistencies and all) and to fix logic. In these cases, this is the least disruptive, the least costly, strategy.

The allure of the paraconsistentist program lies chiefly in the rehabilitation of naive set theory and naive semantics, the only theories of such things that aren't counter-intuitive, *ad hoc*, difficult to work with, and just wrong. Whether the rehabilitations will come off awaits a good deal more investigation. As we speak, the polls are still open and the early returns are mixed.[1]

What the paraconsistentist has lacked, contrary to some unconvincing assurances otherwise, is a primary datum or what Herzberger has called 'a primordial intuition.' He lacks a knock-down demonstration of what no classicist will give him without a knock-down demonstration, namely, that certain things are objectively true and false. He lacks what Galileo had but timorously kept to himself; that is, a knock-down demonstration of the equinumerosity of some classes and some of their own proper subclasses. When the proof did hit the light of day, it changed people's minds radically, and number theorists could start talking about infinities in deep and interesting ways.

My self-appointed task is to try to find for the dialethist his primary datum. I shall look for it in the 'killing fields' of literary semantics, which of course is already a reason not to look there. In doing this, I mean to be guided by an initial symmetry with set theory and semantics. Modern theories of fictionality are at least the messes that the paraconsistentist takes those others to be. So perhaps we should endeavour to return theories of fictionality to *their* long-lost intuitive moorings and start afresh under paraconsistent guidance.

So I begin with what, somewhat tendentiously, I shall call some 'naive axioms' of literary semantics:

[A] Reference is possible to fictional beings even though they don't exist.

[B] Some sentences about fictional objects and events are true.

[C] Some inferences about them are correct.

[D] Reference truth and inference in respect of such things are made possible by the primacy of the author's say-so – by the say-so criterion of truth, as it has been called.

[E] Some fictional truths involve existent objects and real states of affairs.

One of the contentions that endures in the precincts of literary semantics concerns how to construct a story's 'maximal account,' as Parsons has called it (1980). The maximal account is the original text supplemented by what a competent reader would furnish by way of the specification of unexpressed content. By my lights, indispensable for such a task is the employment of what are called 'default logics.' If you tell me, over the phone from Bombay, that you've spied a tiger from your study window, I will attribute four legs and some stripes unless you tell me differently, that is, in default of information to the contrary. When we assign 'default' values to variables whose actual values aren't given, we are guided by the appropriate prototypes. If we didn't do this in general, as in life, we would derange communication and paralyse routine inference. We would also perish probably. Guided by prototypes, I infer that Holmes had a brain, for how could he be a man (and England's most splendid deducer) without one; and that he had a spine, for how else could he stride the moors or stand to fiddle? As for his having a mole on his left shoulder blade, prototype considerations won't be decisive, but the dermatology of the human skin being what it is, either he had a mole there or he did not.

If this is right, something else is seriously wrong. To hold, as Parsons and many others do, that Holmes is objectively incomplete in this regard (and numberless others) is a grave violation of prototype and completely without auctorial sanction. It flies in the face of default reasoning and makes the construction of maximal accounts all but impossible.

Inconsistency arises in discourse about the fictional in at least two ways. First, there are internal contradictions, that is, contradictions expressly in the story or in its maximal account, and underwritten by the author's say-so supplemented by default reasoning. Secondly, there are external contradictions arising from the semantic tension between a fictional being's world and the real world. 'Sherlock Holmes lived in London' is true by say-so but false, or anyhow untrue, by the ways of the world. It would appear that fiction gives rise to internal contradictions only occasionally, but external contradictions are liberally and systematically produced, one each for every sentence of any maximal account made true by say-so or by default considerations therefrom. As for internal contradictions – the advertent ones such as Keith's being elected and not elected president in the year 2005 in the Ray Bradbury story (see Heintz 1979, 92–3) – they are manageable in an underlying paraconsistent logic such as a quantifictional extension of Priest's *PP* (1987, chap. 5) or in John Heintz's adaptation (1979, 92–3) of an early system of Routley and Meyer.[2] And so it would seem that the paraconsistentist has his primary datum, for that contradiction, that necessary falsehood, about Keith is also true, and yet our good old world is as non-trivial as ever.

External contradictions offer even greater dialethic appeal. In Quine's lovely phrase, we have here 'a teeming prosperity' of sentences, each true by say-so and each false by the world. That said, it can be appreciated that a sentence's taking the paradoxical value {T, F} is not an isolated or exotic affair. It is a commonplace.

Not only does the paraconsistentist have an impressive primary datum, it is a datum which gives additional momentum to his cost-benefit strategy. After all, if we could have learned to live with inconsistent fictions, why not with inconsistent sets and inconsistent semantic reference?

But now I must tell you about 'The Mischief of Ricardo Bosque,' a story by Djaitch da Bloo. In this tale, Ricardo has constructed a Semantic Orthocomplementation Device, which he calls Negator. Negator is designed to take as input a proposition together with its truth value and to yield as output the same proposition but now with its truth value changed. This is Ricardo's way of making things better – of changing the world with uttermost circumspection (for Ricardo is, among other things, a coward). Things go wrong at the test stage, and in one careless rapture Negator in-takes all propositions, together with their respective truth values, and spits them all back out again, but now attended in each case by the paradoxical value {T, F}. By the provisions of our present theory, our naively paraconsistent literary semantics, everything is now either true and false and false or true and false and true (or, striking redundancies each time, true and false). The world is trivial and no paraconsistentist can prevent its being so.

The culprit of course is say-so. We have given it too much free sway. Various remedies lie in wait. Let us look at two.

Remedy I: Reconstrue the say-so criterion and reissue it as a condition not on truth but on the correct assertibility of what is false. Correct assertibility? What is this? It becomes a conspicuous feature of Remedy I that our fictional sentences no longer oblige Tarski's Convention T. Let Σ be any maximal account of any text made assertible just by the author's say-so and let S be a member of Σ. In fact, we might as well let Σ be the maximal account of 'The Mischief of Ricardo Bosque,' since it is here that our previous trouble originated. Hard cases may make bad law, but they are the heart and soul of serious philosophy. That said, we have it vacuously that:

(1) If 'S' is true, then S.

But not the other way round. Instead we have

(2) If S then 'S' is false.

And so

(3) 'S' is not true. [By 'S's' membership in Σ and a negation rule not in doubt.]

But from (3)

(4) 'Not-"S"' is true.[3]

and from (1)

(5) Not-S

However, by the construction of Σ

(6) S.

And given the teeming prosperity of da Bloo's Σ, again the world is trivial.

A further retreat is necessary.

Remedy II: We should find for Σ some modest build-up of structure, some syntactic reckoning with its auctorial origins. Attachment of adverbial supplementation, say, of an 'in-fiction' operator, might help. Let us do it: The sentences Σ now present themselves in the reconstructed idiom, not of 'S', but of 'f(S)'.

Questions arise. What is the structure of these artifacts? What are their truth conditions, if any? Do they comport with Convention T? Good questions, and hard ones. One thing is clear in any case. It cannot be allowed for any pair, 'f(S)', 'f(¬S)' that the occurrences therein of 'S' and '¬S' are *false*. Otherwise the following quartet would emerge.

(7) f(S)

(8) 'S' is false

(9) f(¬S)

(10) '¬S' is false

But (8) gives us

(11) '¬S' is true

and (10) gives us

(12) 'S' is true

Whence by the usual conjunction properties

(13) '"S" and "¬S"' is true.

The world is still trivial.

Enter the gapper. The gapper is he whose antecedent inclination was to forbid the sentences of fiction a truth value in the first place. In the present situation he could allow that the 'f(S)' are true and yet direct his gappy designs to the embedded 'S'.[4] It won't work. It may be that the gapper's solution handles well enough those sentences of S in which there is purported express reference to fictional objects (e.g., 'Ricardo was perplexed and very, very angry') and for which, he thinks, there are prior and independent presumptions of reference failure. But the remedy cannot explain at all how our modest adverb 'f' manages to take the robust falsehood, assertible in any story willing to have it, viz.,

(14) London has a population of a hundred million souls

into semantic oblivion. It is even worse with truths about the world which an author borrows for guest-appearances in his f-construction. For, once borrowed,

(15) London is the capital city of the United Kingdom in 1996

likewise goes into a semantic black hole. We must not empower the f-operator prodigally. It is ludicrous to see it as a truth-value annihilator and so as kith and kin to Ricardo's own Negator, only worse. It will work for embedded sentences attracting antecedent allegations of truth valuelessness. It will not work at all for the others.

I lack the space to but sketch our future course. We might have said that (15) has no occurrence in f(15), that (15) though true is not the (15) of f(15) which is neither true nor false. Saying so, we would have mangled the identity conditions for sentences and encumbered f(15) with astonishing structural illucidity. For what could f(15) possibly mean?

We have to follow, reluctantly, the course of Fortress Fiction, using an analogy to Fortress America of some eighty years ago. Fortress Fiction is a policy of harsh semantic isolationism, the austerity of which makes its near-namesake seem a call for world federalism. Fictional sentences are now refused intercourse with any save their own kind in a given maximal account, which in turn is constrained by ungenerous closure conditions. It is a central provision of Fortress Fiction that mingle is not to be tolerated. This is consequential. Its sole pronouncement upon

(16) David Lewis has done quite a lot of thinking about Sherlock Holmes over the years

and

(17) Holmes has had a large cult following in Europe and North America

is to refuse them the status of input to its own theory. If people on the 'outside' want to hazard an opinion, how worldly and how brave, but they are no business of literary semantics. This will strike some people as unfortunate, having all the attractions of the physician's advice to Groucho Marx:

Groucho: Harry, my shoulder hurts when I move my arm like so.

Doctor: Don't move your arm like so.

Fortress Fiction is also terrible news for the construction of a story's maximal account. On the face of it, we cannot even default-reason our way to the inference that Holmes had a spine. For although we have it from the stories that Holmes was a man and from human anatomy that men have spines, Fortress

Fiction is ungenerous about closure. It will begrudge their conjunction, if not ban it outright. Denied now, the guidance of prototype construction of maximal accounts becomes an astonishment and a mystery.

Where does this leave literary semantics? Where does it leave paraconsistent logic? It leaves literary semantics in a cringing state. But is does allow for a paraconsistent treatment of internal contradictions in those cases where their indiscriminate deducibility is not already crimped by closure jitters. Whether this gives the paraconsistentist his primary datum is doubtful. For, although we do have it that 'f(S)' is true and false for some Σ and some 'S', Fortress Fiction conspires to deprive such sentences of the shock and interest of genuine paradoxes. Such is the fate of guilt by association. I can hear set theorists all over the world laughing themselves silly at the very idea that the paraconsistentist would seek or accept solace from anything as half-baked as Fortress Fiction. He can claim the solace if he wishes; but how it will go down with the classicist who, after all, is its intended beneficiary is another matter.

Notice that Fortress Fiction has demolished all but our naive axioms. Primary datum or not, the paraconsistentist cannot claim the further cost-benefit advantage that he claims for paraconsistent set theory and truth theory. They restore their intuitive axioms. Paraconsistent fiction puts the intuitive axioms into permanent retirement. So our 'initial symmetry' is lost.

NOTES

1 The system N of paraconsistent set theory gives all set theory that the ordinary mathematician needs, including the category theorist. The Russell paradox can be proved, but it cannot be proved (yet) whether N is trivial. Impositions of relevance constraints will give provable non-triviality, but how non-trivial is unknown. Perhaps the leading paraconsistent semantics is Priest's theory *Sem*. It is not known whether *Sem* is inconsistent. And if made inconsistent by technical manipulation, it is not known whether it is non-trivial.

2 See note 1.

3 I will consider shortly putting this move in doubt.

4 And, of course, the gapper can now block the move from (3) to (4).

4

Literary Fictions and Philosophical Theories: The Possible-Worlds Story

PETER McCORMICK

Recall a crucial passage in one of the many literary masterpieces Lubomír Doležel considers repeatedly in his long and rich reflections on fashioning more satisfactory accounts of the nature of literary fictions:

But it was above all at mealtimes that she could bear it no longer, in this little room on the ground floor, with its smoking stove, the creaking door, the walls that sweated, the damp floor-tiles; all the bitterness of life seemed served up on her plate, and, with the steam from the boiled beef, there rose from the depths of her soul other waves of nauseous disgust. Charles was a slow eater; she would nibble a few hazelnuts, or else, leaning on her elbow, amuse herself drawing lines on the oilcloth with the point of her table knife. (Flaubert 1950, 78–9)

And recall as well a crucial moment in the complicated history of the interpretation of this passage, an interpretation like that of Erich Auerbach which Lubomír Doležel has criticized searchingly in some of his most recent work:

This paragraph forms the climax of a presentation whose subject is Emma Bovary's dissatisfaction with her life. She has long hoped for a sudden event which would give a new turn to it – to her life without elegance, adventure, and love, in the depths of the provinces, beside a mediocre and boring husband; she has even made preparations for such an event, has lavished care on herself and her house, as if to earn that turn of fate, to be worthy of it; when it does not come, she is seized with unrest and despair. All this Flaubert describes in several pictures which portray Emma's world as it now appears to her; its cheerlessness, unvaryingness, grayness, staleness, airlessness, and inescapability now first become clearly apparent to her when she has no more hope of fleeing from it. Our paragraph is the climax of the portrayal of her despair. (Auerbach 1953, 483)

With these details of the rich complexity of paradigmatic instances of literary fictions and interpretive criticism freshly in mind, I would like to explore critically several key resources in Doležel's work for advancing a widely shared concern with understanding more fully the nature of literary fictions.

DOLEŽEL ON THE LIMITS OF A POSSIBLE-WORLDS MODEL FOR FICTIONS

In some of his most recent work, Lubomír Doležel has provided an important summary of his ongoing critique of various kinds of mimetic criticism as well as a reformulation of his own critical alternative to 'mimetic theories of fictionality' (1988, 475). Doležel's project is the direct result of the inadequacies he finds in mimetic theories of fictionality like Auerbach's. These failings are numerous. But the central problem that generates the need for an alternative theory is the situation of mimetic theories within what Doležel calls 'a one world model frame' (481), a world, mimetic theories construe further, as an actual world only. For a 'mimetic semantics of fictionality' attempts to integrate fictions into a framework that comprises one actual world only. By contrast, Doležel wants to propose a 'non-mimetic semantics of fictionality,' what he also calls a 'fictional semantics,' that replaces the framework of the actual world with a framework constructed from the notion of a possible world. Moreover, in place of only one actual world, the new framework comprises many worlds which are construed as possible worlds. Thus, the non-mimetic alternative to a mimetic semantics of fictionality is in part 'a possible worlds semantics of fictionality' (481). Fictions are to be integrated not into the actual world, but into a multiplicity of possible worlds thereby, the implicit claim runs, obviating the debilitating handicap which afflicts the rival strategy while not incurring similar handicaps of its own.

One central claim in Doležel's work is that certain 'specific features of fictional worlds of literature cannot be derived from the possible worlds model of formal semantics; yet they can be identified only against the background of this model frame' (486). What are those features? Without claiming exhaustiveness, Doležel points out three: 'Fictional worlds of literature are incomplete' (486); 'Many fictional worlds of literature are not semantically homogeneous' (487); and 'Fictional worlds of literature are constructs of textual activity' (488).

The incompleteness of fictional worlds distinguishes them from the usual Carnapian construal of a possible-worlds framework as complete. One consequence is the indeterminacy of fictional worlds that makes undecidable many statements about such worlds (486). Another is the aesthetic significance of different degrees of incompleteness in different kinds of fictional worlds. Moreover, fictional worlds include within structural wholes different complex 'sets of semantically diversified domains,' for example, the domains of multiple fictional agents like Charles and Emma within a particular narrative like *Madame Bovary*. Thus, unlike possible worlds, the claim is, fictional worlds accommodate semantically heterogeneous structures. Finally, fictional worlds, unlike their more general rivals, require a distinction between non-actualized possibles and just those non-actualized possibles that are fictional entities. 'As textually determined constructs, fictional worlds cannot be altered or cancelled, while the versions of the actual world provided by descriptive texts are subject to constant modification' (489). And behind these three structures lies Doležel's commitment to a many worlds view of fictions as opposed to a one-world view.

RECENT CHALLENGES TO DOLEŽEL'S VIEW: AN ACTUALIST VERSION

If these are, on Doležel's recent reflection, the three main constraints that fictional worlds impose on possible-worlds theories, do these constraints require rethinking in the light of recent philosophical differences between possibilists like David Lewis and actualists like Robert Stalnaker? Consider for a moment several actualist claims.

The view I have in mind refuses to subscribe to the possibilist claim that all possible worlds are equally real and that all possible objects equally exist. Instead, this moderate version of modal realism claims that only actual objects exist and all other things including possible worlds and their individuals exist in the actual world (see Loux 1979, 48). The basic idea here is that some objects such as propositions, relations, kinds, and states of affairs accommodate a distinction between existence and instantiation. Thus, possible worlds on this view become instantiable entities. All possible worlds actually exist, but only one of them is instantiated. Thus, 'what we call "possible worlds" are not really worlds but properties the one world might have, states it might be in, or ways it might be' (Stalnaker 1987, 121). Hereafter I will refer to this more moderate variety of modal realism as the actualist version of the world, a related but more sophisticated framework than the one on which mimetic theories of fictionality are said to rely.

The actualist version of the world, like its more extreme rival, is a metaphysical theory that provides a series of philosophical benefits for those concerned with questions like the ones mentioned earlier. The possibilist wants to claim that precisely the metaphysical commitments his theory entails are those that must be made if we are to gain the philosophical benefits to which his theory points. The actualist, in a striking counter-claim, argues that having these benefits does 'not depend on any particular metaphysical commitments' (Stalnaker 1987, 172). Here is the claim in the formulation of Robert Stalnaker, its most persistent proponent.

Any application of the framework to a particular domain will have to say or presuppose something about the nature of the entities – the alternative possibilities – that it quantifies over when it makes modal and intentional claims, but different things. All such applications will have some structure in common, and analyses of modal, probabilistic and intentional concepts are an attempt to clarify that structure. But they need not have an ontology in common, and there need not be a single set of maximally specific possible worlds to fit all contexts. It may be that every attempt to say something substantive about what possibilities are – what structure and constituents they have – will be local in the sense that it leaves out some possibilities that may be relevant in some other context. A general account of possible worlds will be abstract, not in the sense that it says that possible worlds are a special kind of entity, an abstract entity, but in the sense that it attributes to them only a certain relational structure. Possible worlds will be primitive and unstructured in the general theory, not because they have some kind of metaphysical simplicity, but because we want to theorize at a certain level of abstraction. (1987, 122)

On the actualist version of the world, fictionality comprises not just ways things might have been but ways things might still be. These ways are future rather than past possibles in that the time of their possible instantiations in the future is different than that of their similarly possible, but no longer actual, instantiations in the past. Fictional particulars like Emma and Charles in this metaphysical story really exist as possibles, but they are of a different sort than those really existing possibles that are already actualized. Unlike actualized possibles, those that are as yet unactualized are all abstract objects. Moreover, they are not fundamental in the sense of being logical primitives, but depend ontologically on the status of the internal relations of rational agents.

On such an actualist account of fictionality, moreover, fictional individuals are to be understood not as the residue of an ontological reduction, but as the ontological configurations that arise from a redescription of certain as yet unactualized states of affairs. These states of affairs obtain not independently in the confines of possible worlds but within possible worlds which themselves exist within the one actual world. Thus fictional entities are not themselves possible worlds but simply conjunctions of certain possible states of affairs that could be instantiated in the actual world as novel properties of that world. Unlike actual properties, however, these novel properties that the actual world would at some future time exhibit by including both instantiated and novel states of affairs as abstract entities have a generally relational structure only. The consequence is that on the actualist version such abstract objects, far from being metaphysical simples, are to be understood continually as a function of dynamic rational and ethical agents as readers.

Such an account raises a serious challenge to Doležel's thesis that, however we limit the application of possible-worlds theory to our analyses of fictionality and fictional individuals, certain features of fictional worlds can be identified only against the background of a many-worlds interpretation of possible-worlds theory, that is, of a possibilist and not an actualist account. Before coming back to Doležel's views about necessary presuppositions for understanding certain features of fictional worlds, I would like to extend the suggestion so far that some version of an actualist account of possible worlds may be a more satisfactory framework for understanding fictional worlds than a possibilist account such as Doležel's.

EXTENDING THE ACTUALIST ACCOUNT OF POSSIBLE WORLDS

My suggestions arise from reflection on an atomistic framework originally proposed by the early Wittgenstein and Russell and recently amended and developed by Skyrms.[1] Following Armstrong, I take states of affairs as primitive, with both individuals and universals as the constituents of such states, and properties and relations as divisions of universals. This framework yields an account of possibility that will enable us to nuance the actualist version of possible worlds already before us in such a way, I think, as to make a more fruitful critical application of a suitably qualified version of possible-worlds theory to fictional worlds.

Worlds, whether possible or actual, are worlds of states of affairs. Fictional worlds are worlds of particular kinds of conjunctive states of affairs configured in distinctive ways. More simply, there is only one world. This world is the actual world of space and time. Accordingly, possibility is to be subordinated to actuality so that only the actual world and no possible world is, in this idiom, properly speaking 'real.' How that subordination is construed, that is, whether we are to understand actuality modestly in naturalistic terms only ('nothing at all exists except the single world of space and time') or more strongly on some non-naturalistic interpretation ('certain *actual* entities [exist] over and above those postulated by Naturalists'), I will not explore here. Appreciating this framework itself, however, requires more background.

ATOMISM AND THE LOGICAL AND METAPHYSICAL BACKGROUNDS OF POSSIBLE-WORLDS MODELS

Anyone who wants to look closely and critically at a metaphysical notion of the world does well to scrutinize freshly in the context of contemporary discussion what is still among the most influential understandings of this notion in modern times, that of the early Wittgenstein. Hereafter I will refer to this idea somewhat misleadingly as the atomistic notion of the world. Although Wittgenstein propounds this view in the opening sections only of the *Tractatus* as well as in the *Notebooks, 1914–1916* and then in his highly elliptical early manner, this notion of the world with many small qualifications stands behind the movement of English language philosophy from Frege, through Russell, into Schlick's Vienna Circle, and through Carnap and Reichenbach into much of the early work of Goodman, Quine, and Putnam. Although unfashionable, and difficult, it remains even today in its still unfathomed modal versions a powerful and persuasive metaphysical vision that continues to inspire much work in logic, philosophy of language, and philosophy of science together with their respective impacts on artificial intelligence, cognitive psychology, and both linguistic and epistemological naturalisms. What are the elements of this notion of the world and what is its structure?

Perhaps the least misleading way to grasp this account of the elements and elementary structure of the world is to see them by reflection in the elementary structure Wittgenstein believed he had found in language. At successively finer levels, the structure of language correlates with that of the world. At the first level, we may say rather roughly, we find a correlation between what Wittgenstein calls propositions and facts, at the second and deeper level between elementary propositions and states of affairs, and at the third and final level between names and objects. Without taking the time here to spell out the debts Wittgenstein acknowledges to the terminology of both Frege's and Russell's philosophies of logic and language, we can visualize the proposed structure of the world with the help of a recent diagram.[2] The diagram captures the parallelism while leaving out just how the elements are understood to interact whether at the horizontal or at the vertical levels.

WORLD	LANGUAGE
facts	propositions
states of affairs	elementary propositions
objects	names

When we read this schema upwards from the simples through their compoundings into the complexes, we have the notion of the atomistic world as a representation of reality in terms of objects as logical simples built up into states of affairs. These states are taken either as existent and hence positive facts or as non-existent and hence negative facts. Accordingly, the atomistic world is not an aggregate of things or a collection of elementary objects. Rather, the atomistic world is the totality of facts arising from elementary states of affairs from which objects (i.e., individuals, properties, at least formal ones, and relations) can be abstracted. Notoriously, Wittgenstein provides no example of either objects or states of affairs or facts. He does, however, insist that facts consist of states of affairs, their combinations and arrangements, and states of affairs themselves consist of further unanalysable objects. Although these latter can change, simple objects that are not of any one kind only cannot change. Just what are these kinds of simple objects Wittgenstein does not say.

REVISING THE ATOMISTIC ACCOUNT OF THE WORLD

Now much more in this atomistic notion of the world has required critical discussion. For our purposes, however, I want to underline a series of global and local changes that Wittgenstein himself began to formulate in 1929 and 1931 and that he also articulated more fully in the *Investigations*. These changes involve a shift away from the possibilist views of the *Tractatus*.

The local and particular changes in Wittgenstein's views are many but we should stress at least three. He came to see that the truth-functional analysis of properties was exaggerated in that, unlike the definition Russell had provided for the definite article, certain properties such as colour impressions could not be analysed this way at all (see Wittgenstein 1974, 211). Moreover, the understanding of names in his early theory of meaning was inadequate – 'names do not simply attach themselves to things' (Pears 1987, 193). And further, the early theory of language, even without considering the picture theory, exhibited two key related failings. The senses of signs need not be determinate and far reaching, nor need the senses of each factual sentence be separated from that of others – that is, the doctrines of separatism and far-reaching sense both needed overhauling.

More globally and in general Wittgenstein introduced three further changes. The biggest problem in the *Tractatus* version of atomism was the lack of specification for the nature of the objects underlying factual sentences – Wittgenstein's inability to choose between the interpretation of simples as either material points or sense data. This problem had to be solved. Objects had to be seen as not necessarily devoid of internal complexity if the further problem of colour incompatibility was to be dissolved in such a way that, despite 'this is red' and 'this is green' being logically incompatible, both could be taken as elementary propositions. Moreover, the idea of one unique language had to be rejected. As Pears writes, 'what he was rejecting in 1929 was the idea of a unique language, perfectly mirroring the essential nature of phenomena and providing the complete analysis of ordinary factual discourse' (Pears 1987, 99, also 69, 96, 194). Finally, the very strict restraints Wittgenstein had imposed on the doctrine of showing in the *Tractatus* needed to be greatly loosened. Showing had to be understood as operative in many different language games covering the gamut of human activities and not restricted just to the ways in which only elementary sentences display the simple possibilities they assert (cf. Pears 1987, 193).

FICTIONS AND THE ATOMISTIC ACCOUNTS

With these reminders before us, return now to our shared concern with Lubomír Doležel for understanding fictions, say, for coming to terms with Emma and Charles at dinner in their small room *au rez-de-chaussée*.

Now in this context the basic difficulty an unrevised atomistic account has for our concern with literary fictions like these is that nothing can be said about such fictions that makes sense. Talk of fictions is not meaningless; for, after all, whatever the objections may be, at least some of the many suggestions of the modal realists are meaningful. Rather, on the atomistic view, talk of fictions is nonsensical. The reason goes back to the peculiar ways the correlations between language and the world are said to be elucidated. For at the most fundamental level, whatever facts embedded in their states of affairs that would be pertinent for fictional matters still lack any correlation with whatever names could be suitably embodied in elementary philosophical propositions. Fictional matters, like philosophical ones, stand outside the limits of the atomistic world. Emma is beyond us.

But we need not accept this doctrine without qualification given some of the problems just mentioned – its quite problematic reliance on an obscure notion of a 'picturing relation' between language and the world, its insufficiently critical dependence on Fregean and Russellian views about propositions and states of affairs, and its unwelcome consequences of putting even most philosophical matters, and not just aesthetic, ethical, and religious ones, beyond the pale. Rather, instead of accepting the atomistic version *tout court*, or even reflecting on one of its revised forms, we can already explore its peculiar suggestiveness in pointing to some non-elementary states of affairs as showables if not sayables. A first move then would be to supplement an account of fictional worlds with a much less restricted doctrine of what can be shown. The suggestion here would come to the idea that fictions as novel states of affairs exist already as part of the one actual world but in the form of still unactualized fictional possibles. They can continue to be construed as properties of entities and not just of propositions when their proper discussion is understood in terms of what philosophical discourse cannot so much utter as exhibit in uttering. The salient cases here are those of fictional entities in philosophical poetry, such as states of mind in the choral odes of Sophocles, particulars in the cosmological visions of Lucretius, doctrines in the *Paradiso* of Dante, individuals in Shakespeare's speculative dark romances, the dramatic expositions of conflictual relations in Racine, colour terms in the nature mythologies in parts of Goethe's science, and even the patterns Emma draws on the oilcloth while Charles slowly eats his boiled beef.

Besides this needed reminder to specify those kinds of discourse where talk of fictions can be described in other than merely propositional ways, a second lesson comes clear on critically reconsidering the atomistic account of the world. For in its striking and persistent attentiveness to what the atomistic version calls 'facts' and their combinations in complex states of affairs embedding arrangements of objects as logical simples, the atomistic view opens up the prospect of construing simples in literary fictions in less definite terms than those states of affairs a conceptual framework quantifies over in making modal claims. The question here is whether fictional worlds can be understood in less general terms than those on which a modal realism insists. More specifically, if we are to capture more faithfully some of the many ways in which as yet unactualized fictional possibles already solicit our reflections and our energies in the ongoing present, the ways Emma disquiets us, why not construe these states of affairs in what I have called elsewhere such quasi-modal terms as virtuality and intermittence (McCormick 1988, 286–93)? Here, we would say that these future states of the world are to be understood as falling into and out of the actual world to the degree that they are virtual states of affairs that are intermittently actual and intermittently possible.

RECOVERING SEVERAL POSSIBILIST NOTIONS FOR A CONTEXTUALIZED ACTUALISM

In this light, I think we must try to recover several of the continuing contributions of the more extreme, but nonetheless suggestive, possibilist accounts of a modal realism which we set aside earlier.

We need to recall here the possibilist demonstration that the term 'actual' pushes too far the notion of the actual world when it construes the actual world as including, rather than standing as a counterpart to, possible worlds in an indexical expression like 'here,' ' now,' and most significantly 'I.' The term 'actual' points us in the direction of certain states of affairs which include among their many components the reference of 'actual.' More specifically, we need to focus on the metaphysical, and not on the semantic, version of this claim, to wit, the claim that what the adjective 'actual' points to is the relation between the real world and the things existing within that world. Yet *pace* the possibilists, we need to construe the reference of the adjective 'actual' in larger terms than the possibilist alone would ('I and my surroundings') so as to include as well 'the ways things are.' Thus, while endorsing the indexical analysis of 'actual' in the possibilist vision, we need to detach that analysis from its dependence on any commitments to possible worlds and their parts really existing outside the domain of the one actual world, and from their construal as non-redescribable and irreducible logical primitives.

This move, I think, allows us to parse the overly general element in the actualist version of fictions as novel states of affairs that consist in those abstract objects we call ways of relating some future philosophical dispositions of actual rational agents as readers. For now we can take these 'ways of relating' as actual in the double sense of real things existing in the real world and as including in their reference not just the parochial and its regional surroundings of philosophical readers but the universal ways things are. Here nothing need stand outside the scope of those as yet unactualized dispositions of rational agents acting in the future, nor need any human being, however remote in language, culture, space, and even future times, be excluded either.

Yet the composite metaphysical notion of a world that would allow us good enough rational grounds for thinking through talk of fictions, if it now can accommodate possibles within one world only while integrating a sophisticated indexical interpretation of the actual and its manifold references, still lacks some metaphysical purchase on our concerns. For, as a strictly modal vision, this story of the world seems overcommitted to talk of actuality and possibility. In particular, as a *de re* modal vision this account does not yet address the difficult question of whether, in the case of fictional possibles, modality in some way must attach not just to entities but to the propositions as well. And here we need to retrieve in a final move for now some of those features of an atomistic vision of the world we considered in the context of Wittgenstein's own second thoughts about the *Tractatus* – some non-elementary states of affairs as showables and as quasi-modal intermittent virtualities.

Each of these final steps, you will argue, requires much more discussion. But at least for now good reasons urge us to entertain the idea that fashioning fictional worlds depends in some strong ways on construing the world with the help of those non-propositional and more than merely strictly referential accounts of how things stand. Such accounts enable us to exhibit, if not to say, just how the virtual ways philosophical dispositions of rational readers may be directed to the appearance of genuinely novel states of affairs in as yet unactualized fictional domains.

RECONSIDERING DOLEŽEL'S SEMANTICS OF FICTIONS

In the light of these further explorations, however summary, into recent philosophical work on possible worlds and its backgrounds in logical atomism, we can now return to Doležel's reflections on both the 'fundamental theses of fictional semantics' that he derives from possible-worlds frameworks and the specific features of fictional worlds in literature.

When viewed from the recent perspectives I have been discussing critically here, fictional worlds are, I believe, more helpfully construed as conjunctions of possible states of affairs rather than in Doležel's term as sets of possible states of affairs. The difference between these closely related formulations is larger than it seems. For we already have on record a thorough and persuasive account both of possible states of affairs and of conjunction. Curiously, however, the notion of set in non-mathematical contexts remains problematic. Consider this recent and representative comment: 'It seems that sets are supervenient on their members, that is, ultimately, things which are not sets. Supervenience, however, is a notion to be defined in terms of possible worlds and hence in terms of possibility. It seems undesirable, therefore, to make use of sets in defining possibility' (Armstrong 1989, 47; cf. 133–8).

Doležel thinks that the 'most important feature of the possible worlds model' is its providing a 'legitimation of non-actualized possibles' such as fictional particulars like the possible individual Emma. 'Emma is not an actual woman, she is a possible individual inhabiting the fictional character as non-actualized possibles become evident' (Doležel 1988, 482). Now in the more nuanced understanding of a possible-worlds model that does not appeal to sets, a few further qualifications need noting. I think we do better to talk of Emma as a possible individual that cannot exist and not as a kind of fictional particular. This way we can postpone judgment on what remains an especially litigious matter, the understanding of the nature of universals and particulars in non-modal, as well as modal, contexts. Further, we need to enlist the distinction between a possible individual and a merely possible individual – roughly, a distinction between, say, my kinder and gentler self as a possible individual three years from now and Emma as a merely possible individual. The first, my kinder and gentler self, exists in some sense ready to be actualized in the fullness of time and allows of proper reference, whereas Emma, on the sketchy ontology we have been exploring here, does not exist in any way – 'a merely possible state of affairs does not exist, subsist or have any kind of being,' although she does allow of ostensible reference. Finally, Emma as a merely possible individual is better understood not as 'inhabiting the fictional world of Flaubert's novel' (Doležel 1988, 482), but as a constituent of that fictional world in the way that any merely possible individual with properties and relations is a constituent of a merely possible state of affairs.

Besides the nature of fictional worlds and fictional individuals, Doležel also applies his many-worlds version of a possible-worlds model to the problem of the relation between fictional and actual individuals that share the same proper name. Appealing to Hintikka's 'individuation function,' Doležel construes this relation in terms of cross-world identification while holding that the boundary between actual and possible worlds is what protects the identity of fictional individuals. But without going into the perplexities that still surround cross-world identification (as 'trans-world-heir-lines'), we can already notice a difficulty here with the notion itself of such a boundary. On Doležel's model, the nature of this boundary is, despite appearances to the contrary, not so clearly sign-posted as it is in the more recent work. Thus the idea is to draw a boundary between many possible worlds, only one of which is actualized. The alternative we have seen is to draw the boundary within the one actual world among the various possible worlds. We are back, in short, to the old opposition between the many-worlds and the one-world model. But, for reasons which I detail elsewhere, I take the one-world hypothesis together with the combinatorial theory of possibility to be more economical than the many-worlds theory Doležel and others propound. The consequence of adopting my view here is that the relationship between fictional characters and actual persons bearing the same proper name reaches across boundaries but not across worlds. With others, I want to hold that there is only one world, not many, and that one world includes many actual and possible states of affairs, some of which, like the worlds of Flaubert's novel *Madame Bovary*, include merely possible states of affairs such as the character 'Emma Bovary' who did not share her name with her probable once-living counterpart, or others, like the worlds of Shakespeare's play *Hamlet*, that include other merely possible states of affairs such as the character Hamlet, who perhaps did share his name with a once-living prince of Denmark.

As non-actualized possibles, are then all fictional individuals, whether or not their proper names are shared with historical persons, ontologically homogeneous? Doležel thinks so largely because such homogeneity is 'a necessary condition of the existence and compossibility of fictional [first-order] particulars' and also because ontological homogeneity 'explains why fictional individuals can interact and communicate with each other.' And it is this ontological homogeneity that 'epitomizes the sovereignty of fictional worlds' (Doležel 1988, 483). But, in the light of our critical explorations here, this seems too categorical.

The answer, rather, has to depend on one's metaphysics. If we go Doležel's many-worlds route, we have to find a justification for eschewing the more economical alternatives. And the ones Doležel himself provides do raise serious difficulties about the nature of universals, the understanding of possible worlds in the problematic terms of set theory, the location of the distinction between the possible and the actual, and the difference between possible and merely possible states of affairs. So we may, I think, answer yes: all fictional individuals are ontologically homogeneous, so long as we can extend our agreements on just what kind of metaphysics we finally subscribe to in trying to account for fictional worlds. It thus appears, at least on the basis of the few reminders I have assembled here about possible worlds and literary fictions, that more discussion is in order.

CONCLUSION

Recall, then, the scene with which we began:

Mais c'était surtout aux heures des repas qu'elle n'en pouvait plus, dans cette petite salle au rez-de-chaussée, avec le poêle qui fumait, la porte qui criait, les murs qui suintaient, les pavés humides; toute l'amertume de l'existence lui semblait servie sur son assiette, et, à la fumée du bouilli, il montait du fond de son âme comme d'autres bouffées d'affadissement. Charles était long à manger; elle grignotait quelques noisettes, ou bien, appuyée du coude s'amusait, avec la point de son couteau, a faire des raies sur la toile cirée. (Flaubert 1983, 98)

And here again is Auerbach commenting:

The scene shows man and wife at table, the most everyday situation imaginable. Before Flaubert, it would have been inconceivable as literature ... Nothing particular happens in the scene, nothing particular has happened just before it. It is a random moment from the regularly recurring hours at which the husband and wife eat together. They are not quarreling, there is no sort of tangible conflict. Emma is in complete despair, but her despair is not occasioned by any definite catastrophe; there is nothing purely concrete which she has lost or for which she has wished ... Nothing happens, but that nothing has become a heavy oppressive, threatening something ... [Flaubert] organizes into compact and unequivocal discourse the confused impressions of discomfort which arise in Emma at sight of the room, the meal, her husband ... [In] a series of pure pictures – pictures transforming the nothingness of listless and uniform days into an oppressive condition of repugnance, boredom, false hopes, paralyzing disappointments, and piteous fears – a gray and random human destiny moves toward its end. (Auerbach 1953, 488–9)

In the presence of such pure pictures, a final question may arise here: when freshly reminded of the extraordinarily rich complexities of fictional works of art like *Madame Bovary* and nonphilosophical critical masterpieces about fictions like Auerbach's *Mimesis*, what further discussion about theories of possible worlds must we still pursue if we finally are to be able to award philosophical reflection on literature any further serious attention at all? What exactly is wrong, if anything, with skipping what still counts as philosophy here altogether, and especially still another philosophical theory of possible worlds in literature, and surrendering oneself, knowingly, to the inexhaustible pleasures and interest of entertaining Madame Bovary still one more time? For Emma Bovary has a way of requiring of us an account of where she stands, of explaining ourselves, of, as Lubomír Doležel continues to suggest, putting philosophical theories to the test, and of putting slow-eating philosophers, like Charles, at much more than conceptual risk.

NOTES

1 See Armstrong (1989, 145–52) which reprints the earlier article by B. Skyrms from 1981.
2 Cf. Grayling 1988, here slightly rearranged.

PART 2
MODELS

5

On Fictional Discourse

FÉLIX MARTÍNEZ-BONATI

In the following discussion, I use the expressions 'fictive,' 'fictitious,' and 'purely imaginary' as synonyms. The word 'fictional' has a different meaning in ordinary usage, and I want to keep it that way. A fictional text (discourse or narrative or work) is not a fictitious text (although it may represent one). In an obvious sense, a work of fiction (a novel or a short story) exists and is real. However, it necessarily implies a fictitious element, since otherwise it would be improper to call it a fiction or a work of fiction. A fiction, then, is both (in one sense) real and (in another) fictitious, and it is not easy to deal with this double nature. Not everybody agrees on the extent of the fictitious element in, for example, novels. Most people will grant that the characters and events presented by such works are fictitious, or largely so; but many will deny that the novel's narrative discourse itself is fictitious. It is, they will say, the discourse of an author, who is a real person, and therefore a real, actual discourse, which refers to merely fictive events.

For reasons that I cannot try to explain here, it is always difficult to conceive of any discourse as being a fictitious one.[1] In effect, the 'existence' of fictitious discourses has to be demonstrated. The premises, on which everybody can agree, are: (*a*) since novels contain characters that are accepted by the reader as being (entirely) fictitious, their actions must also be thought of as fictitious; and (*b*) some of these actions are discursive. Therefore, we can find fictitious discourses in novels.

This conclusion becomes more significant when we reflect on the fact that, in some novels and short stories, the narrative consists entirely of one character's discourse (for example, a so-called first-person narrative). In this case, we must grant not only that the fiction's content (the story, its action, and agents) is fictitious, but also that the narrative discourse itself is fictitious. The real author, in this case, has to be thought of as somebody who is the scribe who writes down a discourse that he has merely imagined and that he has not imagined as being his own discourse, but the discourse of a merely imagined person.

Let us go further. Let us suppose that the fictitious person who is narrating the story (in the so-called first-person narrative mode) has only a very marginal role in it. In that case, he will rarely use the word 'I' to refer to himself because he will rarely refer to himself at all. His narrative will be almost entirely a third-person narrative, interspersed with brief remarks about his own position and activities. Let us now further diminish the narrator's participation in the world of the story and limit it to one event told in one sentence: 'I was there on that occasion,' or the like. Would that still be a first-person narrative? Formally, yes. Although seen from any relevant aesthetic point of view, that narrative would be equivalent to a third-person narrative. What if we suppress this last narrative self-reference? Would that change the ontological status of this discourse? Would that make it suddenly cease to be a fictitious discourse of a fictitious speaker and become the real actual discourse of the real author? Or should we rather say that the narrative discourse continues to be fictitious, but now its fictitious speaker is silent about himself?

The reader who has followed my argument thus far may now ask: How do we know that our third-person fictional narrator is a fictitious one if he does not participate at all in the fictitious world of his story? He is not now, as he was before, an evidently fictitious part of a fictitious action. Is there a way in which he can be distinguished from the real author?

In their most characteristic mode, fictional third-person narrators display a knowledge that, by its nature or by its magnitude, is inaccessible to human beings. Fictional narrators can perceive the solitary acts or hidden thoughts of others in ways that are literally fantastic, and therefore, *a fortiori*, fictitious. Their discourse, serious in tone as it normally is, cannot be thought of as a possible utterance of a real human speaker. It is a speech that has to be thought of as having an unreal immediate source; it has to be understood as coming from an invented, magical mind. This reflection, however, is, in a sense, unnatural because the reader of fiction is normally paying attention to the characters and events and not minding the transparent medium of the narrative itself.

Of course, third-person narrators do not have to be silent about themselves in order to continue being third-person narrators. They can be imagined by the (real) author as also being authors, be they merely the authors of reports, biographies, or even fictions. These fictitious authors belong to a fictitious realm, that is different from, although connected to, the fictitious world of the story. This separate realm, which is an 'authorial' space of fictive reflection surrounding the fictive activity of narrating and writing, can be easily confused with the real circumstances of the real author, and it may resemble them very much.

I repeat that the reader of fiction does not need to have a distinct consciousness of these formal aspects because the traditional game points in another direction, that of the illusion of contemplated life.

I conclude from these first paragraphs that there are good reasons for assuming that fictional *discourse* is always fictive discourse, although the fictional *text* is a real physical commodity and the fictional *work*, a real part of our cultural life.

A speech-act theory of literary discourse seems to be pointless because literature is not a specific type of speech act (or a specific group of such types), but rather the reproduction, in the realm of the imaginary, of all the types of speech acts that occur in real life. Nonetheless, a question related to speech-act theory may be relevant for a definition of literature. Literature is allowed to present not only fictive beings and events that conform to the types or classes of beings that we find in ordinary experience, but also beings and events of an invented nature: fantastic things. Consequently, a legitimate question would be whether (fictive) speech acts of types not found in actual human discourse occur in literature. It is perhaps not obvious, or perhaps it is too obvious and therefore difficult to grasp, that, as I mentioned earlier, literary language often assumes fantastic forms, which human discourse does not present in actual 'serious' communication. Verse, highly figurative expression, and direct descriptions of solitary acts or internal states of others are examples of speech forms that, either by nature or by degree, exceed the possibilities of real speech. Nobody in real life would seriously communicate with others using these types of utterances. Another striking example are those lyrical utterances in which an often pathetic and solemn speaker is movingly talking to somebody who, as obviously known by the very same speaker, happens to be somewhere else or to be altogether nonexistent.

Fictional narrative assertions of a third-person, authorial narrator (assertions which, like all literary discourse, I conceive of as being fictive discourses) could be considered embodiments of a speech-act form that is not found in real speech. A good reason for granting this distinctive status to assertions of fact made by a fiction's third-person narrator is that they cannot be seriously doubted. That assertions as we know them in real life are either true or false belongs to their nature; the possibility of their being false, or not strictly accurate, is part of our understanding them as speech acts. On the contrary, our understanding of fictional authorial assertions of fact excludes the possibility of their being false and grants them unqualified truth and accuracy.[2]

Of course, one tends to think that it would be better to say that we only playfully and ironically grant them unqualified truth and accuracy, and only in relation to their own fictive world. Certainly, but it is precisely within the game of fiction, and only there, that they happen to be assertions. There is no other way we can take them as serious assertions. And we must take them as authentic assertions in order for the narrative to make sense and to be a narrative in the first place. We playfully and ironically grant them the nature of speech, and that only within the realm of the fictive. They are fictitious speech, and that is why they can assume fantastic forms; for example, they can be indubitable assertions of fact.

Once we accept fictional assertions as being such a thing, (that is, [fictive] speech), and once we begin appropriately reading fiction, the game's rules have to be followed in order to make sense of the text, and thus to make sense of our activity of reading. The irony and playfulness that one has in mind in this regard are outside the realm of the fictitious speech and world, although not outside the realm of fiction, insofar as this realm is understood to be the encompassing frame of mind of the reader. If we were to develop this view, we would have to distinguish between levels of consciousness – say, the real state of knowing that we are reading fiction, and the imaginary mind-set of unlimited credulity. (The game is a *'willing* suspension of disbelief,' but ultimately a 'willing *suspension* of disbelief.') It is within this second frame, and only there, that fictional, literary speech takes place. Only there does the fictional narrative assertion 'exist.' It also follows that the speaker of these sentences only exists on the plane of the fictitious.

Considerations such as the preceding ones caused me to criticize John Searle's characterization of fictional third-person narrative discourse as a series of pretended, non-serious, inauthentic assertions made by the real author (Searle 1975, 319–22; Martínez–Bonati 1980, 425–34). If the reader of fiction would play the reading of the narrative starting from the belief that the real author of the fiction is the one who is speaking, and that his assertions are merely pretended ones, the narrative would have no assertive force. There would be no impulse to follow the tale. Our habits and mental dispositions in following stories have emerged from listening to assertions we take seriously. We would not get very far in the way of narratives if every one of their sentences had to be effectively understood as statements introduced by a 'Let us merely imagine that' or 'Let us pretend that.' As we just indicated, there is precisely no lack of assertive force in fictional narratives; indeed, they possess it to a degree that is literally fantastic.

Another inconvenience of Searle's account is that (as with Käte Hamburger's theory decades ago) it unconvincingly divides literary fictions into two logically and ontologically separate classes (Hamburger 1973). Since some fictional narratives are, partly or entirely, first-person narratives, that is, discourses of 'dramatized' narrators that obviously belong to the fictitious world and are obviously themselves fictitious persons, their assertive speech acts (as well as generally all their speech acts) cannot be thought of as pretended ones (except if they happen occasionally to be jokes, or lies, or, if we follow Searle, third-person narratives considered as fictional in their worlds), but have to be imagined as authentic, serious assertions. We would have, then, on the one hand, fictions that are fictitious serious discourses (consisting mostly of true assertions) of fictitious persons and, on the other, fictions that are the real speeches of real persons (the author) and that only pretend to be serious assertions, without being truly such. As it happens, fictions of both groups can be stylistically and rhetorically indistinguishable, and very similar in their artistic effects, so that often the reader may not remember whether a novel or a story he read long ago was written in the first or in the third person. It seems very improbable that this would be so if indeed these classes were separated by such an enormous pragmatic, logical, and ontological difference.

In many cases, as I noted in the initial paragraphs, first-person narrators have only a marginal role in the story they are telling, and, in those cases, their assertions of fact tend to assume the same authority granted to the third-person narrator. The dividing line between first-person and third-person narratives is truly imperceptible, since the 'dramatization' of the narrator, or his incorporation into the world of his story, only needs one sentence, something like: 'I knew X [here the name of the protagonist, or the protagonist's friend or relative, or a witness to the narrated events, etc.] very well.' It only needs the narrator's self-reference to put him anywhere within the virtually unlimited web of the story's world. Forces of style and structure may impede such a sentence, but, at least in realistic fiction, a sentence like the one above is always logically possible; indeed, sometimes it can be understood as implicit in the narrative discourse. (All narrative is implicitly or potentially first-person narrative, because all speech is the speech of an *I*, of a subject that always can refer to himself.) It does not seem appropriate, then, to suppose that the pragmatic and logical-ontological nature of a fiction would depend on a minor detail like this one. That a logical-ontological abyss could be crossed simply by the always possible explicitation of a latent sentence is a fascinating thought, but it seems highly implausible.

These considerations reinforce my view that there is a systematic continuity of fictional narrative forms, and that they all share the same ontological status, despite their subtle logical and pragmatical differences. Basically, all fictional discourse is fictive authentic discourse of a purely imaginary speaker.[3]

In a recent article, Gérard Genette has presented a description of the pragmatic nature of fictional discourse that is based on Searle's work but intends to overcome some of the difficulties found in it (1990, 59–72). Genette accepts Searle's view that third-person fictional assertions are speech acts of the (real) author, and are only pretended assertions, but he sees them as *indirect* or non-literal speech acts that are parts of another, more complex, and this one serious, speech act. Thus, the description of the underlying, serious and authentic speech act would be something like 'I am asking you to imagine that – [here the fictional assertion].'[4] Alternatively, or complementarily, Genette conceives of the narrative speech act as a directive or a declaration, in Searle's sense (an utterance of assertive form that, by virtue of an institutionalized authority, brings about the thing it describes). If the person entitled to do so says, 'The meeting is opened,' the meeting is in fact opened. When, at least in our cultural space, the author of fiction says, 'A little girl used to live near a forest,' the reader or hearer in fact thinks of a little girl who used to live near a forest. According to Genette, 'the complete assertive formulation of an utterance of fiction would be ... "It is not a fact that once upon a time a little girl, and so on, but by pretending this I make you think of it as an imaginary state of fact."'

I do not intend to deny that these are reasonable ways of explaining what fiction is. Publishing fiction is certainly an institutionalized invitation to readers to imagine the persons and events narrated and described in the published text. Whoever follows the invitation can be expected to resolutely imagine these persons and events and to try to enjoy doing it. Notwithstanding the validity of his view, I see some problems in Genette's account.

First of all, it is plain that this description of third-person fictional discourse can be easily adjusted to fit first-person fictional narratives (which Genette, along with Searle, radically opposes to third-person narrative discourse). We could put it this way: 'It is not a fact that, as the (first-person) narrator is asserting, this and that took place, but by pretending that he is seriously asserting it, I make you think of it as an imaginary state of fact.' Speaking more generally, is it not true that the assertions of an authorial first-person narrator will in many cases have exactly the same illocutionary sense and force that the third-person assertions have? The descriptions of both forms as complex speech acts can be easily assimilated. 'It is not a fact that this took place, but by pretending that I (he) am (is) seriously asserting it, I make you think of it as an imaginary state of fact.' Both types of discourses are equally 'pretended' or equally 'serious.' Genette's (and Searle's) radical distinction of third-person and first-person narratives does not seem to be sustained by his own analysis.

The notion of 'pretending' is, in this context, unfortunate. If (*a*) the author is only pretending to assert, and (*b*) the narrative speech is his, then nobody is asserting seriously those narrative sentences. In basic fictional discourse, we would not have full and authentic narrative language. The shortcomings of such a description of the writer's activity are several, and I will not insist on them now. However, if, in order to describe fictional narrative discourse, one wanted to use the notion of pretending or feigning, it would be better not to say that the author is pretending to assert, but rather to say that he is pretending to be somebody who is seriously making assertions, somebody who *can* make those assertions seriously. Only a being belonging to the world where the fictive action takes place can do so. Writing a third-person fictional narrative, the author fictionalizes and transfigures himself. Then, the assertions are not defective utterances of the author's, but perfect assertions of somebody else, of a speaker or writer who is a merely 'pretended' person (or a person whose existence the author is merely pretending to presuppose). The author, in this view, would be reproducing or imitating somebody else's speech, but this somebody and his speech would be fictive. Since, in the case of fiction, the author creates this fictive speaker by feigning or pretending to be somebody else who is making serious assertions, this act of creation would be equivalent to (*a*) imagining a fictive speaker and his speech, and (*b*) creating a (real) written or oral replica of that fictive speech. This way we can arrive at the description of writing fiction that I have proposed.

Let us go back to Genette's correction and development of Searle's description. What about *factual* narratives in relation to Genette's proposal? Reading the work of a historian (or the newspaper), we cannot help but think of the persons and events it describes. Should we say that factual narrative assertions are indirect, non-literal speech acts whose illocutionary meaning is to be part of a declaration or a demand? All assertive utterances can thus be considered indirect speech acts, covering a complex speech act of declaration or demand. These statements would implicitly be of the nature of (a declaration) 'You now think of ...,' or (imperative demands) 'Think and imagine that ...,' or, as Bertrand Russell once put it, 'Know that ...' Indeed, all utterances, all speech acts, could be understood as indirect ones, forming part of an underlying imperative or declarative act that could be made explicit as 'Hear and understand that ...'; 'You think of this ...'

This seems to suggest that, on a certain level and as a first step, all assertions are not yet assertions, but only directives for thinking, only the content part of a declaration. Thus, Genette's description would not be specific to fictional utterances and even less to third-person, authorial fictional utterances.

If there is a difference, then, between fictional and factual narrative sentences, or between fictional third-person and first-person assertions, it cannot be the one indicated by Genette when he describes the fictional sentence as an indirect speech act.

The only difference left is that the states of fact asserted by the fictional utterance do not exist, while those referred to by factual narratives are supposed to be real. Again, this distinction, as trivially true as it is in a rough, approximate sense, hides several problems. Genette presents this matter in the following way. He concedes that any (assertive) utterance, fictional or not, can be characterized as a description of the states of consciousness of their speakers or receivers. And he adds: 'The specific feature of the fictional utterance is that, contrary to utterances of reality, which in addition [sic] describe an objective state of fact, it describes nothing other than a mental state.' One difficulty of this account is that if assertive fictional utterances are, as he says, 'descriptions of their own mental effects,' one cannot see why they should be called fictional (and less, 'pretended'), since it is assumed that these mental effects follow the sentence almost necessarily and are thus real. The fictional assertions would be or become serious assertions of fact. These assertions (all assertions in this case) would be true statements of fact pertaining to the introspective biography of their speakers and hearers. Thus, third-person fictional assertions would be at first pretended ones and indirect speech acts, and then they would turn out to be serious and true assertions. The author of fictions would be only (or only at the beginning) pretending to pretend. The description I am criticizing seems to collapse.[5]

There is also a more basic problem with the account of assertions as descriptions of the mental states they effect. Does 'Once upon a time there was a little girl living with her mother near a forest' describe a mental state? Some authors deny that there are such things as mental states, but even those who accept their existence will hardly conceive of them as possibly being little girls, having mothers, and taking residence near forests. We certainly do not think of a mental state when we understand the sentence and think of the little girl. We then think of people in the world, while assuming all the time that precisely these persons never existed and precisely these events never took place.

I think that I do understand what Genette means. His position on this point corresponds to a persistent psychologistic tradition. Since the only real thing about these fictive persons and events is the fact that we think of them, it is reasonable to conclude that, insofar as they have any actual substance, they are a transitory part of our mental states. Nonetheless, along with this assumption, the absurdities that always accompany the unavoidable notion of fiction emerge more forcefully than ever. An account of fiction, in my view, has to be hospitable to its essential duplicity. Fictive entities are both actually inside and intentionally outside of the mind; they are seriously believed by the receiver to be occurring, but this belief takes place within an encompassing consciousness of playing, of imagining non-actual parts of the world.

Genette approvingly refers to Plato's understanding of fictional discourse (Homeric epics in this case) as being the speech of an author (Homer). Genette also accepts Plato's view of the direct, quoted speeches of characters as being speeches that are possible because the author 'imitates' the character; that is, he occasionally 'pretends' to be Achilles or others, and lends his (Homer's) voice to the words of the hero. In order to be consistent with Genette's position, we have to understand, I think, that Homer would be pretending to be Achilles speaking *seriously*, since Achilles's speeches are story-internal ('homodiegetic,' in Genette's terminology) ones. Is there a reason why we should not understand Homer's basic fictional discourse as if Homer were pretending to be himself speaking seriously? Or even better, pretending to be somebody else, a seer or a prophet, who is speaking seriously (very seriously, indeed). The view to which Genette alludes is Plato's in *The Republic*. But in the *Ion*, Plato gives a different account. The poet is not speaking his own discourse, but receiving it by way of divine inspiration, and, if writing at all, he is taking dictation. In a formally related sense, I maintain that the act of writing, reciting, or composing fiction is an act of the author's, but it is not a speech act. It is an act of imagining and recording fictive utterances – utterances that may be occasionally playful and non-serious, but that will normally be serious, even when they assume fantastic shapes.

As we see, the characterization of basic fictional discourse (in the third person) as anything other than serious (fictive) assertions is fraught with many difficulties. The advantages of conceiving of the narrator of fiction as always a fictive entity are considerable. The range of types of third-person fictional narrators is also a proof of their fictitiousness. They can be inspired seers, familiar authorial voices, 'omniscient' chroniclers, impassible observers, observers only of physical events, ungraspable, impersonal, inhuman sources of words, fantastic organs of perception and description that lack a normal sense of life, etc.

I have argued in favour of the view that the forms of narrative fiction that differ according to the story-internal or story-external position of the narrator share a basic logical, ontological, and pragmatic nature. The spectrum of these forms is continuous; it does not present an internal ontological chasm. Let me say a final few words about the continuity and homogeneity of the fictive discourse and the fictive world itself. Genette shares with many the view that not all fictional assertions have the same truth-value because not all that is referred to in fiction is fictitious. Novels often describe well-known cities and other real geographical objects, and sometimes they include historical persons as characters. Fictional discourse would thus be mixed of empirically true or false and purely fictional assertions, corresponding to non-fictive and fictive entities. Elaborating on a remark by J.O. Urmson, Genette says that even the assertion 'A little girl used to live with her mother near a forest' must often be an empirically true assertion.

Like all speech acts, assertions are not timeless entities, but contingent performances of beings gifted with language. In the context of this essay, the statement 'A girl used to live with her mother near a forest' is not an assertion but only a sequence of words typical of a class of possible assertions. An assertion of that class exists only when, and every time that, somebody actually says or writes these words with (serious) assertive intent. Fictive assertions of the same class 'exist' when a purely imagined speaker is imagined as uttering those words with assertive intent. This particular act of imagining occurs when we read or hear 'Red Riding Hood.' This fairy-tale assertion, then, can never be empirically true in the real world, since it is, *a priori*, a fictive description of a fictive individual. The highly probable circumstance that actual assertions of the same wording have been true many times does not change the status of the fictional speech act. Generalizing, we can state that fictional discourse is homogeneously fictive, despite the fact that there occur in the real world many true sentences that have the same wording as some fictional ones. The fictional world itself is homogeneously fictive, despite the fact that many individuals exist or have existed (historical as well as publicly unknown persons and places) that can be associated with the fiction, either as models of the fictional items or as ostensible part of the represented world. Within the fictional experience of the world, any historical persons and places will be reduced to their conventional image and to the properties explicitly mentioned in the fictional discourse. No empirical concern about these individuals will enter the realm of literary reception. Within a given fiction, Paris or New York will be fictionalized, and descriptions of them that would be empirically false regarding the real cities will be accepted by the reader as true and definitive for the fictive world of the story.

NOTES

1 This difficulty has something to do with the fact that we regularly do perform real acts of internal, unuttered discourse. Also, there is a strange quality in thinking of a merely invented speech. Are not all speeches invented speeches?

2 Lubomír Doležel (1980, 7–25) has offered a theory of the logical properties of fictional discourse that differs from the one I have proposed but that is in several respects compatible with it.

3 I am speaking of the logical continuity of possible fictional narrative forms. Clearly, only a few of these forms have established themselves as canonical, and therefore, the apparent discontinuity of traditional narrative types does not contradict the a priori spectrum's lack of internal boundaries.

4 This and similar explicitations of the underlying, commanding speech act are naturally ambiguous. The sentence is both a description of what the speaker is doing, 'an act of request,' and the execution of the described request. In order to understand Genette's argument, however, the illocutionary sense of the utterance should be taken to be a demand or request.

5 This figure of thought, a pretending to pretend that results in a straight serious act, is suggestive in our context. It points to the description of fictional assertions that I have offered, since, in my view as in Coleridge's, there is a two-step movement in understanding fiction. First, one understands the text as being fictional and lacking a real referent then, as a fictitious discourse that refers to fictitious individuals and describes them with perfect truth.

6

The Perception of Fictional Worlds

PIERRE OUELLET

The relations between fiction and the world are complex and permit at least two types of inquiry. The first concerns the status of fiction itself, considered either from the point of view of the object (*de re*) or from the point of view of discourse (*de dicto*). In the first instance, the ontological status of fictional beings such as the unicorn, Hamlet, or the Lilliputians is examined, whereas in the second instance, the logical or pragmatic status of the different discourses of fiction such as the drama, the short story, or the lyric poem is investigated. The second type of study focuses not on the fictional in itself, but on its relations, more or less explicit, with the real and unique world or with the possible and multiple worlds that give rise to and support it. And here as well two points of view arise. On the one hand, the fictional text can be seen from the point of the world that precedes and encompasses it and that furnishes the work with the states of affairs that it is capable of representing: the city of Paris, for example, provides the framework for a large number of novels of a fictional nature. On the other hand, the fictional text can be seen from the perspective of the world that it constructs, thus augmenting the exterior world with possible states of affairs which are more or less believable: Big Brother, for instance, is part of a fictional world which now largely exceeds the novelistic world in which it was created, in the same way as we can say of a real person that he or she is a Harpagon, a Lolita, or a Don Juan.

Consequently, we can ask ourselves a number of questions about a character such as Marcel in *À la recherche du temps perdu*: what is his ontological status as a fictive being; what is the illocutionary status of the discourse which he utters or which is uttered about him; to what reality prior to the novel does he refer; and to which new reality, more or less plausible or compatible with the one we recognize as 'real,' does he give rise? To be sure, all of these questions are closely linked, in the sense that fictional beings are accessible to us only through a particular semiotic entity: a proper name, a definite description, a proposition, or a text. This entity refers, regardless of what use we make of it, to an already existing world in which it finds its place, and also to another world, constructed, which it denotes. All questions about fictionality are thus at once *de re* and *de dicto*, for they simultaneously bear on beings and on the expression associated with them, even if only by virtue of their name or definition. Likewise, these questions are also concerned with two distinct states of the world, one which is both anterior and exterior to the fictional utterance, or its reading, and the other, which is its product and which is in some way internal. Hence, we have two states of things, and the links between these states are more or less problematical.

Whether we consider, according to Doležel's categories (1988, 489), a given text as descriptive of an already existing world or constructive of a new world, it is always a question of the text's mimetic relation to the real world: either by means of a process of representation (Proust depicting more or less accurately the Bois de Boulogne at the turn of the century) or by means of the operations of verisimilitude (Cyrano de Bergerac rendering more or less believable a journey to the moon in the seventeenth century). Of course, this process and these operations are realized just as much in the text's structure and form as in its content. In the same way, fictitious beings and fictional worlds, which are always the result of an act of language having a distinct pragmatic status, can possess a logical or ontological status only if we are able to compare them with the world that we know, that is to say, with a certain experience that we have of the world – an experience against which these beings and worlds are found to be more or less compatible, or to contain a varying number of mimetic features. Thus Emma Bovary appears to us as less fictitious than Chamiso's Peter Schlemihl, who has lost his shadow, if we consider the traits that each of these characters shares with those real beings with whom we are familiar. In the end, these fictitious entities possess a stronger or weaker mimetic link with what we call reality.

Moreover, in our representation of fictitious beings, we also mentally represent for ourselves the different propositional forms of the utterances used to designate them. It is not the same thing to say 'a lot of credulous people believe in the existence of the Loch Ness monster' as it is to say 'I saw the Loch Ness monster with my own eyes,' or 'much evidence attests to the existence of something we could call the Loch Ness monster.' The degree of fictionality or verisimilitude varies from one case to another on a scale that moves towards an increasing acceptance of the reality or the possibility of the thing designated. This acceptance itself varies according to the force of the modal expressions applied to the subject 'Loch Ness monster' and to the predicate of existence that subtends it. There is consequently a gradient of fictitiousness, which is a function of the force of modal operators, and factors of verisimilitude, combined with the relative quantity of semantic features that the fictional world or being shares with the real world as we know it. The truth value of fictional utterances depends not solely on their possible verification in the observable world, but also on the argumentative force of the utterance, as well as on the perceived qualities of the represented beings or objects, qualities which are shared to a greater or lesser degree by the beings and objects of the real world which we experience.

VERIFICATIONISM

'Verificationism' (Bouveresse 1976, 365–6), which bases the possibility of signification on a procedure of comparison with the world and the consequent verification, in that world, of the existence of the thing signified, underlies almost all of the philosophical discussions of fictionality, whether or not these discussions arrive at segregationist or integrationist conclusions (Pavel 1986, 12). Yet this is surely not the best way to approach the problem of fiction or even the general problem of representation. Understanding fictional utterances does not consist of comparing names with things as Searle would have it – in his discussion of a suspended or false link between propositional content and particular states in the world (1979, 58ff.) – nor does it consist of simply comparing two worlds, by verifying whether each entity of the constructed world indeed exists in the given world or in one of its possible versions. In fact, we do not understand a fictional utterance in the same sense as we understand a purely informative proposition, such as 'Canada is north of the United States.' Indeed, we can see no value in attempting to situate the country of Lilliput in a geopolitical relation to the flying island of Laputa. I would say that we 'experience' what a fictional text represents much more than we merely identify its reference or simply comprehend its meaning. I do not read Broch's *Der Tod des Vergil* in order to gain information about the poet of the *Aeneid*, or simply to seize the meaning of the words and propositions of which the text is comprised, and to identify their more or less credible reference. I am not concerned with verifying whether the novelistic world constructed by Broch corresponds at all to the possible world in which Virgil could conceivably have lived. Rather, to read *Der Tod des Vergil* is to have an aesthetic experience (from the Greek *aisthesis*, meaning 'to apprehend by the senses or by reason'), an experience which finds its correlate in the world that is constructed and represented by the text. In other words, the work of fiction represents not a real or possible world but rather a cognitive-perceptual experience which has its two poles; first, in real or fictitious objects (which are necessarily perceived, conceived, imagined, dreamed, felt, etc., by subjects), and secondly, in subjects such as characters, narrators, enunciators, and readers who have a cognitive-perceptual experience at every level of the text (the diegetic, the levels of narration or enunciation, or at least the level of the interpretation as such, that is to say, the reading). From the moment an utterance is considered no longer as representing objects but as embodying an experience, the problem of its truth-value ceases to reside in the verification, in a real or possible world, of the existence or non-existence of the beings that the utterance designates. Rather, the truth-value of the utterance depends on the extent to which the experiences described and presented through a given semiotic form correspond to those that we experience or could experience in the phenomenal world.

Any world, real or possible, is thus the correlate of an act of apprehension on the part of subjects, particularly by virtue of those *a priori* forms of intuition which are time and space, in the Kantian sense, and that are the foundation of our perceptual activity, in the broad sense of the term. A fictitious world, for example, is always a world imagined by subjects and, among other things, it is always this particular perceptual process, that we call imagination, which constitutes the real crux of every work of fiction, be it a novel, a poem, or a dramatic text. In the modern novel, the significance attached to the representation of cognitive-perceptual processes – processes which permit us to participate in some way in the activities of consciousness which depict a character, that is to say, a fictitious being such as Broch's Virgil, Proust's Marcel, Musil's Ulrich, Valéry's Monsieur Teste, or Joyce's Molly Bloom – emphasizes the fact that the world of the novel is constituted much more by experiences, in the phenomenological sense of the term, than by objectifiable states of things such as actions, facts, or individual entities. In this sense, the reference of a fictitious character, such as Molly Bloom or Monsieur Teste, is based less on some individual living in a problematic, possible world, which is more or less accessible to our own, than on the representation of an indefinite set of acts of consciousness, which are acts of perception in the broad sense, that the literary work requires readers to (re)create in their own imagination. This question is, of course, very complex, because to enjoin readers to perceive or to imagine a fictitious being also requires them to perceive the semiotic or linguistic item used to represent it, which then requires, moreover, the perception of the discursive universe in which the representation is inserted according to the global thematic organization of the text. Finally, these acts also imply the perception of the exterior world as it normally presents itself to our senses, a world, whose different forms of appearance are represented by the work of fiction in its own way (see Ouellet 1988; 1990). Since I cannot adequately treat the entire problem here, I will concentrate on a few of the limitations of the 'verificationist' theories of fiction and demonstrate how a phenomenological approach, based on the perceptual acts (exteroceptive, interoceptive, proprioceptive) of the different subjects of experience involved in a text, might permit us, if not to resolve, then at least to change our point of view on particular aspects of this problem.

Theories of fiction are characterized by three basic theoretical positions. The first claims that the world – the real world or Kripke's 'world G,' that is, the privileged world of reality which permits access to possible worlds (Kripke 1963) – is perfectly accessible to us, that it is known or knowable in its objectivity, and thus provides a sort of invariant for the identification of possible or fictional worlds.

According to the second theoretical proposal, a world said to be real or possible is a logical world, one possessing a propositional structure of the type defined for the discursive universe of science, for example, according to a logical-empirical epistemology.

The third position characterizes fictional discourse by a particular act of language or by a specific property of these language acts, such as being fallacious, non-serious, or doubtful. Incidentally, this latter characterization is seen as totally independent of the cognitive-perceptual processes that the fictional enunciation may activate in the subjects to whom the discourse is addressed.

THE WORLD AS INVARIANT

Asking questions about the relations between the world and fiction always comes back to the same thing: acting as though we do not know what fiction is and, inversely, assuming to know fully well what the world is. In fact, it is always this latter term, the 'world,' that serves as the point of reference or as the basis of verification, permitting us to distinguish fiction from nonfiction. This is because we suppose that the world possesses a stable definition and that it in no way constitutes, as is the case of fiction, an unknown or a variable to which it would then be necessary to attribute some value. In this sense, the world is understood as being a constant. The real would thus be certain and only fiction might lead us, occasionally, to cast doubts upon it. It is then always with a perfect knowledge of what reality is, in its essence, that we question ourselves, in our ignorance, about what fiction might be in its multiple guises. And yet does the real world or, if one prefers, the phenomenal world – that of appearances – not appear to us in a form that we could call fictitious? After all, we know perfectly well (that is, logically and empirically) that 'the sun never sets,' for example, or that 'the earth in fact rotates,' whereas in the world of common sense, in the real world of perceptual qualities, we act as if 'the earth didn't budge' and as if 'the sun set each night at the horizon.' And speaking of the horizon, could there be a purer fiction than this imaginary line which marks the circular limit of vision for an observer who occupies the centre? The horizon exists, however, as fictitious as it seems; it is that which structures, in actual physical depth, our perception of the real and, conversely, the modes of appearance of the real for the subject's consciousness and sensori-motor apparatus. Deictic space, as demonstrated by the structure of various languages, is largely informed by this perfectly fictitious horizon structure, which renders phenomenological space more heterogeneous than purely physical space.

Fiction is thus an integral part of the real, insofar as it constitutes one mode of representation of a state of affairs, in accordance with our perception of appearances from the point of view of a real or imaginary centre of observation, that we usually identify with our sensory organs. It would be easy to recall to mind the numerous sensorial illusions discussed by philosophers of perception, such as the illusory bend of the stick plunged into water or the desert traveller's equally illusory vision of the oasis, in order to demonstrate that the world is far from being logically consistent, that it is, in fact, subject to a complex perceptual activity which structures it in different and sometimes contradictory ways. For instance, Austin (1962) speaks about the fact that we see a stick plunged into water as being bent, yet we know at the same time that it is straight. What we perceive, says Austin, is not only the stick, that is, an autonomous and objectifiable entity, but also the entire observational situation or, if one prefers, the conditions of perception of this object. These conditions include the totality of the perceptive space in which there is not only a stick, but also the water, the interior and exterior of the water, and likewise the point of observation from where we apprehend the scene, and, of course, the global temporal structure of the event where there is a before and an after, a memory and a future, a moment when the stick is not yet in the water and yet another when it will not be (see Austin 1962, 20ff.). It is clear that there exists not only a present of the present, but also, as Augustine has shown (1912, book 11, chap. 14, 237ff.), a present of the future and a present of the past: I remember that the stick was straight and I expect it to become straight again while seeing it presently crooked in the water. The same thing occurs in front of a mirror or a window in which I see, respectively, my own face and that of a passerby: what is seen, and what enables me to distinguish a reflection from reality, is not only in both cases facial features but also, most importantly, in the first case, a mirror and, in the second, a window. In other words, I recognize the conditions of observation prior to the time or at the same time, that I become aware of the object observed. In the case of the stick, I can see and know, at the same time, two contradictory facts, one of which we could consider as fictitious. In the case of the mirror and the window, I am able to differentiate the perceptual world to which the two observed faces belong (one real and one simulated) so long as I also perceive, at the same time, a clear plate of glass or a mirror.

These paradoxical perceptual experiences may recall the idea of the 'dual structures' of fictional worlds (Pavel 1986, 54), or what Walton (1984, 179) calls 'the game of make-believe' or 'the game of as if,' to the extent that, although we know fully well that the sun constitutes the fixed point of our solar system, we act as if it rotated around the earth, rising and setting each day at the horizon. Likewise, despite the fact that we know that a stick, by virtue of its rigidity, does not bend when immersed in water, we pretend that it does, because both cases – the movement of the sun and the bending of the stick – are the direct effect of our conditions of observation and of perception that create these fictions. These are 'natural fictions,' just as fictional as those created by narratives, stories, and poems. It is in this sense that one should understand Lewis's proposition (1973, 84–91), that holds that the word 'real' is an indexical term since we speak only of the world to which we belong. According to this proposal, each person has his or her own world, not so much in the solipsistic sense of the fundamental impossibility of trans-subjectivity, but rather in the sense that there exists no unique point of view above and beyond the world (or worlds), one that would correspond to some sort of extra-sensory Observer-God, for whom everything would be accessible, that is to say, perceptible. In its place are but a multiplicity of points of view which, together with the situations of observation that characterize them, form an integral part of the states of affairs out of which real or possible worlds are constructed. Worlds are organized around a point of observation that we might call the 'I-here-now,' the point of anchorage of our perceptual-cognitive activity, the structure of which obeys less the laws of logic than it does those of a certain optical geometry, that is, the laws of perspective (in a sense quite different, of course, from that of pictorial perspective, but still similar in a number of ways). Fictional beings, like my face in the mirror, the bent stick, the setting of the sun, every bit as much as Dulcinea's face, Elseneur's castle, or Saint Graal, are in fact the correlates of a complex act of perception to which the conditions of apprehension of mode of appearance of these entities belong. Examples of such conditions would include the fact that the objects are plunged in water, reflected in a mirror or imagined by the author of a poem, told by a character in a drama or dreamed by the narrator of a novel. Indeed, these conditions are far from being insignificant.

FICTA

Now that we have seen that our actual world can be 'invaded' by fictitious entities depending on our complex perceptual activity, we may ask what is the specific status of what we term 'fictionality.' Do the fictional worlds that we fabricate, particularly in literary works, constitute the correlate of particular cognitive or perceptive acts, such that we could say that these acts modify, in some way, our ontology or, at least, that they modalize it? What kind of worlds are fictional worlds? Worlds of a second order? Meta-worlds? And what is the nature of fictitious beings? Shadows of our world or real entities of another world? Speaking of that problem, Husserl (1950, 42–3) and Fink (1966, 56–8) make use of the term 'ficta,' in order to designate that which consists either of a substance we mould (such as wax, clay, or plasticine) or of a feigned or illusory reality (such as a day-dream or a mirage). Indeed, the ontological status of 'ficta' is double: material and ideal. The word 'fictus' derives from the Latin *fingere*, which is the name for a double process – on the one hand, 'to mould,' 'to model,' 'to sculpt'; and on the other, to 'invent,' 'to imagine,' 'to feign,' even 'to lie.' The passage from the first meaning of the verb to the second is made possible by the meaning of another related expression, *fingere animos*, which means 'manipulating the minds.' *Fingere* means 'representing the image of a thing' in the double form of a real statue, made of clay or wax, and of a mental image which appears to our consciousness or in the middle of a dream. Whether it has to do with a statue or with a phantasm, every representation or image involves, as fictus, an action upon the soul, an effect on the spirit or mind, which finds itself manipulated and modelled like a mental wax. The marble statue of Venus that I see before my eyes, like the one I imagine in my dreams, can be represented in my mind only if my consciousness, via my sensory organs, is properly manipulated, handled, and worked in such a way as to enable me to recognize and identify her perfectly. 'Fingite animis imaginem' goes an idiomatic Latin expression: 'allow your spirit to create,' 'imagine such and such a thing.' There, behind all the fiction, is the first and proper meaning of 'ficta,' namely, 'acts of mental perception.' And these acts have to do with the very nature of representation, with what the Greeks called *eidolon* in order to speak at the same time of statues and of phantasms, of phantoms and of ideas, in short, of appearances of all sorts: simulacra of stone or coloured pigments, visions of the mind, or illusions of the senses. The implicit imperative utterance underlying all acts of fictional language is thus of a perceptual kind: imagine ..., represent ..., figure ... The object of these acts is what we can call a fictional world in the etymological sense of the word 'fictus'; this kind of world may take the form of an amalgam of more or less perceptible appearances, which are the correlates of acts of apprehension on the part of a subject.

Our means of access to the real or to a fictional world is thus modalized by our perceptual activity: we represent to ourselves not only the world, but our own way of representing it through different types of perceptive-cognitive experiences. The world is not an invariant but, as Husserl would say, the product of eidetic variations, that is, it is the result of complex extero-, proprio-, and interoceptive experiences of objects and their perceptual qualities. On the subject of dreams, Austin has remarked that we describe them exactly as we would describe reality; surely we can say the same thing of the worlds of novels, because we can speak in exactly the same terms of Emma Bovary and of our neighbour, or of Proust's imaginary Berma and the real Sarah Bernhardt. We must admit that when we move from reality to dream, or from these to the world of fiction, it is not the world as a universe of objects and properties that is sought, nor is it the effect of truth resulting from the correspondence of words to the external world. This effect is just as significant in the narrative of a dream and the fictional text as it is in journalism or scientific discourse. What is sought, in fact, is a mode of perception, a perceptual modality, that is, the way in which Charles, in one case, or Marcel, in the other, or, better still, Flaubert and Proust, respectively, perceive and allow us to perceive those two fictitious beings who are Bovary and Berma. In order to properly understand this phenomenon, we must radically alter our ontological conception of the 'world,' in which the objects are usually seen as independent and prior to experience.

THE PROPOSITIONAL WORLD AND NON-SERIOUS LANGUAGE ACTS

The modern inquiry concerning the ontological status of fiction recalls the ancient quarrel about images: the schism of Byzantium. The stakes in this battle were considerable: just like the debate of today, though in a different style, they dealt with the 'Truth' of ficta or of iconic representations. What would be, it was asked, the reality proper to idols, to *eidola* – to images – that would not be a betrayal, a lie, or trickery with respect to the only reality that exists and that admits no replicas, that is, the divine reality, alone and unique? There too, one notices, there is a constant, an invariable, a 'Great invariant,' in relation to whose spirit all images, real or imaginary, would be but incarnations, forever changing and arbitrary, vaguely contingent and ephemeral. What is the alethic value and the representative status of these icons, which number in the thousands and which are all different, in relation to an immutable Uniqueness? These numerous iconic representations can only be false next to the unique

Being they all claim to manifest. Between this unique Being, which we call God, and the other, which we call the World, there is perhaps only one step to be taken, and we take it unhesitatingly. In effect, does the World – as we call it in our modern ontological debates – not play the role that God previously assumed in those theological dramas that opposed (with arguments still in use) iconoclasts and icon worshippers? Doesn't the meaning of fiction, like that of images, find itself reduced, by our modern Byzantines, to the simple function of truth or non-truth, with respect to the World? It is as if ficta, embodied by the stories we tell and the images we paint, had as their sole and unique function to reveal or to hide the truth – the whole truth and nothing but the truth – about something that we would seize in an instant, knowing from the outset what it is and what it is not, by an innate science.

The relation between world and fiction is not binary, not dual, but compound and plural. Fiction and nonfiction exist, but we never speak of world and non-world. At the most, we speak of a plurality of worlds, just as we speak of a multiplicity of ficta. The question could thus be formulated in the following terms; what is the rapport between fiction(s) and nonfiction(s) in their relation with the world or worlds? Fictions and nonfictions, on the one hand, and worlds, on the other: it is indeed this triplet that underlies the entire debate, just as formerly image and non-image were opposed to God, who could not be negated, no more than the world itself, or even considered as an unknown, someone whose existence had to be discovered or demonstrated.

But what exactly is this world, of which we are so certain? In our debates on the truth and the lies of fiction, can the world be used as a yardstick against which we can measure the degree of accurate correspondence between fictional utterances and actual states of affairs? Within the context of our discussions about the logic of fiction, the world of which we speak appears in fact to be the shadow of what we call a (logical) proposition. The world is seen as merely the reflection of those mental categories by means of which we conceive the structure of our propositional language. It is a world populated with individuals, in the logical sense, that is, with particulars (to which proper names and definite descriptions refer), but also with classes (signified by common or generic names), with properties (designated by their predicates), with relations (which express specific functions), and even with mental or illocutionary attitudes (which modify modalities and the propositional forms themselves). In short, the universe that permits us to compare fictional utterances is in reality the reflection of logical propositions which obey both the laws of analytical truth (the principles of non-contradiction, of symmetry, of reflexivity, of transitivity, etc.) and the laws of synthetic truth (of empirical verification based on what Carnap called an observational language).

Consider the famous incipit of Flaubert's *Salammbô*: 'C'était à Mégara, faubourg de Carthage, dans les jardins d'Amilcar.' A truth-value can be attributed to this utterance by verifying, by means of synthetic judgment, the referents of the proper names contained within it; while at the same time, by means of analytic judgment, the propriety of its logical form can be confirmed. Megara, Carthage, Amilcar have all existed, and Flaubert's utterance, in this sense, could well have served as the opening sentence of a textbook of ancient history or of historical geography were it not for the expression 'c'était' which, just like the classic 'once upon a time' acts here as an 'operator of fictionality.' It is supported in this function by that which Genette (1987) calls the utterance's paratext, by means of which the title, the author's name, and the identification of the genre all act as indices of the text's fictional character and, consequently, of the 'non-serious' nature of the assertions that the text contains. We thus have a double movement which consists of, on the one hand, verifying the utterance by analysing its propositional structure according to logical laws and by matching each of its expressions to the world of individuals, of properties, and of relations to which they refer and, on the other hand, of identifying the illocutionary attitude of the enunciator, which in this instance aims to feign an assertive discourse, a feigning whose effect is to suspend, as Searle would say (1979, 70ff.), any judgment about truth, that is, to sever any possible connection between the words and the world(s).

The example chosen from Flaubert permits us to see that behind every act of language inserted into a fictional context, there is a hidden imperative of prescriptive utterance. This implicit directive, which characterizes all fiction (and which makes us think of the way in which the stick plunged into the water is both straight and bent), states: even if the following utterances are true, they are not. That is, these utterances are not to be considered from the point of view of their 'truth,' in the analytical or empirical sense of the term – just as the stick, from the moment we change the conditions of its observation, is considered from the point of view no longer of its being, but rather of its appearance, which is the correlative of another type of perceptive act that does not constitute its essence or its truth. This means that the demand placed on readers of a work of fiction by the enunciator consists uniquely not, as we too often believe, in pretending as if the utterances presented to them were true, but also, and most importantly, in considering the truthful utterances as if they were not really true. Thus the verifiable proposition that Megara was actually a suburb of Carthage and that Amilcar lived there has to be seen by the reader as a 'false' statement in the specific context of Flaubert's novel. Yet readers of the text are enjoined to imagine, or represent for themselves, that this non-truth constitutes the objective correlate of the perceptual-cognitive activity on the part of the narrator or of the characters of the novel. In all fiction, in fact, there are two situations of make-believe. We are asked, first, to act as if Carthage were not real, or as if the Bois de Boulogne that Proust describes in *À l'ombre des jeunes filles en fleurs* were not the real Bois. At the same time, we are also asked to pretend that these things still relate to some perceived or experienced reality and are not, for example, simply a hallucination on the part of Marcel or a lie on the part of the narrator of *Salammbô*.

Faced with fictional entities such as Flaubert's Carthage and Proust's Bois de Boulogne, we must perform what certain psychologists of perception call a double Gestalt shift in relation with what we currently call double images, like those dear to a Dali or an Escher. We all know Escher's famous drawing of a hand, which seems real, drawing another hand, which appears drawn, and consequently fictional, but which in turn is drawing the preceding hand. This is a sort of vicious circle where reality and fiction engender one another in a perfectly reversible causal relation, one which deeply troubles our normal habits of perception. Does this same kind of perceptual trouble not characterize all fiction, where the real Paris becomes, as depicted by Balzac, a paper Paris, a pure fiction, which itself gives rise to a reality that would have all the appearances of the real Paris? Again, it is not the object – here Paris, inhabited in Balzac's fictional world and also in the real world of the reader – which actually changes its existence, but it is the way in which we perceive it or, more precisely, the conditions under which it is given to us to perceive it. It is these conditions, in effect, which are modified, just as they are when we immerse a stick in water, or when we see the world in a mirror rather than through a window. It is precisely these modifications that modalize, in diverse ways, the beings and states of affairs represented in works of fiction.

One has to admit, then, that not only does the world not consist of a constant, stable, invariable entity, capable of serving as the basis for the verification of our propositions, but, in addition, it is not comprised strictly speaking of individuals, of classes, or of properties and relations whose structure would perfectly match the logical form of a descriptive proposition. The world is not so much logical as it is, first and foremost, 'phenomenological,' or as Peirce would say, 'phaneroscopic,' in the sense that it appears, it places itself, before our eyes or before our mind's eye. The world as phenomenon embodies the very mode in which we experience it, that is, the synthetic form in which it appears to us and through which we apprehend it, by virtue, notably, of those forms of intuition, that is, time and space, whose quality varies according to the perceptual acts directed at particular states of affairs. To imagine is not the same as to see, nor is to imagine what could be seen the same as to imagine what could not be observed. Even within a fiction, then, London and the country of Lilliput do not have the same status, just as Rosinante and Pegasus do not inhabit the same perceptual space. It must be emphasized that the aesthetic event, of which these beings are the objective correlates, is different in each case: I do not have the same cognitive-perceptual experience of the character of Humpty Dumpty, living on one side of the mirror, as I do of Alice, who passes from one side of the looking-glass to the other. In turn, this double experience is quite different from the one I might have of a being, every bit as fictitious, such as Emma Bovary, whose perceptual activity – and perceptible, by virtue of the way the narrator presents her to us for our perception – largely corresponds to the prototypes of my own aesthetic experiences (in the Greek sense of the word *aisthesis*). It is not because Emma possesses a greater ontological weight than do Alice or Humpty Dumpty, but because she sees the world in the same way as I myself might see it, without my having to, so to speak, step through the mirror. It is through the perceptual activity of the narrators and of the enunciator, that a fictional world takes on a greater or lesser degree of veracity. This degree of veracity relates, not to our own objective knowledge of what the 'real' world is – in which Emma exists no more than does Alice – but to our own aesthetic activity (extero-, intero-, and proprioceptive). A given fictional world can represent the most typical or predominant features of this activity to a greater or lesser degree.

An appropriate allegory of this phenomenon, one which allows us to change perceptual spaces and, consequently, visions of the world – without really modifying the objects of this world – can be found in Proust's famous scene of the steeples at Martinville. Here, two versions of a particular state of affairs are both composed of the same individuals, particulars, classes, or atomic properties (to speak in logical or propositional terms), all of which are easily identified and associated with a particular perceptive experience. This experience, however, varies considerably from one scene to the other, thus altering the global vision of the world represented. The passage in question makes us move from the scene presented through the mnemonic activity of Marcel the narrator, writing his memoirs many years after the event, to another, included in the prior scene which depicts the first literary efforts of the young Marcel, the character, who is writing a sort of prose poem only a few minutes after the actual experience. For the direct observer, a position assumed by Marcel the character, the steeples of Martinville represent certain conditions of observation which are filtered by the double conditions, quite distinct from one another, in which Marcel the narrator can observe the steeples anew, in the form of a memory, and the young Marcel, the apprentice writer, can see them again by means of his imagination. These conditions are modalized at several levels by the perception the reader can have of the entirety of the world represented, a perception which itself plays a role in the representation, since the aspect or angle from which a thing is seen forms an integral part of the world in which it is experienced. In this scene, Proust has succeeded in creating an image like Escher's, where we pass, not from a real to a fictive hand, one which is drawn, and vice versa, both represented on the same piece of paper, but from the so-called real steeples to those described, thus fictitious, objects within a literary work, then back again to the real steeples – all of this is represented in the same book, the same work of fiction. The steeples described by the young Marcel are no longer the 'real' steeples but continue to exist in the same way that the Champs-Elysées which Proust describes are false Champs-Elysées, which nonetheless continue to be true – and this process occurs by the reader's passage from one perceptual universe to another. In the memory of Marcel the narrator, or in the imagination of Proust the enunciator, the Paris that Marcel the character sees takes on a different modal value on each different occasion for the reader, who sees or imagines it only through these different perceptual filters that the text of *À la recherche* itself, and its narrative structure, render manifest and inevitable.

One therefore has to take seriously the implicit directive proposed by Levin (1976) or, more recently, by Genette (1989) who would preface all acts of fictional language, whether feigned or non-serious, with the following utterance: 'I imagine or I invite you to conceive of a world where ... Longtemps je me suis couché de bonne heure.' This directive, or any variant of it that we care to contrive, concerns the cognitive-perceptual dimension of fictional worlds: to imagine, to conceive, etc. – a dimension which is intimately linked with the act of *fingere* itself, which lies at the origin of all ficta. One should no longer see worlds and works of fiction as the pragmatic effect of a simple tacit act of language, of a maxim, or of a communicative contract between the two partners of a linguistic exchange, but rather see them as the enactment of aesthetic activity. There, the interest lies surely not in simply making the words 'fit' the things depicted, but in leading the reader to a cognitive-perceptive experience, in which the form and the content more or less resemble the reader's own phenomenological experience of the world. When reading *À la recherche*, I do not use some real or possible world in order to verify the more or less modified state of the individuals, properties, or relations, in short, the 'states of affairs' which are described by the text. Instead, I experience, through the representation of the perceptive activity of the characters, narrators, and enunciators, a whole range of aesthetic experiences which in a way become my own and which correspond more or less accurately to those experiences that I could have outside Proust's fictional world. It is perhaps along these lines – of perceptive modalities of a phenomenological sort, rather than just logical ones – that one must search for the link, close and yet tenuous, between the experienced world and fictionality. It is undoubtedly here that this paradoxical double link resides, which allows us to say (to paraphrase Claudel, according to whom the poet's words are everyday words but they are not the same) that the 'things' about which *À la recherche* or *Salammbô* speak are certainly everyday 'things,' but they are not the same.

NOTE

I would like to thank Larry Marks and Barbara Havercroft for the translation and revision of this article.

7

Beyond Reality and Fiction?
The Fate of Dualism in the Age
of (Mass) Media

SIEGFRIED J. SCHMIDT

'REALITY – EUROPE'S DEMONIC CONCEPT' (G. BENN)

No other problem has vexed European thinking as intensively as the relation between being and cognition, the question whether or not human beings are able to recognize reality objectively. From its very beginnings European epistemology has assumed an indissoluble bond between 'reality' and 'truth' and proclaimed an unbridgeable chasm between subject and object. European thinking remains basically dichotomical and hierarchical compared, for example, to more holistic and rhizomatic approaches as developed in both Asian and postmodernist thinking. Accordingly, dualistic conceptions of reality have been favoured: reality ('objective' or 'true' reality) has been categorically opposed to irreality, dream, falsity, or fiction; and it is, of course, reality that is attributed the highest value among its competitors. This dualism, however, not only impregnates the philosophical discourse: it did, and does, organize Western social, economic, and juridical interactions; it still serves as a relevant basis for power structures and social hierarchies; and it provides a seemingly self-evident gauge for defining 'mental health.'

The ontological question (what is real?) implies or dominates all other basic questions in our society (e.g., what is true? what is necessary? what is good?). Every society is vitally interested in unambiguous answers to the ontological question, since winners and losers in the 'reality game' must be clearly discernible. Accordingly, social groups and social systems are established and can be defined in terms of consensually constituted models of reality which serve as reference frame(s) for all semantic activities in the respective society.

From a pragmatic social point of view the reality vs non-reality dualism is indispensable. The individual as well as society must be able to answer the ontological question virtually automatically in order to preserve cognitive as well as social identity. This practical requirement, however, does not at all predetermine how this dualism can be established, administered, and legitimated. Epistemologically, various options exist. Two of them – known as the ontological and the operational concept of reality – will be epitomized in the next section.

'REALITIES ARE PACIFIERS' (H.R. MATURANA)

The third-century sceptic Sextus Empiricus formulated an idea which since then has never been convincingly refuted: 'We can only compare our perceptions with our perceptions; we can never compare them with the object of our perception in its status before we have perceived it' (Diels and Krantz 1971). The idea that perception and experience are the only ways to reality, and that, conversely, 'reality as such' is inaccessible without or beyond perception and experience, seems to be trivial in logical terms; but the epistemological consequences of the acceptance of that idea are considerable. We have to realize that we are absolutely unable to compare 'reality as such' with the products of our cognitions. In other words, we construe our world by and through living it. And this world is a world of our experience, not an ontologically 'real' world.

In the last two decades, biologists and neurophysiologists have offered plausible explanations for the constructivity of our brain. As their ideas are easily accessible, I shall concentrate on some essentials.[1]

The most fundamental argument in this framework reads as follows: perception takes place not in our sensory organs but in specific sensory domains of our brain which are responsible for the topological distribution of sensory inputs. Our brains see and hear, not our eyes and ears. Consequently perception has to be modelled in terms of attributing meaning to neuronal processes that, as such, are meaningless, that is, perception is construction and interpretation (see Roth 1987a). Our brain is functionally closed and interacts exclusively with its own states. It is connected to the world outside via sensory receptors which, due to environmental perturbations, undergo variations of their electric properties which are then transferred to the brain in terms of impulses (or signals). In other words, our sensory organs translate environmental events which are inaccessible to the (operationally) closed brain into the brain's language. During the translation (and due to it), the original necessarily and unrecoverably gets lost. The brain is forced to rely on those principles and strategies of signal-processing and meaning-construction which have been developed during its ontogenetic and phylogenetic evolution (and which Gestalt theory began formulating in the twenties). That is to say, what becomes conscious has already been modelled and imprinted automatically by our brains. It follows from these assumptions that our brain is not able to mirror or to re-present the reality; it does not represent, it construes.

As the brain has no direct access to the reality, it is – forming part of the nervous system – self-referential, self-explaining, and self-organizing. It recursively operates on its own operations. All perceptions depend on processes of cognitive self-differentiating which are closely connected to processes of learning. Perception, in this approach, is theoretically modelled as a self-description of the brain which is operationally closed.

Roth proposes a very productive distinction between the real brain and the cognitive world: 'The real organism is equipped with a brain which produces a cognitive world consisting of world, body, and subject in such a way that this subject relates this world and this body to himself. This cognitive subject is, of course, not the producer of the cognitive world, which is created by the real brain; instead the cognitive subject is a kind of "object of perception," which experiences and undergoes perceptions. The real brain is just as little existent in the cognitive world as is the reality and the real organism' (1987a, 234; my translation). The cognitive world is the local and temporal reality of and for the cognitive subject. The categories developed in the cognitive world are not applicable to the real world which must be regarded as an absolutely necessary regulative or heuristic device but which can never be experienced by the cognitive subject. The real brain forms part of our body, which in turn can be described and explained as an autopoietic system. Our cognitive operations are determined by this biological basis, but they are not identical with it.

Apart from the innate mechanisms of checking our brain-produced world knowledge, we have to bear in mind that the real brain produces individual knowledge according to social conditions. Though our brain has no window to the world outside, the reality it produces is a social reality.

The cognitive world is the world of the observer. Only the observer is able to distinguish and to describe something as something. Any description requires an observer; and the logic of description is isomorphic to the logic of the operations of an observer.

From a philosophical point of view, this constructivist theory of cognition provides a reformulation combined with an empirical foundation of Kant's idea of transcendentality: our world is the world of our experience, not 'the real world.'

During the 1986 Gordon research conference on the cybernetics of cognition, Maturana reiterated his idea that we cannot distinguish experientially between perception and illusion. This distinction, he insists, is a social distinction. As our language is a language of objects, we can speak about objects as long as we remain in our language. On the other hand, together with the rise of language comes the rise of the observer. The speaking, or – in Maturana's wording – the 'languaging,' observer is the source of objects because languaging means consensual co-ordination of actions and recursion on consensual co-ordination of actions. Maturana emphasizes that validating scientific explanations presupposes not objectivity but only coherence (e.g., provided by the scientific method). Validation explains the experience of observers and not properties of an observer-independent reality. The world we live in is a cognitive one, consisting of different levels of coherence, models, and descriptions. To make experiences and to construe levels of coherence presupposes interaction in consensual domains. That is the reason why we need the other to make our own experiences. Generating a concept of object presupposes that we are able to impute our own experiences successfully to others (von Glassersfeld 1985). Thus it is consensus and intersubjectivity that provide what we experience as objects or facts, not the ontological correspondence of our perceptions and experiences with the real entities. By transforming the concept of ontological objectivity into that of interactive intersubjectivity, the epistemological attention shifts from the real world to norms and criteria for consensuality and intersubjectivity in a social group or in a society as a whole, and to the language by which observers operate on events and activities in their consensual domains.

According to cognitive constructivists, world constructs (i.e., cognitive worlds) cannot, and need not, be true: they only have to be (and can be) viable, that is, they must allow for the survival of the cognizing individual as well as of society.

World constructions have to meet two requirements: they must comfort the cognizing individual, that is, they have to satisfy the claims individuals make on their own constructions; and they have to preserve the cognizer's acting competence without maneuvering him or her into perilous positions. In sum, the cognitive world we intuitively deem 'reality' is a viable social construct produced in the cognizing individual. This construction is achieved according to the social, neuronal, and psychological conditions of cognizing systems in social systems.

MEDIA AND COUPLING

The emotionally heated debate on the mass media is characterized by polarization and simplification. I therefore have to start with some clarifications.

'Medium' is a vague and ambiguous term which is normally introduced by enumerating examples (book, film, TV, computer, etc.). Following these examples it intuitively makes sense to conceive of media, first of all, in terms of material instruments of communication. But, of course, this pragmatic device deserves more explicit description which, I think, systems theory can yield.

In a systems theoretical framework, mass media can be theoretically modelled as social systems. Their components are media activities, that is, activities making use of specific instruments of communication in an organizational and/or institutional social framework, which includes technical, political, juridical and economic constraints. Media activities are manifestations of acting roles which in modern mass media systems have become professionalized and institutionalized, that is, the production, mediation, reception, and post-processing of media offerings or media events. The relations between the acting roles define the structure of a media system. Media activities combine to form media processes (e.g., the production and subsequent reception of a media offering, for example, a television spot).

Media activities are obviously related to each other (production to mediation, production to reception, reception to post-processing, production to produc-tion, etc.), that is, the system is self-referential. In other words, the behaviour of the system is determined by its internal state, that is, by the mutual interaction of the four basic types of acting roles. This is the case because any change in the potential activities belonging to one role brings a shift in those of the other basic roles in the medium system.

Order arising in self-referential media systems is achieved spontaneously and results from the specific features of the components and their relations; that is, media systems are self-organizing[2] and, to a large extent, autonomous.

Of course, media systems are not isolated; they interact with other social systems. But this interaction is realized in terms of the system-internal organi-zation. In other words, all influences exercised on a medium system have to be transformed into system-specific activities and processes. As complex systems, media systems permanently have to cope with both their environment and their internal shortcomings, and are thus forced into permanent self-adaptations. As a consequence, they necessarily develop a kind of dynamic stability (Schmidt 1990a).

Modern societies make use of various media systems which can theoretically be modelled as subsystems of the global media system of a society. The subsystems mutually interact, thus determining the special role each subsystem can play in the global system and in relation to other subsystems (e.g., the mutual interaction of print and audio-visual media in the multimedia system).

From a systems-theoretical point of view all media systems are regarded as social systems, whereas, of course, not all social systems are media systems. Social systems as self-referential and self-organizing (i.e., autonomized) systems are characterized, among other things, by special kinds of communication, including specific stylistics, discourses (thematic units) and genres (regulations of reference semantics)[3] or schemata for staging cognitive reality. Self-organizing systems, as has already been mentioned, can neither merge nor control each other immediately and intentionally, at least not over a longer period (unless physical force is applied). They mutually interact according to their own internal conditions. The function of media systems consists in coupling self-organizing and self-referential cognitive systems and social systems. This coupling is based on intersubjective devices (experiences, rules, conventions, discourses, genres, stereotypes, etc.) which each individual acquires during his or her media socialization. The coupling is successful if the individual usage of communication instruments in a media system fits the standards of socialization in a specific social system.

'DAD, IF A TREE FALLS IN THE FOREST, AND THE MEDIA AREN'T THERE TO COVER IT, HAS THE TREE REALLY FALLEN?' (R. MANKOFF)

Today it is beyond any doubt that mass media play an important role in all processes of world construction. A closer look at audio-visual media systems, for instance, reveals how this is achieved.

From their very beginning mass media had to face the complex task of selection. Selection depends, of course, on criteria, interests, prejudices, etc. Today nobody will contest that news is produced according to the internal structures of the institutions in mass media systems. News editors, for example, must fill a narrow program section at their disposal. Not only has whatever appears on a television screen been selected from among other possibilities, but it has also been staged. Whereas it is obvious that, for example, politicians strive for a perfect *mise en scène* of their television performances, we tend to forget about staging when looking at news, travel reports, or animal films. 'Living pictures' immediately occupy our interest and automatically claim to represent 'reality,' especially when they have reached the perfection of modern television presentations. Our preference for pictures results from the way our visual system operates. The neuronal production of visual impressions requires the activation and connection of several billions of neurons in various brain domains. Visual orientation in our environment seems to be highly consensual among human beings. Normally we rely on visual experience much more strongly than on other sensory experiences, since visual experience has proved to be especially viable and reliable in the past.

Whereas painted pictures in the past overtly conveyed the fact that they had been fabricated, photography – especially film, television, and video – has concealed with increasing effectiveness the constructivity of picture-making.

Though technical devices – for example, camera and screen – effect in a way a double removal from 'natural' visual perception, electronic pictures claim to represent 'reality' in an authentic way. If the usual criteria of plausibility, credibility, and evidence are not grossly neglected, televison pictures make us forget that the television camera is the blind spot in our visual system, and that not cameras and eyeballs but people see pictures other people have produced, via selection and *mise en scène*. At least for those working in a television station, it is obvious that 'reality' as constructed by mass media reflects the conditions and rules of the production of media offerings to a much larger extent than it reflects reality.

Mass media offerings – due to technical and organizational developments – have become very expensive in the last decade. A lot of money is involved, and together with it come economic, political, and juridical considerations and issues of special interests, power, and influence. The small screen has turned into a battlefield of conflicting interests on a large scale. All this bears, of course, on the process of agenda-setting by the mass media. The more attention has become a scarcely available good in the face of a multiplicity of options, the more rigidly media-specific strategies for attracting attention have to be applied. Public opinion, as well as public relations, increasingly depends upon mass media to the degree that what isn't covered by the media doesn't exist. The more the technical facilities have been refined, the more television and other media systems create the impression of omnipresence and of reporting objectively, though staging becomes more and more sophisticated, and techniques such as the 'blue box' rob the recipient of any chance to relate a picture back to its sources and to its contexts. In a way, the picture of reality has become the reality of the picture.

Although, because of the individual's cognitive constructivity, media offerings cannot automatically and causally influence the public in a predictable way, they do, of course, influence their recipients to some extent. Media systems confirm, reinforce, or handicap special ways of perception and communication; they introduce life-styles and constructions of social, political, or cultural 'realities' which can serve as models, entering into private and public communication and provoking either consensus or opposition.

Heterogeneous publics need mass-media-mediated communication. This, in turn, bears on the selection and staging processes in media systems. The constant interplay between mediated and unmediated communication serves as one of the most powerful instruments for creating and consolidating the respective social construction of a reality. Media refer to media, and any congruence in the staging of reality here and there is taken as a testimony for the truth of media offerings by the public. Consequently, the criteria for 'reality' have shifted from truth and objectivity to plausibility, credibility, and consensuality of reports and opinions in the self-referential media system of a society. By their behaviour people make real what they deem real, and this behaviour is increasingly based upon media models of reality and on the credibility of opinion leaders, all the more so since the ratio between personal experience that is mediated by the mass media and personal experience that is unmediated has become unbalanced.

Our look at 'the reality'; our look at the 'media reality'; our media look at the 'media reality': the staging of 'reality' has become extremely complicated. We should therefore deliberately and consequently say farewell to realistic epistemologies, of whatever type, and consciously accept our responsibility for the processes of world construction.

There seems to be a self-organizing mechanism operating on media, communication, and cognition. Every media offering potentially influences communication, which in turn potentially influences cognition, which in turn potentially influences the production of media offerings and vice versa. Mass media also affect the process of 'social memory.' Technological developments have created new kinds of archives where increasingly more documents can be stored on increasingly miniaturized data bases. But here again the 'dialectic' character of mass media comes into play: the more occasions for remembering that archives provide, the more we have to select among these occasions. Optimizing remembering and forgetting necessarily go together.

Mass media, as K. Krippendorff has pointed out, constitute themselves as institutions in the very social realities they create to thrive in. Like other social institutions, they prove Winston Churchill's insight that first we shape our institutions, then our institutions shape us. But Krippendorff draws our attention to some other important differences. Since his ideas on that topic are worthy of discussion, I take the freedom to quote rather extensively.

Other institutions must rely on some kind of communication to constitute themselves in the cognition of its participants but the mass media constitute themselves in their participants' own communication practices, they own their means of constituting themselves and are hence more autonomous and self-directing than any other institution ... As an institution, the mass media constitute themselves at the expense of its participants' cognitive autonomy ... What makes the mass media so different from other institutions is their overwhelming communicative authority: the mass media are able to assemble talent, journalistic practices, scientific research, communication technology, and economic resources to produce what no individual seemingly can. The mass media are able to involve a vast number of willing participants, numerically dominated by its mass audiences of anonymous viewers, listeners, readers, to engage in individual communicative acts (whether simply watching TV, accepting mass media created celebrities as models or being performers themselves) geared to preserve the viability of (their own construction of) the mass media as an institution, making each feel insignificant with little voice in the matter. The mass media are able to make everyone believe to have equal access to an objective reality ('seeing is believing'), a reality they are in fact in the business of creating. All three sources of the mass media's communicative authority, but particularly the claim to have privileged access to a reality largely denied to individuals, institutionally blinds its participants against realizing their own cognitive autonomy more so than any other institution can … As a constitutive part of society, the mass media are far from neutral in … showing particular realizations of communication. Having to be socially accountable for what they say, like all communicators are, the mass media create spaces of possible reality constructions in which their own activity is not likely to be questioned. The kind of realities that accomplish widespread aquiescence (i) can be talked about by everyone and with little effort, fuels ordinary conversation and enables imitations; (ii) elaborates on what everyone wants to hear or already believes in, like amplifying social stereotypes or prejudices; (iii) has few recognizable practical consequences like television genres, entertainment and fiction, and makes the latent consequences difficult to ascertain, like the long range effects of inducing fear through news coverage of violence, food poisoning and mass consumption, or of creating expectations through political or commercial advertisements, like the notion that everything can be bought with the right kind of money; and finally (iv) generates its own industrial and political support through which the mass media are being funded. Thus, what we come to know through the mass media, the social reality constructed therein, is mediated by the role the mass media create for themselves in interaction with the other institutions of society, none of which can escape operating in the same ecology of models, metaphors, and myths the mass media selectively support. The institutions in society are increasingly and surreptitiously monopolized by what the mass media has to do as an institution. (Krippendorff 1990, 17–18)

TOWARDS UBIQUITY OF SIMULATION?

In view of the increasing presence of mass media in Western societies, J. Baudrillard (1985) has launched the thesis of an ubiquity of simulation, a thesis which raises the question whether or not, in an age of mass-mediated social construction of reality, the difference between reality and fiction is simply disappearing. I think this question can only be perused after having clarified the concept of fiction.

As I mentioned above, it is a crucial matter in all societies who is entitled to answer the ontological question. In feudal societies, highly consensual and homogeneous models of reality provided (nearly) all members of society with an ontological, moral, religious, and pragmatic orientation. The administration and preservation of this model of reality guaranteed that state and church held a monopoly on the production of meaning. In the eighteenth century, through the emergence of functionally specified, autonomized social systems, the prescriptive model of reality (which proposed a global interpretation of the world) was shattered. Each social system now developed and administered its own partial model of reality, but these various models no longer added up to only one comupulsory, overarching model. In the long run, each system (and within it every individual cognitive system) had to face the task of coping with the self-referentiality of cognition, emotion, and communication which was inevitably becoming apparent (evidenced by the tremendous success of transcendental epistemology in the eighteenth century).

The differentiation of world models caused by the functional differentiation of society as a whole did not result in a general social schizophrenia (although it did produce many cases of individual neurosis) for the sole reason that the economy had taken over the 'leadership' of society. The objectivity of money, which made all goods and all kinds of labour quantitatively commensurable, responded to the crisis created by the ontological differentiation into types of world models. Money became the guarantee of reality and the objective measure of goods, labour, and human beings. Money became, as it were, the general mode of equivalence. Based on an economy that functioned by means of monetary mechanisms, the state could afford to pass the 'ontological question' along to society and to its various functional subsystems: the need to interpret 'world and life' and to explain disappointments was now delegated to social subsystems as well as to individuals. In addition, the developing juridical system allowed for the coexistence of contradictory world models without jeopardizing state and society, because repressive claims for universalistic world models – as evidenced by the religious wars of the seventeenth century – could no longer be enforced. Consequently, the bourgeoisie could realize its recently detected subjectivity and creativity (incorporated in the figure of the genius) in terms of the communicative freedom of subjective 'world-and-life interpretations' – long before it achieved its political freedom. Yet this freedom was more or less restricted to the private sphere and to special discourses, for example, the philosophical and the literary ones. The poets (at least since Klopstock) insisted on their ability and vocation to develop alternative models of social reality, thus becoming profane priests of the bourgeois public. These alternative models were no longer expected to be reflections of a compulsory prescriptive model of reality. Accordingly, literary communication in the autonomized social system of literature gradually became fictionalized. Fictionalization, that is, the orientation towards possibility instead of truth or probability, became the 'engine' of a thematical and stylistic differentiation of literary productions, resulting gradually in an exclusive orientation of literary activities towards literary norms and values. In this process of aestheticization, the literary code (i.e., literary vs non-literary), and nothing else, served to select literary activities.

At the end of the eighteenth century, the literary system can be described as becoming progressively autonomized (self-referential and self-organizing) and literary communication as being fictionalized. As a result, the literary system and its discourses were sharply separated from other social systems and their discourses, as well as from daily life: any attempt to achieve an immediate application of 'literature' to 'life' became an illusion. This fictionalization and aestheticization of literary discourse gave rise to a proliferation of literary semantics, since all thinkable modes of referentiality that could be contrived and expressed were admissible. This remarkably increased the complexity of the literary system.[4] Fictionalization, in this perspective, suspends the 'referentialability' of assertions or statements in literary texts. Readers are free to relate them to the frames of reference they prefer. Though literary texts are not at all restricted to fictive statements,[5] it is not surprising that many contain a significant number of them.

The fictionalization of the literary discourse allows for a cognitive modelling of alternative worlds, for a cognitive treatment of everything that has not yet been realized, that has been forgotten, or that is being suppressed in a society. It allows for subjective interpretations, projects, and blueprints. Fictionality makes prevailing realities seem changeable.

Fictionality increases individual cognitive, as well as communicative, complexity – thus contributing to creativity. By 'creativity'[6] I mean significant modes of interrupting social communication, interruptions which open up new possibilities of continuation (new forms of connectivity). Creativity enhances the attraction of otherness, of discontinuity and difference, of ambiguity and multi-stability.

From an epistemological point of view, the distinction between reality and fiction results from cognitive operations of the individual which are embedded in his or her social experiences. This operation, however, does not happen in an empty space: people, through socialization and previous experiences, normally know very well which kind of media offerings they encounter at which places and times and in which contexts. Whoever switches on his or her TV does so for more or less automatized reasons. He or she knows what kind of media offerings are distributed in a certain media system and, above all, he or she is familiar with media genres (cf. Schmidt 1987b).

Media genre can be theoretically modelled as a specific type of (intersubjectively shared) cognitive schemata, namely, media–action–schemata. These schemata commit media activities (including their components and results) of all members of a social group or society to socio-historically admissible modes of references to models of reality, thus constituting the degrees of freedom which can then be exploited by socially expected strategies for the production, reception, and evaluation of media activities and their results. This definition implies that the media we are concerned with belong to that set of media whose components can actually be related to reality in an intersubjective, consensual way (thus excluding, for example, music).

Members of a society unfold the socio-historical system of media–action–schemata and define the specialities of the use of media according to socially consensual modes of referring to models of reality. These specialities concern, above all, the thematics of actions in various media–action–schemata available in a society and the modes of performing or realizing and presenting these actions in the process of staging. Media–action–schemata constitute modes of referring to models of reality, that is, they specify what 'status of reality' is assigned to a certain verbal or non-verbal (but referrable) behaviour in the framework of a media–action–schema, and what degree of reliability and authenticity is attributed to someone acting in such a schema (e.g., newsreaders on television vs spokesmen of an industrial company). According to the respective socio-historical conditions, the specification of modes of referring to models of reality can be called 'true, real, authentic, credible, reliable, trustworthy,' etc., or 'false, unreal, fictitious, utopian, unreliable, untrustworthy,' etc.

In our everyday life as well as in our everyday media life, I claim, people normally have no problems recognizing the difference between adultery and adultery on screen. The point in this story is not, I think, whether people are able to make the distinction between reality and fiction; the interesting point is how they handle and evaluate this basic dichonomy.

As I have tried to elaborate in some detail in this paper, every cognitive system, as well as every social system, depends on a clear answer to the ontological question in order to establish and to maintain individual and social identity. The distinction of reality vs fiction has to be made. But this crucial necessity does not at all predetermine on which grounds this distinction can be made, recognized, and legitimated. From a constructivist point of view, the better arguments speak in favour of an operative instead of an ontological explanation. It is not 'reality' that calls for a specific decision; instead it is the cognitive, as well as the communicative, constructivity coupled by media systems which – via self-referentiality and self-organization – settles the ontological question in a pragmatically effective way.

The shift in the mode of dichotomization should have become evident: the distinction between reality and fiction has to be transformed from an ontological credo into an operative function. In other words, we need – for the reasons presented in this paper – an instrument to perform the distinction, but we do not need an ontological basis for that operation – and we actually do not employ such a basis, evidently not in media communication. As I mentioned earlier, the interesting point in this story is people's stance towards handling and evaluating the operative distinction between reality and fiction. A look at our media reality reveals three interesting aspects of this process.

First, experiments and experiences with American as well as German children show that, although they are quite able to handle the operative dichotomy, they seem to be much less interested than the elder generation in constantly applying and confirming this operation. They take media offerings as such; they take them for granted. They suspend, in a way, the automatism of dichotomization. They seem to have acquired the possibility of accepting a plurality of cognitive worlds without further ado. For them 'the real' – in the long run – may acquire the status of non-obligation. They switch from one to the other as easily as they switch from one TV program to another.

Secondly, there are domains in our society where the referential mechanism implied in the dichotomization is deliberately instrumentalized, for example, in the advertising system.[7] Well-known film directors like Jean-Luc Godard have produced television spots for jeans (Closed) which deliberately play with the *art vs non-art* dichotomy. Without a film script, without even mentioning the product, without any advertising message, Godard realizes something like a personal signal. This kind of spot can easily be placed in both systems, art and advertising.[8] Accordingly, only the context (medium, time of presentation, program context, etc.) can serve as indicator for recipients to place the media offering either here or there – or to suspend this decision for reasons of an aesthetic pleasure. In any case, the recipients have to perform a conscious Gestalt switch, a kind of cognitive zapping, in order to cope with that kind of media offerings.

A third possibility of modulating the reality–fiction–dichotomization is chaotization, and its most prominent genre is the video clip. Video clips very often present a seemingly randomized sequence of pictures, music, and language, mocking all traditional strategies of narratives or coherence. The great success of (especially music) videos with young audiences shows that they like to be beyond dichotomies – a tendency which can, of course, also be observed in fashion or hairstyle. Context-bound operative dichotomization can easily be performed, easily be modified, and easily be renounced. I guess that the shift from categorically based dichotomization to an operative handling of context-dependent dichotomization will become one of the signatures of the nineties.

NOTES

1 See the bibliography on constructivist publications in Schmidt 1987a.
2 For a definition of 'self-reference' and 'self-organization,' see Roth 1987b. For details, see Schmidt 1989.
3 Cf. Schmidt 1987b.
4 For details, see Schmidt 1989 (cf. note 2).
5 If a statement p is actually neither true nor false in our current world model WMi, but one can imagine a world model WMx, at another time in which the statement is true, then p is called a 'fictive statement.' (See Schmidt 1976; 1980.)
6 For details, see Schmidt 1988.
7 See Schmidt, Sinofzik, and Spieß 1990.
8 For details, see Schmidt 1990b.

8

Models, Madness, and the Hereafter

CESARE SEGRE

Recourse to notions of world models, anti-models, and possible worlds has proven useful to contemporary criticism. What I propose to illustrate here is our conceptual attachment to the world as it is or, rather, to models we have generated from it. Even when we outline models for something that is alien or totally unknown to us, the influence of the models of our own world does not cease. Furthermore, this is implicit in the notion itself of anti-world (or anti-model), because such a world is usually identical with the actual world even though it is a reversal or a reflection.

In what follows I will focus on the opposition us vs others in two definite usages: the otherness and exclusion that mark mad people; and the unknowability that pervades the world of the dead despite the ardour of our curiosity in seeking to describe it. Finally, I will attempt to examine in the Witz (the witticism) the prime calling-into-question of our models of the world. I consider this calling-into-question 'prime' because it is linguistic and effective, although momentary.

The images of madness have always placed mad people in a mental space that differs from ours – more precisely, that is opposed to ours. For example, in the Middle Ages, one trusted and used the oppositions culture vs nature, noble vs base, clothed vs naked, armour vs staves or arrows, human vs savage, cooked vs raw, speech vs cry. The mad one, having left the community of the civilized world, essentially was situated in an anti-world, in close proximity to the savage man of myth. Among the oppositions just mentioned some were applied to all mad people, others were reserved for knights and lords (most notably, the third and fourth oppositions).

We must add two further elements: a certain ritualness – which is also a constraint – in the assuming of the traits of madness and, contrariwise, a form, which the mad person enjoyed, of freedom from constraints that sages obeyed. Thus world and anti-world continued to mutually determine each other, despite their conflict.

These remarks based on literary texts already rely on a certain – conscious – modelling. A case in point is Ariosto who ascribes to the deranged Roland the traditional attributes of chivalric madness through his device of transferring reason to the moon from where one can recover it. The moon being, above all, a mirror of the earth, he reflects upon the specular relation between the worlds of sages and mad people. The literary nature of the documents also accounts for the rather scarce mining of the linguistic disorders associated with madness. They are not passed over in silence, but they are attributed preferably to love-induced madness, as shown in the multiple tongues and abnormal versification of the *descort*. The abnormalities of language were probably considered relevant only for those in society who had the right to speech, that is, the nobility and the literate.

Furthermore, as Erasmus of Rotterdam before him, Ariosto had also discerned in madness the critical or subversive function that aristocratic society exploited – and yet sterilized – through the institution of the clown, close cousin to the *gracioso* and the fool of theatre. The mental and social operations of the clowns were rather complex: they consisted in decking out the truth in the trappings of falsehood and paradox, in describing the world as if it were an anti-world. This allowed one to say what sages were forbidden to say – a subtle and efficacious anticipation of defamiliarization.

However, what is extremely interesting is that the image of madness and its manifestations change over time. It is true that individual and social pressure contributed to these changes, but above all it is a greater valorization of the unconscious that accounts for these transformations. In Cervantes's novella *El licenciado Vidriera*, it is obvious that the hero has sublimated his libido in a search for glory and fame. When a courtesan causes him to experience genuine sexual aggression, which would return his libido to its normal function, he becomes mad. The madness accentuates his repulsion for all physical contact and makes him believe that he is made of glass and thus extremely fragile. The multiplication of these madmen made of glass between the sixteenth and the seventeenth centuries (dozens and dozens of testimonies) says a great deal about the status of the unconscious during the repressive period of the Counter-Reformation.

The case of the *El licenciado Vidriera* is also significant for the relations between public and private truths. Protected by his madness, Vidriera enjoyed the same authority to speak the truth as did clowns: he made public truths which should have remained private and, more often than not, his opinions caused injury. He may describe the world as it is, even its aspects usually obscured by custom. But when he is cured of his madness and wants to become a barrister, he is barred from doing so by the community: he can no longer bring back to the private sphere what he has henceforth proclaimed in a public form. Briefly, the world will not allow itself to be criticized unless it is presented as the anti-world of an anti-world.

The case of the hereafter is even more suggestive because it deals with a world about which we cannot affirm anything with certitude, not even its existence. The available information has been accepted only by acts of faith, in religion, superstition, myth. Also accepted have been the testimonies from the mouths of ghosts claiming to inform us about life after death, or from mystics describing voyages to lands that await us at the end of our earthly days. If this information that is so difficult to verify is accepted with such readiness, it is because of our unconquerable abhorrence of passing from our all too transitory state to the sphere of nothingness.

The less we know about the hereafter, the more we feel authorized to extrapolate the models of our world to the other. Hence the transfer of our experiences of pleasure and pain to a world which we like to imagine as not only more just than ours but also capable of correcting injustice that down here is almost continuously tolerated. As well, we attribute to the other world a compensatory function in relation to ours: the evil deeds we have committed become inflicted punishment, good deeds, the reward of the just – a movement that culminates in the implementation of an authentic accounting apparatus. We must add that during the Middle Ages, but not only during the Middle Ages, there existed an urge to imagine, with a torturer's curiosity, the punishment of sinners; unfortunately, the possible repertoire of pleasures appears less rich and sometimes boring.

In regards to models, one observation imposes itself at first: souls are attributed a specific place within spatio-temporal co-ordinates that are familiar to us. And it is time, apparently less concrete than place, that maintains its properties whole, although they are often dilated or compressed. Depending upon the case, voyages into the hereafter correlate our hours or our days with years and centuries or become concentrated in such intense contemplation that instants seem like months or years. The most subtle theologians unsuccessfully tried to present the hereafter as a situation, rather than a place, and to expand the notion of eternity by distinguishing it from duration.

Let us turn to the us vs others opposition. If, in the case of madness, this opposition is actualized as delimitation and exclusion, in the case of the hereafter, it is actualized as distancing within a particular cosmology or cosmogony. The deceased, on the other hand, will occupy positions that are differentiated according to the archetypal oppositions high vs low and east vs west. The first of these oppositions, which also implies moral superiority or inferiority, liberty or dependence, etc., has caused men, once they had abandoned the metonymic identification of burial and survival of the soul in the underworld, to imagine an oppositional topography for the blessed souls and the damned. The former were usually situated on high mountains or directly in the heavens, while the latter were pushed more and more deeply below the surface of the earth. As well, another opposition, heaven vs earth, was valorized along with its corollaries, especially light vs darkness – where light can be truth and darkness, sin and disbelief. In this case, the figurative meaning becomes literal.

The opposition east vs west is linked to a series of metaphors inspired by the diurnal cycle. Dawn symbolizes birth and life; sunset, old age and death. As well, it is in the east that the earthly paradise was situated; in more recent times, one looked eastward for the origins of our peoples and languages. Conversely, it is in the direction of the setting sun that many, especially maritime peoples, have seen the souls of the departed leave: the vessels upon which Egyptians and Vikings placed their dead, sometimes set afire, were transformed, in their imagination, into ghost ships sailing towards the west. For this western destination of the dead, an easterly one is substituted when a cycle of life-death-life-death is affirmed either through the belief in metempsychosis or within eschatological conceptions such as those of Christianity. This implies, of course, an identification of bodily death with a more authentic life.

Only modern writers have attempted to disengage themselves from such a rigorous geography. It has been, above all, Kafka and Beckett who have stressed that hell is not in the hereafter but here on earth and that there is no co-relation between failings and punishment. Conversely, the Argentine writer Ernesto Sábato, while ignoring the traditional myths, preserves the symbolic value of the high vs low opposition and accentuates that of the light vs darkness. In his novel *Sobre héroes y tumbas*, the conspiracy of evil is the work of a band of blind people. In placing the messengers of evil in the sewers and subterranean pipes of Buenos Aires, Sábato has superimposed two cities: it is in the catacomb city that crimes are devised and that horrible and incestuous rites are celebrated.

That we are always trapped in the prison of models can be seen if we move on to other thematics. Guido Morselli, for example, in using models as narrative and demonstrative structures, transforms them into alternative worlds which seem to allow us, at least in fantasy, to leave the one in which we live. Morselli imagines a past where events occurred differently from actual history or he hurtles towards a future which turns meaning topsy-turvy. He deals not with outcomes as yet undecidable, but with actual situations that we consider as definitive. He even seeks to imagine a future in which our world has ceased to exist for all people – victims of a catastrophe. But despite his efforts to transport himself beyond the world, we are forced to observe that, if the worlds Morselli encounters display enormous contingent differences in relation to ours, they present almost no ontological changes.

The most striking example of where a veritable collapse of represented worlds, rather than models, seems to occur is the witticism. And this appears natural, if one thinks that language is not only the primary model but also the medium through which we filter all our mental elaboration. The witticism is characterized by an abrupt discursive detour. The eruption of the witticism causes discourse to turn from the lines it was following and take another path. And while verbal elements develop in both parts of the text generally homonymic possibilities, the conceptual elements actualize two types of logical structure, related to two models of the world. This actualization is usually based on synonymy.

This process is described in a particularly astute manner by Koestler, who speaks of 'a sudden bifurcation of a mental event along two usually incompatible matrices.' Koestler writes: 'the underlying model ... is the perception of a situation or an idea, L, in relation to two reference systems each provided with its own internal logic, M_1 and M_2, but normally incompatible. The event L, a point of intersection of two 'planes,' enters in a manner of speaking into a simultaneous vibration on two wave lengths. As long as this unstable situation persists, L is not linked simply to one single associative context but bissociated with two contexts' (1989, 38, 40). In very different, but convergent, terms, Freud states: 'Reason – critical judgement – repression here are the forces against which, each in turn, the *Witz* struggles; it never renounces its primitive pleasure in playing with words, and from the onset of the stage of joking, it causes new sources of pleasure to well up by removing inhibitions' (1938, 735). Even more interesting is an allusion by Groos to a state of 'psychic stagnation' that is triggered in the person hearing a witticism and annulled at the moment of understanding. Whatever the case may be, the unconscious that Freud sees in the genesis of the witticism is a linguistic unconscious or a logopoetic one. It is for this reason we find in it ludic procedures like those of children and slips of the tongue.

In order to analyse the relationship of witticisms to logico-linguistic models and to models of the world in general, one must distinguish between the situations of the sender and the receiver. The sender uses verbal play as a function of forces more or less unconsciously polemic. The sender's enjoyment is that of invention or, if one wishes, that of the successful ruse. For the receiver enjoyment is more intense, for it consists primarily of a prompt restoration of logico-linguistic authority which is menaced by the witticism's assault. The bissociation of matrices which momentarily challenges models of the world appears as a game and thus triggers enjoyment and gratification as in the resolution of a double-bind situation.

Bissociation as defined by Koestler and the double-bind situation as shown by Fry (1963) consist in the apparent contradiction between the final sally of the message and its co-text. The final sally denies reality, the model of the world to which the receiver is most accustomed. The latter (during a brief and long moment) sees the world collapse and is only reassured upon understanding, that is, brought back to their effective terms, the subversive absurdity of the witticism. We must add that the sender of a witticism is not more conscious of witticism's potential. Having thus pronounced it, the sender finds himself partially in the same condition as the receiver: also in a dimension of wonder, psychic stagnation, and illumination, a dimension also involved in the shake up of a reality that soon restores itself. The laughter of the two participants in a witty exchange is a signal of their solidarity in the face of the linguistic unconscious. And it is, at the same time, a renewed act of subordination to the models of the world which our participation in history and the power of archetypes oblige us to accept.[1]

(Translated from the French by François Lachance.)

NOTE

1 The themes in this article have been developed in my *Fuori del mondo. I modelli nella follia e nelle immagini dell'aldilà* (Torino: Einaudi, 1990).

PART 3
NAMES, GENRE, GENDER

9

Characters and Their Versions

URI MARGOLIN

Lubomír Doležel has taught us how to describe and compare fictional worlds, encoded in different texts, in terms of the macrosemantic constraints and modalities that govern them. In this essay, I will describe a way of comparing the individuals (INDs) who inhabit such worlds in terms of the original/version relation.

Quite often, when we read a fictional narrative we encounter in its story world a named IND who can be intuitively regarded as a version of an original, bearing the same proper name, which is located elsewhere. This elsewhere may be another subdomain of the story world represented by this very text, or it may be another fictional, as if, story world represented by another text, or, finally, it may be a socially encoded model of the as is, actual historical world, as represented by a certifying discourse of the culture. The relation between original and version may hence be an *intra*textual, *inter*textual, or *extra*textual phenomenon. Moreover, in narrative, original and version may belong to the sphere of narration (narrator and narratee) or of the narrated (narrative agents). They may even shift spheres, as in John Gardner's *Grendel*, where the monster of the narrated domain of *Beowulf* is now the narrator. But underlying all of these varieties is the same basic phenomenon: 'What was [initially] a name with a single individual as its referent, now has as its reference a function, which for each world [or subworld] defines the embodiment of the individual in question in the given world [or subworld]' (Hintikka 1982, 139).

The study of the original/version relation has at least three dimensions: the discursive, the comparative-typological, and the ontological. In the intertextual and extratextual cases, a fourth, genetic or text-historical dimension, is crucial as well. In the following discussion, I shall limit myself almost entirely to the standard case where the INDs bearing the same proper name are both in the sphere of the narrated and are referred to by a reliable authenticating discourse of the narrator. Genette has discussed the intertextual variety at great length in *Palimpsestes*, but his purely classificatory procedure can be expanded by the other two varieties, and considerably deepened by using insights gained from the work of Doležel and Rescher.

INTRATEXTUAL

A   In some narratives, especially of the postmodernist kind (Borges, Fowles, Goytisolo, Robbe-Grillet), the basic authenticated story world or textual actual world contains several alternative versions of some temporal stage(s) of a named IND's life history, all of which are presented as continuations of a unique original temporal phase. Because of their occurrence in the textual actual world, all of these versions are equally authentic and possess the same ontological status; no choice or ranking among them is thus warranted by the text. We may understand this situation as the creation of a radically inconsistent world in which several irreconcilable strands are superimposed on each other, turning the IND into a plurality of mutually exclusive, simultaneous versions. A more charitable interpretation would regard this situation as a branching or divergence of worlds following a common world stage, with the original IND having several alternative life histories, one in each world. All the different versions have as their essential condition a match of their origins, the same degree of continuity with this common origin, and mutual incompatibility. In other words, each of the versions is possible relative to the common origin, but no two of them are jointly possible. The versions may be very different from the original and from each other, but since they are all equally related to the same original and all bear the same proper name originating with the narrator, they must all be considered as temporal versions or continuants of this original.

B   A more frequent case involves the existence of one or more alternative versions of an 'actual' story IND in the belief worlds of one or more narrative agents. Here, unlike the previous case, there is a clear difference in ontological status between the original IND, who exists in the textual actual world, and its versions, which exist only as objects of belief in the private domains or doxastic spheres of narrative agents. Any narrative agent in a story world may entertain a doxastic version of any other narrative agent, which may diverge slightly or radically from the original, as characterized in the discourse of the narrator. But once again, as long as the discourse of the narrator asserts that this is a doxastic version of an original who exists in the textual actual world, it is to be so considered. This would also apply in a case where different co-agents entertain very different beliefs about the same original, such as the different absurd hypotheses about the identity of Chichikov held by different narrative agents in *Dead Souls*. Narrative agents may also entertain alternative versions of themselves. One amusing example is Thurber's Walter Mitty, a hen-pecked original, who, in his imagination, exists as a series of heroic versions. The difference between the original in the textual actual world and the doxastic versions he or she has of himself or herself is even more striking in stories of madness or delusion. Nevertheless, all such beliefs about oneself, or *de se* beliefs, are to be considered as versions of the original as long as we are told by the narrator that this is how a given IND thought of himself or herself. One last complication: a doxastic version may be believed by a narrative agent who entertains it to be a true version of himself or herself. But it may also be entertained as an unreal condition: how one believes one could have been, had things gone otherwise.

C Doležel's claim that any constructed fictional world depends on the mode of its construction is amply borne out in the case of polyvocal narration (a story with a multiplicity of personalized partial narrators but without a global one above them) as well as that of a story told by a textually marked and unreliable or inconsistent heterodiegetic narrator (e.g., *skaz*). In both of these kinds of discourse, it is not possible to speak of original INDs in the textual actual world. What we are faced with, respectively, is a plurality of doxastic versions of an IND bearing the same proper name in the discourses of the various partial narrators and a single doxastic version stemming from a global narrator. Especially in the first case, we may try to infer and reconstruct a hypothetical original, the IND as it 'actually' is, but this IND will be eternally devoid of the ontological primacy and the certainty which only the authenticating discourse of an impersonal narrator can confer on fictional INDs.

We can say in conclusion that in case *A* the contrast is between equally valid ontological versions, in *B*, between ontological and epistemic, and, in *C*, between epistemic ones.

INTERTEXTUAL

A(1) The initial issue here concerns the identification of the original. In the intratextual case, the identification of an IND in the text's story world as original or version reflects an internal ontological hierarchy or primacy. Thus, the IND who occurs in the textual actual world, defined by the authenticating discourse of the narrator, is the original, while his namesake in the belief world of any narrative agent is a doxastic version. Similarly, in the extratextual case, the actual IND is the original, while the corresponding actuality variant in a given story world is the version. No such ontological hierarchy exists in the intertextual case, so the pragmatic dimension, embodied in the historical genetic context, becomes decisive, and the original is to be identified simply by the earliest text in whose story world it occurs. In Graeme Forbes's words: 'A fictional individual is something which is created at a specific point in time by the originator(s) of the first story to involve this object' (Forbes 1986, 15). When a relative chronology of the pertinent texts cannot be established, there is no original in the strict sense, and the decision is, rather, which IND to employ as point of departure or fixed point of reference. This decision is purely heuristic in nature and depends on the context and purpose of the enquiry.

A(2)   When a textual chronology is available, the following obtains. Any intertextual original/version comparison where both INDs are fictional – or 'supernumerary to the actual world' in Rescher's apt phrase – involves the tracking of INDs across what are *prima facie* different story worlds, encoded in different texts, with the sameness of proper name serving as our *fil conducteur*. The constancy of the fictional name serves here as what Genette calls 'contract of hypertextuality,' referring us back to the hypotext and inviting us to perceive the later version in the light of the original created in this hypotext. But a dyadic model of one original–one version, contained in one hypotext and one hypertext, respectively, is often a theoretical simplification. One ought to distinguish between an absolute original, associated with the first text to involve this IND, and an original relative to a given version. Some fictional INDs created by influential writers have enjoyed a large number of versions over the centuries. A multi-stage anaphoric chain of texts and versions has thus arisen in the course of time. Any late link in this chain may contain a version of a named IND which uses as its original the IND created in the originating story, or this IND plus one or more versions created in intermediary texts, or even just one or more versions created in intermediary texts, without recourse to the absolute original. In the case of multiple textual sources, the later author has at his disposal in fact a synthetic or eclectic second-level original, which may be quite different from the absolute original and which, in addition, is not contained in any one story world.

One important variety of a second-level original is provided by named cultural stereotypes or generic INDs, that is, fictional INDs who are beyond any specific story operator. As Castañeda points out (1979, 44–6), some fictional INDs created by leading authors assume a further life of their own; they undergo a process of culturization, where they finally become common cultural property, such that many or even most participants in the culture do not even know which is the first text in which they occur. In the end, they no longer belong to any particular story world and are part of a living cultural heritage. Notice that the features of a cultural stereotype need not be the invariants shared by all its versions to date. Rather, these features are a conglomeration of salient or core features of several versions. The proper names of such INDs are now well on their way to becoming common names or class concepts, as indicated in English by their use with the indefinite article (a Don Juan). A related phenomenon of a named original functioning midway between unique IND and cluster of properties, that is, midway between the extensional and the intensional, is exemplified by such titles as *Romeo und Julia auf dem Dorfe* (Gotthelf), *Die neuen Leiden des jungen W.* (Plenzdorf), *Doktor Faustus* (Mann), or *Ulysses* (Joyce). The central INDs of all of these stories bear proper names that are different from those occurring in the titles. They also exist in different space-time regions – normally very close to those of their authors – and have different co-agents or world mates. The proper names in the titles, being culturally entrenched or codified, serve therefore as preliminary contracts of intertextuality. They function as a shorthand for a complex of intrinsic mental and physical properties, action-related features, human interrelations, and global life courses shared by the two INDs and first instantiated or exemplified by the INDs named in the respective titles. Such named INDs can be referred to – albeit strictly metaphorically – as 'concrete universals.'

A(3)   And now for a few complementary remarks about versions. Once a fictional IND is created in an originating text, further versions of it may be constructed in subsequent texts by the same author, by different authors, and, occasionally, by both the originator and another writer (Don Quixote by Cervantes and by Avellaneda). But in the modern age, we associate a fictional IND with the circumstances of its creation, hence with its originator. Accordingly, if original and version occur in texts by the same author, and if they and their surrounding worlds can be seen as compatible, we are ready to construe each of these texts as a partial description of one and the same IND's life story. In other words, we are ready to join original and version without much further ado, even though they occur in different texts. Now, how about a compatible version of an IND – be it supplement or sequel – created in a work by a different author? Logically, the case for joining them is no different from the previous one, and yet a positive answer is not automatic. The third case is probably the most puzzling. While it is generally accepted in the modern age that authors own their texts, do they also own their creatures in the same way? Can an originating author claim, for example, that only he or she knows what they are like and what their full life story 'is,' so that supplements or sequels to their life stories, produced by other authors, who sign their own names on these texts, are 'invalid' from the start? And what can 'invalid' mean in this context? In general terms, we grant that each fictional IND is invented by someone. But once it is publicly encoded, does it turn into a public object of cognition and further elaboration, like theoretical entities, or does it still retain a privileged link to its originator? I leave this as an open question.

B(1)   Turning to the ontological perspective, we should now specify the nature of the original/version relation. To begin with, the relation is always in principle one-many. While an original can have only one version in each story world associated with a specific text, it can have *in toto* a large and open-ended series of versions, depending on the course of literary production. One can therefore speak of the open class of all versions to date of a given original, even though some of them may be mutually incompatible. Secondly, the INDs bearing the same proper name occur in what are, at least *prima facie*, distinct and different story worlds, and their property sets are seldom, if ever, identical in all of them. A strict Leibnizian identity of original and version is hence out of the question, especially as supernumerary INDs may have a *quiddity*, but not a *haecceity*. They are abstract entities, constructed from and defined by sets of constitutive properties, and are individuated through their complete descriptive specifications, since there is nothing else to individuate them through. On the other hand, our literary experience indicates that fictional INDs bearing the same proper name are seldom, if ever, totally unrelated in terms of their property sets. So the original/version relation must be located below identity but above unrelatedness. In most general terms, we can say that a version serves as surrogate or counterpart of its original in a different story world. But story worlds are unlike the possible worlds of logic. Neither they nor their inhabitants are maximal or complete, and, in addition, they are temporally restricted. Story worlds are more like what Hintikka calls 'small worlds,' temporal fragments or partial descriptions of worlds. Different story worlds involving an IND of the same name, and encoded in different texts, are therefore not necessarily closed, self-sufficient, or disjointed. On the contrary, it may sometimes be the case that original and version, as well as their limited story worlds, can be combined or joined. In such cases, the minimal counterpart relation is replaced by the stronger relation of sameness. In Richard Routley's terms (1980, 537), the different texts will turn out to embody parts of one and the same source book on the same IND and his world, yielding jointly the 'full life story' of this IND.

As soon as fictional INDs in two or more story worlds bear the same proper name, especially one which is culturally entrenched, the possibility of at least a counterparthood relationship between them must be addressed. A question arises at this point whether there is a minimal degree of similarity required for the counterpart relation to hold and what it may be. One also wonders whether there are any specific (kinds of) essential properties which all counterparts have to maintain in common with their original and what their nature might be. In the rest of this section, I shall concentrate on the questions just raised concerning the relevant dimensions of similarity, their main kinds and degrees, and the possible nature of essential properties linking original and version to each other. The first two questions are typological, while the third, which grows out of them, is ontological.

B(2)   The reader who studies relations of counterparthood finds the INDs concerned and their respective worlds fully constructed in the texts he is comparing. In other words, the structures whose members are being compared have already been articulated as regards INDs, properties, and relations. The properties of the two INDs in question can manifest one of five kinds of set theoretic relations: total overlap, as in Borges's meta-story about Menard rewriting the *Quixote*, inclusion of original in version, inclusion of version in original, intersection or partial overlap, and total lack of overlap, except for a shared proper name. The first and last cases, however, are marginal in actual literary practice. We can model the creation of a version as a process where several operations can be carried out on the property set of the original to turn it into this version. These operations, which in fact give rise to the corresponding set theoretic relations, involve semantic (de)construction, and can therefore be represented by the four cardinal operations of classical rhetoric: addition (expansion, amplification), deletion (depletion), substitution (which is a combination of deletion and addition), and rearrangement. In the case of intensional properties, we would also want to determine whether or not the properties added or replaced bear some semantic affinity to those of the original and, if so, whether or not they are similar, compatible, or at least consistent with them. In order to carry out a disciplined comparison of kinds and degrees of (dis)similarity between original and version, we need first of all a narratively oriented categorization of the properties of fictional INDs, one which bears in mind the *differentia specifica* of stories as temporally restricted and at least semi-ordered sequences of actions and events.

I would propose a tripartite categorization, based on Doležel (1979a). In the first group of properties, I would place space-time location and identity of co-agents (world mates). In the second, action-defined properties or actantial roles and functions, as defined by the overall course of events and interactions. To the third group belong the fictional IND's intrinsic mental and physical properties, supervenient properties like axiological stance, and also nomic and taxonomic properties as defined in Rescher (1975), which are a function of the type of world the IND inhabits (Doležel's macrosemantic constraints). If one accepts this tripartite division, there can be, in principle, eight kinds of (dis)similarity between original and version, depending on the number and nature of the categories which get modified.

Let us review briefly a few examples. The preservation of an original's intrinsic properties, mental and physical, coupled with a change in his extrinsic ones (location, world mates) and actantial role yields a visitor or guest appearance, where an IND, who is native and central to the story world of one text, now has his version appear in a secondary role in the story world of another text. Examples are the appearance of Richardson's Pamela and her family in Fielding's *Joseph Andrews*, the transhistorical party in Fuentes's *Terra Nostra*, and Chamisso's Peter Schlemihl in Hoffmann's *Die Abenteuer der Sylvesternacht*. Note that, if the properties associated with the home world or original environment of the guest are very different from those of the host world, they become highly marked through this procedure. On other occasions, the author of a version may choose to change or even reverse some of the mental properties of the original (axiological stance, intentions, attitudes, goals) while leaving the other categories of properties unaltered. An example cited by Genette (1982, 394–5) is Giraudoux's *Electre*, where Aegisthus is made to act out the same role as in Aeschylus, but now out of patriotic, even altruistic motives, rather than the traditional ones of selfishness, revenge, and lust for power. In Michel Tournier's *Vendredi* (Genette 1982, 237–8), time, space, and world mates are preserved, but in this version Crusoe learns from Friday rather than the other way around (reversal of actantial roles) and prefers pristine nature to civilization (reversal of axiological stance). In both 'high' and 'low' literary and cinematic narratives, we often encounter a modernization of the story world of the original, or its approximation to the contemporary readers' or spectators' world, but without changing the names of the main agents, their patterns of interrelations or their intrinsic properties. One good example is Roger Vadim's *Les Liaisons dangereuses*, set in Paris of the 1960s; another is the string of Sherlock Holmes movies in which he and Doctor Watson are active during the Second World War. Another well-known procedure of version creation consists of the radical reinterpretation or inversion of the original, effected by replacing its central mental properties by opposite ones, 'opposite' being defined as either lexical antinomy or opposition according to some defined cultural model. Byron's *Cain* and *Don Juan* readily come to mind. It is evident that a radical change of this nature entails a corresponding drastic change in the actions and interrelations of the original, and pushes the counterpart relation as a whole to the limit. We shall return to this point later on.

B(3)   Any comparison of original and version along the dimensions just outlined and exemplified must also take into account the crucial role the temporal aspect plays in all story worlds, the fact that the life histories they contain are the verbal representations of time-bound phenomena and INDs. The next step is accordingly to determine in each case the temporal or chronological position of any version relative to its original, by aligning their respective life histories in the corresponding story worlds. In technical terms, the property sets of original and version are to be temporally indexed relative to each other. If the temporal stage occupied by the version is earlier or later than that occupied by the original (*Vor-* and *Nachgeschichte*, analepsis and prolepsis), we may be dealing with a backward or forward temporal extension of the original, even if the property sets of the INDs in the two time frames are incompatible. The main issue now becomes the joining of the temporal stages of the INDs concerned, or trans-temporal continuity (perdurance). On the other hand, if the temporal stages of original and version overlap more or less, we are dealing with a version that is a supplement, complement, or alternative to the original, depending on the degree of their mutual relatedness and compatibility. Here the issue is counterparthood or possible sameness of INDs across temporally parallel story worlds. In a phrase, the first case concerns reidentification over time, the second, identification across story worlds. Once again, we notice the intimate relation between the ontological and the genetic in the case of fictional INDs. Evidently, both sequel and prelude to a fictional life history can be invented only once some initial time frame has already been established in the originating text. As clearly, the two texts must be published on separate dates and under separate covers. Especially if the sequel is by the same author, the original/version relation can be totally obliterated in a later edition in which the initial and the later texts are published as, say, part one and part two of the same text, hence implying a single story world. Individual continuity over time is consequently presented as a mono-textual given, instead of an intertextual problem. In the following section, we shall be dealing with temporal extension, temporal overlap or parallelism, and temporally unordered story worlds, in this order.

C(1)   The addition of life stages to a pre-existing life history of an original, contained in an earlier text, implies minimally the addition of one or more temporal stages with some new events, actions, or situations in them. In the case of the *retour des personnages* (Faulkner, Balzac, Tolkien), we encounter in a later text by the same author a whole cast of fictional INDs, recurring jointly at a later temporal phase, in the same type of world, and preserving their respective basic actantial and internal properties. In other cases ('the further adventures of …'), the added temporal slice is associated with a different location, as well as new world mates. As for action-defined properties, as well as internal and taxonomic ones, they may remain roughly constant between original and version (the Holmes, Bond, Smiley stories). But the original's intensional property set may also get modified through addition, deletion, or substitution, the latter sometimes involving the replacement of the central properties of the original by their opposites, or by semantically unrelated ones. While a temporal extension presupposes by definition whatever we know of its original, and must take it as both true and as background information, it may still deviate from it radically. But since the property sets of original and version/extension have different temporal indices, no logical contradiction is ever engendered by asserting them jointly, even if they are semantically incompatible. After all, actual individuals too change into their opposites in many respects: active into passive, foolish into wise, and so forth. Similarly, one cannot generate a contradictory extension from an original by eliminating any number of its properties at the later phase. To use again Routley's terminology, incompatible sets of properties assigned to an IND with the same proper name can, in principle, be joined into one source book on him as long as they take different temporal evaluations.

In the case of temporal extension, the crucial question concerns the minimal conditions for accepting original and version as forming part of the same IND's life story, or of the same continuant. Differently put, up to which point is it possible to find a higher-level structural principle which will serve as motivation and justification for construing different temporal stages as forming part of one unified chronology, in spite of all the differences between them? The key question here is not what and how much must remain constant or unchanged between original and version, but rather what kinds of change can still be predicated of the 'same' IND. For a possible answer, I take my clue from Hintikka's observation that 'one must consider not only individuals, but at the same time structural (dis)similarities of the entire worlds in which these individuals occur' (Hintikka 1982, 63). I believe, therefore, that the answer in this case depends primarily on the relation between the macrosemantic constraints, or nomic and taxonomic regularities, governing the respective story worlds of original and version. A Holmes who in a sequel is a giant rat or a magician is a most unlikely temporal extension of our detective, primarily because the fundamental laws of natural kinds and of what is possible and impossible at all, governing the world of the original Holmes stories, are quite incompatible with those of a world of fantastic creatures and supernatural powers. This blocks the way for the addition of the corresponding temporal stages into one time sequence or one life history. To effect a transition from the original Holmes world to the kind of world I have just suggested would require what Félix Martínez-Bonati has termed 'the magic operator.' But this magic operator connecting the two world structures is not there in the original, while it is already presupposed by the sequel, making the bridging of the two unfeasible. In other words, we cannot provide any internal motivation for the radical change in individual properties between the two texts or worlds. The same would apply, *mutatis mutandis*, to a strictly realistic sequel to fairy tale.

$C(2)$ Under temporal overlap or parallelism, I subsume cases where the life history of the version in the later text consists of just part of the time span of the original, of the same time span, or of the original time frame plus a temporal extension. Changed endings, as well as changed endings with added stages, also belong here. Genetically, parallel time frames for the same IND are encoded in texts by different authors, but sometimes also by the same author, as in different published versions of the same narrative, for example, Keller's *Der grüne Heinrich*. Even more generally, this phenomenon often exists when published texts are compared with their manuscript drafts.

The addition of properties poses no logical problem, since fictional INDs are always given to us schematically and incompletely. If the additions are consistent with the original, one may regard the version as a supplemented, expanded, amplified, augmented, or enriched original, as 'more of the same IND.' Midrash stories on Old Testament persons are of this kind, but the parade example, cited by Genette, is no doubt Thomas Mann's *Joseph und seine Brüder*: sixteen hundred pages for about sixteen pages in the Old Testament. We note again that the same original can be enriched by different authors in different ways, which are all compatible with it, although they may be incompatible with one another. One ought also to distinguish between added properties that are logically compatible with the original but semantically, especially actionally, unrelated to them, and those that are both compatible and semantically relevant to the initial course of events. This latter case defines an even closer relation between the two, providing variant, rather than new and different, aspects of the original. The addition of details and aspects that are unrelated to the initial course of events may be considered aesthetically detrimental or desirable, depending on the aesthetic norms adopted by different readers and critics. One way of generating compatible and semantically related versions from originals is expansion, based on inference drawing and gap filling. This activity is quite central to traditional literary interpretation, which is more of a literary than scholarly activity in this respect. At the other extreme stand expansions that deliberately add properties that are incompatible with the original, turning it into an internally inconsistent version. Such procedures of logical absurdization are central to literary parody and devalorization in general.

The subtraction or deletion of properties from an original can never engender a version that is incompatible with it, and is often practised in censored versions, versions for children, abridged versions, and the like. But the original may well possess some properties that are neither explicitly ascribed to its version nor inferable from it, thus blocking any relation of access back from the depleted version to its richer original. This process of property-set reduction raises the question of the limits to which one can modify an original in any way and still claim the result to be its counterpart. We shall return to this question in a moment.

Finally, the most crucial case, that of property substitution between original and version. Here we are dealing with what is neither a supplemented nor a reduced original life story, but rather an alternative one, which can no longer be joined to the original to form one source book on the given IND. Whenever properties are changed, we can no longer speak of the 'same' IND, but only of a very close or not so close counterpart of it. This closeness is a function of two factors: the number and nature of the properties changed, and the semantic relation between original and substitute properties. In the case of substitution by unrelated properties (i.e., properties belonging to a different semantic dimension or category), some foothold in the original history, that is, some property overlap, must be maintained, otherwise we may end up with an entirely different, unrelated IND, a mere 'homonym' of the original. But such random replacement is seldom practised by authors anyway, since it bears no literary or general aesthetic significance. Replacement of properties by semantically related ones ranges from replacement by similar ones, yielding a variant, through replacement by different ones, yielding an alternative, to replacement by opposites, yielding an anti- or counter-version, or, quite simply, an inversion of the original IND. Full inversion of the original's central constitutive properties is possibly the most effective and striking original/version relation, as it evokes the original most powerfully, and as it would completely lose its significance and effectiveness if the original were not instantly recognized. Property inversion is normally associated with changes in narrative stance, style, tonality, and genre (anti-legend, anti-märchen), but in many cases also with a shift in the kind of world the IND inhabits, such as de- or re-mythologization.

In all cases of property subtraction and substitution, the question of the limits of the version relation arises. Given extensive changes – especially in action related and intrinsic properties – between original and version, how much overlap between them must be preserved to justify the claim that the latter is still a counterpart of the former? How many properties of the original story, and of which dimensions, are necessary for this purpose, and is there a dimension which is the most important in this context? The traditional way in which these questions are formulated concerns the existence and the specification of the essential properties that all versions must maintain in common with their original for the relation to hold. Turning to Rescher for clarification on this point (1975, 63), I accept his view that all supernumerary INDs must, in principle, have some essential properties, since their tracking along worlds is merely conceptual, and can proceed only through their complete descriptive specifications, which include essential properties. I also accept Rescher's view that essential properties are relative to a description, theory, and perspective (1975, 22–3). But which perspective should we then adopt? I believe we conceive of fictional INDs in literary narratives as INDs who inhabit non-actual story worlds governed by specifiable global semantic constraints, and who, at the same time, participate in certain specified courses of events. Properties essential for the counterpart relation to hold will hence reside in one or both of these areas: narrative sequences and narrative worlds.

Let us first consider narrative sequences. Essential properties in this area are identical with what Eco has termed S-necessary properties (1979, 235–9), that is, properties that create the syntax of the fabula and that are indispensable for its course. The essential properties of an IND in this context are therefore those that can fill in the blank in the sentential form 'this is a story of a ... who ...' This form presents, in principle, a global pattern of an IND, together with a total course of events. The 'who' clause is most intimately connected with the initial stages of the fabula, with that which sets the course of events in motion, and serves as enabling condition for the rest. As for 'the story of a ...,' the IND is defined in this slot in terms of a significant classificatory predicate (Boer and Lycan's 'knowing who') and a fictional role or office. Eco rightly claims (1979, 243) that S-necessary properties are unique to supernumeraries, who, unlike actuality variants, are constructed and defined by the course of events in which they participate. But he also goes on to claim that S-necessary properties are always relational or reciprocal, involving two or more INDs. This, I think, is an unwarranted restriction. Let us look at a few examples of this sentential form at work:

(1) Holmes is an extremely intelligent detective who solves crimes through deduction.

(2) The phantom of the opera is a horribly disfigured man who lives under the opera house and who lures women to his subterranean abode.

(3) Robinson Crusoe is a European castaway on a pristine island, who encounters and interacts with a man of nature.

(4) Emma Bovary is an unhappy and bored provincial wife who takes lovers.
(5) Père Goriot is an aging father who sacrifices himself for his daughters' social success.

As we can see from these trite examples, narratively essential properties may reside in time and place (Crusoe), co-agents (Crusoe), actantial role (Holmes), physical properties (the phantom), mental dispositions (Emma), or interpersonal relations (Goriot as father), depending on what is required to initiate or motivate the particular course of events. This also explains why endings are the easiest to change, even radically, while still preserving the counterpart relation between the INDs in the two stories. But one must not forget that the courses of events just cited are, in fact, extrapolations from the specific texts. The same narrative text can give rise to a number of equally justified narrative schemes, depending on the reader's cultural and literary background and context, familiar generic patterns, codes of reading, levels of abstraction, reading interests, and the like. So, while many readers will probably agree that the essential properties involved in the counterpart relation reside in the original's classificatory predicates and fictional role, they may still disagree about their specific nature in any particular case. While the decision about the kinds of essential properties relevant in this context is semantic and theoretic in nature, their specification in any individual case is context dependent and belongs probably to pragmatics.

INDs also possess features whose kind and type depend not on courses of events, but on the overall nature of the story worlds they inhabit. Such ontological regularities are associated with the literary category of genre, so that genre formations may sometimes suggest the kind of properties that are essential for all INDs occurring in a story domain. In a realistic historical novel, for example, the particular quasi-real space-time region the events occupy may be an essential extrinsic property of all the fictional INDs inhabiting it. In a fantastic narrative, the main macrosemantic feature is the clash between two ontological zones or spheres. Membership in one of them rather than the other may be an essential feature of each story IND. In science fiction, membership in a kind or species functions in a similar manner: is a certain IND a terrestrial or extraterrestrial being? Human or clone, man or android? As for the relation between the two kinds of essential properties, narrative and global-semantic, one may say that the global ones are more general or basic than the narrative ones, and may restrict the types of classificatory properties and of roles any IND can assume in a given story world. This is probably why ontological conditions figure in both temporal extension and temporal overlap, while narrative conditions are essential in the latter case only.

$C(3)$ Finally, in much of ancient literature, as well as oral literature, we encounter cycles of stories about a given IND – from the proverbial village fool to spirits and gods – whose courses of events cannot be temporally aligned in any way, since they may do with vague temporal indications such as 'once upon a time,' 'many years ago,' ' when the world was young,' and the like. What is more, the texts of these stories cannot be chronologically ordered either. The original/version relation is consequently devoid of both external-genetic and internal support, and cannot apply in such cases. What we are left with is the quest for a generic IND, an invariant, abstract pattern which can be extrapolated from the whole series and claimed to underlie all the stories. Since similarity, rather than perdurance or continuity, is the crucial aspect in this kind of investigation, the utilization of features based on individual predicates and roles, together with global constraints, seems to be the best course to follow.

EXTRATEXTUAL

A In many literary narratives, most typically historical novels, we encounter in a major or minor role actuality variants, that is, named INDs whose originals, bearing the same proper name, are actual INDs whose existence is certified by public intersubjective discourses. In a limiting case, all the INDs in the given story world can have originals in the actual world, and the story itself does not contradict any taxonomic, nomic. or historical regularities of the actual world. What is more, the story does not contradict any intersubjectively acknowledged singular facts about the originals, including so-called negative facts (for example, it is not the case that George Bush ever met Stalin). The author has accordingly chosen to move strictly in the interstices between the documented facts, and can only add to what the extant historical records contain. The resultant story will be a supplemented, conjectural chronicle, straddling the borderline between fact and fiction, since all such additions are real possibilities with regard to the actual world. One good example is the series of presumed encounters between Hitler and Kafka in a Prague coffee shop in 1908–9, as portrayed in the Argentine novelist Ricardo Piglia's *Respiración artificial* (1980). Many more examples are provided by the constant stream of stories in the popular press about past or current secret love affairs of public figures who are known to be acquainted with each other.

On the other hand, all actuality variants become strictly surrogates, in the fictional story world, of their originals in the actual world as soon as they have as world mates story relative, fictional INDs. For it is not possible for actual individuals to bear relations to fictional ones who, by definition, inhabit alternate worlds. This distinction will apply, no matter how close the actuality variant is otherwise to his historical original in terms of actantial and intrinsic properties. The intimate relation between the ontological and the text historical, already alluded to in our discussion of intertextuality, is even more significant in the present context. An actuality variant can be produced only to that which already exists. Consequently, no actuality variant in the strict sense is provided by a literary narrative portraying a temporal phase of an actual individual that is future with respect to the time of production of this text (say, a novel written in 1990 figuring Mulroney in the year 2000). There is as yet no fact of the matter to be altered or supplemented by the creative imagination. What we are dealing with in such cases is, in fact, a conjecture, projection, or scenario for an ontically undecided future state, with a degree of initial probability determined by actual past and present states of affairs and by regularities up to writing time.

Unlike the two previous varieties (intratextuality and intertextuality), an extratextual original is actual and, therefore, complete, fully determinate, and independent of any semiotic procedures or mechanisms. An author may also have direct acquaintance with the actual original individual and create his variant or literary version on the sole basis of this personal acquaintance. But to the reader who compares the author's original with his transformed literary version, this direct authorial original is accessible only insofar as it is represented in some public symbolic medium, such as notebooks, memoires, diaries, recorded or taped conversations. In the vast majority of cases, though, the author's knowledge and image of the historical original underlying his work is based on verbal records contained in various certifying discourses of his culture, that is, discourses with institutionalized truth or fact claim, such as newspapers and history books. (We shall neglect here the mixed case, where what the author uses as original is a composite of factual discourses and previous fictional texts involving this figure.) Any such factual source is partial, as it can contain only some of the infinite number of predications that an actual individual takes, and none of these sources can provide absolutely certain knowledge about, say, the inner states of this individual. All sources are also selective and tendentious, depending on the purpose and context of their writing. Since history books rely on one another, probably even more so than literary narratives, the distinction between absolute and relative original is relevant here too, and so are the notions of generic original and of cultural stereotype. What is more, the cultural stereotypes or generic images of most prominent historical figures vary enormously according to the nation, period, race, or ideology that constructs such historical images in its certifying discourses. The upshot of the foregoing is that the image of the actual individual, serving as original for the creative writer, is a complex textual construct or entity, no less than any fictional IND serving in this capacity. Because of the vastly different property sets often attributed to the same actual individual in different historical accounts, there is no question of comparing the actuality variant with 'reality.' The only meaningful and feasible way of discussing the original/version relation in the case of historical individuals is therefore to establish the (nonfictional) texts that were actually utilized by the given author as basis for his imaginative transformation. A classical example of the study of both sources and transformations is Shklovskij's *Material and Style in Tolstoy's War and Peace*. If the writer's historical sources are not known to us, we can still compare his creature of fiction with the standard image of the original in the writer's time and place or in our own. But in either case we will be engaged in hypothetical and purely typological comparisons.

As distinct from the intertextual case, no person can, of course, be said to invent or own actual individuals, so all versions of them in different works by the same or by different authors are on equal ontological footing. The original/version relation is one-many here too, and there are, in fact, large and open-ended classes of versions of major historical figures, versions which may again be mutually incompatible. As long as we regard the original as a textual construct, the five kinds of set theoretic relations between the property sets of original and version, the four semiotic mechanisms involved in the transformation of the one into the other, and the three basic categories of individual properties defined in the previous section are all valid and applicable in the extratextual case as well. The same holds for the fundamental distinction between versions involving temporal extension and those involving temporal overlap. We may consequently proceed without further ado to an examination of these two varieties with regard to actuality variants.

B   As we have already seen, adding future stages to a living individual's life history is a matter of future projection or conjecture, not version creation. On the other hand, one cannot add stages to a life history that is already completed, for instance, through the death of the actual individual concerned. Once again, the way out of this pseudo-aporia is through the distinction between the totality of facts about a given actual individual, the complete source book on him/her, and the totality of facts available in a certifying discourse about him/her, which is always finite or limited. Since only the latter is available to author and readers alike, there may often be temporal gaps in the record of an individual's life course, and total blanks as regards his or her beginning and/or end. So even an author who does not wish to modify any of the socially held facts about a historical figure may add whole temporal stages not historically documented. Examples are Fuentes's *El viejo gringo*, describing the death of Ambrose Bierce in the Mexican revolution, and Broch's *Der Tod des Vergil*. In these added stages, world mates, locations, actions, and properties of all kinds can be added, deleted, or substituted from the image of the historical original. Once again, the question arises as to the minimal conditions for accepting original and extension as forming, at least in principle, parts of the same individual's life story, in spite of all the differences in property sets. But here, unlike the intertextual case, the identity of world mates becomes crucial. As soon as clearly fictional world mates occur in the temporal extension, there is no longer a way of joining original and version into one life history, as the two temporal phases are now located in two different worlds. What one could examine instead is the plausibility of the historically recorded original possessing in the unrecorded phases of his or her life the qualitative intrinsic and interactional properties this temporal extension endows them with. Such probability is a function of three kinds of factors contained in the certifying cultural discourse: singular documented facts about the original's physical, mental, and actional properties; general historical regularities of the original's period and society; universal nomic and taxonomic regularities we believe to hold in the actual world (especially physical and psychological ones). Since the specific contents of all three kinds of factors with respect to the same original change historically, so will the probability of the corresponding extension. A prime example are the stories about the supernatural birth or death of kings and saints.

C   When original and version occupy the same temporal stage, the possession of additional properties by the version vis-à-vis the original is not problematic at all in the case of a fictional original, since it is always given to us as a schematic and incomplete entity. On the other hand, no addition of properties is possible, in principle, in the case of actuality variants, since their actual originals are complete or maximal. No complete description of any actual individual is, however, possible in any certifying discourse of finite length. As a result, what is impossible in theory becomes quite possible in practice. Authors can accordingly add events, actions, world mates, properties, and relations to historically documented stages of actual individuals: secret love affairs, illegitimate children, and the like. Most obviously, the writer can always add mental traits, especially those belonging to depth psychology, to such individuals.

As far as the substitution or change of the properties of the original, as described in specified sources, are concerned, we note that mental properties, states, and acts posited of actual individuals in historical accounts are a matter of inference, conjecture, and hypothesis, so they can always be replaced by different, even opposite, ones in the fictional account without contradicting public facts. Authors may choose to go one step further and preserve just some of the public facts about an original, but otherwise create a counterfactual or alternative life history of this actual individual, a record of how the world would have been had things gone otherwise. A chilling example is Richard Chesnoff's *If Israel Had Lost The War* (1968). In this context we are dealing with revisions of actual individuals, where initial phases of the actual individual's history are preserved, while successive ones are replaced, to diverge emphatically from accepted public facts. In the name of internal consistency, the actions, interrelations, and destinies of all other historically based world mates must also be changed accordingly, so that what we get is, in fact, an alternative version of a whole segment of world history. If all the individuals involved are actuality variants, and if the changes are possible relative to accepted historical and natural regularities, the result will be similar to the alternative world scenarios of modal logic ('suppose Hubert Humphrey had been elected President in 1968'). Interestingly enough, it is artistically easier to change the life histories of actual individuals when they occupy major, rather than marginal, roles in a literary narrative, because in the latter case they serve as the main underpinning for the *vraisemblance* of the whole fictional narrative. As Brian McHale has noted in an excellent discussion of this point (1987, chap. 6), all changes to historical originals we encounter in literary narrative fall into three broad groups: modifications of singular facts, of the socio-historical regularities of the original's time and place, of the laws of nature and logic. McHale names the three corresponding kinds of alternative histories apocryphal histories, creative anachronisms, and historical fantasies. The nature of the change becomes increasingly radical as we move from one group to the next.

Whenever documented properties of any sort of an actual individual are modified in his literary version – rather than being added to or deleted – version and original can no longer be joined together. Such joining is also prevented, as we have already seen, by the presence of purely fictional INDs in the world of the version. The version is now clearly a counterpart or surrogate of the original in some non-actual world. But how long does this relation hold? What are the minimal conditions that any fictional version must satisfy to be considered a counterpart of an historical individual? In the case of fictional INDs, I have proposed two conditions, one based on the specific courses of events in which original and version participate, the other, on the nature of the worlds they inhabit. Now an actual human individual, unlike a semantically constructed one, is defined essentially not by any set of constitutive properties or course of events, but rather by his unique causal origins, biological and spatio-temporal. At the same time, he is also bound to generic regularities of his species or natural kind, which are themselves tied to the overall taxonomic regularities specified by the dominant scientific world model. It would seem, therefore, that match of individual origins and of generic, species-defining properties are the two essential conditions for any fictional version of a particular actual individual to be considered as its counterpart in a given story world. Failure to satisfy the first condition will yield a relation based exclusively on qualitative similarity of properties or general shape of personal destinies, that is, a relation that is purely typological. Failure to satisfy the second condition will yield a wild historical fantasy, in which a human is turned into an angel, animal, or machine, and the counterpart relation will be based entirely on extrinsic factors such as time and place of birth.

The upshot of our discussion is that extrinsic properties play a far more crucial role in literary works involving actuality variants than in those involving the modification of pre-existent fictional originals. Actuality is segregated from fictionality far more than different fictional realms are segregated from each other. As we have seen, the very addition of fictional world mates is enough to turn a possible actuality variant into a merely fictional one, that is, one that is no longer a real alternative with respect to the actual world. With one stroke, the potential transworld identity is replaced by the weaker relation of counterparthood. Failure to adhere to the origins of the actual original seems to undermine even this weaker relation, and reduces the original/version relation further into mere general typological similarity. The preservation of prototypical, species-defining features, on the other hand, seems to be equally decisive for both actuality variants and pure supernumeraries.

10

Naming Names in Telling Tales

PETER W. NESSELROTH

The study of proper names in fiction has a long history.[1] It is not surprising that literary theorists pay so much attention to naming in fiction since, in a narrative network, proper names are the nodal points through which actions and descriptions are interconnected. These, in turn, function as semantic features that define the meanings of the names and produce a type of fictional cluster called 'a character.' Or as Barthes wrote back in 1970: 'On peut dire que le propre du récit n'est pas l'action mais le personnage comme nom propre' (1970, 74), which may be translated as 'It could be said that the distinctive feature of stories is not the action but the character as a proper name.'

But while most studies of names in literature have focused on the logic of naming within the philosophy of language or on the role of imaginary names in a given corpus, say, names in Balzac, Proust, or the Victorian novel, this paper will deal with the use and function of real names in literary contexts, names that are part of our sociolect and appear in fictions alongside names that occur in the idiolect of a single work, or of one author's corpus. This happens not just in historical novels where real names are a requirement of the genre (e.g., Napoleon for the nineteenth century, Hitler for the twentieth), but also in other types of fiction where they are explicitly, or implicitly, present. Fictionalization occurs not only with historical or contemporary names but with literary ones as well, provided, of course, that they have come to represent a type (version of a prototype, in Uri Margolin's scheme). They are consequently transposable to other contexts – Emma Bovary, for example. I shall deal here with three types of names in fiction: historical real names; real fictional names (behind the fictional name, we can identify someone, usually one of our contemporaries); fictional real names (we know them from literature).

HISTORICAL REAL NAMES

Let me begin in the personal mode. When I was first introduced to Lubomír Doležel, some twenty-five years ago, he asked, on hearing my name, if I was a descendant of the famous nineteenth-century Russian diplomat Count Karl Robert Vassilievich von Nesselrode, who served both Alexander I and Nicholas I as Foreign Minister and later became Chancellor of the Empire. Although family lore has it that we do have a kith and kin relationship with this important historical figure (like us, he was of German origin), I have never (or not yet) been able to find hard evidence of any connection. The question about my last name comes up frequently, not always from particularly cultured individuals who think immediately of the famous Russian, but also from ordinary lovers of fine desserts, with reference to Nesselrode pies and puddings, which are, in fact, based on the Count's recipes (in the early fifties, Nesselrode pies were quite common on dessert menus in North American restaurants).[2]

So the name is a good conversation starter. And I often fictionalize about it, creating possible worlds in which I am indeed a direct descendant of the Count and, of course, legally entitled to the title. Last year Lubomír remembered that, in 1929, Tynianov had written a historical novel about Griboyedov, the playwright/diplomat, the author of *The Misfortunes of Being Clever*, who was stoned to death by a mob in Teheran. The novel's English title is *Death and Diplomacy in Persia*, and Nesselrode is one of the characters in it (Tynianov 1975). I was, of course, anxious to see if fiction would provide some juicy details to flesh out the entries of various encyclopaedias and history books, and I did find many descriptive details: Karl Robert Nesselrode is introduced as 'a grey-faced dwarf' with a 'tiny feminine hand, and that white little hand was enclosed in the other hand, which was yellow,' and at one point, Tynianov says: 'The little white hand was laid on the rather large bundle [the Peace Treaty that Griboyedov had just handed him] with its affixed seals. The grey head came to life, the Jewish nose breathed hard, and the German lips said in French: "I welcome you, Monsieur le Secrétaire, and you too, Messieurs, on the occasion of this excellent Peace." Karl Robert Nesselrode did not know Russian' (1975, 33). Now, this is not quite what I had imagined for my family romance. In fact, I would have much preferred the characteristics of a Nesselrode pudding: very rich, complex, sweet, and hard to make. Nesselrode is a real name, identifying someone we know to have been in the world, and it doesn't really matter whether Tynianov's description of him is accurate or biased. The interest of historical novels has never been due to the objectivity of their representation of people and events. On the other hand, the historical novel has to be rooted in real names, as well as places and dates, because its truth effects depend on what we already know, or can easily verify elsewhere, in what Didier Coste has called the certifying discourse of textbooks, atlases, and encyclopaedias (1989, 98–100). Unlike re-enacted dialogues and actions, they tend to be informative and reliable. That is why, for example, children often learn about Richard the Lion-Hearted and his evil brother John Lackland from *Ivanhoe*, and about the history of France from the *Three Musketeers* and its many sequels. Or from *Petit Larousse illustré*, which is the encyclopaedia that those of us, with a French formation, first read for fun and where we picked up a lot of our cultural information. I remember being particularly fascinated by the sequence, in Roman numbers, of the French kings named Louis. There are eighteen of them altogether. This fascination with the French Louis is not uncommon: Prévert has a poem, called 'Les Belles Familles,' which reproduces the entire list in numerical order, and he complains at the end about people who aren't even capable of counting to twenty (1949, 163). But Prévert's list goes from Louis I to Louis XVI, skips Louis XVII, and then continues to Louis XVIII. That is because, within the historic and encyclopaedic sequence, Louis XVII is a diegetical gap. He was the second son of Louis XVI, and he became the Crown Prince after his older brother's death. He was proclaimed king by the Royalists, but he never reigned, and he probably died at the age of ten. Being the last direct Crown Prince of the older Bourbon branch, the name also came to mean, in royalist circles, absolute and divine legitimacy, the purest of the pure, as opposed to not only obvious usurpers like Napoleon, but also to his uncles Louis XVIII and Charles X. In *Le Temps retrouvé*, Proust tells of the disapproval of the Parisian aristocrats for the socially unfit company that the genuine Duchesse de Guermantes keeps in her later life. She is the only one who was entitled to sign 'Guermantes-Guermantes' because she bears the name by blood and not by marriage (as opposed to Verdurin-Guermantes, for example). To her husband's sisters she had seemed to be a miraculous survivor: 'quelque chose de plus précieux, comme un Moïse sauvé des eaux, un Christ échappé en Égypte, *un Louis XVII enfui du temple*' (my emphasis).[3]

  Louis XVII died under mysterious circumstances, and rumour had it that he was rescued from the Paris prison cell where the revolutionary government kept him after his parents' execution. This has enabled many pretenders, throughout the nineteenth century, to claim his identity, and the gap has been extremely fertile for the generation of real fictions. False Dauphins, from Prussian clockmakers to Iroquois Indian chiefs, all claiming their rights to the throne, materialized out of nowhere (see Buleau 1861, 3: 271–322). In Patrick Modiano's 1989 novel *Le Vestiaire de l'Enfance*, the narrator, in order to earn a living, fathers an endless Spanish radio serial called 'Les aventures de

Louis XVII.' This time, our escaped Crown Prince has survived to become a plantation owner in Jamaica.

Modiano is, in fact, a writer who plays the game of the name in an exemplary fashion, especially in his first novel, published in 1968, *La Place de l'Étoile*. This novel was brought to my attention by Gerald Prince who has written a very illuminating article on Modiano in which he shows the relationship between the morphology of names and the thematics of memory and of otherness in Modiano's work (Prince 1986). My comments here will be more concerned with the use and transformation of real names in this particular novel, because its humour depends to a great extent on recognizing them and on knowing what they mean.

The hero-narrator of *La Place de L'Étoile*, named Raphael Schlemilovitch, is a young Jewish writer, the author of a *Psychanalyse de Dreyfus*, wherein he proves, once and for all, that the captain was as guilty as can be. Schlemilovitch dreams of being a respected member of the French wartime collaborationist, and rabidly anti-Semitic, editorial board of the journal *Je suis partout*, of palling around with the likes of Céline, Drieu La Rochelle, Brasillach, and Rebatet. He would like to propose the creation of a Jewish division of the Waffen SS to Otto Abetz, the Nazi ambassador to France charged with organizing the Collaboration. His *maître à penser* is Maurice Sachs. He wants to be an honorary Aryan in the Third Reich and Eva Braun's lover, with Hitler's benign acquiescence. He thinks he has a photo of her with a dedication that says: 'Für mein kleiner Jude, mein geliebter Schlemilovitch – Seine Eva.'

The whole story is based on extreme inversions of what we know about the period and the events. It creates a world we know to be (or to have been) impossible, mainly because the semantic contents of the real names contradict their fictional representation. To the extent that we recognize them, they have various degrees of negative associations for today's readers, but in the story the characters bearing them are all wonderfully warm and gentle. Modiano's strategy here is similar to that of Don Delillo, who in his 1984 novel *White Noise* has a narrator, an academic by the name of Jack Gladney, who has created, and chairs, an extremely prestigious Department of Hitler Studies where he teaches a course called Advanced Nazism, a course of study 'designed to cultivate historical perspective, theoretical rigor and mature insight into the continuing mass appeal of fascist tyranny, with special emphasis on parades, rallies and uniforms, three credits, written reports' (1984, 25).

Both Modiano and Delillo treat the catastrophic events and evil personalities in the only serious way that they can be treated, that is, frivolously, like the 'Springtime for Hitler' number in Mel Brooks's *The Producers*. In *White Noise*, one of Gladney's colleagues, a New Yorker named Murray Jay Siskind, would like to create his own program in his field of expertise: Elvis studies. Gladney tries to help him by visiting one of his classes in the hope that his presence will add prestige to the project. The two professors then give a lecture contrapuntally in alternating voices comparing Hitler and Elvis, who, it turns out, shared many fine qualities, the major one being that they both adored their mother:

'Elvis and Gladys liked to nuzzle and pet,' said Murray. 'They slept in the same bed until he began to approach physical maturity. They talked baby talk to each other all the time.'

'Hitler was a lazy kid,' [said Gladney]. 'His report card was full of unsatisfactorys. But Klara loved him, spoiled him, gave him the attention his father failed to give him. She was a quiet woman, modest and religious, and a good cook and housekeeper.'

'Gladys walked Elvis to school and back every day. She defended him in little street rumbles, lashed out at any kid who tried to bully him.'

'Hitler fantasized. He took piano lessons, made sketches of museums and villas. He sat around the house a lot. Klara tolerated this. He was the first of her children to survive infancy. Three others had died.' ...

'There is not much doubt that Hitler was what we call a mama's boy' [this remark makes 'a note-taking young man murmur absently "Muttersöhnschen"']. (1984, 71–3)

The technique here consists not only in the mock-heroic juxtaposition and Oedipal interpretation of Hitler and Elvis, but also in foregrounding certain well-known but historically trivial encyclopaedic features of the two names. While the real names in *White Noise* are limited to this fairly common and well-known dynamic duo, the names in *La Place de l'Étoile* run the gamut from the universally recognizable ones (Hitler, Eva Braun, Céline) to the ones that require a slightly more specialized knowledge of the period and of the country: Brasillach and Drieu La Rochelle, as collaborationist men of letters, were the 'bad guys,' as opposed to resistance heroes like Malraux and Éluard. Brasillach was executed after the liberation, and Drieu committed suicide. During the postwar period, they were not on the reading lists for courses on modern French literature. You might recall, though, that Paul de Man reviewed Brasillach's *Notre Avant-Guerre* and Drieu's *Notes pour Comprendre le Siècle* rather favourably in 1941 (1988, 130–1, 170–1). And you will find entries for them in the *Petit Robert 2*, today's desk encyclopaedia. Rebatet and Maurice Sachs, on the other hand, are not mentioned there. Lucien Rebatet was the most virulent anti-Semite and pro-Hitler columnist on the staff of *Je suis partout*. He is the author of *Les Décombres*, about six hundred pages of fanatical ranting and raving against the Jews and the decadence of the Third Republic, the first being the cause of the latter, of course. It was the literary smash hit of 1942. The book was republished in the 1970s, under the title *Mémoires d'un Fasciste*. In *La Place de l'Étoile*, he is also referred to under the more emblematic name of Léon Rabatête who writes polemical attacks on Schlemilovitch in Rebatet's style.[4] And Maurice Sachs was, and still is, the epitome of the sleazy character. He had been one of Cocteau's lovers and stole from him and from anyone who befriended him. He was probably half Jewish (during the Occupation, he tried to change the spelling of his name to 'Saxe'). He volunteered to work in Germany, and he became an informer for the Gestapo. He himself was eventually arrested and, given his homosexuality, inevitably earned the nickname 'Gestapette' from the other prisoners. He died in 1945, probably shot by the SS with whom he was fleeing. He achieved some posthumous fame when his books about the 1920s and 1930s were published (*Au temps du Boeuf sur le Toit*, *Le Sabbat*, etc.) But his death, like Louis XVII's, is shrouded in mystery (see Raczymow 1988). He may have survived and assumed another guise. In the novel, Schlemilovitch meets him in the bar of a hotel in Lausanne, and Maurice Sachs confides in him and relates his misadventures since his so-called disappearance. After his stint as a Gestapo agent, he tells of having been successively: a G.I., a cattle trader in Bavaria, a diamond broker in Antwerp, a bordello keeper in Barcelona, and a clown in a Milan circus under the stage name Lola Montès. He has finally settled in Geneva, where he now owns a small bookstore (Raczymow 1988, 27–8).

The book is very funny but only for people who know what these names (and many others from that period) represent and what their cultural connotations are. Even for Modiano himself, all these names come from indirect sources since he was born in 1945 (he also co-wrote with Louis Malle the screenplay for *Lacombe Lucien*, about the same period). That is why, as Prince says, Modiano doesn't travel well, and as far as I know, he hasn't been translated. In another culture, those names would be fictional and the humour would be lost. Because they are esoteric, and will become increasingly so despite their occasional faddishness (Modiano was blamed for the 'mode rétro' in France), they are almost as difficult to decode as those in a *roman à clef*.

REAL FICTIONAL NAMES

But in a *roman à clef*, real names are by definition changed to fictional ones. However, to be successful, that is, sufficiently recognizable for the reader to identify, or to guess at, the palimpsestuous covered real name, enough encyclopaedic features must be actualized in the description of the character so that the proper identification becomes almost inevitable. Sometimes even a bit too obvious: guess who the philosopher Brumhold is in the novel *How German*

Is It? by Walter Abish? At a ceremony to rename small town Brumholdstein in his honour, the town's architect, Helmut Hargenau, is giving the inauguration speech:

'In speaking of Brumhold,' said Helmuth. 'In speaking of a man I greatly admire, I am also, to a degree, explaining or attempting to explain Germany. For aren't we all mirrored in the metaphysical speculations of Brumhold? Not that I wish to imply that we all *equally* shared his thirst for truth and knowledge. No. What I wish to say is that because we are Germans we are closer to understanding Brumhold, closer to what he meant by *Dasein*, for Brumhold's confrontation with this term *Dasein* or "Being" became most tangible, most unresistant to understanding when he, Brumhold, in his mind or in actuality, wandered through the thick forest, his beloved forest, a forest – I must emphazise - that is and remains spiritually close to us. For it was not just any forest. And again, yes again, it was not necessarily one specific forest: it was the German forest in which dwells our spirit, our ideals, our culture, our poetry, our truth.' (1983, 169)

While the name of the philosopher of *Dasein* would be in any modern *encyclopédie universelle*, a less universal one would be required for names in more specialized sub-genres, such as the novels that deal with the Parisian intellectual scenes of recent decades, from mandarins to samurai, or in Anglo-Saxon academic fictions like David Lodge's trilogy *Changing Places* (1975), *Small World* (1984), *Nice Work* (1989). Because names here generally refer indirectly to contemporary personalities who would only figure in restricted encyclopaedias rather than in universal ones, in a *Who's Who* rather than in a *Britannica*. For example, the name Morris Zapp, the American hustling academic superstar who appears in all three of the Lodge novels, stands for the name Stanley Fish, or so the 'authority' of our own 'interpretative' community would have it. As in many traditional novels, the name indicates the character and personality of the man. Morris is zappy in his verbal delivery, just as Stanley is in his lectures and in his writings, and both first names are the markers of an identical New York ethnicity.[5] Morris Zapp also has a contract with his university that guarantees him a higher salary than anyone else in the humanities, so whenever the university wants to bring in another star for big money, his own pay cheque gets automatically fatter. And Zapp's intellectual evolution is very close to what we know about Fish's: Robyn Penrose, the British post-structuralist heroine of *Nice Work*, who is looking for a tenure-track position, writes Lodge, 'was familiar with his publications: originally a Jane Austen specialist in the Neo-Critical close reading tradition, he had converted himself (rather opportunistically, Robyn thought) into a kind of deconstructionist in

the nineteen seventies, and enjoyed an international reputation in both guises'
(1989, 322).

The only alteration, Jane Austen for John Milton, is the kind of displacement
required in a *roman à clef* and doesn't make much difference since both names
share the semantic feature 'canonical English author.' But the change from
a masculine to a feminine name does indicate that Zapp, who has had to
endure much abuse from feminist critics, is above ideological concerns in his
scholarly interests. In fact, during cocktail party chit-chat, he can drop the
right real names (and flirt) better than almost anyone: 'Robyn told him [what
her book was about]. Morris Zapp vivaed her briskly about its content and
methodology. The names of prominent feminist theorists crackled between
them like machine-gun fire: *Elaine Showalter, Sandra Gilbert, Susan Gubar,
Shoshana Felman, Luce Irigaray, Catherine Clément, Susan Suleiman, Mieke Bal*
– Morris Zapp had read them all. He recommended an article in the latest
Poetics Today which she hadn't read. Finally he asked her if she had made
arrangements to publish her book in America' (325).

Even a reader who has never heard of any of these 'prominent feminist
theorists' will gather that Morris Zapp is impressively *au courant*. And, of
course, readers are not required to know that Zapp stands for Fish, although
knowing it adds the pleasure of gossip to that of the text. Morris Zapp is simply
recognizable as the prototype of the hot-shot academic, and this gives him the
potential to become what I call a 'fictional real name,' a name that enters into
our sociolect, our culture, and our encyclopaedias. For, as Umberto Eco has put
it: 'the encyclopedia does not register only the "historical" truth that Napoleon
died on Saint Helena but also the "literary" truth that Juliet died in Verona'
(1984, 83–4).[6]

The difference, though, is that Juliet died in Verona only because Shakespeare
said so. Unlike Napoleon, she made her first appearance in a fictional context,
and this context defined her once and for all. Any writer who uses her
name for a character works either with or against the semantic features that
were first established for that name. In a recent Canadian feminist play by
Ann-Marie MacDonald entitled *Goodnight Desdemona (Good Morning Juliet)*,
Juliet marries Romeo, is instantly bored, and longs for a lesbian relationship
with the Shakespearean scholar who is also the one who imagines this play. It
is significant, though, that the program notes handed to the audience contain
synopses (i.e., encyclopaedic entries) of both *Othello* and *Romeo and Juliet*, on
the assumption that, without a reminder of the definitions, we wouldn't get
it. Or, to stay with Shakespeare but closer to our concerns, Thomas Pavel can
illustrate his discussion of Searle's abbreviation, or cluster, theory of naming
versus Kripke's rigid designator theory with sentences like 'John is just like

Hamlet: neither can make a decision in due time' and 'Had Hamlet married Ophelia, they would have lived happily ever after' because these names, the literary ones, not John, come with encyclopaedic features that enable us to understand their use in Pavel's context (Pavel 1986, 32–4).

When fictional names become part of our cultural knowledge, they acquire the same value and functions as historical names and any number of stories can be written about them: Emma Bovary, as Woody Allen and Philippe Sollers have shown, has generated some particularly imaginative and amusing postscripts. In Allen's 'The Kugelmass Episode,' the title character is a balding New York professor of humanities who has, with the help of a magician, gone back to the past in order to have an affair with Emma who speaks to him 'in the same fine English translation as the paperback.' 'She's young and nubile,' and Kugelmass has an easy time with her because he arrives in Emma's life at just the right moment, when she is most receptive, that is, 'a few pages after Léon and just before Rodolphe.' Emma is starved for excitement, and she loves to hear him tell her stories about Broadway night life, Hollywood, fast cars, and TV stars: 'Tell me again about O.J. Simpson,' she implores, and he obliges: 'what can I say? The man is great. He sets all kinds of rushing records. Such moves. They can't touch him.' But after Kugelmass brings her back to modern-day New York and puts her up at The Plaza, Emma becomes restless and, of course, begins to make demands: 'Get me back into the novel or marry me,' she tells Kugelmass. 'Meanwhile,' she adds, 'I want to get a job or go to class, because watching TV all day is the pits' (1981, 59–78). Similarly, Sollers, in *Femmes* (1983), imagines Emma in present-day Paris. She is 125 years old but she will always be 30. She is still as beautiful, voluptuous, and mysterious as ever. She still gives Charles a hard time about his mother, and she has a migraine every time he tries to come near her. Léon is a centre right deputy and Rodolphe, an influential literary critic. A few years ago, he had convinced Emma to participate in some partner swapping parties with him. She tried to like them to please him, but they soon bored her. Emma greatly admires Flaubert, and she and Rodolphe agree that Sartre, in *L'Idiot de la famille*, which neither of them has read, has shed some remarkable light on poor Gustave's illness (119–21).

Sollers's and Allen's parodies of *Madame Bovary* both exploit what we know about Emma Bovary as a 'character': she is not too bright and therefore interprets life through romantic and pseudo-realistic banalities ('Les affaires d'argent seront toujours, quoi qu'on dise, les seules affaires,' she thinks in *Femmes*). They also exploit what we know about the name Gustave Flaubert, a name whose ready-made associations include his supposedly fierce contempt for bourgeois stereotypes.[7] As canonical literary icons, the name and the novel inevitably generate academic platitudes like the comment about *Madame Bovary* by a Stanford professor in *The Kugelmass Episode*: 'Well, I guess the mark of a classic is that you can reread it a thousand times and always find something new.'

More than any other words in a language, real names, whether historical or fictional, have the potential to produce new stories. That is because they already come with built-in stories (or 'definitions') from other contexts, either fictional or supposedly factual, like encyclopaedias. Because encyclopaedias incorporate the circle of our knowledge, they are generally thought of as being centripetal. But they are centrifugal as well: they not only bring together disparate bits of information, they also keep disseminating them, and sowing new literary seeds. That is why the inside cover of the *Petit Larousse illustré* has a representation of a little Marianne-like girl blowing away at a dandelion with the caption 'Je sème à tout vent.' Real names in a literary text do not just serve to produce an *effet de réel*. They also give us new fictions, from *Rameau's Nephew* to *Flaubert's Parrot*, *Shakespeare's Dog*, and *Foucault's Pendulum*.

NOTES

1 For an overview of the topic, at least up to 1983, see Nicole 1983, 239–53.
2 In Proust, Marcel's parents serve the pudding to Mr de Norpois who tells his host, as a compliment, that such a Lucullus-like meal will force him to take a diet cure at the Carlsbad spa (Proust 1974, 1: 466).
3 'En réalité, elle, la seule d'un sang vraiment sans alliage, elle qui, étant née Guermantes, pouvait signer: Guermantes-Guermantes quand elle ne signait pas: la duchesse de Guermantes, elle qui à ses belles-soeurs même semblait quelque chose de plus précieux, comme un Moïse sauvé des eaux, un Christ échappé en Égypte, *un Louis XVII enfui du temple*, le pur du pur, maintenant sacrifiant sans doute à ce besoin héréditaire de nourriture spirituelle qui avait fait la décadence sociale de Mme De Villeparisis, elle était devenue elle-même une Mme De Villeparisis, chez qui les femmes snobs redoutaient de rencontrer tel ou telle, et de laquelle les jeunes gens, constatant le fait accompli sans savoir ce qui l'a précédé, croyaient que c'était une Guermantes d'une moins bonne cuvée, d'une moins bonne année, une Guermantes déclassée.' (Proust 1956, 3: 1004)

'But the truth was that she alone who could boast of a blood that was absolutely without taint, she who had been born a Guermantes and who when she did not sign herself "La Duchesse de Guermantes" had the right to put "Guermantes-Guermantes," she who even to her husband's sisters seemed to be more precious than they were themselves, like a Moses saved from the waters or Christ escaped into Egypt or *Louis XVII rescued from his prison in the Temple* [my emphasis], she the purest of the pure had now, sacrificing no doubt to that hereditary need for spiritual nourishment which had brought about the social decline of Mme de Villeparisis, in whose house snobbish women were afraid of meeting this or that undesirable and of whom the younger generation, observing the *fait accompli* and not knowing what had gone before it, supposed that she was a Guermantes from an inferior cask or of a less good vintage, a Guermantes *déclassée*' (Proust 1987, 3: 1057)

4 The deformation of an individual's name is, of course, a traditional polemical device; cf. Derrida's reference to John Searle as 'Sarl,' an acronym for 'société à responsabilité limitée' (1988, 36ff.).

5 On emblematic names, see Riffaterre 1990, esp. 33–6.

6 See also Eco 1976, 86–7 on names as cultural units versus names that have only personal references.

7 For an example, chosen at random, see the Flaubert entry in the *Penguin Companion to European Literature*: '[the *Dictionnaire des idées reçues* was] a collection of trite sayings he had kept throughout his life. It was to have been his greatest attack upon the bourgeois and foolishness he loathed so violently' (Thorlby 1969, 273).

11

Fictionality, Narration, and the Question of Genres

FRANCESCO LORIGGIO

Although matters pertaining to the notions of fiction or fictionality have always, almost since time began, tended to bring into play philosophy or the philosophical, the heavy investment by the philosophers of this century in such issues as reference, meaning, truth, possibility has made the point more cogently than before. It is fair to say that, now more than ever, to speak of fiction and fictionality is really, ultimately, to be discussing the connection between one's discipline and philosophy or the philosophical domain.

This is especially so in the case of literary studies. Criticism tends too often nowadays to forget that Plato, Aristotle, and Longinus were philosophers. And it clearly has not meditated as much as it could on Frege's and Russell's biobibliographical data: they too lived in the crucial early decades of the century and were philosophers to no lesser a degree than were those thinkers – like Nietzsche, Husserl, Bergson, Heidegger – most frequently invoked in the histories of literary modernity.

When a novelist and playwright such as Pirandello, who put heavy stakes on the notion of fictionality, announced around 1920 that he had the 'misfortune' of being a philosophical writer,[1] he may have been right in more ways than one. The confession probably has cost him a rank or two vis-à-vis the other great figures of the age, the authors whose obsession with language and linguistic gamesmanship has been elevated into the emblem of all literature. Yet, in looking back now, his statement, however misused or misunderstood, seems to be a pivotal one, one that gives us a more nuanced and appropriate view of the literary history of the past hundred years.

Of course, merely acknowledging that fictionality is one of the places where philosophy enters into contact with literature does not do justice to the full cultural and intellectual measure of the topic.

To begin with, it should be stressed that fictionality is where a certain philosophy touches base with a certain literature or a certain branch of literary studies. Other philosophies, if they show any interest at all in literature, do other things with it or to it. It is well known that the philosophers working within the boundaries of deconstructionist criticism have, in their most representative works, spent quite substantial amounts of energy to prove the irrelevance – philosophical and literary – of the question of reference. Derrida's 'Il n'y a pas de hors-texte' (1984, 84) is the culmination, in proper slogan-like form, of Nietzsche's view of truth and traditional strivings to reproduce a self-sufficient objective reality as a 'mobile army of metaphors, metonims and anthropomorphisms' (1954, 46–7), and it reverberates through many works of literary theory.

Secondly, and perhaps most significantly, in spite of the positioning it implies towards some philosophers and some philosophical strategies, fictionality does proclaim literature's or literary studies' return to philosophy, after flirtations with other realms of inquiry, and therefore the restoration of philosophy's ascendancy over literature.

To just glance at it, the approach of the deconstructionists appears to be more flattering for literary critics. The aim of these philosophers is to undermine the self-descriptions of their discipline by reversing tensions that have always existed, in one form or another from Plato onward, by transforming philosophy into a literary genre. The profession once banned from the city is reinstated with a vengeance. By contrast, philosophers who have sought to entrench fictionality deep in their discipline have burned fewer bridges. They disavow smaller chunks of the tradition and maintain some barrier between themselves and literature.

This, to be sure, is a divergence that risks being over-simplified. There are shadowy areas. In order to conflate literature and philosophy, deconstructionists have had to rely heavily on, and attach a large premium to, the notion of textuality. They have had to privilege those qualities that make all written works texts. Changing 'literature' into 'writing' changes also its relation to the disciplines of which it was reputedly an object of study. Once it has been determined that there is no 'finished corpus' of individual works, but 'a fabric of traces referring endlessly to something other than itself, to other differential traces' (Derrida 1984, 84),[2] in effect the relation is abolished.

'Fictionality' is not quite of such all-encompassing magnitude, and would spare us embarrassing complications, but philosophers have frequently used 'fiction' as a synonym for 'literature,' as a label to override and abolish all differences within the literary domain. To a larger extent than is usually admitted, the disputes between the two camps are thus about the amount of ground covered. Still, this and other intricacies notwithstanding, there is one swerve of the distinction that must be underlined. Curiously enough, precisely because of the limits it sets itself, which affect literature and not the discipline, the philosophy that has most often and most closely interrogated itself about the notion of fictionality finally holds out the greater promise for the critic. The priority deconstructionists grant textuality, while it may chastise a philosophy too sanguine for its own good, also declares literature null and void. The compliments sent to the literary critic are very much left-handed. With fictionality instead, the possibility of commerce, of exchange, is left intact.

As happens with most other items in the basic vocabulary, the basic notional repertoire of the age – besides 'text,' one thinks of such other terms as 'play,' 'dialogue' – at this level too we are confronted with opposing motions. Fiction and fictionality carry with them sedimentations that hark back to a specific discipline, but have become interstitial categories, intellectual buffers which are stop-overs for many and disparate perspectives and which, like those metro stations where lines criss-cross, allow us to travel in various directions and, hence, above all, to go back and forth between disciplines. In the notion of dialogue, for example, linguistics, philosophy, anthropology, and literary studies meet. The discipline responsible for establishing the initial parameters of the notion cannot but take into account the accretions that, whatever their provenance, be they proposed by anthropologists, sociologists, linguists, or other late-comers, now exist side by side with the early, triggering formulations. As a result, a host of comparisons, pulling together now one set of disciplines, now another, lurk in the concept, and they are no less compelling because we choose to gloss over them.

'Fiction' and 'fictionality' are now at a similar stage: issues deriving from disciplines other than philosophy are starting to have an impact on the philosophical core of the notions. Indeed 'fiction' and 'fictionality' recapitulate both the macro- and the micro-features of the process: they remind us that, in the present epistemic circumstances, we will always, when all is said and done, be left with nothing but the play of disciplines, nothing but comparison, and that literary studies will always figure heavily in the comparing.

Some of the fashions in which this occurs, and that show how literary criticism can lend as well as borrow, export as well as import, have been already explored by the theorist whose work the present volume is honouring. In several of the essays Lubomír Doležel has written in the last fifteen years or so, the wherewithal, the toolery that the philosophical debate on fiction and fictionality has helped to forge, inspires neat and elegant revisitations of some very troublesome topoi of literary criticism.[3] Thanks to the reflection on transworld identity, we can understand better the internal mechanics of the theme of the double or of the metamorphoses that literature has often and so poignantly and obsessively described. In other essays, perhaps theoretically of greater interest to us, Doležel has instead taken the opposite route. Philosophy, or at least the part of it that has focused on fictionality, he argued before almost anyone else, must engage literary categories if it is to remain credible. The shift from the sentence to discourse as the unit of analysis is crucial in his own work. For discourse brings back into the picture such components as the narrator, as voice, which, although ancient chestnuts of criticism, have a visible effect on the semantics of the works of fiction one reads or analyses.

The presence of an utterer, of a speaking subject, replaces the emphasis on truth condition and the modes by which to verify it with an emphasis on authenticity and authentication and the modes by which it is implemented in the text. The ontology of the fiction narrated is disclosed by purely formal, discursive categories. Given his role as teller, given his relation to the characters, who are, precisely, narrated by him and whose statements he can validate or rebut, the narrator can indicate to us how to approach, semantically, the worlds of the story. By adding the accessory criteria of reliability and unreliability and of completeness and incompleteness and applying them to the narrator or to the world he or she authenticates, Doležel is able to devise a very sophisticated taxonomy of narrative structures. At the same time, and in a more widely philosophical sense, the focus on authenticity and authentication and on the narrator and his presence or absence within the story squares perfectly with some of the general trends of the last two decades: Doležel's review of literary categories does not simply lead him to speculate on alternatives to correspondence and truth-condition theories or even to the notions of actuality and possibility; it confirms the mind dependency of possible worlds, thereby anticipating some of the aspects of the turn towards the pragmatics of fiction and fictionality, which is, by general consensus, the development we are grappling with today.

The remarks that follow will continue in this vein. They will stay in between literary studies and philosophy and take advantage of both of the directions comparison opens up. They will attempt to expand upon the premise according to which the philosophy of fictionality is inevitably enmeshed with the literariness of fiction the very moment it dwells on literary texts. Specifically, what I would like to suggest is that, as critics or as philosophers, one of the more exquisitely literary problems we are forced to ponder when we install the two concepts within literary theory has to do with genres.

Most rehearsals of the theories of fictionality drawing on philosophy have built this question into their preambles. Literary worlds are created, recognized, or experienced against a whole background of inherited expectations – logical, ontological, representational – which are mediated and encouraged by genres and sub-genres. Similarly, the very fundamental, inspiring contribution by Doležel noted above sends us back to a central axiom of literary semantics: if worlds are stipulated and constructed by and through discourse, then the procedures of construction are crucially pertinent and should not be ignored. For this theoretical lineage, the worlds fiction proposes or otherwise gives rise to are, as Doležel aptly says, 'system-specific' (1980, 10).

One could even, were one in a mind to, ascribe to disagreements about the attributes of particular genres some of the more substantial differences of the various theories. Thus Doležel in examining the particular type of fiction that he calls the *Er-form* tends to stress the presence of a narrator and his or her role as regards the characters and their speech acts, while others, from traditional critics to theorists such as Martínez-Bonati, have insisted on the impersonality of narratorial discourse. As a consequence, for the former it is the narrator's authenticating authority, his or her ability to guarantee or to disprove the value of the sentences uttered by characters that counts. For the latter group, the inability to establish who the narrator is, to specify who is speaking, yields altogether different issues. It minimizes the function of the speech situation, renders the discourse transparent: rather than conceiving the fictional world depicted as being uttered, the reader perceives it, conceives it, as being real. 'We put aside any reflection on the sentences themselves,' explains Martínez-Bonati, 'and turn our attention to the world whose determinate configuration the sentences narrate' (1981, 36).

This is an important divergence, and I shall return to it later, but there are other as theoretically crucial and as much across-the-board sorts of reasons why the question of genres must be confronted.

In literary studies, no less than elsewhere, a theory is as good as the field it presupposes. The works and authors a critic purports to interpret provide the logical motivation of his or her enterprise. Theory is irrevocably synecdochical: it generalizes and legitimizes the limited range of texts it inherits or whose traits it favours. It is not without significance that the New Critics of the thirties and forties used the term 'poem' to allude to any literary artifact: their notion of textuality is poetry-laden; it parallels and corroborates the pre-eminence they accorded to that genre, with which, being often themselves poets, they identified. Nor is it irrelevant that the structuralist attempt to narrativize literature, to see literature *sub specie narrationis*, in the sixties and early seventies, was carried out primarily by theorists whose opinions were shaped by work on folk-tales and myths. In both cases, certain choices were made, certain peculiarities were enlarged and pronounced typical of all literature.

The interest in the philosophical debate on fictionality comes for literary criticism at a time when the novel is the dominant genre. To listen to some, modernity is nothing but the novelization of literature, the carrying over to, the superimposing on, other classes of texts some of the features of the novel, the only genre to reach full maturity in the age of the printing press, of silent reading – during, in short, the last five hundred years.[4] In this respect, for the literary critic, the study of fictionality partakes of, and reinforces, a historical phenomenon reflected in other venues from other angles. That is, literary semantics reaffirms the primacy of the novel over and against other approaches – dialogistic, rhetorical, linguistic, etc. – by bringing to the surface, and/or re-evaluating, some hitherto inadequately, or at any rate not rigorously, conceptualized specific facets of the genre.

This should not be taken as pre-emptive scepticism about the range of applicability of the philosophical apparatus associated with literary semantics. Certainly the idea of fictionality in the guises in which it has developed in recent decades obliges us to accept three postulates: that there are worlds; that these worlds comprise particulars, individuated entities; and that both worlds and particulars have properties. Intended *stricto sensu*, such prerequisites would seem to rule out many of the metaphorical offshoots and prolongations, many of the parallels we often encounter in criticism and philosophy, no matter how stimulating they may turn out to be. In equating fictionality with the sphere of the symbol or with symbolization, as we do when we contend that music and mathematics are also fictional, we stretch the argument, to say the least. But in literature the reverse obtains. It is very difficult to find a set of texts in which the logical and ontological issues raised by literary semantics do not apply.

What is doubtful is the degree of insight the operation would produce. For semanticists sensitive to the demands of literary criticism, the real test has always been lyric poetry and experimental writing. Although we need not be overly worried about the fragmentariness, the compactness, the level of incompletness, of the worlds projected or portrayed by these texts, which are a problem but not an insoluble one, we are still left with doubtful results. Let us assume that we are prefacing such texts with the message 'this is an artifact that the fictional speaker is offering to himself/herself' (Ryan 1984, 133). How would such a prefacing improve our understanding of poetry and experimental novels? Furthermore, how is our understanding enhanced by the statement that in these works 'the only domain left open for contemplation and conjecture is the material quality of the language (which becomes a sign of itself, not a sign of its speaker)' (Ryan 1984, 134)? Does not the fact that we can talk about these texts only negatively, by indicating the criteria they do not meet, mean that we are filtering our appreciation of these texts through those situations in which the criteria do function? Would we still act as we do were the fictional canon other than it is in our times? In other words, is the norm for us – the zero-degree situation in which the criteria are fully, perfectly observed – not the novel?

We clearly can do more with poetry which, although not outrightly narrative, sketches out in cleaner strokes either the world or some characters, some individuated beings. 'The Love Song of J. Alfred Prufrock,' the poems in Edgar Lee Masters's *Spoon River* anthology, Coleridge's 'The Rhyme of the Ancient Mariner,' Byron's 'Beppo,' Wordsworth's 'Tintern Abbey' are easier to deal with in terms of the theory of fictionality than is nonsense poetry or the poetry of e.e. cummings. They, or texts like them, often lend themselves to adaptation, as the appearance of Hugh Selwyn Mauberley, the character from Pound's eponymous poem, in the novel *Famous Last Words* by Timothy Findley, would seem to demonstrate. T.S. Eliot's Prufrock is as representative a type of twentieth-century culture as is Joyce's Leopold Bloom. So that it is possible to detect in the mechanics by which fictionality is utilized a kind of translatability principle: criticism's bias in favour of the novel is confirmed by the tendency by which the texts (including poetry) approached positively, and not negatively, are those that best fit the rules and regulations of novelistic discourse.

To be entirely precise, not only is the zero-degree situation novelistic, but it is so in a very special manner. The touchstone, the inaugurating grid, the grid that acts as benchmark for all texts, is the one that poses the notion of 'world' least problematically within, or in the context of, our cultural norms. The theory of fictionality has helped to bring some order to the age-old controversy about representation in literature by addressing directly and explicitly some of the philosophical preconceptions on which it has rested, by substituting the idea of verisimilitude with the much wider notion of reference, and by revising the notion of 'world.' In the process, it has redefined such fixtures of criticism as realism, romance, mythical narrations. But it has not dislodged realism from the pre-eminence it has enjoyed.

It would be of valuable instruction to relate these literary developments to the more purely philosophical controversies about the logic and the ontology of fictions. The privileges criticism accords realism in its typologies, by making it the category from which classification begins, reiterates, probably independently, the role philosophy has conferred on the actual world. If Russell's dictum that there is only one world and it is the real world has been amended by philosophers to allow for a plurality of worlds, indirectly in that plurality the 'real' world retains some of its prerogatives: we create and experience other worlds through what we know and understand of the actual world. For a literary critic, the syllogism according to which characters are 'real' as fictional entities since they belong to a realm that has to be stipulated and imagined by concrete, flesh-and-blood writers and concrete, flesh-and-blood readers and the polemics about the existence of fictions (which may be 'false' or not 'real' but exist or may exist in the future) echo the attitude that change in literature, even when effected on behalf of apparently non-realistic or anti-realistic modes, occurs always in the name of greater or 'truer' or more adequate conceptions of reality. One reacts to the preceding generation, the preceding decade, or the preceding movement by proposing works that in their outrageous iconoclasm are still in more correct synchrony with the *Zeitgeist*.

A corollary to the concerns I have been voicing could run as follows: to concede the primacy of the novel in theories of fictionality is not necessarily to acquiesce to the primacy of realism, where realism is intended as the zero-degree option in which sentences refer to a fully authenticated world or act as strongly, robustly truth-functional statements within the fictional world. Quite apart from everything else, novels are not just romances or mythical or realistic narratives, if realism is understood in the sense it is in everyday intellectual parlance. These are abstract pigeon-holes; only very seldom do we encounter individual texts in such pure forms. Both the worlds they portray and the discourses by means of which they convey them offer inklings – if not more – of various worlds. And while one may classify the text in agreement with the way it has thematized or hierarchized the worlds it represents and label one sort of thematization or hierarchization 'realism' or 'romance' or 'myth,' one could just as well highlight the co-existence, the mixedness. The simplest narration, one that contains an authenticator and authenticated sentences, with no discrepancies between the narrator's speech and the speech of the characters, is already of composite nature, since the valuating discourse emanates from a world that serves as the world of actuality for that which is being validated.

Exploring the implications of this hybridism has been one of the objectives of recent theory of fictionality. Martínez-Bonati distinguishes between *uni*regional and *pluri*regional worlds, between pure or contaminated regions, between regions that are contaminated by contextual play ('through motifs that evoke another system' [1983, 193]) or by intratextual collusions of systems. Apparently a mere archival exercise, the complex subdivisions that he derives from the combination of these elements reformulate the notion of world.

Similar preoccupations can be discerned in Pavel's discussion of the topology of the imaginary, of the simultaneous presence in the everyday world of sacred and profane, of history and metahistory, of actuality and myth (1989, 251–9).

Neither of these proposals dethrones realism. Instead, they distance themselves from the suspiciously nineteenth-century narrative models that the grids elaborated by theories of fictionality sometimes seem to fall back on. In effect, the many-tiered ontologies of the worlds described in the latest work by Martínez-Bonati and Pavel are best epitomized in literary criticism by the notion of realism as a confusion of styles, as an adjacency of high and low registers, of the sublime and the ridiculous resuscitated in the earlier part of our century by great stylisticians such as Erich Auerbach. Martínez-Bonati establishes the connection overtly: in recalling that worlds come attached with a style, he also alludes to the tradition of stylistics in literary studies (1983, 182–5). Realism in this theoretical tradition dates back to the advent of Christianity, to a historical period that was able to envisage the divine and the human, the otherwordly and the worldly embodied in the same person; that was able to claim, as Pavel might say, that the actuality of the actual world is interspersed with pockets of mythicalness. Most of all, underlying this realism, whose culminating text is Dante's *Divine Comedy*, is a logic as paradoxical as the logic of a world that is composed of many regions, many 'systems of reality,' to quote Martínez-Bonati (1983, 193).

Let me recapitulate: the theory of fictionality steers criticism towards the novel. And within the novel, it has tended to grant priority to models that literary criticism has rightly or wrongly linked to nineteenth-century realism by assigning them the positive markers against which other texts will be classified. On the other hand, it erodes that primacy by postulating models of actuality in which worlds of differing ontological consistency can co-exist and which would lead literary criticism towards other – multidimensional, impure, hybrid – versions of realism. In the light of this, one might ask whether some similar tensions do not imperil the prestige of the novel itself, whether the theory of fictionality, along with the intrageneric, does not embody some sort of intergeneric slippage.

A number of caveats justify such premonitions. The novel thrives – and perhaps this is its most accurate definition – on the incorporation of other genres, literary and non-literary: it appropriates and transforms the essay, the poem, the diary, the letter, the case study, the film script, etc. Understandably, in the face of this openness, this lack of generic stability, of this 'maximal contact with the present,' to pick up on Bakhtin's variation on the theme (1981, 11), the fate of the criticism of the novel could not but have been a highly precarious one. Literary theorists have often succumbed to the temptations the genre has afforded. Novels have been the kind of texts most often spoken about through criteria that relate to other texts: they have been epic novels, confessional novels, lyric novels, historical novels, and so on.

To properly canvass this aspect, which is one of the more pertinent specific dilemmas the theory of fictionality rebounds back to criticism and critics, we can count on one very telling symptom. In their most elementary definitions, fictional worlds do not just consist of individuated entities, are not just furnished; they are circumscribed, they have boundaries. And they are circumscribed and have boundaries *qua* fictions as much as *qua* worlds. Kripke has warned us that a 'possible world isn't a distant country that we are coming across, or viewing through a telescope' (1971, 147). But it would be a mistake to underestimate the salience of this feature. One does, after all, run into articles with such titles as 'How Remote Are Fictional Worlds from the Real World?' (Walton 1979). The postulation of some hiatus, of some gap separating the 'real' from the 'fictional,' is essential to avoid pure and simple cognitive magma. We cannot but consider the initial gesture to be the cut in the flux of experience whereby, as one philosopher phrases it, 'That which *Is* is Contrasted with That which It *Is Not*' (Merrel 1983, 1). In turn, that cut cannot but 'evoke ... the notions of "inside" and "outside" and the suggestion of "near" and "far away", of "object" and "background,"' according to Maurits C. Escher (see Merrel 1983, 1). Artists and writers have also dwelt on this, often pointing out that worlds are accessed, that entrance in literature is negotiated, that literature has its little rituals about the traversing of domains. We are all familiar with the devices – engravings on picture frames, rich illustrations on book jackets or on the title pages – that isolate and give prominence to the threshhold that sets fictional worlds apart from actuality. In Woody Allen's film *The Purple Rose of Cairo*, one of the characters leaves the fictional world by jumping through the screen. Michel Butor has likened reading to travelling; fiction is an elsewhere, to engage in it is to momentarily leave the actual world, to absent oneself from the surroundings in which the writing or the reading is taking place (Butor 1972). In the first pages of Italo Calvino's *If On a Winter's Night, a Traveller*, the speaker, who, we are informed, is the author of the book, entreats the reader, who is the protagonist of the story, to put his or her legs up, set the light at the right intensity, and generally get comfortable before continuing on.

The boundedness of fiction is duplicated inside the story among the regions of a world. Mirrors have this function in Jean Cocteau's films: one walks through them and enters the beyond, a second life, the world of dreams, or some other dimension. If the pluriregionality is not solely underscored but represented, some passage may be involved. In Pirandello's short stories and novels, the whistle of a train is enough for the protagonists to imagine far-away lands and intricate hypothetical, counterfactual, or fictional situations. In science fiction, one can find oneself another world to explore through simple mechanical wizardry, by just concocting a time-travel machine.

In all of these instances, whether the frontier separates the fictional from the actual, or one region from another, the notion of world acquires an almost anthropological valence. Fiction is the realm of difference; it is the *alter* of actuality, the site where animals talk, metamorphoses are cheap and fast, and where, if nothing strange or unexplainable happens, individuated entities will at any rate stay the same, they are 'fixed forever,' as one of Pirandello's characters expresses it.[5]

Pragmatically, we can play fiction against actuality, and vice versa, to learn about either or both. We read in a book about the possible worlds of fantasy: '[In] trying to understand the world of *Little Grey Rabbit* or *Winnie the Pooh* in terms of human beings, we may extend and transform our notion of human beings by associating them with the timidity of rabbits, the boisterousness of hares, the dejection of donkeys; and hence realising with greater clarity that such characteristics are indeed exhibited by human beings, that in some ways they can be rabbit-like or hare-like' (Maitre 1983, 73). Fantasy, however, only exploits features inherent in every fictional narrative. That tradition should have judged the lowering of the distance tantamount to practising specularity or reiteration does not make mimetic fictions any less asymmetrical to the actual world, ontologically and anthropologically. Reflections are enantiomorphic; they project images in inverted order. Instead of just reproducing 'reality,' they too, like fantasy, complete it, underscoring facets of it we might not have noticed without their proddings.

How does this tie in with genre contagion? When it is textualized, when it is in the story, the anthropological push-and-pull between worlds or portions of worlds will return us theoretically to some of the themes of the narratology of a few decades ago. More particularly, pluriregionality brings back to mind the theories of narration centred on the function Propp labelled 'transference.' In Tartu school semiotics, Propp's most direct progeny, for a story to have a plot its structure must encompass at least two differently marked cultural spaces, two topographies. An event, the basic unit of narration, is defined as 'the shift of a persona across the borders of a semantic field' (Lotman 1977, 233). Just as the hero of fables departs from home, from the world of domesticity, and runs into that strange world in which animals and dead persons talk and magic rings allow one to fly, so the protagonists of novels move from the countryside to the city, from a lower to an upper class, and can have mystical or oneiric experiences. Regionality thus reinstalls the tale into the novel. Or, said less stenographically, in as much as the notion of world parallels the notion of semantic field, the debate on fiction and the fictional celebrates at once the novel and the narrational within it, hence the genre by which the narrational is most forcefully conveyed.

But as far as generic contagion goes, the more purely semantic relation between actuality and fictionality is a more fruitful one for criticism to explore than the one between regions. What is most striking critically, and most intriguing and enticing about the notion of world is its scenographic qualities. Worlds of fiction are there, beyond some hiatus; we are here. We can experience them when we identify with a character and see everything through his or her eyes, and we can bear witness to them when we have no privileged outlook to hang on to. Regardless of the range of focus, or the position we assume towards the states of affairs the worlds narrate, we are the spectators of that which they elicit, much like we are at a play. Vocabulary about visualization, about spectacularization, is generally overlooked, although it is the main underlying tropological strain of the theory of fictionality. The fictions that literary semantics describes occur on a mental stage; they are mental theatre.

This source of contagion has precedence over tales, for pluriregionality can replicate the actual-world/fictional-world duality. To a foreigner, a country or a city may be a strange and unreal site, a manifestation of an 'otherness' as ethereal and uncanny as dreams or fictions: they oblige one to position oneself, to respond from a nearness or a farness. In ordinary day-to-day life, sacred places have, for believers, a distinctly other-wordly cast. Everything that occurs in them appears choreographed, theatrical: one is now a participant-character, now a witness-observer, one identifies and is within the mysterious realities being evoked and/or enacted, and one is a person who will soon leave and therefore will stand on the outside looking in. Point of view, focalization, and such cognate devices of novelistic narration betray their theatricality in the spatialization of meaning they force upon us; they oblige us to recognize space and to meditate on its function as we construct and reconstruct the events the book is telling.

Drama, then, inevitably insinuates itself in the criticism that defends or is guaranteed by the overwhelming preponderance of the novel. And if literary semantics is a chapter in occidental poetics, as Doležel has taught us to think of the discipline, it is so also to the extent that it demonstrates, in a fashion both modern and non-trivial, that literary theory and the philosophy of literature are imbued with dramaturgical models, as they have been from the beginning, since Aristotle. Semanticists dealing with fiction appear to be Aristotelians not only because in their endeavours they have returned possibility and such other neglected notions to their rightful theoretical status, but also, and perhaps most of all, because they have willy nilly, without realizing it, inherited the conceptual and tropological baggage of those notions, the language, the metaphors, the generic bias that permeate the *Poetics*.

It comes as no surprise that in semantics-oriented approaches lyric poetry should be the odd genre out: except for a brief period, during early Romanticism, the history of Western literary theory has always been, for better or for worse, a history of the predominance of narrative and theatre and of their complicities.

One phase of this coinciding of vocations will suffice as illustration. During the nineteenth century – the heyday of the novel – very few and scarce were the narrators who did not also write for the stage. The novelists who occupy the zero-degree slot in much of the theory of fictionality (the novelists of impersonal realism, especially) aspired to the condition of a 'theatre of textuality' in which no one but the characters speak, and the work, as one of them states, 'makes itself.'[6] Only the myopia of a criticism unable to forgive the nineteenth-century impersonalists for their ideological allegiance – their naturalism, their positivism – could ignore the suggestiveness of their formal, their literary, interests. 'Le poète est dans le drame comme Dieu dans la création ... Le poète dramaturge est le grand invisible ...' (Bigazzi 1978, 329), a minor contemporary of Flaubert tells us, summarizing with concise if somewhat grandiloquent simplicity and *ante litteram* the adaptations of the analogy between theatre and writing on the part of the naturalists and their generation. But there isn't much difference between such musings and the more careful and more elaborate proclamations of the twentieth-century modernists, who theorized that the dramatic monologue was the perfect formal antidote to unmediated, first-person effusions, and whose descriptions of impersonal narrative shade off into descriptions of drama. The passage in which Stephen Dedalus conjures his celebrated image of the artist as one who 'like the God of creation, remains within or behind or above his handiwork, invisible, refined out of existence, indifferent, paring his fingernails' is a passage about drama (Joyce 1963, 215). Even the defences of pure poetry by those great purists that were the Symbolists become suspect once we hear them asserting 'Il en est de la mentale situation comme des méandres d'un drame' (Mallarmé 1943, 165).

It is this historical intertwining between concrete literary genres, this construction of models of literature and theory that needs to be properly spelled out. As befits a profession that operates by incongruity, that displaces a question, that takes it away from its original intellectual environment and addresses it from a new disciplinary angle, philosophy would contribute to such an investigation the gift of simplicity. I have up to now, much like everyone else, stressed the scenographic, world-centred features of the philosophical notion of fiction. It would be more correct to say that philosophy in this century has hovered over two views: the analysis of possibility, of fictionality, and of the scenic properties of a story, the analysis of the action narrated, has had as counterpart, as alternative or complementary option (especially in recent years, in the wake of the rise of speech-acts theory), the analysis of the devices by which a fiction is enunciated. The duality re-enacts the contrast between Plato and Aristotle on the classification and description of fictions, except that speech-acts theory does not moralize in placing the enunciation of stories under the aegis of a logic of simulation: in narrating, one pretends, and that is neither good nor bad; it just is. What is more, speech-acts theory nuances antinomies, since it deems narrating to be an action, and a pretended action at that, thus insinuating theatricality into the very gist of story-telling.

The lessons such a survey of the contagion of genres would provide are not, I must repeat, drastic ones. They will not redirect the course of the disciplines they most affect. There are, nonetheless, benefits to be gained. In a general way, it is difficult not to be impressed by the persistence of ideas related to mimesis or action within the discourse on fictionality, whether they be connected to representations or to speech. In a specific way, the staying power of theatre and theatrical subtext helps us resolve more satisfactorily some of the critical tangles that have accompanied this notion. To mention perhaps the most obvious instance: the presence of a narrator in a story and the ensuing authenticating processes do not render a work of fiction any less mimetic. We continue to perceive the words composing it as transparent, as true, irrespective of the narrator or any authorial stand-in participating or resonating in the story. The breaking of the illusion by devices that accentuate the constructed, lingual nature of a story can itself be recuperated, absorbed. All that is required is to simply extend the notion of mimesis to cover also the act of narrating or the act of telling or of authenticating a narration. Both are functions supplementary to the story narrated, but they constitute a supplement that can be imbedded in it and, most of all, that can be represented. The words of the author or the narrator ultimately can be viewed as imitated language, simulations of an author doing his or her job, no less so than the words of the characters. This is the upshot of such plays as *Six Characters in Search of an Author*: the making of a story can itself be a good mimetic story. Anything that is narratable can be converted into theatre. Again, we can do it by expanding our conceptions of reality or our conceptions of action to include the reality of fictions and the activity by which they are made. It is why critically the relation between realistic fiction and so-called self-referential fiction is more complex and enticing than other generations believed it to be or why Pirandello, who moved between the short story, the novel, and theatre with deliberate passion, is one of the seminal figures of the century.

NOTES

1 See the preface to *Sei personaggi in cerca di autore*: 'Ci sono scrittori ... di natura più propriamente storica ... ve ne sono altri ... di natura più propriamente filosofica. Io ho la disgrazia di appartenere a quest'ultimi' (Pirandello 1958, 36).

2 But possibly the most cited title on this issue is Roland Barthes's article 'De l'oeuvre au texte' (1984, 67-77).
3 Among his many articles on semantics written in the last fifteen years, I point out Doležel 1976a; 1980; and 1988.
4 The major proponent of this view is M. Bakhtin; see his 'Epic and Novel' (1981, 39).
5 'Non cangia, non può cangiare, nè esser altra mai, perchè già fissata ... per sempre ... realtà immutabile' (Pirandello 1958, 105).
6 See Giovanni Verga's preface to *L'amante di Gramigna* (1969, 228): '[I]o credo che il trionfo del romanzo ... si raggiungerà allorché ... l'opera d'arte sembrerà *essersi fatta da sè.*'

12

Narratology, Narratological Criticism, and Gender

GERALD PRINCE

Fifteen years ago, Susan Sniader Lanser noted disapprovingly that narratology, in its exploration of narrative voice, paid no attention to gender: 'Nowhere in modern narrative theory is there mention of the author's or narrator's gender as a significant variable ... [yet] surely the sex of a narrator is at least as significant a factor in literary communication as the narrator's grammatical person, the presence or absence of direct address to a reader, or narrative temporality' (1981, 46–7).

More recently, after examining some of the possible reasons why the feminist and the formalist investigations of narrative have ignored each other (everyday terminology versus technical language, mimetic orientation versus semiotic approach, reliance on context versus bracketing of it, distrust of binary logic and universals versus confidence in them), Lanser called for a feminist narratology whereby 'feminist criticism, and particularly the study of narratives by women, might benefit from the methods and insights of narratology and ... narratology, in turn, might be altered by the understandings of feminist criticism and the experience of women's texts' (1986, 342).

To start the movement towards such a revised narratology, to pose some of the questions and focus on some of the textual aspects that a gender-conscious study of narrative would have to confront and discuss, Lanser analysed a short (fictional) letter, written by an unhappy young bride to an intimate friend. The text selected, as Lanser herself admitted (1986, 355), was not exactly appropriate since it hardly made up a narrative. But Lanser's analysis was interesting, nonetheless, especially when bearing on questions of voice and tone. Besides, better (more pertinent) examples than hers have been provided by Robyn Warhol in a splendid study of narrative discourse and gender in the Victorian novel. Lanser's proposal for an 'expansive narratology' was vehemently taken to task by Nilli Diengott, who argued that gender is not a *differentia specifica* of narrative and that, quoting from the abstract to her article, 'there is no need or possibility to reconcile feminism and narratology,' given that the former constitutes an interpretive, critical enterprise, while the latter is a theoretical activity. In her response, Lanser renewed her call for dialogue among 'feminists, narratologists, and feminist narratologists' (1988, 59) and maintained that gender-inspired questions about the nature, scope, methodology, and goals of narrative poetics could lead to its positive transformation.

In what follows, I do not intend to consider what narratology might bring to feminist- and gender-oriented theory or criticism, though I will mention that both Lanser and Warhol find the precision and systematism of poetics helpful (Lanser 1986, 346; Warhol 1989, 6). Nor do I intend to consider most of the reasons (adduced by Lanser and others) for feminist resistance to narratology, though I will say that at least some of them strike me as nostalgic (the longing for a transparent language, the stance against 'deathly' science), as facile (the dependence on a strategy of 'both ... and' though 'neither ... nor'), and even as misguided: thus, an argument for the existence of universals need not be regressive (in fact, it can sometimes be progressive), and a belief in certain universals need not entail a belief in others (I believe that all human beings die; I do not believe that all human beings enjoy Mozart); similarly, though they often constitute a symptom of, or basis for, prejudice, distortion, and repression, binary oppositions do not necessarily lead to the creation of hierarchies or hegemonies; besides, narratology does not always depend on binary pairs (think of its account of narrative speed or of narrative frequency) and it does not always exclude the middle (think of free indirect discourse). What I want to discuss, rather, is why some of the challenges posed to narratology by a category like gender must be addressed.

It is important to note at the outset, I think, that the very domain of narratology is (and has been) in flux and that the discipline keeps on changing as its boundaries are (re)drawn. As Michel Mathieu-Colas has argued, if narratology is a theory of narrative, its scope depends, first of all, on the definition of narrative. When the latter is viewed primarily as a verbal mode of representation (the telling of events by a narrator as opposed to, say, the enacting of them on stage), the narratologist (e.g., Gérard Genette) pays little or no attention to the story, the narrated, the 'what' that is represented, and concentrates instead on the discourse, the narrating, the 'way' in which the 'what' is represented. This view may well have tradition on its side: the Latin term *narrare* designated a *language* act and, in the Western tradition, the opposition between *diegesis* and *mimesis*, recounting and representing, epic and drama, narrative and theatre goes back to Plato and is still very common. Furthermore, this view may well capture the specificity of a purely verbal representation of events by a narrator and, in particular, account for the many ways in which the same set of events can be told (compare 'Mary ate before she slept' and 'Mary slept after she ate'). But it neglects the fact that non-verbal or mixed modes of event representation (e.g., movies or comic strips) are often taken to tell stories, to recount them, and are often referred to as narratives; besides, it forgets that the story too makes narrative whatever it is (without story, no narrative). When, on the contrary, narrative is defined not so much in terms of mode (a narrator narrating) or substance (linguistic as opposed to non-linguistic) but rather, as in Paul Ricoeur's *Temps et récit*, by its object (events), the narratologist focuses on the structure of represented events and their possible combinations. But she or he would then be unable to account for the various forms a given story can take. There is – as always! – a third possibility. Since both story and discourse, narrated and narrating make up narrative, a number of narratologists (e.g., Jean-Michel Adam) define narrative as the representation (verbal or non-verbal, with or without a narrator) of one or more events, and they attempt to integrate the study of the 'what' and of the 'way.'

Of course, even if all narratologists agreed on a definition of narrative, they would still have to determine what in narrative is specific or relevant to narrative. Narratology is not so much a theory of narrative as it is a theory of narrative *qua* narrative: it tries to account for all and only possible narratives to the extent that they are narrative (that they exhibit features distinctive of, or pertinent to, narrative). If temporal relations, say, are clearly essential to narrativity and if comic power or psychological insight are not, the relevance of certain other elements or aspects of narrative texts is much more difficult to fix. Think of style, for instance, which can help to characterize and differentiate narrator and characters; or think of tone, which can affect the very way a novel or a tale makes sense. Though neither of these elements constitutes a *differentia specifica* of narrative, the same can be said of character, description, or even focalization; and only much further study can determine the narrative and narratological pertinence of stylistic or tonal qualities. In other words, the argument against making room for the feature 'gender' in narratological accounts on the grounds that this feature is not specific to narrative hardly seems compelling.

If the distinctiveness criterion is not determinative, what about the necessity criterion? Narratologists pay (infinitely) more attention to a narrator's diegetic situation or degree of covertness than to a narrator's sex or gender presumably because every narrator can be described as extra- or intra-, homo- or heterodiegetic, and as more or less overt or covert, but not every narrator can be characterized in sexual or gender terms (what is the narrator's sex in 'Mary ate before she slept'?; or, more generally, if narratological categories constitute and designate a narrating subject, must this subject be gendered?). However, narratologists pay considerable attention to narrative space, say, though it is quite possible to narrate without referring to the space of the story, the space of the narrating instance, or the relations between them (consider 'John thought of Peter before he thought of Sally'), and they pay even more attention to characters though it is not difficult to find (minimal) narratives without characters (consider 'First it rained and then it snowed'). In other words, the argument against making room for gender because gender is not integral to narrative also proves unpersuasive. Besides, gender could be coded in terms of necessity: narrators and narratees must, after all, be gendered or not gendered, and their gender can be specified or remain unspecified.

Other criteria prove just as problematic. Simplicity, for instance, is not only a function of the measures selected but also a function of the results yielded; and elegance should be left to the tailor. In the end, perhaps the most consistently applicable criterion is that of productivity. The inclusion in narratological models of such categories as character or description was motivated and vindicated by their traditional and continued importance in 'adequate' accounts of narrative possibilities as well as by their capacity to raise new and narratively pertinent problems (on plot structure, say, on narrative domains and energetics, on narrative speed and frequency). Sex or gender (and race, class, age, ethnicity, or height and weight) may prove to be just as effective (even if they do not have 'tradition' behind them). Moreover, it would be easy to start incorporating them explicitly in a narratological model, for instance, by subsuming them under the rubric 'distance' (the space obtaining between narrator, characters, events narrated, and narratee, a space that can be temporal, intellectual, emotional, etc.) or even by subsuming that rubric under them.

Just as gender-inspired arguments can challenge the basis of narratological categories, they can put into question the actual nature of the narratological corpus. Narratology tries to account for the form and functioning of all and only possible narratives. Ideally, its methods and arguments do not therefore depend on a particular set of narratives (great ones, literary ones, or even extant ones), and narratologists have been known to invent narratives in order to bolster their demonstrations and prove their points. Still, there is a narratological canon (a set of texts repeatedly used as illustrations), and this canon is undeniably androcentric: Robyn Warhol points out, for instance, that, in my 'Introduction to the Study of the Narratee,' there are as many as eighty examples 'and only two of them are from female-authored works' (Prince 1989, 7). Narratology is indeed a theoretical activity (favouring the constructed) but – *pace* Diengott – it is far from being indifferent to critical enterprises (just as feminist critical practice is not detached from theory in general and feminist theory in particular).

On the one hand, narratology provides tools and ideas for investigations of specific texts (and leads to so-called narratological criticism). On the other hand, these investigations – in turn – test the validity of narratological categories, distinctions, and reasonings; they identify (more or less significant) elements that narratologists (may) have overlooked, underestimated, or misunderstood; and they (can) lead to basic reformulations of models of narrative. Even a quick study of Giraudoux's *Bella*, for instance, is enough to make it clear that that there is no essential contradiction between a homodiegetic narration and an omniscient point of view; similarly, an energy-centred analysis of the interaction between the plot architecture of Maupassant's *Bel-Ami* and the world-view that it conditions and is conditioned by brings out the importance of an element narratology has overly neglected and should take into account: that of the length of the narrative text; and a careful examination of Robbe-Grillet's *La jalousie*, which involves temporal distinctions and presents events while resisting chronological ordering, shows that narratologists would be wrong to assume that the fundamental order of narrative sequencing is bound to chronology. Thus, it can be argued that a modification of the narratological corpus in favour of female-authored narratives may significantly affect the very models produced by narratology; and, should it turn out that it does not, the models would be all the more credible.

If narrative poetics ought to be more alert to the implications of the corpus it privileges, it also ought to be more sensitive to the role of context – and, in particular, to the possible role of gender – in the production of narrative meaning. The allegiance of classical narratology to strategies inspired by structural linguistics or generative-transformational grammar and its scientific ambitions (its desire to isolate narrative universals, which transcend context) resulted in the narratologists' reluctance to make pragmatics part of their domain of inquiry and in their neglect of the contextual dimensions of meaning generation. During the last few years, however, partly because of the growing awareness that narrative must be viewed not only as an object or product but also as an act or process, partly because of the need to account for the variability of narrative message and point, and partly thanks to the work of scholars like Lubomír Doležel on problems of meaning and authenticity in narrative (1976; 1980), a number of narratologists have begun to address explicitly context-dependent questions. In *Le texte narratif*, for example, Jean-Michel Adam has attempted to build a model that takes into consideration the contract between sender and receiver underlying an act of narration. Similarly, in 'Narrative Pragmatics' (1983), I have argued that one way of accounting for the multiple interpretations that a single narrative (or non-narrative) can yield is to consider its context as part of its text; and I have stressed that narratological models ultimately should include a pragmatic component, along with a syntactic, a semantic, and a discursive one. In 'Toward a Feminist Narratology,' Lanser goes so far as to state that narratology ought to 'study narrative in relation to a referential context that is simultaneously linguistic, literary, historical, biographical, social and political' (1986, 345). Her statement is, to say the least, more appropriate to (narratological) criticism than to narratology. The latter tries to describe the ways in which all and only narratives make sense rather than the meanings of particular narratives in particular circumstances. It can indicate that narrative signification is a function of context; it cannot specify how a certain meaning results from a certain context (it cannot list the infinity of possible contexts). Still, Lanser's statement helps to remind us that, since one of the goals of narratology is to explain the functioning of narrative, narratologists must not only characterize the general pragmatic/contextual principles affecting this functioning but also devise ways of testing the possible influence of factors like gender on narrative production and processing.

In short, without yielding to the interpretive temptation and without renouncing the ideal of a description of narrative and its possibilities that would be explicit, systematic, and universal, narratology should and can take into account calls for more self-awareness, flexibility, and attention to the concrete. Indeed, it is on this condition that it will perfect the fit between its models and the texts they strive to characterize and that it will find a place in a generalized semiotics.

13

The Renaissance Dialogue and
Its Zero-Degree Fictionality

EVA KUSHNER

Among the many territories that can serve as testing grounds for fictionality, I should like to single out the dialogue, fully realizing that it begs for a definition. However, because of the manner in which dialogue forces us to problematize, it may prove fruitful. If, prior to any definition, any verbal exchange between or among speakers can be dubbed dialogue, it must be recognized that it can be narratologically problematic, because among all the elements of fiction dialogue is often perceived as being the least separable from mimesis.

On pourrait se demander jusqu'à quel point les répliques actorielles sont calquées sur la langue parlée commune car [...] il semblerait que les paliers plus spécifiquement pragmalinguistiques soient susceptibles de rester intacts, pour autant que l'évocation linguistique (le code oral) par du linguistique (le code écrit) ne porte atteinte, a priori, ni à la syntaxe, ni aux articulations logico-sémantiques, ni aux isotopies présuppositionnelles inhérentes à tout dialogue dit normal. Il s'ensuit que, automatiquement soustraite aux opérations de travestissement subies lors de la représentation scripturale d'entités non linguistiques – objets, événements, lieux, êtres –, la parole écrite présenterait une homologie parfaite avec le système dialogal réel qu'elle ne ferait que 'reproduire' sans aménagement aucun. (Lane-Mercier 1990, 11)

In the end, however, the dialogue component appears just as integrated in a closed semiotic system and just as constrained by the logic of the text as the more diegetic or descriptive components. But, undeniably, direct transcription (or simulated transcription) of utterances appears to constitute unmediated mimesis and to carry the least complete degree of fictionality.

That is perhaps why narratology in its analyses and its theorizing has privileged indirect over direct discourse. Shlomith Rimmon-Kenan, following Genette (1972, 185–6), reminds us that no text of narrative fiction can 'show' or 'imitate' action; language signifies rather than imitates. 'Language can only imitate language, which is why the imitation of speech comes closest to pure mimesis ... there is a narrator who quotes the character's speech' (1983, 108). Even as it conveys the impression of mimesis, the narrative creates an effect or illusion of it, and the question is only how this illusion is created; in order to answer this question, Rimmon-Kenan, following McHale (1978, 258–9), proposes a progressive range of types of speech representation, from the purely diegetic to the purely mimetic: diegetic summary; a somewhat less diegetic and more representative summary; indirect content paraphrase or indirect discourse; discourse that is indirect but mimetic to some degree; free indirect discourse; direct discourse quoting dialogue or monologue; and free direct discourse. Of these seven possibilities, free indirect discourse appears to have received most attention because of its distinctive features and functions leading, or so it seems, to a different status: a certain treatment of the reporting verb, a certain tense scheme, deictics, etc. Free indirect discourse works in different voices, speakers, attitudes without having to identify them with the implied author yet inviting such identification because it is based on mimesis; in fact, it seems to constitute a reflection on the representation of reality so that it has been taken as emblematic of representation and of literariness, treated as an important exemplum of what is most characteristic of narrative fiction (Rimmon-Kenan 1983, 109–15 *passim*). This is easily linked with Bakhtin's thought on juxtaposition of various discourses from various times in polyphony.

As Genette updates in *Nouveau discours du récit* (1983) the positions he had taken in 'Discours du récit,' he revisits the term *diégèse* as opposed to the Platonically based diegesis and states that 'diégésis, c'est le récit pur (sans dialogue) opposé à la mimésis de la représentation dramatique, et tout ce qui, par le dialogue, s'en insinue dans le récit, ainsi devenu impur, c'est-à-dire mixte' (1983, 13). It is clear that Genette does not (nor do I) espouse this historic and genre-based contrast which makes dialogue into a narrative impurity. But the very fact that he mentions the problem shows that narratology, even quite recently, is still preoccupied with this insufficiently embedded, imperfectly fictional set of elements. The narrative transmission of discourse, in order to be admissible and escape the threat of *mimétisme*, has to be *discours rapporté*, while *discours transposé* and *discours narrativisé* do not run the same inherent risks. Genette, with Dorritt Cohn and others, espouses the view that free indirect discourse better serves the expression of inner monologue and represents more successfully than the direct quotation of utterances having actually occurred; it bears visible marks of embedding or grammatical subordination which the direct one does not. Throughout Genette's reflections on Dorritt Cohn's comments concerning his earlier work, there runs an agreement about what is more appropriately fictional: the 'free indirect' form paradoxically governed by subordinating devices, while direct discourse is simply not *régi*, that is, grammatically subordinated. This free-standing status is part of its less complete fictionality.

Although the vocation of narratology is to model, rather than to ascribe, values, we must recognize that aesthetic preferences are shown, at least statistically, in the choice of cases and the gathering of desirable results; thus according to Perry, the 'plurality of speakers and attitudes, the co-existence of "alternative patternings" contributes to the semantic density of the text' (quoted by Rimmon-Kenan 1983, 114), that is, to more demonstrable literariness. With respect to direct discourse, whether that of the narrator narrating or transposing or that of a character reporting the discourse heard, we are still in the area of verbal creations transforming so-called everyday discourse. When it comes to dialogue itself, in which exchanges of utterances occur, the implicit accusation is that, inasmuch as they stem from the need and the will to communicate, they belong to everyday conversation and therefore can only become fiction on condition that the narrator needed to heavily emphasize the down-to-earth nature of a given character. Currently, a dialogue excerpt in a novel runs the risk of not quite fitting the fictional world, of being simply excerpted, as a recording might be, from everyday speech, just as it is often said that photographic reproduction is not an object of pictorial art.

But the cases we are considering here are extreme cases in which the exchange of words between or among characters is dogmatically ascribed immersion in the experiential world and its ideology. In my view, this notion contravenes the conception in some ways inherited from structuralism, according to which in a multi-layered text all elements belong together as parts of a diegetic whole. What, then, would make the dialogue so foreign? There are a variety of reasons why critics or readers might feel that way: we have already mentioned the most obvious, namely, the excessive resemblance of that which is fictionally said to what might be said in everyday speech. Such readers fail to see the integration of this 'extrinsic' element into a radically other whole: that of a fictional world. Above all, the conversational passage may serve as an incipient communicative device involving the reader; it might be heavy with hermeneutic potential.

But here we must take into account Lubomír Doležel's thoughts on the manner in which fictional worlds are accessed from the actual world or, rather, how that access is to be conceived if we are consistent in our differentiation between the actual and the fictional world and if we accept his 'possible-worlds semantics,' which implies 'a legitimation of fictional worlds vis-à-vis the actual world' (Doležel 1990b, 120–1). The whole concern about an incestuous relationship of immediate identification between the reader and what may be said in a fictional world stems from an incomplete mutual definition of the two worlds; in the hypothesis of a radically other possible world, it becomes groundless. 'In the reception stage, the fictional world is reconstructed by actual readers in the information processing of the fictional text. The reader, depending on his own way of reading, *extrapolates* the empty domains either by filling them in, or by integrating them into the world's structure. Finally, according to the purpose of his reading, the reader either appropriates the fictional world by dissolving it in his own experiential world, or he expands his experiential world by preserving the fictional world as a possible alternative experience' (Doležel 1990b, 121). The very integrity of the process depends on the specificity of the fictional world: 'A theory of reading which annihilates the literary text blows up the main bridge between actual readers and the universe of fictions' (122).

Thus, possible-worlds semantics not only removes the grounds of the perception of dialogue as leading away from fictionality; it provides a positive role for the dialogue as a frontier area for observing the workings of fictionality, as long as it continues to be understood that the fictional setting opens up for the reader the possibility of exploring an alternative experience rather than reliving an imperfect copy of his own experience.

A corpus that I have studied intensively is that of sixteenth-century texts partly or entirely in dialogue form. Because of its implicitly or more often explicitly didactic intent, the genre has been regarded as a thinly disguised tool for direct intervention in the actual world. Renaissance poetics, as well as modern scholarship, have stressed its mimetic nature: the discussants, their topic, their interrelationships, their style, their mode of argumentation are strongly reminiscent of historical equivalents; furthermore, that is their basic ambition. Yet there is another factor to be considered: curiosity about alternative modes of thought on the part of the author as well as the reader. The minimal fictionality with which the dialogue is endowed – the characters are succinctly developed, the circumstances of the encounter are often barely indicated – starts from the premise that, in humanistic writing and even more specifically in doxographic writing, the scriptor has the choice of encoding his message in a treatise that will be univocal on the surface. But despite this, his voice in the treatise may be in discussion with other, often less audible voices, or in addressing a more visible and audible protagonist in the form of a dialogue where such protagonists are actualized. And the *effet de réel* that permeates such dialogues (and we said earlier that the *effet de réel* is tantamount to illusion) requires that the voices of the less dominant actors are not only heard but given a hearing, that the reader's imagination is given access to them – in varying degrees, of course – rather than being totally absorbed and finally persuaded by the dominant voice. To what extent that can occur at that particular time, and in that form of writing, relates to the typology that is being developed here and in other research. But first we must ask what is at stake.

In looking back to the sixteenth century, we speak of a time when, in meditation upon classical poetics and aesthetics, creators were only beginning to take for granted the indivisibility of the 'pleasant' and the 'useful' in poetry and art. The dialogue tradition incited imitation by providing models, rather than theoretical prescriptions, according to Plato, Cicero, and Lucian. Even in distinguishing the three models and their Renaissance reincarnations, we must admit that rhetorical role-playing, rather than the understanding of the intra-diegetic protagonist(s) or those whom he or they represent, is the game. Subordinated to rhetorical needs, at least from the point of view of genuine or feigned intentionality – one also has to remember the reality of censorship and indexes in the Renaissance period – does the dialogue then ever soar towards fictionality? The answer must be two-pronged: imagination knows few fetters when we consider the abundant pictorial and poetic use of mythology, be it ornamental (and we know better today that ornament was not dispensable, but a luxurious necessity rather than a necessary luxury), or in the romances and folk-tales, not to mention narrative fiction, poetry, and drama. On the other hand, the dialogue at the outset is given absolute austerity of the imagination as its compulsory starting point, since it is designed to instruct; and whatever elements of fiction are allowed are meant to be regulated by this primary role. But, however minimal the part of fiction, it gives rise to a dynamic of its own, to a possible world in which the other who is given a role however modest – that of pupil or casual listener, for example – and that other unknown who will gather in the resultant of the dialogue, namely, the reader, relate to one another. What we have, then, is a rhetorical impulse towards fictionalizing and varying degrees of undecidability as to whether the fictional will or will not overcome the initial instrumentality of this kind of dialogue form. Although the minimal degree of fictionality that is invested has often been noted, this should not dissuade us from examining it; on the contrary, the very fact that it is so minimal provides us with a laboratory case of some historical importance: for it was by way of humanistic conferencing – *le colloque continu des humanistes* – that dogmaticism was being countered and examination of alternatives instilled. That is why even minimal signs count: the very fact that access to speech is granted to the opponent and that the opponent can state his case, for example. Now this was also the case in the medieval debates and disputations, which, however, were often allegorical in nature, and intended more to strengthen argumentative skills than to induce a new result. In Renaissance dialogue, the mimetic imperative signals very strongly that there will always be an osmosis with the world of experience, be it in the historically recognizable identity of the speakers, in the timely problem discussed, in the stylistic animation, in the symbolical *locus amoenus*. Such is the paradox of the Renaissance dialogue: in pragmatic terms, it arises from a need to understand and confront new worlds, philosophically, theologically, scientifically, even geographically; but in that very activity, fictional entities are created the status of which defies their pragmatic genesis (or the will of their authors to imitate Plato, Cicero, or Lucian as one was encouraged to do).

From a diegetic point of view these texts appear limited: action, circumstances, character are minimally indicated, present to the poetic imagination more intensely than in the text, and setting the stage for the real event which is the adventure of ideas, the true diegesis of the dialogue. From that point of view, the theoreticians of the time – such as Speroni, Tasso, Sigonius, and Erasmus (the three former at least struggled with the fact that Aristotelian poetics held no direct advice to offer this would-be genre, beyond the general requirement of mimesis and decorum) – understood well enough the power of transformation that lay in the form of this instrument. There are dialogues in which truths are imparted; others, where they are sought and negotiated as long as the argumentation continues, where the emphymematic corridor remains open. It might be said that even this is a matter of perception, and of *effet de réel*, rather than of acceptance of alternative viewpoints, let alone world-views. What I am saying here is that any degree of fictionality, however limited it appears to us today, would have the double effect (in the world of experience) of expanding the writer's and the reader's perception of the other and, in the world of fiction, of expanding the realms of possibility. Could we say that experience and fiction alternately precede each other in giving birth to new mentalities?

Implicitly, I have, of course, espoused the view that the specificity of the fictional is in no way damaged by endowing it with functionality and with an order relating to that of the world of experience but distinct from it in ways that can also be inventoried. From the history of Renaissance dialogues let me take two examples of texts that used the dialogue form to force the imagining of the other, the less known. One is Nicolas of Cusa's *De pace fidei* (1453) which, in connection with a whole range of theological problems, even that of the Trinity, permits Jews and Moslems to participate in the discussion. There is no doubt as to the trinitarian Christian view that triumphs in the end; it remains that foreign elements have been invited to the discussion table. A century and a half later, this also applies to *Colloquium of the Seven* by Jean Bodin, who stages a far more encyclopaedic discussion in a setting that is globally encyclopaedic: the *panthotèque*, which claims to contain a sample or representation of everything in the world, from the mineral to the animal and human realm. It is also a dialogue, the *Universe* of Pontus de Tyard, which in 1558 introduces for the first time to French society the Copernican view, turning into fact the fiction of heliocentricity.

My brief presentation of the literary and philosophical dialogue of the Renaissance oscillating between fiction and experience was done, for the sake of expediency, in reverse, in the sense that I alluded immediately to the dynamic it generates between the author and the reader, without describing that which mediates it in the body of the text, upon the stage of ideas. In the broadest terms, Renaissance dialogues can be said to be articulated according to three traditions bearing the names of Plato, Cicero, and Lucian of Samosata. It happens that texts of the very pervasive Platonic tradition often feature a central voice which will, very gradually, silence others and emerge as the dominant voice despite the maieutic illusion according to which innate ideas are drawn from the participants. The Ciceronian tradition has fostered a far more balanced type of examination of arguments because of Cicero's encouragement to *in utramque partem disserere*. The final resolution will still, in the end, follow the favoured path of the author's thought but not until arguments on all sides have been heard so that philosophical dialogues written in this tradition will stimulate the mental examination of alternatives. As to the Lucianic tradition, its satirical elements and its theatrical bent, emphasized by Lucian himself in *The Double Indictment*, make structured comparisons difficult with the other two traditions inasmuch as sarcastic downgrading, rather than argument-building, seems to be its basic mode. It has even been thought that such dialogues are no longer dialogues but satirical sketches, if sequential argumentation is indispensable to dialogue. In the spirit of Bakhtin one might say, however, that Menippean writings are as deeply, or more deeply, dialogical as texts constructed in dialogue form. It is evident that the three traditions generate intimately related, yet different types of fictionality or at least degrees of fictionality. For example, both Platonic and Ciceronian-type dialogues make abundant use of historically known or recognizable characters and ascribe to them words, actions, ideas reminiscent of the corresponding historical characters; yet, more importantly, the reader knows that they are fictional not despite, but because of, the power of the illusion: the Morus of Utopia is not Thomas More, nor is the Ronsard of Caron or de Brués the historical person we know. The fiction begins to generate its own world.

In an article entitled 'A Pragmatic Typology of Dialogue' (1977), Lubomír Doležel identifies three types of dialogue. He does not deal exclusively with texts entirely in dialogue form, but with dialogue in a more general sense that is applicable to such texts. In a paper devoted to Erasmus's *Colloquies* (Kushner 1988), I showed a correlation between the three traditions embodied in Renaissance dialogues and the three narratological types identified by Doležel:

1 Certain dialogues feature harmonious relationships and a spontaneous collaboration among interlocutors, both or all of whom have equal access to speech. They construct semantic concord by balancing alternatives and building consensus. This model, in my view, corresponds to the Ciceronian model as practised in the Renaissance.

2 Another category of dialogues is characterized by the dominance of one voice. Here access to speech is asymmetrical; the teacher speaks far more than the taught one. Semantic concord occurs, but it is of a monological kind; we recognize the Platonic model.

3 The third case is that of active, often satirical contradiction among speakers and of disharmony, projecting semantic discord, features characterizing the Lucianic model.

The literary dialogues of the Renaissance, particularly those with predominantly philosophical themes, have been dubbed incomplete fiction (cf. Wilson 1984). On largely Aristotelian grounds, that incompleteness relates to the sketchiness of the genre and to the fragmentary fashion in which representation is handled in it, mimesis being conceived as a means to a figurative end. If, however, we accept with Veltrusky the specificity of the literary dialogue, these characteristics cease to matter: 'The dialogue used in a literary work is not the dialogue which it evokes (or represents). Similarity is not sameness, nor even imperfect sameness; it is another thing altogether. Whatever its form, literary dialogue is highly organized ... Nor does the reader perceive literary dialogue as the dialogue it represents' (Veltrusky 1984, 599).

More than just to install a distance between the representing and the represented, this would claim, for the dialogues of the Renaissance, a level of reality or world of their own in which imagined communication takes place. The main question is whether such a concept does not fly in the face of everything we know from history about a European episteme trying to come to terms with expanded horizons geographically, scientifically, spiritually. How can dialogues, as part of the doxographic literature of the time, not be instrumental in this process of change?

And so it is a case of the mode of separation of possible worlds from the actual world. From the viewpoint of possible-worlds semantics, there is indeed separation; the mode of communication in the literary dialogue is allowed to evolve on its own and to generate alternative models the better to act upon communication in the actual world. Undoubtedly, the status of this viewpoint is only hypothetical; but the hypothesis happens to be congruent with the trend of humanistic discussion in the Renaissance.

PART 4
FICTIONS AND HISTORIES

14

Signposts in Oral Epic: Metapragmatic and Metasemantic Signals

NANCY FELSON-RUBIN

This paper attempts to describe a dynamic aspect of the communication between the performing epic poet (Homer[1]) and his listeners in the audience.[2] It focuses on the phenomenon from the oral poet which suggest how his listeners might take the events and figures of the fictional world he presents. *Metasemantic signals* tell audiences about the fiction they are experiencing and *metapragmatic signals* suggest how they might respond.[3] These two signal types, though quite distinct as categories of analysis, are usually intertwined in practice. For example, internal audiences behaving either gullibly or sceptically could alert Homer's audiences to listening strategies that are both descriptive (metasemantic) and prescriptive (metapragmatic). Such scenes, then, exemplify the two types of signposts that the oral poet sends his listeners.

Of the several theoretical works that have helped me formulate the problems set forth in this paper, I mention in particular the studies of possible-worlds semantics by Lubomír Doležel (1976; 1980), Thomas Pavel (1980; 1986), and Marie-Laure Ryan (1985), and an essay by Vincent Crapanzano in which he distinguishes metasemantic from metapragmatic signals (1989). Henceforth, whenever I refer to content, I am in the metasemantic realm, and whenever I refer to reaction or response or behaviour, I am in the metapragmatic.

Homer's *Odyssey* includes a variety of embedded structures – in particular bardic scenes and spectacles – mirroring its own oral performance. Such scenes would have invited live audiences, in archaic times, to reflect on their ongoing experience and perhaps to alter their own behaviour as listeners. As modern readers, we can also feel the metasemantic and metapragmatic impact of these embedded structures.

According to a principle that Odysseus articulates among the Phaeacians, inhabitants of the island of Scheria, the best narration is told by one who has experienced it firsthand or has heard it from one who was there (8.492–3).

Thus, first-person diegesis, with the character as narrator and actor, outstrips narration by a third person, especially one who is outside the narrative world. Using Genette's terminology, we could recast Odysseus's valuative statement as follows: the best narrator is intra-diegetic (on the same narrative level as the characters in the story he tells) and homo-diegetic (a participant in that story), especially if he is also auto-diegetic (the subject of his own story).[4]

Odysseus himself exhibits all these attributes when he tells his challengers at the games in Scheria of his own excellence (*aretê*) at athletics. His narration (8.214–33) is intra-homo-auto-diegetic: without naming himself, he hints at his importance as a war hero just back from Troy and as a skilled bowman. Moreover, by the very standards he has just set forth, his elaborate tale of his own 'Adventures' (spanning Books 9–12) is of the highest order, even overtaking Homer's own narration.

It is through such extended first-person character narration that Homer enlivens his own diegesis. Otherwise, his position outside the character world, as an extra-diegetic narrator, might make his story bland. He uses dialogue to animate his epic tale. So does the Phaeacian bard Demodocus in his second song, 'Adultery on Olympus,' sung at the games on Scheria to the all-male competitors. Demodocus alone of the internal bards (and only in the second of his three songs) dramatizes the events he narrates, like Homer, by representing the various divinities speaking.

The literal bards (*aoidoi*) in the text, Phemius of Ithaca and Demodocus of Scheria, are extra- and, hence, hetero-diegetic like Homer.[5] That is, they are at a different narrative level from the characters whose stories they tell and they do not participate in these stories. The unexpected presence in Demodocus's audience of a character celebrated in his first and third tales (at 8.75–82 and 8.500-20), namely Odysseus, breaks the frame separating singer and characters, almost in the manner of an apostrophe or an aside at a dramatic performance. This rupture may suggest to Homer's audience a potential identity between fictional characters and themselves. Moreover, when Odysseus responds to the first and third tales by weeping profusely (cf. 8.83–9 and 521–2), his behaviour opens up the possibility of weeping for Homer's listeners, sending the metapragmatic signal: 'You can weep profusely too.' In the case of the third story, the 'Trojan Horse,' Odysseus's weeping is compared to that of a woman bemoaning her husband who has fallen before the city and his people, while fending off the pitiless day for his city and parents (523–30). This reverse-gender simile, elaborating Odysseus's response, might suggest to men in Homer's audience that to weep like a woman is a legitimate response to powerful song and further, perhaps, that the boundary between male and female, husband and wife, is not so impermeable as they might have thought.

In another bardic scene, an unnamed bard in Argos, assigned by Agamemnon to protect Clytemnestra and keep an eye on her, is banished to an island to die.[6] This unfortunate bard becomes a victim in an exposure tale that he does not live to tell. Nestor incorporates the bard's story within his narrative (at 3.265–72) to his young visitors, Telemachus and Pisistratus. Thus, not only does he appropriate the role normally belonging to a bard, but he even takes the bard's sad fate as his theme. This appropriation might signal to Homer's listeners that the poet is human and vulnerable, like themselves, that he might even become a character in a tale, rather than always remaining safely above and outside it. This suggests, as a metasemantic message, that the boundary separating the singer from his audience may sometimes be crossed, that a member of the community, like Menelaus, might make the singer his topic in song.

No bard in the *Odyssey* rivals Homer, though Demodocus comes the closest in his 'Adultery on Olympus.' Put differently, Homer nearly always summarizes bardic songs without relinquishing centre stage: this is true of Demodocus's first and third songs, 'The Quarrel' (8.75–82) and 'The Wooden Horse' (8.500–20), as well as of the 'Returns' which Phemios sings to the suitors (at 1.326–7). The song that Phemius resumes, much later, as Odysseus approaches the palace with Eumaeus (17.262–3) has no reported theme. Later, when Odysseus spares Phemius and bids him lead the festive wedding dance to deceive the villagers (23.133–6), the Ithacan bard becomes the one who executes Odysseus's scheme, just as Odysseus in Books 9–12 is Homer's instrument. The metasemantic message of these hierarchies might simply be that Homer, as oral poet, 'gives orders to' all his characters (including bards), as Odysseus does to Phemius.

The theme of poetic reciprocity in Homer's presentation of bardic performances sends a metapragmatic signal to his listeners that they treat him well. Thus, when after hearing two songs ('Quarrel' and 'Adultery'), Odysseus deliberately gives Demodocus a choice portion of meat and affirms the honour due to the race of bards (8.477–81), Homer uses a subtle tactic (known to occur at song breaks in many contemporary oral performances) perhaps to request his meal and honour. In this scene, when Odysseus asks the bard to change his theme and to sing of the device of the wooden horse, again a metapragmatic signal goes to Homer's audience: 'You can affect my selection of theme.'

In the same scene, Odysseus establishes poetic reciprocity between himself and the Phaeacian bard. What they have to exchange is complicated by Odysseus's bardic talents. Odysseus pledges: 'If you can tell me the course of all these things as they happened, I will speak of you before all mankind, and tell them how freely the goddess gave you the magical gift of singing' (8.496–8).

On the one hand, Odysseus has accomplished the very deeds that Demodocus celebrates. Yet the one deed he specifically asks Demodocus to sing – the ruse of the wooden horse – is an artistic achievement, emphasized by the word for 'device' (*kosmos*). Since carpentry and poetics are parallel semantic domains,[7] Demodocus's song of the wooden horse celebrates Odysseus's artistic excellence (*aretê*) in language suggesting craftsmanship; thus Homer implants the idea that, if Odysseus praises Demodocus in song for his song, that praise will be of the highest order. Odysseus will match Demodocus's excellence with excellent song.

In fact, Homer fulfils Odysseus's promise to celebrate Demodocus's poetic deeds by honouring the bard in his *Odyssey* as 'Odysseus' entertainer in Scheria.' By celebrating Demodocus, particularly his ability, through the Muse's divine gift, to recount accurately what he has not seen, Homer authenticates his own poetic voice and communicates to his listeners his on worthiness of renown.

As a wayfarer on Scheria, Odysseus enjoys reciprocity with his hosts. They provide food, shelter, gifts, and escort home. In return, they hear his 'Adventures' and gain 'unquenchable glory' – *asbeston kleos* – in his song.[8] This glory might compensate for the suffering that Poseidon will exact from them for escorting one too many wayfarers over the seas. The Phaeacians will suffer and win renown, in a single move, through the intervention of bardlike Odysseus, the hero whose own identity is bound up with both causing and enduring trouble.[9]

Odysseus, as a bardic figure, uses poetic ploys to strengthen his position vis-à-vis his hosts and audiences, no matter where he is or what his disguise. His behaviour illuminates the ploys of the performing poet Homer, for whom the dynamic of performance likewise depends on an equilibrium between himself and those for whom he sings A formulaic line at the intermission of Odysseus's 'Adventures' (11.333–4), repeated at the completion of his tale (13.1–2), expresses the enchantment Odysseus is perpetrating on the Phaeacian listeners. During the first break, just after this formulaic description, Alcinous explicitly likens Odysseus to a singer: 'Odysseus, as we look upon you, we do not imagine that you are a deceptive or thievish man, the sort that the black earth breeds in great numbers, people who wander widely, making up lying stories, from which no one could learn anything. You have a shape (*morphê*) upon your words, and there is sound sense (*phrenes agathai*) within them, and expertly, as a singer would do, you have told the story of the dismal sorrows that befell you yourself and all the Argives' (11.363–9).

Alcinous's compliment to Odysseus for the shape of his words and the sound sense within them, and for his expertise in singing, as a bard would, the story of his troubles, introduces (and delineates) an aesthetic dimension of oral poetry. Certainly, to Homer's audiences the compliment is primarily ironic, since Odysseus does descend from the thief and social outcast, Autolycus (19.395–8), and is an arch-trickster.[10] Amidst all the irony, however, Alcinous's emphasis on the shape of words, on noble thoughts and on poetic skill, invites Homer's listeners to infer that the greater an epic's aesthetic power, the more it will enchant. This constitutes a metapragmatic warning to them not to be readily taken in.[11] At the same time, it is, in a sense, self-promoting, since it subtly recommends criteria for evaluating Homer's *Odyssey* and for judging it superb.

In Ithaca, too, Odysseus is commended for his poetic talents. The swineherd Eumaeus tells Penelope how the beggar enchanted him (*ethelge*) in the halls as he sat beside him and how he would also charm (*thelgoito*) her heart with what he tells, if the Achaeans would be silent (17.514). He compares the stranger to a singer 'who has been given from the gods the skill with which he sings for delight of mortals, and they are impassioned and strain to hear it when he sings to them' (17.518–21).

Just before this, to deflect the suitors' blame from him for leading the beggar to the palace, the swineherd distinguished the beggar from the class of *dêmiourgoi*, 'those who do public works' – like the bard, the seer, the healer, and the carpenter (17.382–7). According to Eumaeus, the *dêmiourgos* has a reciprocal relationship to his constituency: he performs a service and receives recompense. The bard, for example, sings for hire and food, and in turn uses his gift of song to enchant and delight his listeners and put them again in his debt. His poetic skills and poetic ploys offset the political and social powers of his constituency; thus bards, who literally depend on their listeners for sustenance, transcend their subordinate roles as *dêmiourgoi* through poetic devices, manipulating their listeners, exploiting their hunger for song.[12] In Eumaeus's social hierarchy, the beggar occupies the lowest rung, but Odysseus, as a consummate liar, songster, and entertainer, has a loftier status, and wins more sympathy, than his clothing and role usually admit. His transcendence of his disguise as beggar may suggest (metasemantically) to Homer's listeners that, even though he is dependent on them for sustenance, he is by no means their inferior.

While the Phaeacians recognize Odysseus's worth even though he is a wayfarer and treat him accordingly; the suitors pay him no such high regard. One of their offences, seldom noticed, is their insusceptibility to the stranger's power to enchant. In their presence, Odysseus exercises a dramaturgic role, of sorts. He stages his combat with Iros – an event which Antinous calls an 'entertainment' or 'delight' (*terpôlê*) – and thereby offers the suitors the possibility of reciprocity, which they decline. They are not his ideal audience, since they are impervious to his charms.

Besides straight bardic scenes and scenes in which Odysseus manipulates his audiences for a variety of ends, internal spectacles vividly unfold before the eyes of internal spectators, providing additional signposts to Homer's audiences. These stagings – sometimes contrived ahead of time by a character, or arising spontaneously – contain elements pertinent to dramatic enactment, such as intonation, disguises, and costumes.[13] Some appear in the narrator's diegesis, others within a character's speech or tale or in a bard's song.

In Menelaus's account of Helen's attempt at allurement, told as a corrective to Helen's self-promoting tale, Odysseus is an exemplary, discriminating listener.[14] He resisted Helen's beguiling words at Troy, when she was 'likening her voice to the voices of the wives of all the Argives' (4.279), whereas other sons of the Achaeans nearly succumbed to her enchantment. Addressing Helen (in Sparta), Menelaus recalls how he and Diomedes and great Odysseus sitting inside the wooden horse 'heard you crying aloud, and Diomedes and I started up, both minded to go outside, or else to answer your voice from inside, but Odysseus pulled us back and held us, for all our eagerness.' After that, only one Achaean was ready to answer, Nestor's son Anticlus, but 'Odysseus brutally squeezing his mouth in the clutch of his powerful hands, held him, and so saved the lives of all the Achaeans ...' (4.280–9).

The heroes whom Menelaus names as susceptible to Helen's alluring words (and Menelaus includes himself) are all 'gullible auditors,' taken in by illusion. The young Anticlus even had to be brutally restrained from responding, since he lacked self-restraint. The message designated especially for young listeners is clear: 'Beware of dangerous female allure!' and 'Do not act impetuously!'

In his song 'Adultery on Olympus' (8.266-366), Demodocus depicts a spectacle wherein Hephaestus both contrives the drama and constructs the 'stage-set' in which it is enacted. For Hephaestus as dramaturge, Demodocus uses epithets elsewhere reserved for Odysseus, *polumêtis* 'much-devising' (355) and *poluphrôn* 'of much intelligence' (367); the lame god, like Odysseus on numerous occasions, 'fashioned a deceit' (286). 'Famed for his art' (286) and 'much famed' (287), Hephaestus triumphs by his devices in a competition in which the slow, through cleverness and art, overtake the swift. The male gods standing around as spectators respond with unquenchable laughter as they look upon the devices of very intelligent *poluphronos* Hephaestus (327). Their laughter expresses their solidarity as males, enjoying a joke at the expense Aphrodite and the cuckolded Ares. Out of that laughter comes a second joke: Hermes acknowledges his desire to be in Ares's place. He alone of all the gods watching is lenient and light-hearted towards the betrayal. When Apollo asks him, 'Would you be willing, pressed tight in mighty bonds, to sleep in bed beside golden Aphrodite?' he replies: 'Lord who strike from afar, Apollo, I wish it could only be, and there could be thrice this number of endless fastenings, and all you gods could be looking on and all the goddesses, and still I would sleep by the side of Aphrodite the golden' (8.339–42). Hermes the voyeur wishes to enter centre stage at any cost. His attitude is anti-heroic, since to be the object of laughter is the worst fear of a hero. His words, 'and all you gods could be looking on and all the goddesses,' have implications for the possible inclusion of women in Homer's audience. In Demodocus's song, the goddesses did not watch the act of adultery but stayed away out of embarrassment (*aidôs*). Moreover, Demodocus sings his bawdy song, it seems, in the midst of a contest attended by males alone, just before the dancing and acrobatics; Arete is back at the palace (cf. 8.368–9 and 419–20) and Nausicaa is clearly not present. In Hermes's fantasy, however, goddesses may watch. This raises the question of what is proper for women in Homer's audience to hear and see. If present, they will overhear Demodocus's Hermes include women as voyeurs of his hypothetical prolonged sexual union with Aphrodite. Moreover, Odysseus is soon to outstrip Demodocus – and perhaps even Ares and Hermes – by telling of his love exploits in front of Arete; 'I mounted the surpassingly beautiful bed of Circe,' (10.347) is a virtual leitmotif in the 'Adventures.' Though Arete is a single female auditor in a primarily male audience, she is included as addressee. This inclusion sends a message to Homer's auditors about the appropriateness of certain topics for mixed company.[15]

A third spectacle is the adventure with the Sirens, first delineated in Circe's speech to Odysseus:

You will come first of all to the Sirens, who are enchanters of all mankind and whoever comes their way; and that man who unsuspecting approaches them, and listens to the Sirens singing, has no prospect of coming home and delighting his wife and little children ... but the Sirens by the clarity of their singing enchant him. They sit in their meadow; the beach in front is piled with boneheaps of men now rotted away, and the skins shrivel upon them. You must drive straight past, but melt down sweet wax of honey and with it stop your companions' ears, so none can listen – the rest, that is; but if you yourself desire to hear them, then have them tie you hand and foot on the fast ship, standing upright against the mast with the ropes' ends lashed around it, so that you can have joy in hearing the song of the Sirens; but if you supplicate your men and implore them to set you free, then they must tie you fast with even more lashings. (12.39–54)

The forewarned Odysseus repeats Circe's instructions to his crew (12.158–64) but changes 'if you yourself are wanting to hear them' to 'but only I, she said, was to listen to them' (160). By this substitution, he passes responsibility for his privilege onto her. The Sirens, seeing the ship approach, direct their sweet song towards Odysseus:

Come this way, honored Odysseus, great glory of the Akhaians, and stay your ship, so that you can listen here to our singing; for no one else has ever sailed past this place in his black ship until he has listened to the honey-sweet voice that issues from our lips; then he goes on, well pleased, knowing more than ever he did; for we know everything that the Argives and Trojans did and suffered in wide Troy through the gods' despite. Over all the generous earth we know everything that happens. (12.184–91)

'So they sang,' Odysseus recalls, 'in sweet utterance, and the heart within me desired to listen, and I signalled my companions to set me free, ... but they fastened me with even more lashings and squeezed me tighter' (192–200). Here his men use force on him as he used force on Anticlus, but in this instance he has orchestrated their behaviour ahead of time. After they sailed past, Odysseus tells the Phaeacians, and could no longer hear the Sirens' voice and song, his companions released him from bonds, obeying his instructions.

Thus, at Circe's bidding, Odysseus shields his men from dangerous enchantment as he had earlier protected the sons of the Achaeans within the Trojan Horse from Helen's beguiling words. Yet he himself indulges his desire to hear the dangerous song. Curiously, Homer only includes the song's prelude, as if to tantalize both the Phaeacians and his own listeners through aposiopesis. Odysseus alone among his (or any) men survives after hearing the Sirens sing a song too awesome, and too dangerous, for any other ears.

The tale of the Sirens underscores the pitfalls of *thelxis* 'enchantment.' Odysseus covertly warns the Phaeacians of this danger as Homer, rather playfully, signals his live audiences to beware. Or the message is, perhaps: 'Listen and be enchanted, but exercise caution, and know what dangers lie ahead.'

One spectacle described by the Homeric narrator, the combat between Odysseus and Iros before the crowd of suitors, sends a warning to listeners not to root for the wrong side. The suitor Antinous credits a god for bringing on this entertainment (*terpôlê* [18.37]), and the suitors all watch the two beggars battling with their hands and wits. Iros, the authentic beggar, says that the roguish wink of the suitors (18.11) stirred him to combat in the first place, but really it is Odysseus, disguised as a beggar, who stages the combat and determines which turn events will take. During the contest, the raucous suitors interrupt to rebuke or embolden Iros, providing a negative (metapragmatic) model for Homer's audiences. After he defeats Iros, Odysseus dramatically drags the loser to the front of the courtyard and dresses him up as a scarecrow to ward off boars and dogs. This use of costume contributes to our sense of the whole event as a spectacle. While the suitors do not enjoy Odysseus's gesture of setting the loser up for ridicule, Homer's audience may: the scene may prod them to disparage Iros, as a scapegoat, and to applaud Odysseus, who not only wins the contest that he has staged but even metes out to the vanquished a just public reward.

These and other spectacles in the *Odyssey* display diverse responses by internal audiences – Achaean warriors in the wooden horse, Odysseus and his crew aboard ship, Olympian gods (especially Hermes), and the band of suitors. Two spectators (Hermes in the 'Adultery on Olympus' and the suitors in the 'Beggar's Combat') actively participate in the unfolding event and express their individual attitudes towards the participants. On two occasions, in the 'Wooden Horse' and the 'Sirens,' Odysseus is an ideal auditor: he resists the enchantment of beguiling words and survives. In 'Adultery on Olympus,' the internal spectators delight in the use of a contraption (called a *dolos* 'deceit') to heighten the drama. Two protagonists (Hephaestus as a craftsman of beds and Odysseus as an inventor of the Horse) use devices to gain an end, enhancing the status of an artist. Thematically, the spectacle scenes tend to promote or discourage possible external audience responses.

In addition to bardic scenes and spectacles, characters hearing and imagining events, using their ears and eyes to apprehend, supply models for Homer's listeners. For example, Athena alights at the palace in Ithaca just as Telemachus is envisioning his father's return (1.115). He fantasizes along a syntagmatic axis, imagining his father returning, then scattering the suitors, and ultimately reclaiming his honour and being lord over his possessions. Here Telemachus literally envisions a narrative sequence; the 'return' plot of the *Odyssey*, as Homer expects his audience to do.

The weaving metaphor so prevalent in the *Odyssey* (especially for crafting epic poetry) also suggests a visualization of the actions, characters, and places of which Homer sings. The poet weaves events into strands of plot and images into descriptions; the audience 'sees' the final product, a variegated tapestry. The weaving gesture and the woven product entrap, like a spider's web, like lies and disguises.[16] Weaving diction locates poetry within the female domestic domain, since the poet as weaver resembles the Moirae spinning destiny. As the three sisters spin, so the poet weaves, inspired by the Muse. Moreover, several dangerous female characters in Odysseus's 'Adventures' weave as they sing, notably Calypso (at 5.61–2) and Circe (at 10.220–3); conjoined, these two activities (singing and weaving) herald danger for Odysseus. Oral poetics and mythological metaphysics alike embrace the image of women weaving and singing destinies that are fraught with danger; when Homer aligns himself metaphorically with these weaving singers, or singer weavers, he sends metasemantic and especially metapragmatic signals to his listeners to beware of the power of his song. The metapragmatic message might be: 'Remain cautious!' and 'Don't believe everything I say!'

From my examples of internal bardic scenes and spectacles, it becomes clear that Homer uses a specialized vocabulary for oral poetics, and each time he uses such a word he alerts his audience to think about his epic performance and react appropriately. Some key words and phrases are *thelxis* 'enchantment', *terpsis* 'delight' and its opposite *penthos* 'grief', *euphrosunê* 'merriment', *morphê epeôn* 'the shape of words', *epeessi + meilikhoisi* 'with gentle words'; also, by metaphoric extension, *pharmaka* 'drugs', *huphainô* 'weave'; *teukhô* 'fashion, construct', *tekhnê* 'craft, art', *polumêchanos* 'much devising', *polumêtis* 'of many plans'. *Euphrosunê* arises from a successful interaction between poet and audience, which has a reciprocal quality, a give and take.[17] The singer – as a *dêmiourgos* – depends on communal acceptance, yet he also manipulates his community through poetic ruses of all sorts, offering them pleasure (*terpsis*) in return. For *euphrosunê* to occur, power between poet and audience must be in equilibrium; all the listeners must experience pleasure and no one can be begrudging, disgruntled, or discontent. Begrudging listeners have no share in communal festivities and would detract from the final harmonic effect. If dissension arises, enchantment (*thelxis*) resulting in persuasion (*peithô*) may soften the rift in time.

Homer's listeners must have ranged from gullible to sceptical, like the audiences he portrays within his epic. They also probably were diverse in age and gender. The metasemantic and metapragmatic signals in his performance poem may have targeted particular segments of his audiences, sending special messages to turbulent youths, now to staid elders. The method I have proposed and illustrated should help modern readers of the *Odyssey* 'hear' these often covert messages and appreciate more fully the dynamic between Homer and his listeners.

NOTES

1 By Homer, I mean the flesh-and-blood poet in his role as singer of tales and as narrator of the *Odyssey*. Because he is present at performance, the narratological distinction between author and speaker is less distinct than for written texts. That is, the physical presence of the poet standing before his audience takes on some importance in the case of performance texts.

2 The arguments presented here are further developed in *Regarding Penelope: From Character to Poetics* (1994). The Greek text I use is that of Stanford, and the translations are from Lattimore, but I generally use Romanized transliterations, like Telemachus and Nausicaa, where he uses Hellenized ones.

3 On the distinction between metapragmatic and metasemantic signals, see Felson-Rubin 1990 (121–38), with citations.

4 For these particular discriminations, see Genette 1980.

5 On bards, storytellers, and liars in the *Odyssey* see especially Thalmann 1984, 113–84; see also Scully 1981, 67–83, Scott 1989, 382–412, and Trahman 1952, 31–43.

6 The Argive bard and Phemius both operate in conditions of political disarray, and the social disorder impinges upon their safety.

7 This parallel between poetry as a craft and carpentry goes as far back as Indo-European 'poetics'; on the Indo-European use of *tek(s)* – in the semantic realms of poetics and carpentry, see Schmitt 1967, 296–301, and Nagy 1979, 298–300, 311. Nagy quotes a simile from *Rig-Veda* 1.130.6ab, which he translates: 'the sons of Ayu, wishing for good things, fitted together this utterance, just as the skilled artisan (fits together) a chariot.'

8 The glory (*kleos*) that Odysseus offers to the Phaeacians when he tells them his 'Adventures' he later bestows upon them by recounting their deeds to Penelope (23.338–41). The Phaeacians' interest in being remembered by Odysseus once he is home is expressed repeatedly by King Alcinous, particularly at the athletic event (e.g., 8.101–3, 241–5). Moreover, Odysseus mentions *kleos* in his first speech to Alcinous, a prayer that the king may accomplish everything of which he spoke (namely, conveyance of Odysseus), and so may have imperishable or unquenchable glory (*asbeston kleos* [7.333]). In this remarkable prayer, Odysseus intimates that, in return for their hospitality and gifts, he can offer not only entertainment in Scheria but also a permanent place in epic song.

9 Odysseus suffers trouble and brings trouble to those he encounters; on this double aspect (active and passive) in relation to the etymology of Odysseus's name, see Dimock 1956; 1989 and Peradotto 1990.

10 Indeed back in Ithaca, Athena will praise him for the very qualities of which Alcinous absolves him: his profiteering and his thievery (cf. 13.291–5). Odysseus's 'Adventures' are not innocent in intent, as the king imagines, but aimed at profit. He wants safe escort home and plenty of gifts; he pitches his stories so as to entice already willing hosts and auditors to comply and, once they have promised escort, to keep that promise.

11 Earlier, Odysseus had used a similar expression to criticize the rude Euryalus on whose words the gods place no shapeliness (*morphên* [8.170]). Euryalus, who did

not speak fittingly (*kata moiran* or *kata kosmon*) and had no shape on his words, had to make amends to Odysseus to restore balance.

12 Svenbro (1976) makes much of the subservient position of the *aoidos*, whereas I see the relation between singer and society as more reciprocal, more dynamic, and less stable. At one moment, the bard serves his audience, at another, he manipulates and thus dominates them.

13 Costumes, though not thought to belong to Homer's repertoire of activities as he composed in performance, certainly agree with the spirit of epos, which can be imagined to include every sort of impersonation short of actual disguise.

14 Menelaus's motivations in telling this tale are complex. First, he wants to correct Helen's self-depiction in her matching and preceding tale. Secondly, he wants to praise Odysseus, before Telemachus, as a model not only of self-restraint but of leadership: not only did he resist Helen's enticement, presumably in Penelope's voice, but he also restrained the hearts of his companions and saved the Achaeans from disaster. Thirdly, he provides Anticlus as a negative exemplum for Telemachus, who is in the same age group: 'Though young, do not succumb to female wiles.' As Homer's listeners, especially the unmarried youths, visualize Helen acting out her impersonations, they might be prodded to reflect on mimesis and its dangers, as well as on the dangers of female inconstancy. On the pair of speeches by Helen and Menelaus, see Olson 1989, 387–94.

15 On gender-specified audiences, see Doherty 1992; note how Penelope's lone presence at the Contest of the Bow intrudes in the 'men's club' atmosphere of the event.

16 Hephaestus's contraption resembles the web of a spider; Telemachus connects spiders' webs on his parents' marriage bed with his mother's betrayal.

17 The words *thelxis* and *thelktêria* and *kêleuthmos* occurs fifteen times in the *Odyssey*, mainly in the contexts of song and eros. Odysseus states that in 9.6 that the noblest thing is when a bard achieves *euphrosunên kata dêmon* 'communal merriment'; this is achieved through *thelxis* as well as *terpsis*.

15

Of Worlds and Nutshells:
On Casanova's *Icosameron*

DIDIER COSTE

'Possible' is the fine line that tantalizingly separates and unites a single inexorable 'real' from other worlds that, for all their high risk, would provide the subject[1] with relief and release, time to breathe as well as space to entangle its limbs.

How does one, then, treat and tread this line, how does one trip and trade over it? The question is all the more delicate and poignant when the line in question is no longer a horizon (impalpable, ever displaced) but the very earth we stand on. What happens when we drill the foundation of the real? Is a dark continent going to well up to our mouths, or are we going to be driven into a bottomless pit of speechless desire? How initiatory can be a voyage to the origins? How original can be a trip into 'otherland'? How relativistic can the 'history' of here and then become?

Casanova's *Icosameron* could be an ideal test case, insofar as its text lay undiscovered – ignored – under our feet for some two hundred years, buried in an eighteenth-century Prague edition and a 1928 Italian edition. Even in its current 1988 Paris form, it is a 'complete-but-for' text. Ever since Casanova's *Histoire de ma vie* was eventually published in a decent – almost complete, but not critical – edition in the 1960s, we have been waiting for some literary and cultural reassessment, but biography remains master of the field. Will the publication of *Icosameron* change this state of affairs? It is too early to conclude that the resistance of our ignorance is coming to an end, but we can be sure that we are dealing with one of the very major productions of the European Enlightenment, that is, one that encourages a thorough revision of some widespread ideas on this cultural set.

The location of the telling 'vers le bord du canal de Saint-George du côté de Monmouth, dans la belle maison du comte de Bridgend'(Casanova 1988, 7) is not indifferent. Saint George is paired with the Dragon; Monmouth stands for 'my mouth' in Frenglish; and the end of a bridge is definitely the appropriate place on the return of Édouard and Élisabeth from the nether world. This tale, like so many others – although not always of the fantastic kind – is almost equally dedicated to telling its own success, to construct itself as an object of desire and seduction, as it is to divulging its contents. When, in the introduction, Édouard and Élisabeth enter unannounced into their venerable parents' apartment, they immediately awaken the dormant curiosity of the centenarians: 'qui êtes-vous donc …? Qui vous a donné notre adresse? D'où venez-vous? Que voulez-vous? Informez-nous bien vite de tout ceci …' (7). The generic nature of the forthcoming narrative – *fable, roman,* or *véritable histoire* – will be discussed for some time until the entire audience becomes convinced of the truthfulness of the account. Édouard and Élisabeth appear to be in their early twenties, while they were born, respectively, ninety-five and ninety-three years before. In spite of the physical marks of recognition they give in the best melodramatic tradition (a dog's bite on the left elbow, a pineapple birthmark – 'une grosse envie d'ananas' – on the right thigh), the explanation they provide is so unbelievable at first that the father disdainfully exclaims: 'Voici le commencement d'une fable,' to which Édouard replies that the physical anomaly of his and his sister's youth should be considered, on the contrary, as additional evidence of the 'wonderful truths' conveyed by their story. Casanova makes his characters participate (sometimes halfheartedly, at other times, enthusiastically or ironically) in generic discourses to which they do not belong, so that they take them experimentally, as clever games, and, at the same time, he removes them from the illusion of identification with their own verbal flesh, thanks to disturbing displacements of the enunciative investment.

Rather strangely, in fact, although Édouard and Élisabeth have already spent six months on earth after their forced return from the other world, the hosts and future audience of the tale begin with a historical account of England during the eighty-one years of absence of the travellers. For the external audience – the 'reader' – the two worlds are placed on equal cognitive footing. They are true antipodes of each other. Each is the unconscious of the other. Viewed from a theoretical position, untenable in principle and in praxis, but not in discourse, their coexistence will present no serious problem while its reliance on mutual inaccessibility presents a fascinating if intractable paradox.

It is true that the greater universe of the tale becomes increasingly contaminated by the symmetries and geometry that rigorously apply to the protocosm and have deeply transformed the lives of the English people there. A transgressive process of unification of narrated and narrational is at work from the very beginning, metaphorically attempting the junction of here and down below. This process, while fully successful on the narrational plane on which it uses self-regulated audience participation and collaborative commentary until it hushes all possible manifestations of dissent, has eventually little or no effect on the outer world of referential *realia*. Édouard, the storyteller, validly concludes: 'Et nous voici parvenus à l'accomplissement de nos voeux et à la fin de notre histoire' (762). However, telling the whole story to the 'beloved authors of their beings' was never a principal or even a clear motivation in Édouard and Élisabeth's courageous fight for survival, climbing back here, any more than it was a clear landmark on their horizon of expectations when they first reached the protocosm. The final indeterminacy of purpose is indeed what marks the completeness of the open work.

Physical access from the outer world to that of the Mégamicres and back being barred, except for that one time which is the object of the first and twentieth day of the telling, any project of conquest is not 'dans le nombre des possibles. Le monde d'où nous venons est sûr de ne jamais devenir la proie des conquérants de celui-ci' (22). Not only the Mégamicres themselves, but some six hundred thousand Englishmen would be ready in any case to defend the freedom of that world. Although the overt critique of colonialism in the *Icosameron* is apparently far less radical than in *Gulliver's Travels*,[2] and Édouard foresees its complete occupation by his lineage, Casanova protects his netherworld as a real fortress, guaranteed by the earth's crust, many miles thick, and heavily armed. A terrestrial audience will never be possessed of more than a mere description of the place. However detailed and complete – it rivals and exceeds most actual explorers' accounts in length and precision – such a description will only operate on its addressees as the portrait of a dead beauty on a potential lover, constructing an 'impossible,' inaccessible object of desire, an object of nostalgia. Lemuel Gulliver's evident didacticism turns his discourse towards the future; it offers a program, the Houyhnhnm way of life, and several counter-programs such as those of Lagado and Luggnagg. Casanova's Édouard, who had promptly become a patriarch and a powerful monarch in his 'own' world, rarely engages in giving lessons or examples to his fellow Englishmen.

This is the case not only because he ruled and decided more than he taught in that world: few if any of the laws, customs, health precepts, etc., of the underworld are applicable to the outerworld, because of their different configurations in terms of time and space. I would like to show how such differences are over-determined with regard to gender, sexuality, and food, and over-symbolized by inversions of colours, and so on. But the fundamental alteration of our judgmental criteria is undoubtedly that which results from the euphemistically put 'different manner of computing time' enjoyed by the Mégamicres and their guests. The Mégamicres take exactly so many seasons to develop, know exactly how long they will all live (forty-eight of our years), while the earthlings occupying their world have never died or aged there. As soon as Édouard and Élisabeth reach the surface of the earth, they start aging again, rapidly and irreversibly; it takes them just twelve years to catch up on their eighty-one years of unchanging youth, become old, and die at 110. The *Icosameron* is far more daring than any ordinary time machine, it does not merely attempt to struggle against the time flow or develop alternative time frames: it alters the very concept of time simply by exposing different possible 'constructions' of time.

In order to better apprehend the dialectics of closed and open, alternative and concurrent, we must understand that the lifetime adventure of Édouard and Élisabeth and their telling it are presented as singular and fortuitous. The teenaged brother and sister had asked their parents' permission to travel by sea on a ship that was looking for new lands in the far north of the northern hemisphere. As the ship is sucked by the Maelström, they happen to be locked into a large and thick leaden box that is thrown overboard. 'Landing' at the bottom of a river on the other face of the earth's crust, released from their telescope-equipped coffin thanks to a bath of red mercury that corrodes it, they now belong to dimensions that are really beyond or better, beside death and all expectations, not just because they somehow fit a drunken distorted image of paradise, but because this knowledge, this experience is uniquely and exclusively theirs. Should they have died during the fall, Élisabeth rightly explained that there was no reason to regret their not communicating their new knowledge to England: 'Man should be content and satisfied with knowing truth in order to make use of it himself, without caring in any way for the rest of mankind naturally inclined to accept the lies of imagination rather than the demonstrations of the wise ...' (51; my translation). The apparent lack of necessity of the telling, which is not financially or gloriously rewarded and is never made known to the general public, although it is recorded in writing and the manuscript corrected and amended by Édouard the teller, makes it just as self-contained as the world it presents.

Lemuel Gulliver grows a little wealthier after each of his trips, except the one to the land of the Houyhnhnms that raises him to a lasting plane of moral sublimation, well above all the other Yahoos, just when he is sufficiently well established in England as not to need to make more money overseas. He has brought back material evidence of his adventures, including samples of Lilliputian animal life which prosper on English grass. In spite of his repudiation of colonial exploitation and destruction, the economic model of his subsistence and progress combines ancient adventure and plundering, Ulysses style, with the modern pattern of profits derived from unfair trading practices and one-sided 'discovery,' a pattern largely initiated by Columbus.

While the Alfrède family expands at an alarming rate in the world of the Mégamicres, Édouard and Élisabeth, on their return to the outer world, have nothing but a couple of glowing jewels or carbuncles which they will sell in order to buy a vast estate for one of their nephews, whose heirs will be later knighted. They have themselves no descendants here. Their epitaph will almost literally reproduce the subtitle of Casanova's narrative. We seem to be dealing with a structure of value production that mimics the convention of the hero who went away, saw, learned, and returned to leave his story engraved in stone. But it overlaps and remains at odds with the fundamental heterogeneity of the scene of private telling in the presented world.

The telling occurs in the year 1615, well over one and a half centuries before the publication of the novel. The publication of extraordinary and imaginary adventures and voyages, from Swift and Defoe to Eugène Sue through Jan Potocki, is usually somehow justified in terms of its origin. In the *Icosameron* no explanation is given of the fate of the manuscript in all these years, of its conservation and transmission; no mention is made of a later editor or his right and motivations to divulge this text. We, the readers, are left out in the cold not only with respect to the world of the Mégamicres, which has sutured its tiny accidental openings behind Édouard and Élisabeth, but also to the cozy English lounge where the tale is told and, by extension, to the presenter's intentions. Uninvited, we shall be obliged to dig desperately into the textual body if we care to participate in his scheme. The encapsulation of the tale closely resembles the 'world in a nutshell' that is its constructed object/referent and purports to be its subject matter. In other words, the careless lack of tradition of the text we read eliminates any other referential support for its existence but the very world it presents. It is now our task to determine whether the homology of narrational and narrated structures betrays a specific mode of fictionality that would afford a comprehensive interpretation of the ideological relation of *Icosameron* to one or other selected 'real' of reference or whether it is just another deceptive trick.

The *Icosameron*'s overall thematic, narrational, and narrated structures are characterized by a fascinating combination of symmetry, equivalence, and asymmetry. On the one hand, the telling by Édouard and the panel discussion with his audience after each session, the balance of personal events and didactic or critical discourses on subjects of general interest, the institutional equivalence of social organization above and below are carefully respected. On the other hand, there is no way of communicating between worlds but the tale itself, which is of the past, and judging underworld behaviour by our standards is barely tolerated, as a temporary learning process that will lead to better thinking in the world above. One of the keys to this apparent incoherence is certainly to be found in the central role played by the peculiar fantasy of incest that pervades the entire textual universe of the book.

Édouard and Élisabeth, unashamed husband and wife, are also brother and sister. Their young desire to travel at sea was presented to their parents, who understood it, as 'une inclination.' The introduction by Édouard of Élisabeth as his wife elicits, very strangely, no reaction at all on the part of the audience, as if such a situation were to be expected and accepted quite naturally by a group of early seventeenth-century English people, several of them quite elderly. The later justification of the event of Édouard and Élisabeth's mating is so simple and matter of fact that it projects its candid 'lack of rhetoric' on the love life of the pair. Nature, in the underworld, never queried this incest; the couple was blessed, year after year, with perfectly formed newborns, all of them twins, one male and one female, one blond and one dark-haired, who, in turn, show the most fervent desire towards each other, are married at the age of nine years and three months, and start producing new twins immediately. Early marriage between twin brother and sister becomes a constitutional rule of the Alfrède tribe in the underworld until, many years thereafter, things begin to undergo some subtle changes, with a few possible signs of moral decadence in the race. In fact, the feeding and reproductive systems of the Mégamicres themselves take narcissism *à deux* one big step further: there is no physiological gender differentiation among them; on the contrary, married twin brothers/sisters who are supposed to spend their whole lives together – they are called *inséparables* – feed on each other's breasts and lay twin eggs simultaneously by their mouths. It is only in the rare case of one of them being born red (fecund and noble) and the other a different colour that the non-red twin may be exchanged for a red from another family in the same situation. In that world, the serpents that feed on the fruit that will become human sustenance are also twins, symmetrically perched on the trees, and they will be killed by the Alfrèdes with twin-barrelled rifles. As the number of humans grows, the number of serpents decreases until their total extinction will be achieved. In a very practical sense, then, humans are not only enemies but also heirs to the serpents, at the same time as their reproductive and family behaviour comes to resemble that of the Mégamicres as closely as their physiology will allow it.

Many modern readers would probably concentrate on a Freudo-Lacanian interpretation, considering that the demonstration once again of the return of the repressed is a remarkably unifying tool of interpretive reading. They would certainly find more than a measure of encouragement in the *Icosameron*'s numerology: 'car l'homme veut compter, et *animal qui compte* pourrait fort bien être sa définition,' says Édouard (177). In an extremely obsessive text, accounting, rather than recounting, is the most obsessive feature of all. Biographical explanations (Casanova the gambler and inventor of France's national lottery, etc.) would not do justice to a striking characteristic that is a peculiar combination of the decimal and duodecimal systems, so that 'round' and even numbers prevail everywhere. The Génie of Helion, king of Heliopalu and eternal-cum-invisible-cum-non-existent pope of the solar religion of the underworld, has one hundred ministers, each of them commanding fifty bishops who command twenty-four *alfaquins* or canons, each with a retinue of twelve priests. The total, not given in the text, is one million four hundred and forty thousand people, the square of twelve hundred. The number three is still present, but almost as well buried as the world of the Mégamicres itself. So what interests me more than the desire of incest as a motivation for the rules of this fictional world are the modalities of incest as they shape and define the relation between the two subworlds of the fiction, and between both of them and untextualized other possible worlds.

Even if we should accept that it is, in the individual's story, a displacement of primitive filial dependence, etc., incest between siblings and coevals is radically different from incest between parents and children in that, rather than upsetting chronology, it reinforces it. A paradoxical gesture against the Law, it does much more to support it in its principle than the anarchy of exogamic unions. Édouard and Élisabeth's initial intercourse answered the deepest call of Nature – in which the Law appears to be grounded:

Nous étions seuls l'un vis-à-vis de l'autre, et nous ne pouvions pas craindre ce que notre innocence ne nous laissait pas prévoir: si nous l'eussions prévu, il ne nous serait pas arrivé de violer une loi, que nous étions nés et élevés pour respecter, et nous serions peut-être morts plutôt que d'y manquer; mais nous nous trouvâmes devenus mari et femme sans avoir fait aucune résistance et sans avoir prêté le moindre consentement à le devenir. Pouvons-nous avoir offensé la nature, tandis que ce fut la nature elle-même qui nous fit agir ainsi sans le concours de notre volonté? Et si notre volonté ne s'en est point mêlée, notre union peut-elle avoir été un crime devant Dieu, dont la nature est l'ouvrage (60).

Beside some very old theological arguments and romantic themes that date back to *Daphnis and Chloe*, the spontaneous intercourse of Édouard and Élisabeth is dictated by a mitigated dream of equality, so powerful that it causes a carefully stressed slip of the pen of the author of their epitaph, almost a century later. The epitaph says that they died the same day and the age they were. What it does not say is that 'Élisabeth was two years younger than her brother and husband.' The Σ-narrator proffers a seemingly indifferent and light-hearted remark on this: 'mais ce n'est pas la première fois que dans une inscription de ce genre on sacrifie à la brièveté une circonstance importante.' Since it is obvious that the longish epitaph that mentions 'that they saw their eighth generation and over four million of their descendants' does not sacrifice anything to brevity, the question is, why state that they were the same age and at the same time underscore that their actual age difference was an 'important circumstance'? At least two different interpretations come to mind. First, if they were the same age, it would be more biologically natural that they died the same day, while their dying together, not programmed by nature, is an achievement of the mind, whether you want to call it will, love, or imagination. Second, this age difference remains a metaphor of gender difference in patriarchal society and, by way of consequence, a trace, however tiny, of the father-daughter incest pattern in our world. The overdetermination of the Σ-narrator's statement results in the condensation of compromise formation ('for the sake of brevity'); transplanted in the netherworld, Édouard and Élisabeth go part of the way, but not all the way, towards the geminality of the Mégamicres and their snakes – even Édouard and Élisabeth's race will back away from it after a number of years, apparently for the sake of stabilizing population numbers: a typical rationalization.

It is fascinating to note that the geminality of the two worlds – the outer world and the inner world, the open world and the closed world – is similar to that of Édouard and Élisabeth, except in one key visible respect: mutual knowledge. According to Mégamicric tradition, for instance, their world was created by the Sun some eight thousand human years ago, approximately at the same time as our world was created by God, according to the Bible. But the two worlds are perpetually hermetically sealed and live in mutual ignorance of each other: being true antipodes, they turn their backs or rather their feet to each other. The in-and-out game of Édouard and Élisabeth with the inner world means an irreversible loss of virginity for both worlds but in a very asymmetric manner. The fortuitously visiting-invading human couple functions as a male sexual organ; with a staying power of eighty-one years, it impregnates the womb-world with its myriad embedded babies. But the consequences for the outer world, to which the organ belongs, will be essentially of the order of knowledge. The Mégamicres will have acquired some new techniques and, in some cases, increased their riches, particularly the kingdom of Ninety, but it is at the expense of a loss of autonomy that could end up as total domination by the giant race. A stable world has been destabilized, the profit for the underworld is never clear; the politics of secrecy practised by Édouard, combined with the religious prohibition of curiosity on the part of the Mégamicres, produces results not unlike the overwhelming preponderance of the Father in human societies. Despite the reader's required identification with the human protagonists, one often wonders whether the Mégamicres would not have been wiser to kill Édouard and Élisabeth on their arrival or to let them starve. On the other hand, the act of penetration by the outer world, using Édouard and Élisabeth as its tool, is definitely pleasurable for the penetrators; their initial feeling is one of bliss, they doubt that they are still alive because this is too much like Heaven. When they return to the surface of the earth, blown up with a Mégamicric couple, one of these Mégamicres is found dead, killed by the explosion; the other one, who helps them with unfailing devotion throughout their hard journey, cannot survive despite all the efforts of Édouard and Élisabeth: a Mégamicre, constitutionally, cannot live alone. Life on earth is a lonely life; life on earth is forbidden to the Mégamicres.

The underworld, with its own sun at its centre and its unvarying light, its geometric division of the land, both physically by streams of red water and politically by constant borders, its fixed lifetime for people, animals, and plants, is largely stationary and ahistorical. In fact its 'history,' from the archives of the Grand Génie, although translated by Édouard over many years, is never developed for the reader of *Icosameron*. At best we can guess that the few republics in this world, of which one is particularly corrupt, are relics of an ancient state of affairs. The protocosm, however intellectually and spiritually developed, culturally regulated, and politically organized, is before all else a natural and physical world in that it is functional and customary, two features that the Enlightenment would see as attributes of nature, and it is a female world, bound by and contained within its own body – the Mégamicres are gracious, their language is a kind of singing, and their poetry pure vocal music – although its femininity does not extend to the capriciousness that male chauvinism would consider at that time as a woman's defect. The outer world, ours, is a world of conflicts, wars, greed, erring desires, adultery, and an unpredictable world, the plaything of special interests, irregular atmospheric influences, and so on; it combines the negative stereotypes of masculinity and femininity, while the protocosm amalgamates ideals of a virile femininity. The outer world is the prey of time; its dominant discourse is narrative. In this sense, the protocosmic 'utopia' offers no alternative history, nor does it even offer an alternative to history that would be valuable and accessible to the world above: the concept of progress is largely alien to a world in which chronology is seen as an equal and constant division of durations; the more such a world changes, the more threatened it is in its integrity and its validity as a model. Conversely, its influence (through Édouard's narrative) on the outer world will be severely curtailed, if not negligible, because – just like Mégamicric semantics – it is attached to a lyrical language that begins where harsh consonantic elocution and the eventful arbitrariness of history end.

This is not to say that Casanova's discrimination of the two worlds is Manichaean, nor that his vision of two regimes of fictionality is ever clear-cut and unambiguous, but the images of the inner and the outer world he provides, related as they are to dominant poles of reality and imagination, historically distorted space, and the spatialized temporality of a monotonous landscape, the native disorder of narrative discourse, on the one hand, and mythic-descriptive-lyrical order, on the other hand, has much to teach us about the contradictions and limits of utopia (including dystopias) as a premodern genre of fictionality. Moreover, the very unusual enunciative structure that includes dialogical commentary and dialogical philosophical disquisitions at two enunciative levels, maintains vividly efficient, and leaves generously open, that position of third party that we can only occupy when we practise an argumentative form of theory and which is where freedom resides, if anywhere.

NOTES

1 See Joseph Bya 1990.
2 'J'aime tendrement la liberté de tout ce monde-là, *soit qu'elle doive se conserver, soit qu'elle doive être la proie de mes descendants*,' declares Édouard (22; my emphasis).

16

Ironies of History:
The Joke of Milan Kundera

PETER STEINER

In his musings on the subject of history during recent interviews, Milan Kundera repeatedly used the expression 'half-time.' The evolution of the novel, he claimed, consists of two half-times with a hiatus between them occurring somewhere at the beginning of the nineteenth century. The same is true, he asserted elsewhere, about European music where the magisterial figure of Bach personifies the caesura articulating its development into two distinct segments. But it is not only the supra-individual history of art that, according to Kundera, exhibits such a bipartite structure. Human life often breaks into two halves as well, as can attest Kundera's own biography or that of Gombrowicz, one of his favourite novelists.

These remarks indicate that Kundera's understanding of history differs from the traditional progressivist view (whether romantic or positivist) which conceives of change as an orderly, accretive process unfolding according to some preordained *telos*. Kundera suggests that there is a certain degree of discontinuity among entities belonging to the same developmental series, that the fabric of time is sundered in places. This, however, does not mean that he subscribes to the catastrophic model of history characteristic of that modernist thought which fractures the past into a succession of disconnected states lacking any overall logic. By calling historical segments 'half-times,' Kundera obviously wishes to suggest that their autonomy is merely relative, that they ought to be interconnected somehow, that only together do they comprise the totality of history.

In these discussions and elsewhere, Kundera addresses the most basic metaphysical issue of Western historiography, the problem of sameness and difference. How can something, so the question goes, be considered self-identical if with the passage of time it has changed? For Kundera the answer to this question lies in the relationship between the successive temporal segments. He describes the relationship, first of all, in psychological terms. Like childhood, the first half-time is the source of all obsessions and traumas which the second half-time (the age of maturity) strives to forget, repress. However, Kundera regards as unhealthy these attempts at obliterating the past. Not only can the process of repression cause severe mental complexes but that which is repressed also does not vanish from history: it remains there as a subversive potential, a hidden charge ready to explode. Secondly, the relationship between the two half-times also has for Kundera its ethical aspect. For him, the rejection of the past is morally wrong and he speaks of the necessity of paying old debts, of the 'sin' of forgetting, or of historical 'betrayal.'[1]

This model of history is idiosyncratic enough to suggest that it might be related somehow to the existential experience of its author, to Kundera's efforts to come to grips with his own traumatic youth. His biography points directly to the source of his anxiety. 'My generation,' Kundera explained in 1967, 'matured in the period of Stalinism.' And it was the ethical double-bind of this period that stigmatized him for the rest of his life: 'Stalinism ... was based on a grandiose humanistic movement which even amidst its Stalinist disease retained many of its original attitudes, ideas, slogans, words, and dreams. It was an enormously confusing situation. The moral orientation was more than difficult if not impossible at times ... The danger of Stalinism for all virtues and ideals stems from the fact that while originally based on them it gradually perverted them into their opposite: the love for humankind into a cruelty toward humans, the love for truth into a denunciation, etc.' (Liehm 1988, 56).

The moral confusion created by Stalinism had a devastating effect on the majority of Kundera's generation. It made them behave in a manner they subsequently regretted and it implicated them in crimes of which they were initially unaware. For them, to connect the two half-times of their lives was an involved and painful process of reflecting about a shameful past and drawing from it discomforting conclusions for their present actions. *The Joke*, I will argue, explores the possibilities opened to the members of Kundera's generation in the search that he elsewhere termed a 'stalking of a lost deed.'[2]

According to Lubomír Doležel, *The Joke* 'can be designated an *ideological novel* for the narrators of *The Joke* are representatives of various systems of "false" ideologies – myths' (1973, 115–16). Let me elaborate on this observation in some detail. 'Ideologies,' in Karl Mannheim's definition, 'are the situationally transcended ideas which never succeed *de facto* in the realization of their projected contents' (1936, 194). But, Mannheim argues, there are two basic ways in which every world-view is ideologically skewed. On the one hand, there are sets of collectively shared beliefs rooted in a given social situation to such a degree that they ignore all facts that could destabilize or change the status quo. Mannheim calls such mental constructs ideologies proper. To them he juxtaposes another type, a collective unconscious drive of the opposite nature: to destroy or transform a given society. This utopian mentality, as he calls it, is 'guided by wishful representation and the will to action' to such an extent that 'it turns its back on everything which would shake its belief or paralyze its desire to change things' (40).

The four narrators of Kundera's novel represent the three forms of Mannheim's utopian mentality: the chiliasm of the Anabaptists, the conservative idea, and the socialist-communist utopia. These three modes of utopian thought differ from each other, Mannheim claims, in their perception of time, and in their orientation towards specific dimensions of temporality. The distinctive feature of chiliasm is its absolute presentness. Neither what has happened nor what will be motivates the representative of this mentality; instead, he is motivated by the atemporal Logos, the voice of God which speaks in his soul. 'For the real chiliast,' Mannheim concludes, 'the present becomes the breach through which what was previously inward bursts out suddenly, takes hold of the outer world and transforms it' (215). For the conservative utopianist, the past is of cardinal importance. The present is legitimized only insofar as it has evolved organically from some prior existence. All particular historical configurations are connected because they are the embodiments of the spirit that unfolds through the collective creation of a community, whether tribe, nation, or state. Finally, the socialist-communist utopia is future oriented. It shares with the conservative idea the belief in historical determinism; but rather than as a validation of the present, it sees the past as a blueprint for the future. Furthermore, for the conservatives, history is propelled by a spiritual force; for the socialist mentality, economy is projected into that role.

The Christian Kostka fits well the image of the chiliastic type outlined by Mannheim. Significantly, the text furnishes no clues to his religious denomination: Kostka's church, it seems, is the communion of those ruled by the Word of Christ. His behaviour is not governed by customary social considerations but by the Gospel alone; thus, paradoxically, in the struggle between Communism and the Church, Kostka sides with the former. He sees its push towards social justice, as though apparently atheistic, as being closer to Christ's message of universal love than is the benign neglect of the disadvantaged which is practised by the organized Church. Outside minor involvements with mundane concerns of the day, Kostka lives outside time in the communion with God's absolute presence. 'The help offered by religion,' he explains, 'is simple: Yield thyself up. Yield thyself up together with the burden under which thou stumblest. This is the greatest relief, to live, giving yourself to others. And, to yield oneself up,' he continues, 'means to lay aside one's past life. To pluck it out of one's soul' (218–19; 216).[3] The same holds true, Kostka maintains, for the future as well. Hearing Jesus' words (Matthew 6: 36), 'Take therefore no thought for the morrow: for the morrow shall take thought for the things of itself' (209; 206), he leaves his comfortable academic position to assume a menial position at a state farm.

If in *The Joke* Kostka personifies the chiliastic utopianism, the character Jaroslav embodies the conservative idea. He derives the meaning of his existence not from divine presence, but from a bond with the spirit of his people, that 'age-old tradition which got hold of man after man and pulled him into its sweet stream. In this stream everybody became like everybody else and merged into mankind' (143; 139). Moravian folklore in general and the Pentecostal ritual 'The Ride of the Kings' in particular are for Jaroslav the perfect media through which the past projects itself into the present. For the conservative mentality, the length and the continuity of tradition are of signal value. Hence Jaroslav's quasi-scholarly foray into the history of Moravian folk music (omitted from the first English edition of the novel) which links it to ancient Greece and the mystical jubilation of Dionysus. And whereas Kostka supported the Communists because of their affinity with the purport of Christianity, Jaroslav's membership in the party was a function of its massive support of folklore as a desirable alternative to bourgeois decadence.

The socialist-communist utopia is represented in Kundera's novel by two protagonists, Helena and Ludvík. One reason for this doubling, it seems, rests in the fact that these characters illustrate two different motivations for embracing the Marxist doctrine: an intellectual and an emotive one. Ludvík's utopia is axiomatic, governed by the internal logic of Marxism as a totalizing system of knowledge. In this respect Ludvík is similar to two other male narrators. Helena's utopia, on the other hand, is a response to her sexual experience and is therefore less rational. As she puts it herself: 'I'm not ashamed of the way I've always been. Until I was eighteen all I knew was being cooped up in a convent, two years in a TB sanatorium, another two years catching up on the schooling I'd missed. I didn't even go to the dancing lessons; all I knew was the tidy apartment of tidy Pilsen citizens and learning, learning; the real life was beyond seven walls. Then in '49 when I came to Prague it was all of a sudden as a miracle, a happiness which I'll never forget' (19; 22). Helena identifies the social revolution with her sexual liberation. Her *Weltanschauung* was formed by the orgiastic experience of the May First demonstration when she fell in love, and by the party's intervention which delivered her coy partner to matrimony. The future for which Helena fought thereafter in the name of Marxism was a world of full and requited love.

Ludvík too drifted initially towards the party for certain personal reasons. Yet his were definitely more class-conscious than Helena's. By embracing Marxism, Ludvík protested against the denigration he and his mother suffered at the hands of his rich uncle during the war. But for him the communist utopia was above all a global project transforming fundamentally the human situation in the world. It stemmed, he recollected later, from 'an altogether idealistic illusion that we were inaugurating the era of mankind when man (every man) would neither be *outside* the history, nor *under the heel* of history but would direct and create it' (72; 73). The basic tenets of Marxist mentality and the perception of time peculiar to it are captured in a nutshell by Ludvík's disquisition on the renaissance of folk music in the socialist Moravia presented in front of his old friends just after the Communist coup. As Jaroslav, a witness to this event, summed it up: '[Ludvík] had an air all the Communists had at that time. As if he'd made a secret pact with the future and had the right to act in its name' (136; 134).

But there is yet another, more significant reason why there are two characters in *The Joke* subscribing to the same type of utopian mentality. Helena is a captive of the *Weltanschauung* she adopted in her youth, unable to transgress its limits, to change the cognitive optics with which she sees reality. In this respect she is quite similar to Kostka and Jaroslav whose world-views are equally singular and unitary, though each in its own particular way. Ludvík, on the other hand, represents in the text a sceptical, post-utopianist attitude. A fatal joke transformed him from the member of an élite to a social pariah, and this experience revealed to him not only the limitations of his own beliefs but also the relativity of all ideological constructs. Thus, as Doležel points out, in the novel 'Ludvík is assigned the role of destroying his own myth but also contributing substantially to the destruction of other characters' myths as well' (1973a, 119).

If we now apply Kundera's view of history as an essentially bipartite process to the biographies of his four protagonists, we might say that it is only Ludvík whose existence seems truly historical. The lives of the rest are merely prehistorical, consisting solely of their first half-times. As the gaps between their beliefs and reality increase, they are unwilling to reflect upon the past from a new perspective and desperately cling to their original identities. Helena's words repeated several times throughout the text, 'I don't want my life to break in a half, I want it to be one life from beginning to end,' illustrate well this aversion to accommodate one's existence to new circumstances.

'One's destiny,' Ludvík meditates as the novel closes, 'is often completed before death, the moment of its end need not coincide with the moment of death' (292; 288). And though it is only Jaroslav he has in mind, his observation pertains equally to Helena and Kostka. The unwillingness to scrutinize one's past critically is considered in *The Joke* to be a fatal weakness, and those afflicted by it are symbolically sentenced to death as their respective utopias collapse. Helena attempts suicide and, disgraced, leaves the town with a man she does not love. Kostka commits a mortal sin and, unable to discern God's voice in the polyphony he is hearing, loses his contact with Him. Jaroslav suffers a crippling heart attack which will forever prevent him from performing with his folkloristic (or, rather, folk) band. We part from these injured beings convinced that they will not be able to construct anything positive from the shambles of their lives.

But Ludvík's fate is different because he shed his youthful utopia relatively early in his career. In the penal battalion to which he was sent, he 'realized that the thread tying [him] to the Party and his comrades had hopelessly slipped out of [his] hand' (53; 55). At this moment, the decisive rupture in his life occurred and his second half-time began. But, as I argued earlier, what interests Kundera is not merely the articulation of history into distinct segments but also the connection of the two, the recuperation of the past from a present perspective. Thus, we must ask, what is the relation between the two halves of Ludvík's biography? How did he manage to incorporate his traumatic experience into his subsequent behaviour?

The story of Ludvík's life unfolds according to the principle of inversion. His innocent joke became a personal tragedy which then transformed both his infatuation with the Marxist utopia into revulsion and his former friends into enemies. Accordingly, the only link that connects the two halves of his personal history is purely negative. In Ludvík's own words: 'And the main bond with which I'd tried to tie myself with the past which hypnotized me was vengeance' (270; 267). The entire motivation for his present actions is the desire to revenge himself upon those who punished him unjustly. The Czech word *lítost* best describes this particular mental state.

'What is *lítost*?' Kundera asks in his *Book of Laughter and Forgetting*. It is a word 'with no exact translation into any other language. It designates a feeling as infinite as an open accordion, a feeling that is the synthesis of many others: grief, sympathy, remorse, and an indefinable longing ... Under certain circumstances, however, it can have a very narrow meaning, a meaning as definite, precise, and sharp as a well-honed cutting edge. I have never found an equivalent in other languages for this sense of the word either, though I do not see how anyone can understand the human soul without it' (130; 121). The mystery of the word *lítost* which Kundera puts on display has a linguistic basis. It is a homonym that shelters two incompatible meanings: the feeling of pity or grief, and the state of fury or ferocity. Curiously, this freak of semantics grasps perfectly the peculiar psychic mechanism that intrigues Kundera: a self-pity vented into an aggression. As he explains, 'Lítost works like a two-stroke engine. First comes a feeling of torment, then the desire for revenge' (132; 122).[4]

The story of *The Joke* parallels the sequence of mental states in *lítost* as Kundera describes it. Ludvík was humiliated, denigrated, his career ruined, and his life derailed. With an injured ego, he seeks to settle accounts with the culprits. An accidental meeting with the wife of his chief tormentor provides him with a welcomed opportunity. He seduces her and during their sexual encounter treats her sadistically. But the principle of inversion strikes again. Ludvík's revenge turns into another joke, and instead of getting even with the villain he merely hurts innocent bystanders. *Lítost*, the novel suggests, is not the best mental condition for accessing one's own past. It is another form of 'false consciousness,' of a distorted world-view which, in contrast to its collective counterparts, is strictly individual.

Earlier I quoted Mannheim's definition of ideologies as 'situationally tran-scended ideas which never succeed *de facto* in the realization of their projected contents.' Utopias, then, are futuristic schemes which, in the name of a par-ticular certitude, wish to transform the world. Ludvík's quest for correcting previous wrongs is the mirror image of the utopianist undertaking. It substitutes for the myth of transcendental Truth that of transcendental Justice and strives to project it into the past. With the same tenacity with which Helena, Jaroslav, and Kostka hold to their ideals until time makes the gap between the utopias and reality untenable, Ludvík maintains his belief that former injustice can be rectified – until the outcome of his action proves him wrong. The intervening fifteen years have changed everything. Those who once punished him for his ideological deviation are now thinking very much like him, and his carefully prepared plan turned into the mockery of itself: 'Delayed revenge,' Ludvík realizes, 'becomes something unreal, a personal religion, a myth detached more and more from the lives of the participants ... the blow which I dealt today, after all these years is an unintelligible blow, and because of its unintelligibility it assumes a completely different significance, it becomes something other than I intended, it can turn into many directions and I cannot govern it and even less justify it' (270; 267). Thus, Ludvík's quest for justice becomes as illusory as his earlier quest for a better world.

With this experience, history appears to Ludvík as a series of jokes, an endless irony over which he has no control that transforms every deed of his into something else. The past cannot be recouped because it is an incomprehensible mystery which ought to be purged from memory: 'all that has been done, has been done and cannot be undone ... nobody can redeem the injustice which has happened but all will be forgotten' (271; 268). This recognition breaks the tedious link that held together Ludvík's biography. Yielding to blissful oblivion, he imagines himself falling into the timeless chiasm which suddenly opened in his life: 'I felt myself falling ... down into the depth of years, the depth of centuries where love is love and pain is pain. And I told myself with astonishment that my only domicile was this very falling, the searching, longing fall and I abandoned myself to it and felt its delicious vertigo' (291; 287).

It must be stressed that the image of vertigo employed in the above passage has a special significance for Kundera: 'Vertigo,' he explains to one of his interviewers, is 'the intoxication of the weak. Aware of his weakness, man decides to yield to it rather than to oppose it. He is drunk with weakness, wishes to grow even weaker, wishes to fall down in the middle of the main square in front of everybody, wishes to be down, lower than down' (Salmon 1987). This metaphorical interpretation of vertigo suggests that Ludvík's sudden desire to dissociate himself from his past is a sign of weakness, a form of suicidal drive. But the source of this weakness is not immediately obvious from the text. To pinpoint it, let me return once more to the notion of *litost*.

The similarity between *litost* and the utopian mentality does not end with the fact that they are two forms of a distorted world-view. More importantly, both are manifestations of wishful thinking, the manipulation of reality according to the needs of the group or the individual who project them. The source of Ludvík's weakness, I would like to argue, is the repressed aspect of his personal history, that part of his previous life censored by the feeling of self-pity.

Throughout the novel Ludvík presents himself, above all, as a victim of the Marxist utopia, the avenger of injustice to which he was subjected. But what comes out only rarely in the text is the fact that as a former party member, he was involved in the abuses of power occurring after the Communist take-over. This repressed guilt emerges in *The Joke* only several times in Ludvík's internal dialogues between his two selves; the victim and the victimizer:

'Again and again in my reminiscences I returned to that hall with its hundred people raising their hands for the destruction of my life ... From that time on and each time I've met a new man or woman who might become my friend or lover, I have mentally transported him to that assembly hall and asked whether he would have raised his hand. No one has ever passed that test.' And now the second voice comes in: 'Perhaps it was cruel of me to submit my acquaintances to such severe scrutiny ... Some may even say that this procedure of mine had only one purpose: to elevate myself above all others in my moral complacency. But such an accusation of arrogance would not really be justified. I've never myself raised a hand to vote for anyone's destruction, and, I've tried for a long time to convince myself at least that if I'd had the opportunity I wouldn't have taken it. But I am honest enough to laugh at myself for this. Would I have been the only one not to raise his hand? Am I the only just man? Unfortunately, I found no guarantee within myself that I'd been any better.' (76–7; 77–8)

The logic of this utterance is quite revealing of Ludvík's ambiguous attitude towards his past. He steadfastly refuses any complicity in Stalinist crimes because he never raised his hand to condemn anyone. Yet the feeling of guilt hovers in the air. He did not have to decide anyone's fate, but if push came to shove he would have behaved like the rest of his comrades. The guilt is there because Ludvík's hands are not altogether clean as another of his inner dialogues reveals: 'If asked by various commissions, I could invoke dozens of reasons why I became a Communist, but what enchanted me the most about this movement, even hypnotized me, was *the steering-wheel of history* in whose proximity ... I found myself. Among the faculty were very few Communists then and, therefore, in those early years the Communist students governed the universities deciding virtually alone about the personnel, the reform of education, the syllabi' (71-2; 72). Ludvík among others participated in the purges after the coup, firing professors who did not fit the new ideological mould, thus, in the name of the highest humanistic principles, ruining their lives.

However, Ludvík is not willing to face this responsibility. He is eager to paint himself as a victim of Stalinism, not as one of its promoters. This status furnishes him with the moral ground for his vendetta. Only after his attempt at avenging himself turns him into a victimizer does another connection between his past and present begin to dawn on him. Running away from the place of his unsuccessful revenge, Ludvík realizes that 'every time I tried to redress wrongs, I ended with wronging others. I was chasing away these thoughts because I knew myself for a long time all they were telling me' (285; 281). This old knowledge, never revealed in the text, is Ludvík's suppressed guilt for the deeds of his youth. His utopian quest for social justice by joining the party resulted in an injustice similar to his later action which was intended to correct a personal wrong. But Ludvík is too weak to admit his complicity in the misdeeds of the Stalinist era. Unable to stand up to his past, he gives up to his weakness and in a 'delicious vertigo' obliterates it from his memory.

So far we have seen that none of the characters from *The Joke* manages to come to terms with his/her own history, to somehow connect the two half-times of his/her life. Some are unable to transcend the utopias of their youths; others, unwilling to deal with the shameful memory of the past, recoil from it. But for the members of the generation that matured in the confusing era of Stalinism is there any way out of this dilemma? In writing his novel, I would like to argue, Kundera provided one possible answer to this question.

In his interview with the Czech novelist, Alain Finkielkraut pointed out what he saw as Kundera's greatest contribution to the critique of the Communist utopia: 'In your novel *Life Is Elsewhere* you speak as if it were an era where "the poet reigned along with the executioner." If the New Philosophers find the roots of the Gulag in Fichte and Hegel, you yourself find them in poetry' (1982, 22). Kundera's discovery of a latent affiliation between lyricism and totalitarianism is, no doubt, connected to his own biography which, it is worthy to mention, exhibits some points of contact with the life of his hero Ludvík. Like him, Kundera joined the Communist Party before the coup only to be expelled from it shortly thereafter for an ideological lapsus. But in contrast to Ludvík's, Kundera's career rebounded rather quickly. Already in 1953 he managed to publish a collection, *Man – A Wide Garden*, a book very much attuned to the ideological ambiance of the time; and two years later he published *The Last May*, an equally tendentious poetic composition about the Communist hero of the anti-Nazi war resistance Julius Fučík.

It was the next book of poems, *Monologues* (1957), which heralded the transition in Kundera's creative career. In its verse form it was a continuation of his earlier poetic output, but in its deliberately antilyric mode it hinted at the subsequent stage of Kundera's writerly biography: the shift from poetry to prose. In the late fifties Kundera produced his first short story, the embryo of his next collection *Laughable Loves*, where he abandoned verse never to return to it again. 'My life,' he recollected some quarter century later, 'took flight with the first story for *Laughable Loves*. This was my Opus 1. Everything I'd written prior to it can be considered prehistory' (Elgrably 1987, 8). But even the short story did not entirely satisfy Kundera. In 1961 he published a scholarly monograph, *The Art of the Novel*, about the Czech avant-garde prosaist Vancura, and it was in the novel that Kundera finally found his artistic domicile. *The Joke*, which Kundera began in 1961 and finished in 1965, was his first novel.

The dichotomy of verse and prose, the lyric and the novel, is for Kundera more than a matter of form. These modalities represent for him two incompatible mentalities, two opposite attitudes towards the self, others, and the surrounding world. The lyric, Kundera claims, is unreflective, emotive. It is a direct self-expression of the poet who, through empathy, strives to merge his ego with the audience's collective spirit: 'In rhyme and rhythm,' Kundera writes in one of his novels, 'resides a certain magic power. If a woman *weary of breath* has *gone to her death*, dying becomes harmoniously integrated into the cosmic order … Through poetry, man realizes his agreement with existence, and rhyme and rhythm are the crudest means of gaining consent' (1979, 231; 1980a, 193). To the poetic yearning for an all-embracing unity, Kundera juxtaposes the prosaic awareness of an all-pervasive difference: 'An anti-poetic posture grows out of the conviction that between what we think about ourselves and what we actually are exists an infinite distance, just as there is an infinite distance between what we wish things were and what they are, or between what we think they are and what they are. To apprehend this distance, this abyss, means to destroy the poetic illusion. This is also the essence of the art of irony and irony is the perspective of the novel' (Liehm 1980, 49).

This analysis explains Kundera's argument of a close affinity between social utopianism and the lyric. Both correspond to the deep-seated human need for stability, predictability, harmony. They create a totalizing universe of discourse that is closed to any critical scrutiny. Social utopianism does so through a quasi-rational argument which reduces the complexity of the world to a simple formula whose self-evidence is beyond doubt; the lyric does so through a poetic pathos to which we yield joyfully. It was the period of Stalinism, Kundera maintains, when this latent kinship became manifest: 'The totalitarianism of the '50's was not just oppression alone. It was not by means of its execution posts that it attracted the masses, the young, the intelligentsia. It was by its smile. We tend to forget this today; we are ashamed of this. We no longer say: the bloody totalitarianism of the '50's had a poetry that we succumbed to. If we blame it on the Gulag, we feel pardoned. If we speak of the poetry of totalitarianism we remain implicated in the scandal' (Finkielkraut 1982, 23).

This condensed statement provides, I believe, a clue for understanding Kundera's attitude towards his own past. The word he chose to designate Marxist totalitarianism has powerful connotations. Marcel Detienne reminds us of the curious: '"machine" hidden in the Greek *skandalon*: the deadfall of a trap in which bait has been placed ... the site of scandal, its own space, is made up of a dual motion, repulsion and attraction. One points the finger, one becomes outraged, one makes a scene in order to eloign, to put a distance between oneself and others – between oneself in the eyes of others – that very thing by which one is in danger of being attracted, seduced, or trapped. Like a double bind whose hieroglyph would be one hand cutting the other' (1986, 13–14).

Thus, for Kundera the scandal of Stalinism is not merely the barbed wire around the Gulag – the steel jaws which crushed its victims – but also the allure of lyricism which made many enter the snare voluntarily. The moral opprobrium directed against this troublesome period might distance us comfortably from it, yet it trivializes what happened, obliterates what should be remembered, mutilates the past. We cannot, Kundera argues, walk away from the *skandalon* of Stalinism in disgust; we must return to it and explore it from within, fully and responsibly.

It is clear that Kundera's hostility towards the lyric has its roots in his personal history. 'My youth (my lyric age),' he told an interviewer the same year *The Joke* appeared, 'my lyric activity and interests coincide with the worst season of the Stalinist years.' To put it more bluntly, in the epoch 'ruled hand in hand by the hangman and the poet,' he played a less than an innocent role (1979, 309; 1980a, 270). Kundera's awakening coincided with the first serious crisis of the Communist movement in 1956, and since that time he has been among the most vociferous critics of the party's hegemony. But what could he have done about his own past, the first half-time of his biography implicated in the very idea that he now decried? The figure of Ludvík suggests some possible reactions: the feeling of *litost*, the suppression of guilt, amnesia. Kundera, however, rejected the quiet fatalism of his hero who is resigned to the knowledge that history is the master ironist playing jokes on him. Taking the challenge of standing up to his past, Kundera turned the joke on history. He returned to his 'lyric age' and reinterpreted it ironically, from the novelistic perspective.

The figure of the joke thrives on the essential ambiguity of language. It highlights the fact that words can say something other than what they purport. Ludvík, for example, hailed Trotsky but what he really wanted was to get his reluctant girlfriend into bed. The hidden agenda of Kundera's own joke is the dialogue between the two halves of his life, between the poet and the prosaist. The ongoing polemics between the views its author held in the fifties and those which he holds now are obscured by the fictional universe which the novel projects. We must not overlook that *The Joke* reiterates a number of motives and themes which occurred previously in Kundera's poetry: devotion to the homeland and the friends, the redeeming power of love, the celebration of youth, to mention just a few. But while in his poems these topoi are presented lyrically at their face value, as expressions of eternal ideals in *The Joke* they become novelistic material. They are examined from various perspectives, dissected in a detached manner, debunked.

I will illustrate my thesis with one detail from *The Joke*, the controversial figure of the Czechoslovak national hero Julius Fučík who appears in the novel on several occasions. This Communist journalist participated in the resistance movement during the war, and for about ten months he edited the party's main underground paper. Arrested by the Nazis in 1942, he was executed a year later. Fučík's behaviour at the Gestapo's hands still remains to be assessed objectively, but there are reasons to believe that it was less than honourable. The bone of contention is Fučík's extensive record of his captivity devoted above all to his unswerving heroism, which he mysteriously managed to write during his interrogation and have smuggled out of prison. After the war, this text, which has yet to be fully authenticated, was published by his widow. *Notes from the Gallows*, as the book is known in English, furnished Communist propagandists with fuel for the campaign which launched Fučík as the premiere resistance fighter of his people and the role model for Socialist youth.[5]

Earlier I mentioned that Kundera joined the chorus of Fučík glorifiers in 1955 with his *The Last May*, an imaginative amplification of a small episode from the *Notes*.[6] For roughly forty pages, the poem depicts a mental duel between Fučík and his Gestapo interrogator Böhm. This takes place amid the fragrant beauty of the blossoming spring in a garden restaurant overlooking Prague where Böhm took the stubborn captive, believing that sudden exposure to sensuous nature would undermine Fučík's resolve and make him trade his life for party secrets.

The title of Kundera's composition is a clear allusion to the most famous Czech romantic poem, Mácha's *May*. But, besides its prominence, Kundera selected this subtext for a very specific reason. The main protagonist of *May*, the robber Vilém, shares Fučík's predicament: at the height of spring this condemned felon waits on death-row for his imminent execution. Through such an analogy Kundera is able to draw a distinction between two existential stances, two attitudes towards *thanatos*. For Vilém, alienated from society, death is the ultimate horror, the gate to the void and nothingness. And nature in *May* reminds him how cruel is his fate. For the Communist Fučík – the herald of historical optimism – death is merely a personal sacrifice, a contribution to the final victory of the Cause, outside of which life is meaningless. In an indirect dialogue with Vilém, he asserts: 'Those who live for their own life alone, / for themselves for their fleeting journey, / live like a vain meteorite, / falling into the darkness to perish' (1955, 25).

As in *The Joke*, in *The Last May* folklore plays an important role. It is a folk-song about another robber – the legendary Robin Hood of the Slovak mountains, Janosik – that nourishes Fučík's strength to deflect Böhm's temptation: 'After the death of a fighter his life / changes into a fire on mountains. / And even a small droplet of betrayal / would extinguish this big bonfire. / Am I to dissolve myself in darkness? / Am I to betray? Am I to become a suicide?'

These rhetorical questions are definitely non-aporetic, for Fučík goes on: 'Shoot me! Well! / But after I fall to the ground / the hands of friends / will lift my ax [*valaška*]. The fight will not cease' (29; 32). Caressed by the loving spring, an envigorated Fučík joyously marches back to his cell to face sure death.

In the next decade, though, Kundera's attitude towards Fučík changed considerably. *The Joke* presents him, first of all, as a symbolic participant in

Ludvík's ordeal. During the fatal meeting resulting in his expulsion from the party and the school, the chief prosecutor Zemánek dramatically juxtaposes Ludvík's postcard to his would-be girlfriend, which equates 'optimism' with 'the opium of the people' (36; 38), to Fučík's message to his wife from the *Notes*, whose unbridled pathos makes Ludvík's joke look particularly perfidious.[7] Furthermore, the meeting takes place in a classroom prominently adorned by Fučík's portrait. And the narrator, recounting this event from a distance of fifteen years, does not fail to draw attention to the idolized falsity of this image, 'almost girlish, effervescent, pure, and so beautiful that perhaps those who knew Fučík personally preferred this drawing to their memory of a real face' (188; 185).

But a full-fledged attack against the cult of Fučík which *The Last May* helped to build comes only in the later part of *The Joke*. Infuriated by a quasi-Moravian folk-song about the martyred resistance hero performed by Jaroslav's band, the injured Ludvík speaks his mind. The author of the *Notes*, he blurts out, 'though far from famous, seemed to think that it was of enormous importance to inform the world how he thought and felt in prison, what he was going through and what messages and recommendations he had for mankind.' Ludvík startles Jaroslav by saying that, contrary to the party *doxa*, Fučík wrote the *Notes*, not out of his inner strength, but rather out of 'his weakness. For to be brave in isolation, without witnesses, without the reward of affirmation, in front of just oneself, required too great a self-esteem and strength. Fučík needed the help of an audience. In the solitude of his cell he made up at least a fictitious one. He needed to be seen! To draw strength from applause! At least a fictitious applause! To change the prison into a stage and to make his lot bearable by not only living it but also by displaying and acting it! To adore himself in the beauty of his own words and gestures' (152; 149).

This novelistic reinterpretation of Fučík, it is easy to detect, stems from Kundera's vehement rejection of the Stalinist era for which this figure stands as a prominent symbol. Thus, from the larger-than-life hero of *The Last May*, in *The Joke* Fučík is transformed into a pitiful exhibitionist insecure of his identity, a laughable representative of the 'lyrical age ... when man is still an enigma to himself and others are for him the mirrors in which he seeks his own significance and value' (Liehm 1988, 58). The narcissism of his *Notes* makes Fučík a close relative to Jaromil, the immature poet/police informer from *Life Is Elsewhere* whose lyrics were the product of a similar self-obsession. This kinship is further underscored by the poet's name which, whether intentionally or perchance, harks back to Mácha's and Kundera's songs of May. Not only is the name Jaromil a male counterpart of the name Jarmila – Vilém's *femme fatale* – but also, in its literal sense, it is a designation for him 'who loves the spring' as well as for him 'who is beloved by the spring' – the characteristics of Fučík's in *The Last May* (Kundera 1980a, 7).

The irony of Kundera's treatment of his own poetry in *The Joke* rests in his ability to subvert the past through its preservation: it is neither repeated nor denied, but reinscribed, voided of its lyrical appeal and rendered ambiguous. Despite their scandalous origin – or, rather, precisely because of it – these texts served Kundera as the perfect object for his 'meditative investigation' of the old myth – the Communist utopia – to which he once subscribed. As he put it himself in 1967: 'What we've lived through in the last thirty years was no honey, but all these experiences are a great capital for art. The story of this nation between fascism, democracy, Stalinism, and socialism contains in itself all the essentials that make the twentieth century the twentieth century. It enables us to ask perhaps more essential questions and create perhaps more meaningful myths than those who did not live through this whole political anabasis' (Liehm 1988, 63).

NOTES

1 'In Kafka, Broch, Musil, Gombrowicz there is no disdain for "tradition," but another choice of tradition: they are all fascinated by the novel preceding the nineteenth century. I call this era the first "half-time" of the history of the novel. This era and its aesthetic were almost forgotten, obscured, during the nineteenth century. The "betrayal" of this first half-time deprived the novel of its play essence (so striking in Rabelais, Cervantes, Sterne, Diderot) and diminished the role of what I call "novelistic meditation"' (Oppenheim 1989, 8–9).

'Between the Bach of the Art of Fuga and the classical music that follows there is the greatest caesura that music has ever known. The average melomaniac of today still lives within the aesthetic created by Hayden, Mozart and developed later by the Romantics. What preceded, he experiences as an archaism as foreign to him (though a little more agreeable to the ear) as the modernism of Boulez or Stockhausen. The forgotten past of the first "half-time" acted on nineteenth-century music like a hidden charge, like a repression, like a complex. This is what bears witness to the greatness of Webern or of late Stravinsky ... The history of the novel, it seems to me, also knows this kind of division into two "half-times." Somewhere between Sterne and Laclos on one side and Scott and Balzac on the other, a radical change in aesthetics took place and the memory of the first half-time was concealed or repressed. When, in the fifties and sixties, the partisans of the so-called new novel criticize what they call the "traditional novel," what are they alluding to with the word "traditional"? ... One cannot dispute the nineteenth century and at the same time participate in its greatest "sin": in its forgetting of the half-time of Rabelais and Sterne' (Oppenheim 1989, 14–15).

'It is very interesting to see just how rooted we are in the first half of life, even if life's second half is filled with intense and moving experiences. Not only is there the question of experience (Gombrowicz did indeed have many important experiences in Argentina), but of obsessions, of traumatisms which are inextricably tied to the first half of life – which includes childhood, adolescence and adulthood' (Elgrably 1987, 10).

2 Kundera, *Kniha smíchu a zapomnení*, 15; *The Book of Laughter and Forgetting*, 9. Subsequent references to this text appear in parentheses with the first number indicating the pagination in the Czech original and the second, the pagination in Heim's translation.

3 The first number in parentheses refers to the pagination of *Žert* (1967); the second number to *The Joke*, translated by D. Hamblyn and D. Stallybrass (London, 1969). My quotations are taken, with some alterations, from this translation. Passages omitted in this edition are my own translations.

4 The antinomic nature of this word did not escape the attention of some other Slavic writers. Isaak Babel, for example, named the main protagonist of his novel *Red Cavalry*, Ljutov, to underscore the paradoxical character of this Jewish intellectual turned Cossack. Freud's famous essay of 1910, 'The Antithetical Meaning of Primal Words,' offers a psychoanalytic interpretation of this phenomenon.

5 For the conflicting views on Fučík's resistance activities see for example Fučíková 1961, and Cerný 1977, 321–33.

6 Kundera, in fact, creatively merged several of Fučík's and Böhm's excursions outside the prison: to a Bráník pub and to Hradcany. However, according to the *Notes*, these took place in the summer of 1942, not in May. Cf. Fučíkova 1947, 87–8 and 96; 1948, 66–7, 74–5.

7 Ludvík's reply to his accusers might be mentioned profitably here for it illustrates another facet of the interaction between Kundera's early poetry and *The Joke*. Instead of paying the expected homage to the victims of Nazism and committing a public *auto-da-fé*, Ludvík charged. 'The dead comrades,' he declared, 'were not petty, to be sure. If they had read my postcard, they might even have laughed at it' (190; 186). These words are a distinct echo of Kundera's apostrophe to the dead communist poet Biebl, 'You, Konstantin, Had Never Believed,' from the section 'Critical Verses' of his collection *Man – A Wide Garden* in which the author reproaches 'those gloomy priests / who closed themselves into Marxism as if a cold castle' (Kundera 1953, 49). For Kundera's relationship with Biebl, see Finkielkraut (1982, 23–4).

17

The Politics of Impossible Worlds

LINDA HUTCHEON

We live today in a culture where there exist computer-generated fictions – like Robert Pinsky's *Mindwheel* – which forcibly expand our notions of what an imagined world can mean to both writers and readers; it is a world in which, thanks to recent advances in computer-generated Virtual Reality, one can actually put on what is called a DataGlove and 'feel' an electronic image (Siegle 1989, 400). In such an intellectual climate, the very concept of problematizing the idea of possible worlds in literature may seem tame, not to say, out of date. And yet the problematizing does go on today – and not only by poststructuralist theorists, suspicious of any totalizing ontological structures. Within the novel form itself, there has been a much noted, general interrogation – through politics – of the nature of fiction and its worlds. I mean 'politics' here in the sense of the politics of gender, race, class, ethnicity, and sexual preference, to mention only the most obvious. In the work of writers as diverse as Maxine Hong Kingston and E.L. Doctorow, or Kathy Acker and John Berger, or Daphne Marlatt and J.M. Coetzee, the question of the cultural 'constructedness' of fiction has complicated considerably our notions of the identity and function of its possible worlds.

In order to illustrate in how complex a manner this question can be posed and with what consequences, I want to look at a novel that has been described as being 'at the intersection of feminist, post-colonial and post-modern discourses' (Dovey 1988, 11), a novel in which 'the narrator occupies shifting positions that reproduce both the contradictions and conspiracies within and amongst these discourses' (331). This 'intrinsically contradictory world' – what Lubomír Doležel and others would call an 'impossible world' (1983, 516n) – is created in a novel called *Foe*, published in 1986 by South African writer J.M. Coetzee. A work by Coetzee is a provocative test case for possible-world semantics for many reasons, not only because of his academic background in linguistics, computer science, and literature: he is professor of General Literature at the University of Cape Town and teaches often in the United States. In fact, he was in the United States when the overtly political, engaged work of South African writers like Gordimer and Paton and then Brink and Breytenbach first began to appear. Coetzee has consistently refused to pronounce publicly on the role of the South African writer today, and has come under attack for this silence; similarly, his novels have been indicted as evasively indirect about South African political realities. Nadine Gordimer saw the use of allegory in his early novels as the sign of 'a kind of opposing desire to hold himself clear of events and their daily, grubby, tragic consequences in which, like everyone else living in South Africa, he is up to the neck, and about which he had an inner compulsion to write' (1984, 3). I would like to suggest, however, that another way of looking at the specifically ironic functioning of allegory in Coetzee's fiction is to see it as one of the few possible, non-realist, and non-appropriating modes of address available to a white male who wants to negotiate the tricky waters of postcolonial and feminist politics, without falling into the many traps of bad faith that appropriation can set.

The complexity of the impossible world of Coetzee's novel *Foe* lies in its self-conscious fusion of novelistic and critical, fictive and political discourses, and also in its exploration of this particularly awkward subject position. This is the problem I want to set as a 'friendly challenge' to possible-worlds theory today. What Lubomír Doležel recently called a 'cognitive anarchism' in contemporary literary theory that sees 'a pack of hidden authoritarian conspirators' turning semiotic, cognitive, and interpretive activity into 'a tool of ideological domination' (1989b, 257) is, in the novel *Foe*, thematized, allegorized, ironized, and historicized. What Doležel ironically calls the popular 'pragmatic prime movers' – class, race, gender, history, language – are here given flesh, so to speak, within the fictional world, as Coetzee relentlessly probes the process of legitimation of representations of various kinds of imperialism (historical, sexist, racist, linguistic, hermeneutic) in his investigation and enactment of the political positioning of the white male living in South Africa.

This novel's fictional world is almost instantly recognizable as a rewriting of Daniel Defoe's eighteenth-century one in *The Life and Adventures of Robinson Crusoe*. Coetzee's narrator, however, is a woman named Susan Barton, a castaway on the island where Cruso (as it is spelled in Coetzee's text) and Friday have been living. The quite unignorable intertext is quickly ironized, however, as Susan's story begins to differ from the one the reader has heard before – and for interesting reasons. For instance, Cruso is made to die on the rescue ship on the way to an England that he did not wish to see again. Trying to get some money to survive in London, alone with Friday, Susan tells (and sells) her story to a writer, a Mr Foe. Since we know that Daniel Defoe himself added the 'De' to his name, we can recognize the author of *Robinson Crusoe* in fictionalized form. But Susan's story is not the story the historical Defoe actually wrote: among many other things, she herself has been edited out. She does foresee this possibility, even in her own narration: 'When I reflect on my story I seem to exist only as the one who came, the one who witnessed, the one who longed to be gone: a being without substance, a ghost beside the true body of Cruso. Is that the fate of all storytellers?', she asks (Coetzee 1986, 51). As she too tries to write, however, she comes to understand the difficulties facing the novelist. As she says to Foe: 'More is at stake in the history you write, I will admit, for it must not only tell the truth about us but please its readers too. Will you not bear it in mind, however, that my life is drearily suspended till your writing is done?' (63). The irony is that her life will continue to be so suspended in Defoe's final text.

Of course, it is nothing new to read *Robinson Crusoe* politically, as I am suggesting Coetzee does, but it has usually been read as a novel about capitalism and Protestantism. Its hero has been described as 'a generalized type of the resilient and self-reliant entrepreneur. His interactions with Friday signal a superiority that is rooted not in any distinct particularity but in his assured status as a "natural" (that is, European, male, bourgeois) leader' (Foley 1986, 122). Coetzee's ironic rewriting of this interpretation intensifies the role of Empire in that description and adds a complicating politics of gender. At one point, Susan tries to explain to Friday (who in this version is, significantly, mute) that Foe is a writer and that '"at this very moment he is engaged in writing another story, which is your story, and your master's, and mine. Mr Foe has not met you, but he knows of you, from what I have told him, using words. This is part of the magic of words. Through the medium of words I have given Mr Foe the particulars of you and Mr Cruso and of my year on the island and the years you and Mr Cruso spent there alone, as far as I can supply them; and all these particulars Mr Foe is weaving into a story which will make us famous throughout the land, and rich too"' (58). For the reader, the ironies here are multiple. Aside from the obvious one that Susan – though extremely liberal for her age – is using a tone that suggests she is speaking to a child, the most potent irony is that deployed through intertextuality. We know from Defoe's novel that the 'magic of words' can obliterate as well as record (and this is Susan's fate); it can subject as well as liberate (and this is Friday's second selling into slavery). Inscribed as a slave and silenced as a woman, Friday and Susan do not quite find the place they mean for themselves in *their* notions of what world might be a possible one in their story. In a passage heavy with retrospective intertextual irony for the reader, Susan tells Friday: "'Is writing not a fine thing, Friday? Are you not filled with joy to know that you will live forever, after a manner?'" (58). Foe becomes their foe, in the sense of antagonist, as he exercises the power of what Foucault once called the author's role as 'regulator of the fictive' in a capitalist, bourgeois, patriarchal, imperial society (see Dovey 1988, 334).

Both *Robinson Crusoe* and *Foe* are what Barbara Foley has called 'pseudofactual' novels, fictions that invoke 'an intrinsically ironic, even parodic contract' (1986, 107), that is, an agreement to flout the conventions of familiar modes of nonfictional discourse, such as letters, confessions, or memoirs. Indeed, Susan's story is told in the form of her letters, dated (journal?) notes, and her first-person witnessing narrative. The pseudofactual novel, though, as Foley points out, asks to be read as one kind of discourse but mobilizes 'perceptual habits and responses routinely associated with another kind of discourse' (107). *Foe* complicates this by adding a layer of intertextual recall between the nonfictional and the fictional, and by having the verifiably historical world impinge upon this (doubly) fictional one. One result is that each of the defining questions by which Thomas Pavel suggests we can begin to describe fictional discourse suddenly becomes problematic (1986, 12). For instance, the 'demarcational' questions about the possibility of establishing sharp boundaries between fiction and nonfiction turn out to be complicated, not to say dizzyingly so, in a novel where, if you 'scan the universe' for someone called 'Foe,' you might come up with a person with a related name – Daniel Defoe – but if you scan for 'Cruso,' you will find a book, not a person, with that name (or, again, with a slight variant of it). The case is somewhat different for Pavel's 'institutional' questions about the place and importance of fiction as a cultural institution because these are self-reflexively dealt with within the novel itself, though not without considerably historical irony, an irony which is multiplied when Coetzee's position as a white, male, South African novelist and academic is recalled. And what Pavel calls 'metaphysical' questions about fictional beings and truth here get reformulated into ideological questions about fictional beings and truths, in the plural, and the most important of these questions becomes: whose truth?

These are not the only issues of fictional-worlds theory that get problematized in a novel like *Foe*. How, for instance, could we characterize a fictional world that contains (to use Parsons's terminology for non-existent objects) 'native' characters (those invented in and by the text) such as Susan Barton, 'immigrant' characters from elsewhere – such as Cruso and Friday from another novel – and 'surrogate' or fictional counterparts of real people, such as Daniel Defoe? Susan cannot be a 'compossible narrative agent' (Doležel 1979b, 196) with the Friday and Crusoe we know from the novel *Robinson Crusoe*. Nor can Foe himself, of course. Lubomír Doležel asserts that '[p]ossible-worlds semantics correctly insists that fictional individuals cannot be identified with actual individuals of the same name' (1989a, 230) and that they are not dependent on actual prototypes for their existence and properties. Yet, for *Foe*, it is essential to the plot's structure and detail – as well as its politics and its ironies, as we shall see later – that it *not* be irrelevant that the real Daniel Defoe (or Foe) did write a version of Crusoe's story and that his own life both resembles and differs from that of the character in Coetzee's novel. The nature of the cross-world identification here is problematic; the referential complexity even on the level of naming makes *Foe* very much a 'mixed bag' (Doležel 1989a, 231) and contributes to the 'impossibility' of its fictional world.

Problematic and complex as it is, the fictional world of *Foe* poses problems for narrative semantics in still other ways, ways that are inseparable from the political dimensions of the novel and which have their echoes in much contemporary literary theorizing. Voicing a familiar postcolonial critique, Wilson Harris points to a semiotic problem, one that feminist and Marxist theorists have also noted: 'A narrative tool or habit of command that exercises itself as perfectly natural, perfectly beautiful and normal within a *homogeneous* cultural imperative, where it is rooted in consenting classes and common values, builds into itself an equation of inner eclipse as it generates the suppression of others in a *heterogeneous* situation' (1981b, 115). And here is my 'friendly challenge' to possible-world semantics: Could it be, by analogy, that semiotic urge to universalize rules and descriptions of narrative systems might also prove to be based on a '*homogeneous* cultural imperative' that in fact works to normalize the heterogeneous and different? Could the fictional world of a novel like Coetzee's be usefully described, for example, according to Doležel's four-part model of narrative worlds based on modal systems (1979a)? Let us take each in turn. Is *Foe*'s fictional world 'deontic': that is, are its narrated actions governed by modalities of permission, prohibition, and obligation? The expected plot structure of prohibition–violation–punishment, however, is not so much present as absent, or at least previous to the novel's action; it is also overtly challenged. It appears to emplot the story both of Friday's fate (slavers are said to have removed his tongue) and of Susan's (cast off a mutinous ship with the body of her dead lover, its deposed captain), but the causality of this plot structure is what both put into question: do Friday and Susan know why and how their 'punishment' came upon them at the hands of the more powerful? The other possible deontic plot form – of assigning a task, fulfilling it, being rewarded – is also subverted: this is what Coetzee's Cruso refuses in his deliberate, seemingly futile work on the island, and it is also what Susan is frustrated (in and by) when she takes on the task of teaching Friday to speak and write. In *Foe*, the clear norms necessary for a deontic structure are never present.

Could the novel's world, then, be better described in 'axiological' terms, in terms of goodness, badness, indifference? Here the requisite quest structure (lack of value–acquisition–possession) is indeed invoked, but it is also undermined time and time again in the novel. Antagonists and helpers, who by this theory are supposed to be clearly separate and opposite, merge as Susan is forced to question her own motivation in 'helping' Friday. As a good humanist, she claims: 'I talk to Friday to educate him out of darkness and silence.' Yet she also has to admit at once: 'I use words only as the shortest way to subject him to my will' (60). Who is the foe of whom here? Should the novel's world, then, be thought of in 'epistemic' terms of knowledge, ignorance, and belief? In a way, *Foe* is a mystery story, but the reader is constantly frustrated in any attempts to make final sense of that mystery, to transform ignorance into knowledge. If Susan's humanist desire is to help Friday, to teach him to express the 'urgings' of his heart in language, Coetzee rejects such paternalistic, imperial gestures and frustrates any attempts either to simplify the social or literary functioning of language or to reach any final stability of interpretation. The novel ends in what is called 'the home of Friday' – underwater, at a (significantly dated) 300-year-old shipwreck, where an unidentified first-person narrator tries to force open the drowned Friday's mouth, from which comes a 'slow stream ... dark and unending: But this is not a place of words. Each syllable, as it comes out, is caught and filled with water and diffused. This is the place where bodies are their own signs' (157). Friday's mouth – like his body – has been a silenced space in this novel and there is no easy knowledge that can explain such gaps.

This leaves us only the fourth, the 'alethic' system wherein possibility, impossibility, and necessity work to allow alternative or intermediate possible worlds. Perhaps the novel's final scene, mentioned earlier, constitutes an 'ambiguous world' in Doležel's sense, that is, one with uncertain truth-value, 'deprived of authentication' (1979a, 550). But the fictional universe of the rest of the novel is also deprived of any customary authentication too. Susan Barton's entire story is denied even the degree of conventional 'authentication authority' (Doležel 1980, 11) said to be granted to first-person narrators. It is primarily our knowledge of her absence from the *Robinson Crusoe* intertext that jeopardizes her credibility in the establishing of 'narrative facts,' although, as a narrator, she herself is neither particularly ironic nor lacking in consistency (two of the devices seen as annihilating authenticity). But that is surely the point: the novel suggests that it is not her tone or her narrative skills but her gender that has everything to do with her lack of narrative authority – and with her being written out of the male narrative we know as *Robinson Crusoe*.

Doležel has argued that fictional worlds can also lack authenticity if they are created by 'self-voiding' narratives that are formally either metafictional or ironic (1989a, 238). And, of course, *Foe* is nothing if not metafictional and ironic. Does this mean that the world of the novel should simply be categorized as an 'impossible' one? Or – and this is another way of putting my 'friendly challenge' – does it mean that the categories of semiotic description here are not flexible or subtle enough to deal with this kind of fiction? In other words, is this a question of a limitation of the novel's world or of the critical categories used to describe it? More specifically, can these narrative categories account for the world of a novel that is structured on two referentially contradictory tropes – allegory and parody – tropes that offer conflicting referential nods, in the first case, to an empirical, political world (past and present) and, in the second, to the intertextual world of Defoe's fiction? What happens when a novel like this flouts both consequences of the special (textual) ontological status of narrative worlds? After all, to use Doležel's formulations, *Foe*'s world is neither '*fully determined* by the text in which it is described' (1979b, 195) nor 'an *autonomous* semiotic entity existing independently of the "actual" world' (195–6). These two narrative 'universals' are, in fact, implicitly contested by the novel's intertextuality and allegory, respectively – two elements perhaps not yet fully theorized by possible-worlds semantics, but which are rife in contemporary writing and which thereby pose interesting conceptual challenges to any generalized theory about fiction. The added complication that both the intertextuality and the allegory in *Foe* are radically ironized only makes the challenge all the more provocative.

There are a number of levels on which intertextuality can be seen to function here. On a biographical or historical textual level, Daniel Defoe is known to have been politically active as a journalist and novelist: *The Shortest Way with the Dissenters* (1702) earned him a fine and a few trips to the pillory. Ironically, Coetzee's politicized novel plays down this side of the writer: Foe flees authorities here too, but this time on account of his debts. Likewise, the historical writer's wife and seven children do not appear in *Foe*, no doubt only to make easier his symbolic seduction of Susan. On another level, literary history would have it that Defoe constructed *Robinson Crusoe*'s narrative out of a real castaway tale told to him by Alexander Selkirk (or from Selkirk's tale in Edward Cooke's *A Voyage to the South Sea, and Around the World* [1712]), with added details of the accounts of marooned men from Dampier's *Voyage Round the World* (1697) and Woodes Rogers's *A Cruising Voyage Round the World* (1712); Coetzee's fictionalized version would have the source be a silenced, absented woman. A fiction? Yes, but one that raises an important political question about other silenced females in eighteenth-century travels – real and literary.

The preface to the first volume of *Robinson Crusoe* makes a point of stressing that the 'Editor believes the thing to be a just History of Fact; neither is there any Appearance of Fiction in it' (Defoe 1975, 3), yet the preface to the next volume admits that part of it is 'invention or Parable' (258) though true in 'Application,' and claims that to call it a fiction is to rob the 'Proprietor of this work' of its value (259). Signed by Crusoe himself, it asserts: 'the Story, though Allegorical, is also Historical' (259). The tension here between claims of truth-value and fictionality in the construction of Defoe's narrative world is carried into Coetzee's, but with added retrospective ironies. The version of Crusoe's life that we have come to know from Defoe's novel is one presented in Coetzee's as a tissue of fabrications – necessitated by the demands of fiction and its audience, not by any 'facts.' As Susan protests to Foe: 'You remarked it would have been better had Cruso rescued not only musket and powder and ball, but a carpenter's chest as well, and built himself a boat. I do not wish to be captious, but we lived on an island so buffeted by the wind that there was not a tree did not grow twisted and bent' (55). Similarly, the famous journal Defoe claims his Crusoe kept is only a wishful thought entertained by Susan: Coetzee's Cruso had no interest in recording his island life for posterity. Susan, in fact, suspects that Foe believes the story would be 'better without the woman': 'Yet where would you be without the woman? Would Cruso have come to you of his own accord? Could you have made up Cruso and Friday and the island with its fleas and apes and lizards? I think not. Many strengths you have, but invention is not one of them' (72). Given our knowledge of the intertext, Susan is here ironically made to subvert at once the fictiveness and the factuality of Defoe's novel.

This intertext is omnipresent and the ironic discrepancies between it and the novel we read are always as politically provocative as they are hermeneutically disruptive. Susan's depressive, silent, compulsive Cruso is not the entrepreneurial, inventive castaway who came to feel 'King and Lord of all this Country' (Defoe 1975, 80), who saved Friday from the cannibals because it was 'my Time to get me a Servant' (158); yet reading *Foe* contextually today – as the novel of a white South African novelist – the imperialist, class, and racial politics of Defoe's text are made to stand out in those ironic discrepancies of detail: Coetzee's Friday has 'woolly' curly hair, making his racial origin unmistakable, while Defoe's Friday had long, black hair that made him look 'European' (Defoe 1975, 160); Coetzee's mute Friday is also unlike Defoe's, who learned English and could converse with his master and even tell him much about the island's geographic position. What the muteness of *Foe*'s Friday foregrounds is both the physical suffering of slavery (ironically muted, so to speak, in Defoe's version) and the function of language in enslavement. In Coetzee's novel, Foe the novelist offers a theory of language that goes like this: 'It is enough that we know the names of our needs and are able to use these names to satisfy them' (149). But on the island, Cruso had taught Friday to understand only the words of his – Cruso's – needs. As Susan ironically suggests: 'But as there are not two kinds of men, Englishman and savage, so the urgings of Friday's heart will not be answered by *Fetch* or *Dig* ...' (149).

Clearly, the colonial politics underlined here go beyond the politics of those other feminizations of the Crusoe story – such as Jean Giraudoux's *Suzanne et le Pacifique* (1921) or Catherine Woillez's *Robinson des demoiselles* (1835) (see Genette 1982, 345–50). But this is not to say that the gender politics are ever absent here: Coetzee's initial fictional premise of Defoe writing Susan out of the castaways' story sees to that, and the presence of another Defoe intertext – the novel *Roxana* – makes it even clearer. Not only is Roxana's real name Susan, but the strange scenes in Coetzee's novel, where Susan is followed by a strange child (also named Susan) who claims to be her daughter and a maid (Amy), are straight out of *Roxana*. In rejecting the veracity of this maternal claim, Susan Barton symbolically rejects Defoe's male emplotment of women's lives. Susan may have originally been a castaway from a boat on which she was travelling to find her daughter, but she is utterly unlike fictive Roxana, who leaves her children behind. Rebuffing the girl, Susan says: 'She is not my daughter. Do you think women drop children and forget them as snakes lay eggs? Only a man could entertain such a fancy' (75). As is the case with Defoe's other novel, *Robinson Crusoe*, here *Roxana* is both invoked and ironized, recalled and politicized.

Such intertextual multiplicity alone would create referential contradictions that are not easily resolved into one coherent fictional world; in addition, however, the semantic doubling that all irony entails is also operative here, working to complicate even further any neat semantic categories of 'possible worlds,' even if they are taken only as models to identify against (see Hart 1988, 341). The same is true of the narrative doublings of allegory, another rhetorical form that demands a kind of 'binocular vision' on the part of the reader and, as one critic wittily notes, 'binocular vision enables depth perception' (Slemon 1988, 160). But Thomas Pavel has argued that, because of its complexity of correspondence and the difficulties of artistic economy, allegory is seldom used in fiction, though it is frequently found in the construction of sacred worlds (1986, 60). Today, however, it would seem that the site of allegorical play is in the construction of political worlds, where the ideological replaces the religious – though not without the intervention of irony.

Stephen Slemon has written at length about the resurgence in allegorical writing (especially in postcolonial cultures) and about the renewed interest in allegory in criticism because of 'the increasing purchase of poststructural codes of recognition in Western society – the valorisation of textuality, irony, and the arbitrary in the theory of meaning' (1988, 157). But in postcolonial writing, he argues, the functioning of that allegory has changed: instead of depending on a shared cultural base to enable 'correct' allegorical decoding, this kind of writing challenges that process, asking us to consider just what kind of grounding actually is required for particular allegorical communication to take place. What does it mean to say that we must understand the racial politics of Empire – both historical and contemporary – in order to decode the political allegories of *Foe*? The answer is not as simple as it may seem, and the reason is that, as many have pointed out, allegorical thinking has also been structurally part of the imperial and neocolonial process (Slemon 1988, 162), a process that *Foe* tries to dismantle, even as it appears to underwrite it. In other words, much postcolonial theory today points to various forms of double articulation – irony, allegory, mimicry – as both modes of colonial discourse and disruptions of it, as at once strategies of imperial authority and of postcolonial appropriation of, and resistance to, that authority (see Bhabha 1984 and 1985; JanMohamed 1985). But the fact that Coetzee is not a black South African cannot but condition his response to, or even 'creative reappropriation' of, allegory. This is where the ironizing of allegory – the doubling of doubling – comes into play. It is through irony that Coetzee can try to avoid the bad faith of either repeating the imperial or reappropriating the postcolonial power of allegory – and thereby destabilize both extremes at the same time as he negotiates a space for himself somewhere in between. The addition of gender politics functions to subvert as well the monologic of either extreme. Instead of the expected similarity, his ironic allegories consistently point to difference and even to multiplicity of interpretive possibilities, in an attempt to avoid both imperial and oppositional single-voicing. *Foe*, in fact, offers multiple levels of allegorical reading – none of which explains all and many of which ironically play off and contradict one another. Are we to see Cruso's island as South Africa, and Cruso as the imperialist colonizer, stubbornly set in his ways, unwilling to change, self-contained and strangely satisfied, if uninvolved, with life as it is lived far from the metropolis, suspicious of all and therefore giving full reign to his mastering impulses in terms of both the land and its people (Friday)? Or is it, perhaps, only a more general allegory of any imperial situation or of the power relations in any basic social unit?

At yet another allegorical level, the metropolitan centre of the British Empire turns out to be a foreign place for both women and blacks, as Susan and Friday discover on arriving in London and finding themselves as much castaways in the city as they were on the island. If Friday is, perforce, silent about his fate, Susan is not. But she comes to see that her storytelling too is a mode of mastery and control – over her life, but also over Friday's. Is this, then, another (more contemporary) allegory of 'the way in which the colonized subject [and, one could add, the racial Other] has been appropriated by feminist discourse' (Dovey 1988, 356) – or vice-versa? The issue here is the potentially problematic allegorical alignment – as Other – of women and the black/colonized as victims of oppression (patriarchal and imperial). There are even other possible levels of allegorical meaning relating to contemporary theory. Could we not read Susan's troubled relation to both Friday's silenced and absent tongue and his textually erased penis as a kind of ironic Lacanian allegory, as has Teresa Dovey (1988, 372–4)? Dovey also suggests that the final descent of the narrator to the submerged shipwreck is both an intertextual echo of Adrienne Rich's feminist poem, 'Diving into the Wreck' and an allegorical exploration of the unconscious (395–7), but if so, it would again have to be with a certain irony, given the author's own gender. My point here is that, in *Foe*, the allegories are never single or unironic, nor is the possible world engendered ever non-contradictory and stable. The novel's self-subverting ironies forbid any such reduction of complexity in the name of a coherent fictional world.

Allegory and irony have been considered together before – by Cicero and Quintilian – but perhaps most provocatively in Paul de Man's essay 'The Rhetoric of Temporality,' where it is argued that, while both are doubled tropes – saying one thing and meaning another – and while they share a historical connection, they are opposite faces of human experience of time and split subjectivity. The allegorical sign may indeed always refer to an anterior one, as de Man insists, but Coetzee's novel shows that the conflation of irony and allegory can problematize both the sign and its anteriority, making doubled meanings resound and rebound off one another. Instead of creating an autonomous and coherent possible world, however, this double play of ironized intertextuality and allegory moves outward into history – the reader's, the author's, the text's. Like Kafka's hybrid fictional world, Coetzee's too undermines 'the credibility of our banal and stereotyped interpretations of the *actual* world' (Doležel 1984b, 82). It also undermines our formalist tendencies to deprive the fictional world of a political dimension of relevance to the actual world.

Thomas Pavel once used an interesting metaphor to describe a similar process of contact with the actual:

The mobility and poor determinacy of fictional frontiers is often part of a larger pattern of interaction between the domain of fiction and the actual world. Fictional domains can acquire a certain independence, subsist outside the limits of actuality, and sometimes strongly influence us, *not unlike a colony established overseas that develops its own unusual constitution and later comes to affect in various ways the life of the metropolis.* Such is the case of the fictions of wisdom, parables ... [and I would add, novels like *Foe*]: their fictional content hastily rebounds, so to speak, in what could be called the semantic mapping of their contents upon the actual world. (1986, 84)

The colonial metaphor of the relation of fiction to actuality is obviously a convenient one for me here, but it can also serve as a partial answer to Coetzee's critics who see his work as not going far enough in openly castigating the South African apartheid system, in showing the economic and racial conditions of oppression, in projecting the defeat of the oppressors (see Vaughan 1982, Rich 1982). To these and to those who see his use of allegory as a sign of some 'stately fastidiousness' (Gordimer 1984, 3), I would reply that the indirectness of allegory and intertextuality is not necessarily a sign of evasion or cowardice. In Coetzee's hands, it is instead an ironized and pluralized mode of 'semantic mapping' onto the actual world that avoids the dangers of appropriating postcolonial strategies of resistance, while still addressing social and political issues about which, as a white South African, he too can feel strongly. His awareness, however, of what Wilson Harris (1981) calls the problems of 'liberal pretensions' that mask ambitions to power leads him to thematize overtly those problems within his novel itself. Susan Barton sees herself as what we today would call a liberal: she does care for Friday after Cruso's death and genuinely wants to free him. And yet, ironically, even she cannot evade her culture's ideology. She tells us, for instance, that whenever she spoke to Friday she was sure to 'smile and touch his arm, treating him as we treat a frightened horse' (Coetzee 1986, 41–2). While she can guess that upon 'the sorrows' of Friday's life 'a story entire of itself might be built,' she omits them from her narrative to Foe (though indeed, Friday's muteness would prevent her knowing much of those sorrows, however liberal her humane and humanist imagination). At times even Susan appropriates Friday's role vis-à-vis her 'master,' as she calls Foe, telling Friday that his physical labour for Cruso on the island was less taxing than is her writing for Foe. The ironies abound and rebound in her address to Friday: 'Sometimes I believe it is I who have become the slave. No doubt you would smile, if you could understand' (87). Yet at other times, she rejects any such facile connection. When Foe identifies her silences with those of Friday, she protests: 'Friday has no command of words and therefore no defence against being re-shaped day by day in conformity with the desires of others. I say he is a cannibal and he becomes a cannibal; I say he is a laundryman and he becomes a laundryman. What is the truth of Friday? You will respond: he is neither cannibal nor laundryman, these are mere names, they do not touch his essence ... But that is not so. No matter what he is to himself (is he anything to himself? – how can he tell us?), what he is to the world is what I make of him' (121–2). The multiple ironies here include the fact that Friday will be to the world what Defoe (and Coetzee), not Susan, makes of him. When she asserts, 'It is still in my power to guide and amend' (123), she is wrong, for Foe will symbolically rob her of her tongue as surely as the slavers have literally robbed Friday of his. But another ironic level is added when Susan's 'liberal pretensions' fall away and she has to admit, even after she has officially granted Friday his emancipation: 'If he was not a slave, was he nevertheless not the helpless captive of my desire to have our story told? How did he differ from one of the wild Indians whom explorers bring back with them ...?' (150).

Or, to put it in another (allegorical) context, how does he differ from the woman and black whose silenced stories the male, white Coetzee chooses to tell? How can their stories be told without acknowledging the inevitable distance that biology and history entail, that culture and ideology construct and reflect – and that irony embodies and enables. The dilemma of the white, male South African – not postcolonial resistance – is what the novel *Foe* presents in its semantically 'impossible world' of fiction in which the often contradictory agendas of gender and racial politics meet and clash. There is a challenge here both for possible-worlds theory (as the 'modal logical delineation of relations' [Hart 1988, 321]) and for fictional world theory (as the way to analyse how fictional texts are read). And the challenge simply is to find a more satisfying way of dealing with such 'impossibility' in politicized metafictional novels such as this. Robert Siegle suggests that this combination is becoming the norm in fiction today. He claims that '[w]riting narrative without a real critical edge may well come to feel like crafting jeweled eggs for the Romanovs' (1989, 399). The danger for narrative semantics is that, because of its seeming reluctance to go beyond this category of 'impossible' to describe worlds created in (and with) that 'real critical edge' of things, it will not stretch its explanatory power to include these political dimensions, and thus risk irrelevance. I offer this paper, then, as a respectful challenge and perhaps as a somewhat subversive footnote to the final words of Lubomír Doležel's Nobel Symposium lecture, but I am going to apply his words about the 'ultimate impossibility of constructing a fictionally authentic impossible world' (1989a, 239) in Robbe-Grillet's work to the even more apt world of novels like *Foe*: 'Fiction-making becomes

PART 5
POETICS

18

Thoughts on Aristotle's *Poetics*

UMBERTO ECO

THE *POETICS* IN ITALY

Italian culture has produced the great Renaissance commentators, and during the Baroque period, it was with the *Cannocchiale aristotelico* that Emanuele Tesauro offered to the world of post-Galilean physics the poetic and linguistic theories of Aristotle as the unique scientific guide for approaching the main issues in the humanities. However, in the third decade of the next century this same Italian culture was shaken by Giambattista Vico's *Scienza Nuova*, which challenged all Aristotelian precepts, as well as those only prefigured by Aristotle. Vico came to tell us of a language and a poetry that developed beyond any rules. While in France, from Boileau to Batteux, from Le Bossu to Dubos, up until the *Encyclopédie*, the rules of taste, the rules of tragedy, were still being sought. Vico unwittingly opened the door to a philosophy, a linguistics, and an aesthetics of unforeseeable freedom of spirit. Rather than emerging in the genteel and classic French *esprit*, this freedom characterizes the Romantic and Hegelian *Geist*, which is created by and as History. Hence the refusal of all rhetoric and poetics in the idealism of the twentieth century, and particularly in that of Croce, who dominated our culture for almost a century. Idealist aesthetics understands the whole of language as founded from the outset on aesthetic creativity; in this conception, the poetic phenomenon could not but be described as a deviation from a pre-existing norm, rather than as the emergence of language itself which established rules that a subsequent poetic act would destroy in turn. The few pages that Croce devotes to Aristotle reveal immovable prejudice. Since aesthetics begins with Baumgarten and with his notion of *scientia cognitionis sensitive, gnoseologia inferior*, and since Aristotle did not know Baumgarten, the Stagirite appears to have said nothing about art.

FROM ARNOLD TO JOYCE

I remember the delightful shiver I felt when, marginalized to the point that I felt like a little homosexual in Victorian society, I discovered that the whole Anglo-Saxon tradition had without a break continued to take Aristotle's *Poetics* seriously. I was not surprised to find traces of Aristotle in Dryden or Hobbes, Reynolds or Samuel Johnson, not to mention the references to the *Poetics* however imprecise and contradictory in Wordsworth and Coleridge, as I was not surprised to find them in Lessing, Goethe, or Nietzsche. However, it was in reading the critics and theoreticians and even the Anglo-Saxon poets who were contemporaries of Croce that I found myself before a culture for whom Aristotle was still a living model.

One of the classics of American critical theory, Richards's *Principles of Literary Criticism* (1924), opens with an allusion to Aristotle's literary criticism. If Wellek's and Warren's *Theory of Literature* (1949) succeeded in blending the principles of Anglo-Saxon criticism with the investigations of the Russian formalists and the Prague structuralists, it is because nearly every chapter of this book follows Aristotelian standards. During the forties, the masters of the New Criticism measured themselves against Aristotle.

I discovered the Chicago school, which defined itself without reservation as neo-Aristotelian, and also a theatre theoretician, Francis Fergusson (*The Idea of a Theater*, 1949), who used notions of *plot* and *action* and interpreted *Macbeth* in terms of the imitation of action. I also discovered Northrop Frye, who, in *Anatomy of Criticism*, worked with the notion of *mythos*.

However, it suffices to cite here the influence of the *Poetics* on a writer such as Joyce. Not only does he mention the work in the 1903 *Paris Notebook*, written while reading at the Bibliothèque Sainte-Geneviève, but in 1904 he dedicates an ironic poem to Katharsis. He told Stuart Gilbert that the 'Aeolus' episode in *Ulysses* was based on the *Rhetoric*. In a letter to his brother Stanislaus, dated 9 March 1903, he criticizes Synge for not being Aristotelian enough for his taste (1966, 2: 35). In a letter to Pound dated 9 April 1917, he says about *Ulysses*, 'I am doing it, as Aristotle would say, by different means in different parts' (1957, 2: 101). Finally the theory of literary genres in *Portrait of the Artist* is clearly of Aristotelian origin. In *Portrait*, Stephen Dedalus elaborates a definition of pity and terror deploring the fact that Aristotle had not done it in the *Poetics* while ignoring that he had done so in the *Rhetoric*. By some sort of exceptional elective affinity, the definitions he invents are very close to those of the *Rhetoric*. But he was studying with the Jesuits and, through his twice-removed Aquinas, some three-times-removed Aristotle must have come down to him – not to mention the English-speaking cultural milieu in which he lived and whose Aristotelian tendencies I am now tracing.

POE

I believe that I had my definitive Aristotelian experience upon reading *The Philosophy of Composition* by Edgar Allan Poe, wherein he analyses word by word, structure by structure, the genesis, the technique, and the *raison d'être* of *The Raven* (a poem, not a play, although it is a narrative poem). In this text Aristotle is never named, but his model is always present even in the use of certain key words.

While taking into account a unified impression (which is materially the time unit of reading), place, and emotional tone, Poe's project consists in demonstrating how the effect of an 'intense and pure elevation of *soul*' (which is Beauty) is gained at the cost of a meticulous ordering of the metrical and lexical structures in order to show how 'the work proceeded, step by step, to its completion with the precision and rigid consequence of a mathematical problem' (Poe 1965, 21, 22). What is scandalous in this text is that the author explains the rules by which he was able to give the impression of spontaneity. However, this represents the great lesson of the *Poetics* against all poetics of the ineffable.

This Aristotelian lesson is even found in Pseudo-Longinus's *On the Sublime*, which is always held up as an example of the celebration of an aesthetic of *je ne sais quoi*. *On the Sublime* certainly wants to speak to us of poetic effects that are based not on rational or moral persuasion, but on sensations of wonder and marvel that are produced like ecstasy and flash. But from the very first page of the treatise, the anonymous author wants not only to define the object of his inquiry but also to tell us by what means it can be produced. Hence, in the second part of the treatise, a detailed analysis is developed, which regards the rhetorical strategies to be set in motion in order to attain that effect which one cannot define. It is worth reminding that, in Pseudo-Longinus, this effect is obtained through definable devices.

Poe proceeds in a similar fashion, except that *The Philosophy of Composition* is a fascinating and ambiguous text. His *Philosophy* offers a set of prescriptions given to other poets; at the same time, it is an implicit theory for all art extrapolated from the personal writing experience of an author who plays the role of critical reader of his own work.

The fertile ambiguity of this text was noted by Kenneth Burke, who first approaches Poe's text in explicitly Aristotelian terms (Burke 1966). If there is a discipline named Poetics, it has nothing to do with criticism understood as market-place reviewing or as the distribution of praise or blame. It deals with one of the dimensions of language, and in this way it is the object of the critic proper, in the same way as the poem is the object of the poet. 'An approach to the poem in terms of Poetics is an approach in terms of the poem's nature as a kind (a literary species or mode).' In this fashion, Burke's definition is close to that of the members of the Prague school, for whom poetics is the discipline that explains the *literaturnost* of literature, that is, the property defining literary texts and literary texts alone.

Burke knows that to define the literary rules and procedures of a genre can lead to the transformation of a descriptive science into a prescriptive list of rules to follow. Burke himself, ourselves too, cannot escape from the duty of formulating the precepts that are implicit in the poet's praxis even if the artist is not conscious of them.

Poe, in contrast, was conscious of them and thus worked as a *philosophus additus artifici*. Perhaps he did it as an afterthought. Perhaps he did not realize what he was doing while writing, but, I surmise, upon reading his own text, he became aware of his own praxis. Poe's analysis could have been done by a reader such as Jakobson.

In formulating certain writing practices which a given work exemplifies, Poe identifies the general strategies that characterize all artistic processes.

Poe's essay is Aristotelian in its spirit, aims, results, and ambiguities. Lubomír Doležel has recently written an essay entitled 'Aristotelian Poetics as a Science of Literature' (1984), published as a chapter of his *Occidental Poetics*. There he asks himself if Aristotle's *Poetics* is a work of criticism (which seeks to evaluate works) or a poetics (which seeks knowledge of the conditions of literariness).

The *Poetics* (here Doležel cites Frye [1957, 14]) challenges an intelligible structure of knowledge that is not poetry itself nor even an experience of poetry. Appealing to certain distinctions in the *Metaphysics* (6.1.1025b, 1026b), Doležel considers poetics as a productive science which seeks knowledge in order to create objects.

In this way the *Poetics* does not interpret individual works to which it would have recourse only as a repertoire of examples. What it wants to find is a universal mechanism present in different works. Doležel does not fail to see that this dream of the *Poetics* falls prey to a paradox: in seeking to capture the essence of poetry, it loses its essential characteristic, the unicity and variability of its manifestations. He notes that the *Poetics* is, at one and the same time, both the founding of the study of literature and the founding of Western literary criticism. This double characteristic points to the fundamental contradiction of Aristotle's work. The *Poetics* establishes a critical metalanguage of tragedy and allows critical judgments to be based on the knowledge it supplies. However, this result is gained at a certain price.

A poetics of an ideal structure, which needs to ignore the particularities possessed by individual works, is nevertheless a theory about works that the theoretician judges the best. The *Poetics* is fated to be a disguised axiology, and Aristotle betrays his critical preferences at the very moment he chooses his examples. According to Else (1957, 233), quoted by Doležel (1990a, 178 n. 8), only one-tenth of all Greek tragedies could be made to fit the structure outlined by Aristotle. Vicious circle: an intuitive critical judgment precedes the choice of a corpus upon which is elaborated the general description which will critically justify this corpus. Doležel notes that even Else's statement is the result of a prior critical choice but that the argument still holds because it brings to light the existence of a vicious circle which will probably vitiate the entire history of poetics and criticism.[1]

So we do not find ourselves in front of what has been believed to represent a debate between a prescriptive poetics ('one must do this and this') and an aesthetics which moves at such a level of generality that it escapes any compromise with the reality of works. In fact, 'beauty as the splendour of gathered transcendentals' is a definition that allows one to explain either *Oedipus Rex* or Disneyland. With Aristotle, we find ourselves in front of a descriptive theory and a critical practice, the one presupposing the other.

ERGON

However, Aristotle does give one very explicit criterion of judgment. He does not speak of criteria of measure and order, of verisimilitude and necessity, or organic balance (1450b21 ff.), but of that other criterion which will upset any purely formalist reading of the *Poetics*. The fundamental element of tragedy is plot, and plot is the imitation of an action whose end, its *telos*, is its effect, its *ergon*. And this *ergon* is *katharsis*. A beautiful or well-executed tragedy knows how to provoke the most complete purification. Thus the cathartic effect is a kind of final crowning of the tragic enterprise which does not reside in tragedy as either written or performed discourse but as a discourse that is received. The *Poetics* represents the advent of an aesthetics of reception.

Does the basing of the final evaluation of a work upon its reception mean that the final meaning of a work derives from the spectator's freedom of interpretation?

We know that catharsis can be interpreted in two ways. Both are invited by this enigmatic expression which appears in 1449b27–8: 'Tragedy realises *ten ton toioùton pathemàton kàtharsin*.' Too much ink has been spilt by this terrible phrase. It is either a purification that frees us from our passions or, as it might be suggested by the *Politics*,[2] a purification understood in traditional medical terms, as a homeopathic action liberating spectators through their participation in the characters' passions. And, thus, catharsis imposes itself as the acceptance of that which we cannot do without and of that which purifies us against our will. In this manner tragedy is a corybantic and psychagogic machine. (If detachment is possible, it can only be produced through comedy. Alas, about that we know so little.)

Or catharsis is understood in its allopathic meaning as a purification undergone by our passions themselves as represented and perceived from afar as the passions of others by the cold gaze of the spectator who becomes a pure and dispassionate eye on the text on which it feasts. In this case, the spectator would possess the freedom to judge if the purification really did happen and ascertain the pleasure or refuse the cathartic effect. However, if tragedy is approached from its victorious strategy, freedom is reduced. The empire of (tragic) sense captures those things that escape the empire of the senses.

Of course, in both cases one could certainly say that everyone possesses his or her own manner of either purifying themselves or contemplating the purification of others. But this would deconstruct Aristotle more than he allows for. I think that for Aristotle there was only one correct way to attain either purification or pleasure, if it is indeed true that any *pharmakon* can be either poison or medicine. But once it is taken as medicine, its operation follows a prescribed course.

Furthermore, the rules to produce pity or terror are rather well delineated in the *Rhetoric* (2.1380a). The operations work according to the formula of the excitement of passions. These operations already have been confirmed through Aristotle's study of *endoxa*, that is, common opinions and inclinations.

The ambiguity of 'catharsis' is due to the sources to which Aristotle referred. One cannot avoid the Pythagorean sources of the notion of catharsis: 'at other times they [the Pythagoreans] used music as a medical treatment. There are certain melodies created for the soul's emotions which, in fact, were designed to be most helpful against despondency and mental suffering; and, again, other melodies against rages, angers, and against every mental disturbance of a soul so afflicted; there is also another kind of musical composition invented for the desires' (Jamblichus 1991, 135§111). And Pythagoras used for cathartic functions poetic texts: Homer, dithyrambs, epicedia, and threnodies. It is likely that Aristotle wished to speak about purification that comes about through an act of vision free of the prodigious sequences of the great tragic animal. Yet, at the same time, he was fascinated by the psychagogic forces which his cultural milieu described for him. We should not make him more modern than he was. And thus at the heart of the *Poetics* is played out the drama of a freedom of interpretation conquered by the rhetorical power of the text's discursive strategies.

PLOT

There are other fertile ambiguities that make the *Poetics* present to us. Although a product of its time, the *Poetics* does not serve to understand Greek tragedy. The Hellenistic Aristotle no longer quite grasps the spirit of the fifth century whose religious sentiment he has lost. He works somewhat like the modern Western ethnologists who look for universal invariants in tribal tales which fascinate them but which they only understand from the outside. And here thus is the other, very modern, reading of Aristotle, but one that Aristotle vindicates. In pretending to speak about tragedy he in fact delivers to us a semiology of all narrative possibilities.

A tragic performance contains *ethos, muthos, lexis, melos, opsis, dianoia* but 'the most important of these elements is the systematic ordering of events, *mégiston de toùton estìn e ton pragmàton sustasis ... oste ta pràgmata kai o mythos tèlos tes tragoidìas'* (1450a15–23).

Ricoeur (1984) says that in the *Poetics* it is the case that what was in principle the species of a genus (narration based on plot), this capacity of composing a mythos as *e ton pragmaton sustasis*, becomes the general genus through which epic is transformed into a species. The genus with which the *Poetics* deals is the representation of an action (*pragma*) through a plot (*mythos*) from which the species of epic diegesis and dramatic mimesis are derived.

Thus the theory of plot embodies perhaps the most profound influence that the *Poetics* has exercised in this century.

The Russian formalists, who gave birth to the first modern theory of narrative, proposed the distinction between *fabula* and *sjuzet* and the decomposition of the *fabula* into a series of narrative functions and motives. It is difficult to find direct references to Aristotle in the texts of Skhlovsky and Veselovsky or Propp, but the first study on the Russian formalists, that of Victor Erlich (1969), clearly demonstrated the indebtedness of the formalists to the Aristotelian tradition even if, as Erlich rightly remarks, the formalist notions of *fabula* and *sjuzet* are not strictly co-extensive with Aristotelian concepts. In a similar vein, one could say that Aristotle's narrative functions are less numerous than those of Propp. However, undoubtedly, the principle was already there. All this had been noticed by the structuralist critics of the sixties. Yet it would be unfair not to recall here the dramatic situations described by Polti and Souriau, with their nebulous filiation to Gozzi – ergo one eighteenth-century Italian who had not forgotten Aristotle. 'The narratives of the world are numberless ...,' wrote Roland Barthes. 'It is thus legitimate that, far from the abandoning of any idea of dealing with narrative on the grounds of its universality, there should have been (from Aristotle on) a periodic interest in narrative form and it is normal that the newly developing structuralism should make this form one of its first concerns ...' (1977, 74, 80).

In the same celebrated issue of *Communications*, readings of Aristotle were the basis of Genette's essay 'Frontières du récit' (1966). They also served to launch Brémond's narrative semiology, which could be interpreted as a detailed working out of formal structures suggested by Aristotle (interestingly, Todorov who demonstrates in his later work a sound knowledge of Aristotle will base his *Grammaire du Décameron* solely on grammatical categories).

I am not saying that a theory of plot and narrativity has imposed itself only in this century.[3] The problem is rather to understand why contemporary culture returns to this 'potent' aspect of the *Poetics* at the very moment when we are told that the form of the novel is disintegrating.

However – if it be true – listening and telling tales is a biological function. One does not escape the charm of pure plot. Joyce escapes the rules of Attic tragedy; he does not escape the Aristotelian theory of narrativity. He challenges it, yet he acknowledges it in undermining it. The non-adventures of Molly and Leopold Bloom result in comprehension because they are outlined against the background of our memories of Fielding's *Tom Jones* or Fénelon's *Télémaque*. Even the refusal of the novel Nouveau Roman to make us experience pity and terror becomes exciting against our deep conviction that a story must produce pity and terror. And thus biology exacts its revenge. If literature does not supply us with plots, we find them in American made-for-television films or by default on the front page in the news stories from Kuwait.[4]

However, there is another reason why our age is fascinated by the theory of plot. That is, we have managed to persuade ourselves that the model of the *fabula-sjuzet* pair, *pragma* and *mythos*, serve not only to explain the kind of literary narratives called 'fiction' by the Anglos. That is, all discourse possesses a deep structure which is narrative or which can be deployed in terms of narrative structures. I could cite the analysis of Dumézil's introduction to *Naissance d'archanges* done by Greimas who shows that the scientific text manifests a polemical structure that is produced by academic stunts, struggles against opponents, success and failure. Instead, I will refer to *The Role of the Reader* (1979), where I attempted to demonstrate that one can find *fabulae* hidden even in the opening text of Spinoza's *Ethics*, a text shorn of any story line: 'Per causam sui intelligo id cujus essentia involvit existentiam; sive id cujus natura non potest concipi nisi existens.' Here are nested at least two *fabulae*. The one concerns a grammatically implied agent – *ego* – who accomplishes the action of understanding or signifying and who, in doing this, passes from a state of confused knowing to a state of clearer understanding of what god is. Let us note that if *intelligo* is interpreted as 'I understand' or 'I recognize,' god remains an object unmodified by the action. But if the same verb is understood to mean 'I wish to signify' or 'I wish to say,' then the agent institutes through the action of its own definition its own object as a cultural unit (i.e., makes it *be*).

This object with its attributes is, furthermore, the subject of the nested *fabula*. It is a subject who accomplishes an action by which, by the very fact of being, exists. It seems that in this adventure of divine nature nothing 'happens' because there is no time gap between the actualization of the essence and the actualization of the existence (and that the latter does not change the state represented by the former). As to being, it does not appear to be an action through which that which exists is produced. However, this is a limit example. In this story the action as well as the passage of time are at a *zero degree* (infinity). God always acts through automanifestation and persists forever, always producing the fact of his existence through the very fact that he is. This is meagre for a thriller, but it is enough to allow us to indicate at a zero degree the essential conditions of a *fabula*. The Model Reader of such a story is a mystic or a metaphysician, a type of textual co-operator capable of feeling intense emotion before this non-adventure which, however, does not cease to amaze by its very singular character. And if nothing new happens it is because *ordo et connectio rerum idem est ac ordo et connectio idearum*. All has been said. *Amor Dei Intellectualis* is also an ardent passion. And the inexhaustible wonder of the recognition of Necessity exists. This *fabula* is, in a manner of speaking, so transparent that it leads us immediately to a fixed structure of pure actants.

If in our time it is being discovered that all philosophic and scientific discourse can be read as narration, would it not be because in other times philosophy and science, having lost their faith in their own specificity, have attempted to refashion themselves as great tales? And if these great philosophic tales are not enough, is it not true that contemporary philosophy is conducted not through analysis stemming from past philosophies but through narrators, be they Proust's or Kafka's, Joyce's or Mann's?

MASS MEDIA

The *Poetics*, as we have said, has many faces. It cannot be a fruitful book without having at times produced contradictory results. Among my first discoveries of the contemporary presence of Aristotle, there was a certain Mortimer Adler who had established a film aesthetic on Aristotelian bases. In *Art and Prudence*,

Adler gave this definition of film: 'Motion picture is an imitation of a complete action, having a certain magnitude, in the conjoint medium of picture, words and sound effects, musical or otherwise' (1937, 486). Perhaps the definition was a bit scholastic – Adler was a Thomist who later inspired Marshall McLuhan. But the idea that the *Poetics*, if insufficient to define great literature, appeared to be able, in any case, to be a perfect theory of popular literature was supported by other authors.[5]

I do not find acceptable the idea that the *Poetics* is incapable of defining high art. However, it is certain that it can be, with its laws of plot, particularly adept at describing the underhanded means of the mass media. The *Poetics* is certainly a theory, among others, of the Western à la John Ford and not because Aristotle was a prophet but because if one wants to depict an action through a plot, which a Western does without surfeit, one can but do what Aristotle had already defined and described. Since telling a story is a biological function, out of this biology of narrativity Aristotle said what he did.

So the mass media are not in opposition to our biological tendencies. On the contrary, we could blame them for being 'human, all too human,' for remaining purely biological. The problem is whether the pity and terror that they sell truly lead to catharsis or whether we are to understand catharsis in the minimal state of 'cry and you will feel better.' In any case, pity and terror take after the homeopathic and Pythagorean side of the *Poetics*.

And think – following Aristotle's advice for the construction of a *mythos* which produces an efficacious *ergon* – that one can fall into the purely biological. To come back to Poe, just reading the pages he devotes to the production of the emotion at which he aimed, he may appear to be a *Dallas* screenwriter. In wishing to write in a little more than a hundred lines a poem that produces an impression of melancholy ('since Melancholy is the most legitimate of the poetic tones'), he has asked himself: among all the melancholic topics, which is the most melancholic if one confines oneself to the universal inclinations of human beings? But, of course, death. And which death is the most melancholic of all? It goes without saying: the death of a beautiful woman. She is 'unquestionably the most poetical topic in the world.' If Poe had confined himself to this topic alone, he would have really written something to make everyone cry as they did watching *Love Story*.

Luckily, Poe knew that, if the plot is the dominant function of any story, tragic or not, it must be tempered with other elements. So he escapes the mass media net because he has purely formal ideas which apparently have nothing to do with what the narrow-minded Messieurs Homais of this world identify with poetry, ideas such as placing the black bird on the white statue of Minerva. Why?

I made the bird alight on the bust of Pallas, also for the effect of contrast between the marble and the plumage ... the bust of *Pallas* being chosen, first, as most in keeping with the scholarship of the lover, and, secondly, for the sonorousness of the word, Pallas, itself ...

And the Raven, never flitting, still is sitting, *still* is sitting
On the pallid bust of Pallas, just above my chamber door. (Poe 1965, 29, 32)

Lexis, opsis, dianoia, ethos, melos, all at once. What a beautiful way to arrange a mythos. The mass media can provoke tears, but they do not produce this form of purification through the contemplation of a well-fashioned, great, and beautiful animal. And if they do succeed at times, then it is John Ford and *Stagecoach*, that is, the *Poetics* understood and relived.

METAPHOR

Let us come to the last ambiguity. The *Poetics* is a text that establishes for the first time a theory of metaphor. Regarding this issue, Ricoeur cites Derrida's 'Mythologie blanche': 'Every time a rhetoric defines a metaphor, it implies not only a philosophy but a conceptual network in which *philosophy* is constituted ... The defined is thus implied by the definer of the definition' (1975, 25). Ricoeur notes that 'to explain metaphor, Aristotle creates a metaphor borrowed from the domain of movement.' Indeed, it is at the very centre of this theory that we find ourselves facing the basic problem of all philosophy: is metaphor a distance from an underlying literariness or is it the birthplace of all future literarity? If I remain faithful to a theory of interpretation that in the face of texts which are already written must at least presuppose a zero degree of the literal, then metaphor would be the gap to interpret. But if we situate ourselves in line with a glottogogic point of view (either at the emergence of all language, as Vico wished, or at the emergence of a text in the process of creating itself), we must take into account the moments where creativity emerges and language arises through metaphoric waves that name an object or a plurality of objects as yet unknown and unnamed.

The cognitive power of metaphor upon which Aristotle insisted – in the *Rhetoric*, not in the *Poetics* – is deployed either as metaphor presenting us with something new by working pre-existing language or as metaphor inviting us to discover through its meaning the rules of a language to come. But the latest Aristotelian heirs, the heretical currents of Chomskian linguistics and George Lakoff in particular, today present the problem in a much more radical manner, which, by the way, is already present in Vico. The problem is not to examine what a creative and artistic metaphor does to a language which is already there, but rather to examine how existing language can be understood only by accepting – in the dictionary that explains it – the presence of the vagueness, the fuzziness of metaphoric bricolage.[6]

ACTION

Which brings us to our concluding remarks because it may perhaps be coincidental, but nevertheless interesting, that Lakoff is among the authors who have begun – on the ruins of a naive semantics wherein definition was based on a series of atomic properties – to elaborate a semantics wherein definition is represented under the form of a sequence of actions. One of the pioneers of this tendency was Kenneth Burke who acknowledged his debt to Aristotle. In his analysis of the grammar, rhetoric, and symbolism of motives, Burke presented philosophy and all of literature and, furthermore, language in a 'dramatic' fashion through the play of six motives, that is, act, scene, agent, agency, purpose.

At the very heart of a theory of imitation of the *pragmata*, one already finds in Aristotle the beginnings of a theory of action. We are beginning to understand today that even the definitions of so-called essences cannot be proposed other than in terms of underlying actions.

Not to mention Greimas who makes no effort to hide that a theory of narrativity presides over all semantic comprehension. I am thinking of case grammar which works a narrative structure by agent, counter-agent, goal, instrument, etc. (Fillmore, Bierwisch) and of many models in frame theory and artificial intelligence. Dominique Noguez has recently published a nice humorous piece (in which I play the role of one of the heroes or victims) on the semiology of the umbrella. He did not know that reality surpasses fiction and that one of the most famous studies in artificial intelligence is that of Charniak who, in order to explain to a computer how to interpret sentences containing the word 'umbrella,' supplied the machine with a narrative description of what one does with an umbrella, how it is manipulated, and how it is made. The concept of umbrella resolves itself into a network of actions.

Aristotle did not manage to suture his theory of action with his theory of definition because, being imprisoned in his system of categories, he believed that there were anterior substances which permitted or bore any action. The crisis of the concept of substance had to be awaited to rediscover a new semantics implicit not in his works on logic, but in the *Ethics*, the *Poetics*, and the *Rhetoric*.

To conclude, I would like to relate a myth, a philosophical myth. According to this myth, Adam (or, in the original Greek version, *Nomothète* or 'maker of names') was looking at things and giving them names. The comic situation of the first man sitting under a tree designating a flower or an animal and declaring, 'This will be a daisy, this a crocodile,' became dramatic when the first philosophers of language had to decide if these names had been given according to a convention (*Nomos*) or according to the nature of the things (*Physis*). The semantic analysis of the expressions using primitive atoms as a stenographic *extrema ratio*, the use of definitions such as 'tiger = carnivorous mammal or big yellow cat with zebra stripes,' is only taken seriously in an academic milieu.

According to an example of Peirce (1932, 330), '*lithium*' is defined not only by its position in the periodic table nor by an atomic number, but by the description of the operations which must be carried out to produce a specimen. Peirce's definition also predicts the possible contexts in which the expression 'lithium' may be found. If, for the sake of the story, we trust that Adam knew and named lithium, then we must say that he did not simply assign a name to a thing. He was inventing a given expression to act as a hook upon which to hang a series of descriptions, and these descriptions depict, along with the sequence of actions done with and upon lithium, the series of contexts in which he encountered and expected to encounter lithium.

According to my revised version of the myth, Adam did not perceive the tigers as simple individual specimens of a natural species. He saw certain animals, equipped with certain morphological characteristics in proportion to which they developed certain types of action in interaction with other animals and their natural environment. Thus he decreed that a subject x acting habitually against other subjects to attain certain goals, usually displaying itself in such and such circumstances, etc., was only a part of a story X – the story being inseparable from the subject in question and the subject being an indispensable part of the story. This single section of knowledge about the world, this subject x in action, could be called a tiger.

By the light of this version of the myth, we can understand better all the arguments that Plato enumerates in the *Cratylus* in order to support a theory of origins motivated by naming. All the examples of motivation that he gives concern a mode by which the words represent not the thing itself but the thing as the source or result of an action. Take the example of Jupiter. Plato says that the strange difference between the nominative and the genitive in the name 'Zeus-Dios' is due to the fact that the original name was a syntagm expressing the habitual action of the king of the gods, *díon zen*, the one who gives life.

In a similar fashion, man, *anthropos*, would be reducible to the one who is capable of reconsidering what he has seen. The difference between man and animals is that man not only perceives but also reasons, reflects upon what he has perceived. We are tempted to treat Plato's etymology seriously when we recall that Aquinas, when considering the classical definition of man as a mortal and rational animal, maintained that 'mortal' and 'animal' (the *differentiae* of what distinguishes man from other species of the animal genus) are not atomic accidents as is usually believed. They are the names that we give to a sequence of actions or behaviours through which we recognize by inference that men are a kind of substantial form fundamentally unknown and otherwise unapparent. We discover that men are capable of reason because we accept, in considering human activity, the existence of such a quality, as in a similar fashion we infer a cause from its habitual symptom (*Summa Theologica* 1.79.8). We know our faculties *ex ipsorum actuum qualitate*, that is, through the quality of the actions of which they are the origin (*Summa Contra Gentiles* 4.46).

Myths are what they are – still, we need them. I have simply placed in opposition to a bad myth, a good one, wherein christening names not things but the stories that produce their own actors. This is what the *Poetics* of Aristotle inspired in me.

NOTES

1 Furthermore, Else has noted that in chapter 18 (1455b25 ff.), Aristotle traces the typology of four types of tragedy, each defined in respect to a dominant structural tendency (complex tragedy, tragedy of violent effects, character tragedy, and tragedy of spectacle). There would thus be an open structure with major variables and as a function of to what extent the various parts of a tragedy can assume a leading role there would exist the different types of tragedy and hence different evaluation criteria. If the definition of tragedy seems static, its typology supported by different examples recognizes the possibility of structural mutation and destroys all axiology.

2 Unfortunately, the *Politics* sends us to the *Poetics* for an explanation which is not there.

3 Quite the opposite, any culture that has produced great novels has always produced theories of plot. To come back to the great rejection of Aristotle that has characterized Italian culture since the seventeenth century, I would not want to discredit myself by saying which was the effect and which was the cause, but it is certain that Italian culture produced neither good theories of plot nor good novels. Beginning with Boccaccio, this great civilization of the story has produced novels, but with a considerable lag behind other cultures. We have a very short and insignificant history of the baroque (but in that period Aristotle was still followed), and after that nothing interesting until the twentieth century. In the modern era, there have been excellent narrators, from Manzoni to Verga all the

way to Moravia and Calvino, but in an infinitely smaller quantity than in France, England, Germany, and Russia. It is certainly true that the novel is a product of the bourgeoisie and, although Italy had a medieval bourgeoisie in Boccaccio's time, it had not had a modern bourgeoisie until long after the rest of Europe. However, be it effect or formal cause, Italy had no theory of plot and, therefore, no novels, which were in large part nothing but disguised essays. This is why Italy has never presented great detective novels. Because every detective novel is but the *Poetics* reduced to its essential components: there is a sequence of events (*pragma*), the strands of which are lost, and the plot relates how the detective reconstructs this sequence (except detectives do not invent the plots of which they are characters in order to produce the illusion that there were *pragmata*; but Borges had his Aristotle).

4 The author wrote the paper during the pre–Gulf War period.

5 For example, Langbaum 1956.

6 See, in particular, Lakoff and Johnson 1980; also Lakoff 1987.

19

Chronotopes in Diegesis

MICHAEL RIFFATERRE

My point of departure is Bakhtin's concept of the chronotope, defined in his own terms as 'the intrinsic connectedness of temporal and spatial relationships that are artistically expressed in literature' (1981, 84). Bakhtin specifies that, under the conditions of this inseparability of time and space, 'time ... thickens, takes on flesh, becomes artistically visible; likewise, space becomes charged and responsive to the movements of time, plot and history' (85).

The problem with this definition is that it fails to indicate the specific points at which, in a verbal sequence, the chronotopes can be observed. Bakhtin himself seems to be inviting confusion when, under the spell of Kant, he asserts that 'the image of man is always intrinsically chronotopic' (85; cf. Morson and Emerson 1990, 366–9). Tzvetan Todorov has pointed out that such a broad concept makes it difficult to distinguish between chronotope and genre or subgenre (1981, 128–31; cf. Morson and Emerson 1990, 372–479). A corrective may be Henri Mitterand's narrower definition: he has shown that chronotopes function as distinctive traits of a specific work of fiction and are perceived as such by ordinary readers (1990, 89–104).[1]

The problem raised by Bakhtin's broad concept is that, if chronotopes become synonymous with generic categories, we cannot differentiate them from the diegesis at large, from the whole space-time universe in which the narrative unfolds.[2] The difficulty is answered, it seems to me, if we limit the chronotope to a specific, contextually restricted component of the diegesis. Such a unit will be to the diegesis what a word is to a sentence or a sentence to a text. It will be coterminal with the representation of one moment of the story, of a specific situation, of an instance of interaction between characters. This may go a long way towards explaining how chronotopes become 'artistically visible.'

But it is not enough to focus on the actual representation of chronotopes (rather than on chronotopes as the 'ground essential for the representability of events'[3]). We must also define the conditions for the relevancy of such units to the narrative. The principal mechanism of narrative is time and its impact on characters and situations. This impact translates as a sequence of transformations of an initial given in order for the story to reach its assigned telos. Each chronotope is a sign system, a representation designed to make readers aware that such a transformation is taking place.

There are two ways time may be represented: indirectly by speaking about it and, more specifically by analysing its chain of events in the abstract, as would be the case in the discourse of dynamics. Or, directly, through the mimesis of how the passage of time affects people and things. Since the effects of time must be concrete to be visible, their description bears on shapes, on objects, that are all defined in spatial terms and situated within space. Therefore, the only way that time can be represented is through the mediation of space. This, of course, is precisely what the compound word 'chronotope' implies. Furthermore, any fictional story demands an interpretation that depends on the views embodied in characters and in the narrator – in short, on subjectively experienced objects and interactions. Time made visible as it is translated into space is time significant for someone from someone's point of view, a subjectivized object, as it were. This significance of time must be such that any reader will have to accept it as plausible and applicable to common experience. As a code for time, space has three functions: narrative, hermeneutic, and aesthetic. The first two are obviously related: the vector-like sequence of events leading to a telos actualizes narrative structures and simultaneously dictates its interpretation. And these two functions are as basic as they are related; thus they cannot be relevant to the differences or oppositions between genres.

I suggest, therefore, that generic characterization depends only on the aesthetic function, for it is the only one that admits of variations. Bakhtin's requirement that the chronotope should not just represent time but should do so artistically does not reflect these variations. And the reason is the all-encompassing generality of his adverb. Suppose we replace the phrase 'artistic representation' with 'literary representation.' 'Literary' subsumes two variants, for it refers to verbal artifacts and these fall into two categories: they are either figurative or literal. If they are figurative, genre will be defined by tropology. If they are literal, based on referentiality in the same way as everyday utilitarian language, the artifacts will be conventional themes and motifs, and these will determine generic identity. Combinations of the two may yield yet another category of genres.

I shall discuss first an instance of thematic chronotope: the staircase, a conventional topos, the architectural nature of which should make it an exclusively spatial component of the chronotope. Its vertical axis, however, gives it symbolic values that are the equivalent of a time dimension (cf. Morson and Emerson 1990, 375).

Every member of the household has to use the stairs in the course of the day. A stairway is to the characters of a novel what the peristyle of a palace is to actors in the French classical drama. Whoever enters or exits must go through the peristyle. These synonymous topoi impart verisimilitude to encounters between people whose role or status makes it unlikely that they should meet – hence, the role of the stairs as a device for legitimate and illegitimate interaction between social classes in *Upstairs, Downstairs*, the television series so popular in the sixties. This interaction entails the future subversion of the present hierarchy.

The two areas of the house that are the extreme poles of the staircase, the attic and the basement, happen to be psychological, and thus temporal, entities as well. They are the repressed collective unconscious of the family, the storage space of time, so to speak, where the flotsam of a family's past accumulates, waiting for ominous and unwholesome resuscitation. The role of the stairs leading to the attic in the Gothic novel or to the basement in modern horror stories[4] connect the present and the past, everyday life and the uncanny; they are the loci of anxiety and suspense.

The stairway I have chosen for my example may not necessarily be gauged in psychoanalytic terms, but it serves as the chronometer timing the household's collective life and, for the readers, as the scale on which time becomes significant for an interpretation of that household's family, of its members' tempers, and for setting the pace of everyday life. Once this norm has been disturbed, it will take a whole novel to tell the consequences. Following a baleful event (the accidental death of the paterfamilias), the behavioural norm set by the stairs becomes the standard by which readers will measure how the characters cope with disaster. In short, this chronotope guides and informs readers' evaluation of the actors, of their capacity for pathos, and provides a deceptively peaceful context for the imminent *coup de théâtre*. Here is the first page of *No Name* (1873), one of Wilkie Collins's mysteries:

The hands on the hall-clock pointed to half-past six in the morning. The house was a country residence in West Somersetshire, called Combe-Raven. The day was the fourth of March, and the year was eighteen hundred and forty-six.

No sounds but the steady ticking of the clock, and the lumpish snoring of a large dog stretched on a mat outside the dining room door, disturbed the mysterious morning stillness of hall and staircase. Who were the sleepers hidden in the upper regions? Let the house reveal its own secrets; and, one by one, as they descend the stairs from their beds, let the sleepers disclose themselves.

As the clock pointed to a quarter to seven, the dog woke and shook himself. After waiting in vain for the footman, who was accustomed to let him out, the animal ... appealed to the sleeping family, with a long and melancholy howl. Before the last notes of the dog's remonstrance had died away, the oaken stairs in the higher regions of the house creaked under slowly-descending footsteps. In a minute more the first of the female servants made her appearance, with a dingy woolen shawl over her shoulders – for the March morning was bleak; and rheumatism and the cook were old acquaintances ...

Seven o'clock struck; and the signs of domestic life began to show themselves in more rapid succession.

The house-maid came down – tall and slim, with the state of the spring temperature written redly on her nose. The lady's-maid followed – young, smart, plump, and sleepy. The kitchen-maid came next – afflicted with the face-ache, and making no secret of her sufferings. Last of all, the footman appeared, yawning disconsolately ... (1)

After an interval to let the staff begin and check on the housework, the master of the house appears, cheerful and self-confident, ordering breakfast for 10 o'clock rather than for 9, referring to a concert the night before to explain the ladies' lateness. But at 9 sharp, as testimony to the fact that 9 is indeed the proper time for breakfast regardless of circumstances, the prim, stern, governess appears, maturity incarnate. At 9:20, the mother and elder daughter come down, suitably late to avoid any moralistic self-display. Portraits follow each appearance and tidbits of conversation, the tone of which is in keeping with the characterizations suggested through description. Topping this paradigm of successive entrances, the exception to the rule confirms the logic of the narrative: the whimsy and cuteness readers expect in a youngest, favourite daughter are embodied in her noisy late arrival: 'When the minute-hand had recorded the lapse of five minutes more, a door banged in the bedroom regions ... light, rapid footsteps pattered on the upper stairs ... In another moment, the youngest daughter ... clearing the last three steps into the hall at a jump, presented herself breathless in the breakfast-room, to make the family circle complete' (15).

This coda 'family circle complete' concludes the exposition in truly narrative terms, that is, in temporal terms, since family members are described not objectively in a set portrait, but through actions and demeanour. Thus the descriptive truly yields to the diegetic, since the topos serves only as a stage for the flow of time. Even when the relative waywardness in the previous night's sequence of events is described, it is not presented as a state of things, as a situation, but again as chronology, except that, in this sequence, it is clear that the stairs as chronotope are truly a unit of narrative significance, because they weld together place, time, and characterization. Let me emphasize that this unit, and the requisite functional unity of purpose of its components, does not depend on an arbitrary decision of the author, or on a logic the inferences and consequences of which would be limited to, and motivated by, the context. If that were the case, the chronotope's significance would be questionable, a pattern proposed to readers but one that would leave them free to accept or to reject it.

The unit is genuine and natural because the topos of the chronotope is already impregnated with time in common usage. For in the inner world of the house, any passageway that does not reveal at the first glance the space it opens onto is time-oriented: a closed door, a curtain, a window (at least one unlit and seen from outside or with drapes behind it), a corridor with a turn (or darkened at the end) are indeed openings, but openings that depend on further exploration, on movement, the minute the action has begun. As much as they are passages, they are dramatic time on the verge of revealing something. In short, stairs stir suspense, actualizing in the written story a semiotic system akin to the pregnant moment in a painting.

This time that already takes the form of space in the sociolect – that becomes meaningful because of the nature of its space, because of the progressive discovery or exploration imposed by its space – is a subjectivized time. Coming downstairs early is, again at the level of the sociolect, the symbol of a moral stance: facing the tasks of the new day. The converse, coming downstairs late, is an equally accepted symbol of the contrary: capriciousness in a woman, sloth in a man. The governess, a standard character of Victorian novels,[5] is exemplary of the former behaviour both at the narrative and at the descriptive level, as is suggested by her moralistic punctuality: the coalescence of hall clock and stairway transforms plain time into ethical time-to-get-up. As for the daughter, she verifies what it means to be spoiled and a young lady by using the same chronotope conversely. We readers react positively to this, not in terms of an experience of such people which may elude our limited knowledge of a long-gone society, but in terms of grammaticality. The syntax uniting time with space is here faultless because a single overdetermination governs both sequences.

While the Wilkie Collins chronotope is characterized by one space and several time variations on that scale, a chronotope may take the reverse form and represent one time in several spaces, one time experienced by several characters simultaneously, albeit from their own distinct perspectives. The function of such a structure is to solve a problem peculiar to the narrative, the problem of representing variety and differences within simultaneity. Descriptive texts do not require simultaneity. Non-literary or para-literary narratives may do with some metalinguistic, marginal, extradiegetic comment, not unlike parenthetical stage directions, such as the almost parodic 'meanwhile back at the ranch' in comic strips.

Such is the case of *Mrs. Dalloway*, in which the clocks of London follow the lead of Big Ben in eight different passages throughout the second half of the novel. In the third instance, noontide is proclaimed, but with two different audiences singled out that nothing else has yet brought together, and that everything seems to keep apart – a rich, idle socialite preparing a big party for the prime minister and an unhappy proletarian anonymous couple, the Warren Smiths, preparing to see a psychiatrist for the distracted and indeed suicidal husband: 'It was precisely twelve o'clock; twelve by Big Ben; whose stroke was wafted over the northern part of London; blent with that of other clocks, mixed in a thin ethereal way with the clouds and wisps of smoke, and died up there among the seagulls – twelve o'clock struck as Clarissa Dalloway laid her green dress on her bed, and the Warren Smiths walked down Harley Street. Twelve was the hour of their appointment ... The leaden circles dissolved in the air ...' (Woolf 1953, 142).[6]

The bells are the metonymy of time itself, and constitute a theme as well established as that of the stairway, but with a more decided moral coloration: from the medieval period on, the clocks striking together have reminded people of their mortality. Beyond this philosophical and literary specialization, the mechanics of many characters simultaneously sharing an experience is a well-established narrative cliché even in common parlance. For months after a celebrated power failure in New York, the emergency still provided conversational fodder at cocktail parties where the question remained: 'Where were you when the lights went out?' In the sensational press, the stylistic tabloids usually spin out the story of a major disaster by recording many eyewitness accounts of the same event – the degenerate form of a practice first experimented in literature by Bulwer-Lytton in *Last Days of Pompeii* (1834): the narrator tells the characters' diverse reactions, from the cowardly to the sublime, to a volcanic eruption. Woolf goes one step further by ending her novel on the same clocks now striking midnight and with only one survivor to listen to them. The clausula, a loaded silence, is the same as the last sentence of the overture, twice repeated in the second and third instances of the chronotope:

It was fascinating, with people still laughing and shouting in the drawing-room, to watch that old woman, quite quietly, going to bed. She pulled the blind now. The clock began striking. The young man had killed himself; but she did not pity him; with the clock striking the hour, one, two, three, she did not pity him, with all this going on ... she repeated, and the words came to her, Fear no more the heat of the sun. She must go back to them. But what an extraordinary night! She felt somehow very like him – the young man who had killed himself. She felt glad that he had done it; thrown it away. The clock was striking. The leaden circles dissolved in the air. (283–4)

In the intervening instances, the protagonist hears the bells and so does her husband who is returning from a luncheon to which she was not invited. What is the function of this unanimity of several persons, or bodies, or topoi where a similar consciousness is experienced? We cannot assign here a specific symbolism to the clocks, one that would elicit the same thoughts in the different listeners. But the repetition of the motif and the identity of the sensory experience each time undoubtedly invites readers to compare paths of life, to find them parallel and therefore comparable, like several versions of one experience, one being the parody of the others. Hence, for the reader, an ability to find a lesson, a significance for the whole novel, an aim foreign to the actual sensory experience but common to the treatment of the various characters. Clarissa's triumph in society juxtaposed with ridicule of Lady Bruton's social affairs (the latter is the person her husband had lunch with) is therefore caricatured, made to appear inane. The parallelism posited by the fact that she and Septimus Warren are co-listeners of the same bell certainly suggests that her own snobbish ennui is just as depressing as the acedia that ails the poor helpless misfit.

This, then, would be the telos of the story, and the telos, of course, is precisely the difference that distinguishes the narrative diegesis from a mere description. In short, the repeated chronotope is a hermeneutic index, even though it is in itself open or empty, as would be the title 'A Day in the Life of a London Housewife.' All it symbolizes, it does by pointing to its teleological motivation.

The Collins and the Woolf chronotopes have this in common: despite their eventual symbolism (in the sense I just outlined), they are, both temporally and spatially, literal statements. Neither is a trope. The reverse is true with a second type of chronotope, whose effect on the narrative may not be as far-reaching as with the literal type but which, on the other hand, is felt immediately and compellingly. Indeed, this effect is conspicuous in the context directly following the chronotope, and in the narrower compass of a sentence, a paragraph, or, at most, of a couple of pages.

This type I will call derivative. Time is first posited explicitly and literally, but this given serves only as a matrix from which a spatial representation unfolds, developing and expanding on the peculiarities of what is unique in this particular experience of time.

The derivation is like a rhetorical *amplificatio*, and the longer and the more complex it is, the more it emphasizes the role of time in the story. But it does so figuratively: since time is a literal given, and since space, the only other axis in this two-dimensional reality, is not perceived as complementary to the first but is proposed as the equivalent of time in a different code, as its translation, space can only be metaphorical.

This tropology, this imaginary space, remains entirely within the realm of narrative, for whatever it describes is true not because it rests directly on referentiality to the real world, but because its sensorial representations refer only to a character's or to the narrator's pleasant, or more often painful, awareness of time. Between the temporal experience recounted here and reality, there intervenes a screen of subjective reactions which retroactively either make time a symbol of something else, like mortality, or tailor it, so to speak, to the character's or narrator's circumstance, replacing evenly flowing time with accelerated or protracted psychological duration.

To return once again to Mrs. Dalloway, a first toll of the hour over London occurs seventy pages before the series is resumed. Although it is different from the clocks that delineate a structure of parallelisms, it obviously valorizes the motif, giving it the momentum needed for the series to unfold. This first toll also motivates the motif (inasmuch as the sound is heard jointly by the two principal actors), integrating it into the plot and thus delaying our perception of its actual import as a structural hermeneutic guide for the reader. In this first occurrence, the bells are heard by a single character, a former flame of Clarissa's, but he is one character split into two listeners: he hears the bells now after seeing her again for the first time in years, and this brings back the memory of listening to the bells together: '[It was] as if this bell had come into the room years ago, where they sat at some moment of great intimacy, and had gone from one to the other and had left, like a bee with honey, laden with the moment' (74–5).

Thus the time lapse is annulled by memory, and passion flares anew. If there was no more to the text, it would be a lyrical passage, not a narrative chronotope. In fact, the passage is metalinguistic, or metatextual, since the whole sentence depends on 'as if' – a poetic parenthesis. The true chronotope resides in the splitting of the Clarissa persona into a literal representation of herself (a woman) and a symbolic one (the remembered bell of the time when she and he were a couple): at the beginning of the passage we are told that the bell rings right on time 'like a hostess who comes into her drawingroom on the very stroke of the hour and finds her guests there already. I am not late. No, it is precisely half-past eleven, she says. Yet, though she is perfectly right, her voice, being the voice of the hostess, is reluctant to inflict its individuality' (74).

This unexpected personification of the bell seems to take place for the sole purpose of introducing an odd allusion to coldness. But the very oddity of this personification compels the reader to remember that Clarissa's spurned lover used to reproach her for holding back. He would tell her, with bitter irony, that at least her reserve entitled her to the appellation 'the perfect hostess.' The narrative given, therefore, meshes with the punctuality that in Wilkie Collins had served to define a well-bred woman, or breeding in a woman in clock code, as it were. We now have a complex derivative sequence. First, time is made explicit at the narrative level. Then, there is a spatial derivation in which space (the room) is derived from the sound that inundates it. In a final transcoding, this space determines one more metaphor of time, now its personification as the punctual hostess without whom a reception room would not be complete. Hence, at the level of narrative, a characterization of the protagonist as a frustrating female who keeps her lover at arm's length. To put it another way, her sense of propriety precludes time from turning into the flexible duration of whimsy, let alone the timelessness of passion. The chronotope has become a figure for characterization, for human interest, for a literary image of desire foiled, using only narrative discourse within the bounds of the genre, without any parenthetic concession to lyricism.

The subjective and tropological nature of the derivative chronotope must be linked to the special productivity of this type: indeed, there is a relation between the mechanism of the derivation and the inscription of the subject in the text (*énonciation*).

In literature, derivations from a given have a momentum of their own. This is apparent in the ease with which an isolated metaphor begets an extended metaphor. The chronotope's spatial component is no exception: a derivation from it tends to expand faster because two forces combine to prolong it and develop the rhetorical *amplificatio* further. One is the associative power of the descriptive systems that substitute for a matrix word several periphrases built with the metonyms, synecdoches, and paronyms of that word. The other is the motivation for generating such substitutes: the *cathexis* of the object by the speaking subject. As the object becomes a figure for the subject, the disparity of the two and the need to erase that disparity for the figure to be plausible incite periphrastic developments. These repeatedly privilege the points of the descriptive system of the object where some analogy can be found with the descriptive system of the subject. Such was the case with the imaginary room pervaded by chimes identifiable with the subject's fixation on Clarissa: hence, a room for Clarissa, and an exclusion for it by Clarissa.

The subjectivization of time determines a hypertrophy of the figurative spatial component. Specifically, the difference between time and its subjectivized form, psychological duration, gives rise to images of parallel spaces, one for time, one for its annexation by the self. A case in point is a Baudelaire prose poem (actually it is a tale, for the emphasis is truly on the narrative), which is revealingly titled *The double room* (*La chambre double*). Two spaces are juxtaposed, one euphoric, the other dysphoric. The first is a luxurious love nest the narrator sees in his dreams. The other is the actual bedroom he wakes up to, when morning displaces his erotic fantasies with the companion of his waking hours, a disgusting hag. The room now appears dirty and worn out, with 'stupid furniture' (Baudelaire's very words) reflecting the nonsense of his life.

One space is divided into two not only because of the need to parallel and contrast the room of dreams with the hovel of reality. Such a parallelism would merely be the rhetorical *amplificatio* of the antithetical commonplace I have described. The change is a *coup de théâtre*, at once dramatic and narrative, determined not just by the daylight following night but by a depressive bout. Two rooms in one exteriorize the splitting of the hysterical subject.

One might object that, in Baudelaire, the lyric adulterates the generic integrity of the narrative (and perhaps this is true also of Virginia Woolf), but Marcel Proust offers similar instances that are entirely novelistic. There is a four-page, double description in *Sodome et Gomorrhe* in which waking and sleeping generate two apartments. One is complete with staff, bells for summoning servants, and visitors: we might think it the real one until we learn that the other apartment, an empty one, symbolizes life and that the busy place is that of illusion. Such is the power of parallelism that even the characters undergo splitting and duplications: 'the race of people who dwell in this apartment is androgynous. A man appears who changes into a woman. Things turn into men, men split into friends and foes. The sleeper's time is totally different from that of a man awake' (my translation).[7]

Before concluding, let me pursue briefly my demonstration of the literarity that separates the narrative representation of time from its non-literary representation. This literarity is relevant to fiction because it is entirely based on a discourse of time.

For the chronotope's figurative derivation to be totally integrated into the narrative, even its metaphors, its code must be somehow connected with time (as we have seen in Wilkie Collins), although they serve to translate time into its spatial counterpart. The integration facilitates, smoothes out the jump from one to the other, the boldness of what, in any other genre, would be a contradiction in terms or a gratuitous choice. The transformation still gives readers a jolt, but, despite the aesthetic tension it creates, the sociolect soon reassures them that there exists an unconsciousness of time in this new spatial discourse. We have noted a similar integration in the Wilkie Collins example, in which the space of the stairs was, in a way, a time machine of its own discourse. A last example, again from Proust, may clarify the point. The narrator is pining away, alone, sexually frustrated, on a rainy day. The day itself is personified as a seamstress: weary, resigned, occupied for several hours still with its immemorial task.

The words 'immemorial task' may sound metaphysical, but they can also be understood as referring to the endless cycle of actual time and to the archaic discourse about the duties of women in the household, about their daily, indeed hourly, routine – a sexist but well-established way of representing time. On the other hand, *passementerie* the French word for 'needlework,' is so technical that it clearly marks a shift to figurative discourse. The sentence goes: 'it saddened me to think that I was to be left alone with that day [literally, with *her*, *journée* being a feminine word] that acknowledged my presence no more than would a seamstress who, sitting by the window so as to see better while she works, pays no attention to the person present with her in the room' (my translation).[8]

No established theme will help us here, and the scene, with its Dutch School connotations – this has the feel of a Vermeer painting like *The Lacemaker* – is so strikingly real that it blots out any consciousness of a metaphor, of a convention which would cushion the shock of a personification. Nowhere, it seems, could the distance be so great between the subjectivized passing of time as a figure of empty melancholy and this space devoted to no-nonsense feminine industry. The bearer of the mood, the lonely narrator, would seem to be a stylistic interloper. And yet nothing is gratuitous here; the components of the chronotope are sewn together most compellingly by language itself. Two pages earlier, the path to the truth of the figurative code was cleared by an accepted image of rain as a web (*filets*): 'The grey light, falling like a fine rain, wove ceaselessly a transparent web through which the Sunday strollers appeared in a silvery sheen' (my translation).[9] 'Weaving' is *tisser* but also *filer*; 'web' is *filets*. But the true, pun-like connection, is that *filer*, the verb for 'weaving' as well as for 'lace-making,' for the *passementerie* that is to adorn with embroidery the imaginary space of the metaphorical room, can have 'day' or 'hours' as its predicate. The Parcae are shown to spin out days (*filer des jours*). These immortal spinners are the forerunners of Proust's lace-woman. Even without the authority of mythology, *filer des jours* and *filer des heures* are commonplace for whiling away the days or the hours. *Au fil des saisons* is another cliché for the leisurely unravelling of the thread of Time.

Readers have no room here to disagree because they cannot decode one meaning of the word without being aware of the other meaning. This is a syllepsis, the only trope that can make two separate or contrary meanings co-exist in one word, one context. We have on the near side of the syllepsis, on the surface of the sentence, a tableau of lace-making, in the room needed for that activity. On the other side, the slow flow of Time bespeaks the idle melancholy of an idle, lonely, jilted lover. The syllepsis unites narrative time with diegetic space, a linkage that is as grammatical as the sophisticated artifice of the trope is unnatural, as grammatical in fact as the morphological bond that welds together the two halves of the word 'chronotope'.

In conclusion, I would like to make two points in defence of narrowing down Bakhtin's bold concept. First, by reducing the chronotope's range, not only do I avoid the perils of superficial generality, but I reflect the psychological, or even the physical, realities of reader response, when it is allowed to function freely, individually, and unaided, or perhaps unencumbered, with concerns such as genre or type. It is not clear that these play as strong or permanent a role in reading as they do in the teaching of literature.

Second, I am trying to understand the control the text has over the minds of its readers, over the way they conceptualize, and empathize with, what they read. This control takes effect when the text's presuppositions mobilize the readers' sense of the associative sign systems with which the sociolect has equipped their imaginations. The generative power of the chronotope results from its rewriting time in spatial code and from filling the space thus gained with those signs that further translate chronological time into logical time: namely, the ordered and imperative sequences of presuppositions and entailments. As I see it, the chronotope generates the fictional text. The text merely unfolds and puts side by side loci and topoi that exist in potential or compressed form within the chronotope: the change from the initial infrasegmental predication implicit in the chronotope to the text, from sentence to textuality, gives rise to the diegesis and to its occupants, the characters. We may summarize the backward-forward alternation of presuppositions and entailments by saying that the topoi are filled with past time, while the future is filled with diegetic space.

NOTES

1 Mitterand also points out that fiction borrows ready-made chronotopes from the sociolect's pool of themes and motifs. Such borrowings seem to suggest that chronotopes can be perceived independently of genres.

2 I borrow Gérard Genette's definition of diegesis (1972, 239; 280).

3 Bakhtin's own formula; cf. Holquist 1984, 250.

4 See, of course, Sandra M. Gilbert and Susan D. Gubar, *The Madwoman in the Attic*.

5 A near synonym, at a slightly lower social level, is the female housekeeper of a country seat (e.g., Darcy's housekeeper in *Pride and Prejudice*).

6 The previous two instances are simultaneous with the moment when Clarissa meets again after a long absence with her former, never-forgotten suitor, Peter (59 ff.).

Significantly, there are two instances, because they translate into a 'bell,' that is, into a time code two important facets of the lover's personality: (*a*) Peter upsets Clarissa because he is still an aggressive presence invading the peace, or desert, of her married life: 'the sound of Big Ben striking the half-hour struck out between them ... as if a young man, strong, indifferent, inconsiderate, were swinging dumb-bells this way and that' (71); (*b*) Peter is upset by Clarissa's insistence on her social duties, a propriety that contributed to their separation five years before: 'Remember my party, remember my party, said Peter Walsh ..., speaking to himself rhythmically, in time with the flow of sound, the direct downright sound of Big Ben striking the half-hour ... Why does she give these parties, he thought' (72).

7 'La race qui l'habite ... est androgyne. Un homme y apparaît au bout d'un instant sous l'aspect d'une femme. Les choses y ont une aptitude à devenir des hommes, les hommes des amis ou des ennemis. Le temps qui s'écoule pour le dormeur ... est absolument différent du temps dans lequel s'accomplit la vie de l'homme réveillé' (Proust 1956, 2: 981).

8 'Lasse, résignée, occupée pour plusiers heures encore à sa tâche immémoriale, la grise journée filait sa passementerie de nacre et je m'attristais de penser que j'allais rester seul en tête à tête avec elle qui ne me connaissait pas plus qu'une ouvrière qui s'est installée près de la fenêtre pour voir plus clair en faisant sa besogne et ne s'occupe pas de la personne présente dans la chambre' (2: 350).

9 'Le jour gris, tombant comme une pluie fine, tissait sans arrêt de transparents filets dans lesquels les promeneurs domimicaux semblaient s'argenter' (2: 347).

20

Deconstructing Bakhtin

LADISLAV MATEJKA

The international prominence of the Soviet phenomenon known as the Bakhtin school, or simply as Bakhtin, has grown to a truly spectacular magnitude. Nowadays it even threatens to overshadow the fame of the Russian formalists, who were the primary target of Bakhtin's criticism in the twenties. At that time, young Mikhail Mikhailovich Bakhtin ideologically rejected the Russian school of the formal method in terms of neo-Kantian antimaterialism, while his friends Valentin Voloshinov and Pavel Medvedev were attacking the formalists from the eclectic platform of Marxism and Hegelianism.

The fame of Bakhtin and his school has produced a large body of literature that reflects the contemporary neophilological revival not only in Russia but also in the West. Yet the Bakhtin scholarship is still seriously hampered by problems of authorship and textological authenticity, and implicitly by the danger of ideological manipulation of the data about Bakhtin and his activities. And for that reason we continue to question the nature of the cooperation among the most prominent members of the Bakhtin circle, especially Bakhtin, Voloshinov, and Medvedev. It is still unclear whether certain of their essential contributions were produced by several brains or by a single brain full of contradictions bordering on schizophrenia. In the continuous dispute, Bakhtin, who survived both Voloshinov and Medvedev by a quarter of a century, has turned into a sort of mystical golem, if not into a Frankenstein monster, as some of the sceptics would prefer to call him (Titunik 1984, 561).

The profoundly antimaterialistic neo-Kantian views of young Bakhtin are best documented in his comprehensive discourse 'The Problem of Content, Material, and Form in Verbal Art.' This lengthy study was allegedly completed in 1924 for A.M. Gorkij's *Russkij Sovremennik* but remained unpublished for half a century, so that it is still unclear when it acquired its final shape. Its abridged version first appeared in 1974 in the almanac *Kontekst*, known as an outlet for the Soviet party-line aestheticians. The abridged text was given the title 'Toward an Aesthetics of the Word' and not the slightest hint about the time and the circumstances of its origin was supplied (Bakhtin, 1974). Since Bakhtin was still alive in 1974 and the abridged version did not contain any clear-cut temporal markers, the article potentially led its readers to believe that this was old Bakhtin's contribution to the ongoing Soviet attacks on the legacy of Russian formalism. However, in 1975, the Preface to the posthumous volume of Bakhtin's studies, *Voprosy literatury i éstetiki*, obliquely suggested that Bakhtin's article in *Kontekst* was merely an edited selection from a comprehensive manuscript which had allegedly originated fifty years earlier, in 1924 (Bakhtin 1975, 4).

In its entirety, the printed version of Bakhtin's paper covers sixty-five pages. It is two-thirds longer than the abridged version of twenty-three pages in *Kontekst*. Yet it has very few footnotes and presents a challenge to anyone who believes citations and references are a guide for an adequate interpretation of Bakhtin's philosophical development, his personal profile, and his conceptual dialogue with Medvedev and Voloshinov in the early twenties. Perhaps the most striking fact is that in his paper Bakhtin never once refers to Broder Christiansen's neo-Kantian *Philosophie der Kunst*, although he uses this book in a way that, according to western European standards, could be viewed as plagiarism.

Christiansen's *Philosophie der Kunst* was very influential in Russia, especially after 1911 when it appeared in a Russian translation. It is the same book that enriched the terminological inventory of the Russian formalists with such entries as 'differential quality' (*Differenzqualität/ differencial'nyj znak*), 'foregrounding' (*Wahrnehmungshintergrund/ oscuscenie/ vosprijatie na fone*), and 'dominant' (*die Dominante/dominanta*). Sklovskij himself cites Christiansen's *Philosophie der Kunst* in his famous *Theory of Prose*. However, unlike Sklovskij and other Russian formalists, Bakhtin extensively borrows from Christiansen without giving him any credit.

The title of Bakhtin's lengthy study 'The Problem of Content, Material, and Form in Verbal Art' ('Problema soderzanija, materiala i formy v slovesnom xudozestvennom tvorcestve') is, in fact, nothing but Bakhtin's translation of Christiansen's summary, in which 'material, content, and form' are cited as three distinct factors in a work of art (e.g., 'Unsere Analyse hatte im Kunstwerk drei ungleichartige Faktoren angefunden: Material, Inhalt und Form' [Christiansen 1909, 116]). In Bakhtin's translation only the word order is changed: Christiansen's 'Material, Content, and Form' became Bakhtin's 'Content, Material, and Form' (Bakhtin 1990). These three distinct factors are investigated in relationship to the internal structure of art which Christiansen calls 'das ästhetische Objekt' (the aesthetic object) and Bakhtin 'esteticeskij ob'ekt' (aesthetic object).

According to Christiansen, 'an aesthetic object is a formation in a subject, while an external work of art, an artifact, merely provides material and guidance for a superstructure but, by itself, is not a complete object of aesthetic evaluation' (1909, 50; my translation). Echoing this patently subjectivist view, Bakhtin insists that an aesthetic object has to be distinguished from an artifact, the external material work of art. In his formulation, the task 'of aesthetic analysis is to understand the external material work as that which actualizes an aesthetic object, as the technical apparatus of aesthetic execution' (1990, 267; my translation). According to Christiansen, an aesthetic object 'arises through an act of recreation' (1909, 41), while, in Bakhtin's paraphrase, it 'is realized in the process of creation and contemplation' (1990, 286; my translation). In order to define an aesthetic object, both Christiansen and Bakhtin use the term 'to enter' into an aesthetic object (e.g., *geht in* and *vxodit*, respectively). According to Christiansen, 'the material does not enter into the aesthetic object directly (1909, 127; my translation), while Bakhtin elaborates Christiansen's view by saying 'the extra-aesthetic nature of the material does not enter [*ne vxodit*] into the aesthetic object, created by artistic contemplation, that is, into aesthetic being as such, into the ultimate goal of creativity' (1990, 295; my translation).

Both Christiansen and Bakhtin agree that the concept of the aesthetic object puts a special emphasis on the teleological principle. 'For an aesthetic object a teleological structure is essential' (1909, 130; my translation), says Christiansen, while Bakhtin says 'one has to work by means of the teleological method' (1990, 267; my translation).

Christiansen's *Philosophie der Kunst* discusses the concept of aesthetic object in a special chapter which consists of eighty-four pages and constitutes the pivot of his radically anti-materialistic philosophy of art. Paraphrasing (or more exactly plagiarizing) his source, Bakhtin devotes two-thirds of his lengthy paper to Christiansen, but does not mention his name one single time. Equipped with Christiansen's neo-Kantian concepts, he turns his paper into a fierce attack on materialist aesthetics in general, and on the Russian school of the formal method in particular.

The differences between Bakhtin's short version in the party-line-oriented *Kontekst* and the version in the posthumous volume are not solely textual abridgements. In some instances, the lexical selection is affected as well. For example, the word 'religioznyj' (religious) in one passage of the full text was replaced in *Kontekst* by the word 'duxovnyj' (spiritual), or vice versa. It would be certainly of interest to know more about the editorial process which replaced 'religious' by 'spiritual' or 'spiritual' by 'religious'. Was it an act of stylistic refinement or a semantic provision motivated politically? Was it done by

Bakhtin himself or by his editors? If this was done by the editors of *Kontekst*, did Bakhtin agree with this change? Was he dying as a free man or as a prisoner of editorial manipulations?

Of course, the problems of editing pertain not only to the abridged version, published in 1974 in *Kontekst*, but also to the long version published in the posthumous volume *Voprosy literatury i èstetiki* (1975). Does this version really represent a text as it was completed in 1924, or is it a text which was gradually modified during the following fifty years? An adequate answer to this question is an essential prerequisite not only for our understanding of the Christiansen/Bakhtin relationship, but also for our interpretation of the texts which repudiated Bakhtin's neo-Kantian aesthetics and were published under the names of Valentin Voloshinov and Pavel Medvedev. Clearly, some of these problems could be resolved if Bakhtin's original manuscripts were made accessible without any doctoring. They could shed light on some enigmatic aspects of Bakhtin's circle in the twenties and especially on Bakhtin's intellectual co-operation with Voloshinov and Medvedev. Bakhtin's editors, and especially V.V. Ivanov, should be more co-operative in this respect. It was Ivanov's exegesis that most audaciously assigned to Bakhtin several texts published under the name of Voloshinov and Medvedev and that turned Voloshinov and Medvedev into Bakhtin's pen-names (Ivanov 1973).

V.V. Ivanov's help could be particularly important for the article 'Po tu storonu social'nogo (o frejdizme)' (Beyond the social [concerning freudianism]). This paper was published under the name of V.N. Voloshinov in *Zvezda* in 1925 and must have been written about the time Bakhtin was ready to publish his adaptation of Christiansen's neo-Kantian aesthetics. Voloshinov's paper was primarily concerned with the Freudian concept of the subconscious, but it emphasized the validity of dialectical materialism 'in all areas of ideological creativity,' and was necessarily on a collision course with the Bakhtin/Christiansen anti-materialistic aesthetics. In sharp contrast with Bakhtin, the author of this article appears to be a docile disciple of materialistic monism, impressed by I.P. Pavlov's reflexology and Jacques Loeb's materialistic insistence on a physio-chemical basis for psychology. While Bakhtin/Christiansen was attacking the principles of materialism from the idealistic and subjectivist positions of the neo-Kantians, Voloshinov was rejecting Bakhtin/Christiansen's subjectivism from the Marxist position of dialectical materialism. Consequently, the article necessarily documents a sharp ideological conflict in the Bakhtin circle or in Bakhtin's own head, if it was written by Bakhtin himself. Or should we perhaps read the texts signed by Voloshinov as a buffoonery concocted by a group of clowns who ridiculed the principles of dialectical materialism and the life in Russia after the Revolution by using a special kind of Aesopian language –

a cryptic mixture of seriousness and mockery? As long as this question remains unanswered, adequate understanding of Voloshinov's texts will be seriously hampered, and the Bakhtin enigma will continue to challenge our critical standards.

In 1927, a major part of this same article reappeared in *Frejdizm: Kriticeskij ocerk* (Freudianism: A critical sketch), a book published under the name of V.N. Voloshinov but cited by the Soviet experts and their fellow-travellers as a book by Bakhtin. Here the attack on the idealistic subjectivism is further elaborated and strengthened. Its author points out that 'the psychical is only one of the properties of organized matter and, therefore, it does not allow to be placed in opposition to the material ...' (Voloshinov 1976, 22).

This is, of course, a direct rejection of Christiansen/Bakhtin's concept of an aesthetic object produced by subjective contemplation and divorced from a material artifact. As a matter of fact, Voloshinov's emphasis on the materialistic principles of Marxism clashed with Bakhtin's neo-Kantian paper on every point including human language and its role in art and culture. While Bakhtin, in his adaptation of Christiansen, insists that 'language for poetry, just as for cognition and for an ethical action ... is merely a technical moment' and that 'language in its entirety is not necessary to any domain of culture,' Voloshinov emphatically insists that 'the human consciousness operates through words – that medium which is the most sensitive and, at the same time, the most complicated refraction of socioeconomic governance' (1976, 87).

The crucial role of verbal language which, according to Voloshinov's critique, has not been adequately understood by Freud and the Freudians, was further highlighted in *Marxism and Philosophy of Language*, originally published in 1929 under the name of Voloshinov but claimed to be Bakhtin's book by both the Soviet editors and their fellow-travellers. There we read: 'The word functions as an essential ingredient accompanying all ideological creativity whatsoever. The word accompanies and comments on each and every ideological act ... All manifestations of ideological creativity ... are bathed by, suspended in, and cannot be entirely segregated and divorced from the element of speech' (Voloshinov 1973, 15).

While Bakhtin's text of 1924 was clearly inspired by Broder Christiansen and the German neo-Kantians, the texts signed by Voloshinov were influenced by the doctrine of dialectical materialism and the German Hegelians. Unlike Bakhtin, Voloshinov readily reveals his sources. As a matter of fact, a substantial part of *Marxism and Philosophy of Language* is a critical review of German linguistic studies dealing with verbal interaction and dialogue. Moreover, many of Voloshinov's sociological ideas actually represent the rewording of the German sociologists into the Marxist jargon or, as Voloshinov himself prefers to call it, 'into the language of scientific materialism' (1973, 15). A closer comparison of Voloshinov's text with the numerous sources listed in the footnotes of *Marxism and Philosophy of Language* reveals that Voloshinov's views on the social interaction were shaped by the German sociologist Georg Simmel, while Voloshinov's studies of ideologies were inspired by Gompert's and Weininger's 'Weltanschauungslehre.' Moreover, it is clear that Voloshinov's philosophy of language in general and his semiotics in particular found a powerful source in Ernst Cassirer's *Philosophie der symbolischen Formen*, a book which Voloshinov had decided to translate into Russian (Clark and Holquist 1984, 265). Even the ideas of the Viennese philosopher Karl Buehler, who played an important role in the development of modern linguistics, were found by Voloshinov to be 'ingenious' (Voloshinov 1973, 68).

Yet the formation of Voloshinov's views on linguistics and culture were most decisively affected by Karl Vossler and his school, notably by Gertraud Lerch's study 'Die uneigentliche direkte Rede,' which was published in the Vossler Festschrift in 1922. Referring to this source, Voloshinov says: 'we have been using and shall continue to use Gertraud Lerch's term *uneigentliche direkte Rede* as the most neutral of all the terms proposed and the one entailing the least amount of theory' (1973, 141). It could be added that Voloshinov's translation of Lerch's 'uneigentliche direkte Rede' as 'nesobstvenno prjamaja rec' enriched the Russian linguistic terminology and was even accepted as a standard term in the Russian grammar of the Soviet Academy of Sciences.

Curiously enough, Bakhtin did not use Lerch/Voloshinov's term in his book on Dostoevsky (*Problemy tvorcestva Dostoevskego*), published 1928, the same year as Voloshinov's *Marxism and Philosophy of Language* was originally published, although both books discuss reported speech (*cuzaja rec*) and its treatment in literature. As I.R. Titunik points out in his paper 'Bakhtin &/or Voloshinov &/or Medvedev,' Voloshinov's calque of Gertraud Lerch's term was first used by Bakhtin in 'Slovo v romane,' allegedly written in 1934–5 but first published in 1975 (1984, 544). *Marxism and Philosophy of Language* was written before 1929 when Voloshinov, as a linguist, was affiliated with the Institute for Comparative History of Literature and Language in Leningrad, while the problem of reported speech was a topic of his doctoral thesis. At any rate, the discussion of reported speech constitutes the entire third part of *Marxism and Philosophy of Language*. Therefore, if we should accept that this book was written in co-operation with Bakhtin, then we have strong reasons to assume that Voloshinov's role in this co-operative venture was not marginal but pivotal. In fact, whoever prefers to use a slash between the names of Bakhtin and Voloshinov should probably reverse the order of names to distribute the credit justly.

Both Voloshinov's *Marxism and Philosophy of Language* and the first version of Bakhtin's book on Dostoevsky appeared in 1929. While Bakhtin's book was widely reviewed and positively received even by the Soviet commissar on education, Voloshinov's book was virtually ignored by the Soviet press. Only in Czechoslovakia did Voloshinov find a positive, even enthusiastic, reception by the members of the Prague Linguistic Circle, particularly by Petr Bogatyrev, Roman Jakobson, and Jan Mukařovský, and later a critical reception by Lubomír Doležel in his book on the style of modern Czech prose *O stylu moderni ceske prozy* (cf. Matejka 1978, 167). In the Soviet Union, the only noteworthy review was written by Marr's disciple R. Šor, who pointed out that Voloshinov's survey of linguistic trends in the West was preoccupied with the German scholarship and neglected the French and English contributions (Šor 1929). In fact, Šor's criticism could be extended to all the writings of the Bakhtin circle in the twenties and especially to Pavel Medvedev's book *The Formal Method in Literary Scholarship*, which was originally published in 1928, a year before Voloshinov's book *Marxism and Philosophy of Language* and Bakhtin's book on Dostoevsky appeared.

Unlike Bakhtin in his rejection of the Russian formalists from the neo-Kantian platform, but like Voloshinov in his book on *Marxism and Philosophy of Language*, Medvedev sees the main weakness of Russian formalism as its inability to study literature and art as a dialogue within a given social context. In his view, 'a dialectical conception of the "intrinsic" and the "extrinsic" relations of literature and extraliterary reality (ideological and otherwise) is an obligatory condition for the formulation of a genuine Marxist literary theory' (Medvedev/Bakhtin 1978, 26).

Clearly Medvedev's Marxist orientation had to clash head on with Bakhtin's neo-Kantian speculations about aesthetic object as 'artistic contemplation in its aesthetic purity' and about aesthetic form which transposes content 'to the plane of detached (isolated) and consummated being, axiologically self-contended being – to the plane of beauty' (1990, 296; 282). If we should believe, as some of our colleagues do, that Medvedev's book on the formal method was written by Bakhtin, then something truly remarkable must have happened to this disciple of Hermann Cohen and Broder Christiansen.

The differences between the Bakhtin/Christiansen paper from 1924 and the writings of Medvedev and Voloshinov from 1925 to 1930 are as striking as the similarities between the texts of Voloshinov and Medvedev and specifically between Voloshinov's book *Marxism and Philosophy of Language* and Medvedev's work on the formal method. As I.R. Titunik points out in his postscript to the English translation of Voloshinov's work, 'the two books significantly complement each other, share complete identity of assumptions and outlook, concepts and terminology, and even closely coincide in the very wording of the argument in a number of passages' (Voloshinov 1973, 178).

One of the features these two books have in common is their dependence on the same German sources. In fact, the very core of Voloshinov's and Medvedev's ideas was Marxist reinterpreted German scholarship with the emphasis on the Marxist underpinnings in general. According to Medvedev, 'only Marxism can bring the correct philosophical direction and necessary methodological precision ... Only Marxism can completely coordinate the specific reality of literature with the ideological horizon reflected in its content ... And only Marxism can do so in the unity of social life on the basis of the socioeconomic laws which totally permeate all ideological creation' (Medvedev/Bakhtin 1978, 26).

If this passage was not written by Pavel Medvedev, then it must have been written by Valentin Voloshinov rather than by Mikhail Bakhtin. Yet, in the seventies, both the enigmatic Bakhtin and his eloquent wife insisted on Bakhtin's authorship of both Medvedev's work on the formal method and Voloshinov's on Marxism and philosophy of language, although the dying Bakhtin refused to endorse the copyright claim with his own signature, thereby depriving his wife and the Soviet copyright agency of the international royalties.

At any rate, conceptually, terminologically, and stylistically, Medvedev and Voloshinov had much more in common with each other than with Bakhtin. But there are certain common denominators that all of them share. There cannot be any doubt that the most striking common denominator linking the three authors is their dependence on the school of Karl Vossler and, above all, on Leo Spitzer, who was certainly the most prominent among the Vosslerites.

Although Bakhtin does not readily give credit to his sources, his book on Dostoevsky quotes an entire passage from Spitzer's *Italienische Umgangssprache*, which was published in 1919. It begins: 'When we reproduce in our own speech a portion of our partner's utterance, then by virtue of the very change in speakers a change in tone inevitably occurs: the words of "the other person" always sound on our lips like something alien to us, and often have an intonation of ridicule, exaggeration, or mockery' (1984, 194; cf. Bakhtin 1929, 120).

Commenting on this passage, Bakhtin says: 'Someone else's words introduced into our speech ... become double-voiced.' Hence, a quote from Spitzer is used by Bakhtin to illustrate his concept of a double-voiced word which is the pivot of his methodological deliberations.

But it is not only Spitzer's 1919 book that made a decisive impact on Bakhtin's thinking. We have to assume that Bakhtin was aware of other writings by Spitzer even if he ceased to quote him. He certainly knew Spitzer's studies on medieval laughter, on carnival, and specifically on Rabelais, who was the topic of Spitzer's doctoral thesis in 1910 and who continued to attract Spitzer throughout his entire career not only in Germany but also at Johns Hopkins University in Baltimore. It could well be that Spitzer's decision to emigrate from Nazi Germany to the United States and to become an American citizen was the chief reason why Bakhtin did not dare to refer to him as frequently as Spitzer deserved. For that matter, Bakhtin also consistently ignored Roman Jakobson's studies in poetics and literary theory, including 'Medieval Mock Mystery,' his remarkable contribution to the Spitzer Festschrift in 1958, where Jakobson discusses medieval laughter, mock nativity, and mock resurrection. Indeed, the parallels between Spitzer's and Jakobson's comments on medieval laughter and Bakhtin's observations about medieval laughter in his book on Rabelais (1965) are rather striking. Of course, we do not know whether Bakhtin had access to the Spitzer Festschrift. What we know is that Bakhtin's Rabelais was first published in 1965, seven years after the Spitzer Festschrift.

Unfortunately, the Soviet records about Bakhtin are not readily available. We can only sympathize with Bakhtin's biographers, Katerina Clark and Michael Holquist, who complain that one of the difficulties of the Bakhtin files is the paucity of reliable data: 'not all the official documents can be taken as reliable. Some of them, particularly his work records, were drawn long after the period covered, by which time Bakhtin himself was vague about the facts ... There are also inconsistencies and contradictions among the extant documents, right down to the conflicting version of his birthdate' (1984, ix–x).

It is a pity that our American colleagues who study Bakhtin's legacy are not especially concerned with textual criticism. A rather shocking example of textual sloppiness appeared in 'Forum on Mikhail Bakhtin,' which was published in 1983 in *Critical Inquiry* and was republished in 1986 in *Bakhtin: Essays on Dialogues on His Work*, a book edited by Gary Saul Morson. Here we find 'Shouts on the Street: Bakhtin's Anti-Linguistics,' a paper by Professor Susan Stewart which begins with a reference to Lenin's New Economic Policy in the early twenties:

During the period of the New Economic Policy, as Lenin sought, rather abashedly, to approach communism via a new form of 'state capitalism,' ... the contradictions between synchrony and diachrony, between 'sincerity' and 'irony,' between insistences simultaneously upon meaning and 'multivocality' were in full flower. The work of the Bakhtin school may be located within this milieu of contradictions. It is clear that Mikhail Bakhtin's project was not linguistics but, to use his word, a 'metalinguistics' ... (1986, 41)

To illustrate her interpretation, Professor Stewart quotes Bakhtin's book on Dostoevsky and chooses a passage with the term 'metalinguistics':

The point is not the mere presence of several linguistic styles, social dialects, etc., a presence which is measured by purely linguistic criteria; the point is the dialogical angle at which they (the styles, dialects, etc.) are juxtaposed and counterposed in the work. But that dialogic angle cannot be measured by means of purely linguistic criteria, because dialogic relationships, although they belong to the province of the word, fall outside of its purely linguistic study. Dialogical relationships (including the dialogical relationships of the speaker to his own word) are a matter for metalinguistics. (1973, 150–1)

It is obvious that Professor Stewart and her editor, Gary Saul Morson, were unaware that the entire passage quoted does not appear in the book on Dostoevsky published by Bakhtin in 1929 (Problemy tvorcestva Dostoevskogo) but only in his book on Dostoevsky published in 1963 (*Problemy poetiky Dostoevskogo*). The term 'metalinguistics' was never used in Bakhtin's 1929 book on Dostoevsky and, for that matter, in any text of Bakhtin or his school in the twenties (cf. Titunik 1984, 544). Bakhtin's usage of the term 'metalinguistics' was inspired not by the milieu of Lenin's New Economic Policy, but quite possibly by the linguistic discussion in the fifties and sixties in the United States, if not directly by Jakobson's 'Shifters,' published in 1956 and ingeniously elaborated upon in 1957 by V.V. Ivanov in his 'Kod i soob-scenie' (1957, 48–50), published in Moscow six years before the publication of Bakhtin's *Problemy tvorcestva Dostoevskogo*.

Professor Stewart and her editor should know that accurate textual criticism is of paramount importance, especially if the history of ideas is the topic. For the sake of critical scholarship, it is also important to know who deserves credits and for what. It might well be that the real credit for the most powerful ideas of the Bakhtin school should go not to Bakhtin, Voloshinov, and Medvedev, nor to Karl Marx, Friedrich Engels, and Lenin, but to the German philosophy and philology of the late nineteenth and early twentieth century, to Broder Christiansen, to Ernst Cassirer, to Karl Vossler and his school, and especially to the Austro-American scholar Leo Spitzer (cf. Wellek 1970). At any rate, their impact on the formation of the Bakhtin school in Russia was essential and should not be forgotten.

21

Scratching the Bronze Mirror: Looking for Traces of Fictionality in Chinese Poetics

DOUWE W. FOKKEMA

Various authors in the last two or three decades have emphasized that the world we know consists of texts, thus undoing the oppositional relationship between linguistic sign and extralinguistic world. Derrida's well-known phrase 'il n'y a pas de hors-texte,' is symptomatic of a tendency towards linguistic (textual, narrativistic) determinism (Derrida 1967, 227), which even made school among historians (LaCapra 1983). Obviously, if the idea of a world outside language is denied, or more precisely if human beings are denied the capacity for knowing the world except through the medium of language, it makes no sense to discuss reality as something independent of language. The notion of correspondence to reality (or non-correspondence to reality) can no longer serve as a criterion, since knowledge of reality is not directly accessible and always tainted by the vehicle of language. It is clear that this ends the discussion of fictionality, in which, at least in the occidental tradition, the notion of non-correspondence to reality plays a crucial part.

Derrida's view, however, is only one of the more recent and more outspoken stages in a long chain of opposition to Fregean semantics. We owe a clear description of Frege's conception of semantics to Lubomír Doležel (1990a). Gottlob Frege posited that sentences that lack reference, that do not refer to an entity in the world, are neither true nor false. Such sentences can be found in fiction; they have no reference (*Bedeutung*), only sense (*Sinn*). Doležel concludes that Frege distinguished between '(a) the semantics of referential languages, which studies the truth conditions and reference relations of verbal signs; (b) the semantics of sense languages ('images'), which is concerned with the rules and patterns of sense organization' (1990, 93).

At least four objections could be made. (1) Why should the notion of truth be restricted to correspondence with reality? (2) Do we have consensus on what the term 'reality' means in this context? (3) It is counterintuitive to postulate that fiction does not refer to the world we live in (reality). (4) Frege's dichotomy may serve as an analytical model but cannot explain why the same utterance can be considered referential by one person and non-referential by another. Differences of cultural knowledge or conventions are not taken into account. Let us discuss these objections in more detail.

Gustav Špet distinguished between three kinds of truth. Apart from 'tran-scendental or material truth' and 'logical truth,' he postulated a third kind of truth: 'poetic truth.' In the play of poetic forms, the complete emancipation from reality can be attained. But these forms maintain an internal poetic logic, a logic sui generis, as well as a sense (*smysl*), since the emancipation from the familiar situation does not imply that the text makes no sense (Špet 1923, 2: 66). This internal poetic logic comes close to 'the rules and patterns of sense organization' (Frege, as rephrased by Doležel) in a hypothetical world. If some given data and rules are accepted, the rest of the narrated world will or will not be accepted as a truthful elaboration. 'Truthful' in this context means not, 'in conformity with existing reality,' but 'in conformity with a possible reality.'

There is no consensus about what reality means. Where is the borderline between knowledge of reality and superstition? Are we talking of the reality of molecules and atoms, or of a Buddhist view of reality? The evasiveness of the reality concept is probably the main cause behind the silence around the notion of fictionality. Certainly, my concept of reality differs from Daoist or Buddhist conceptions. In Europe, both *Sprachskepsis* – from Nietzsche onward – and the sociology of knowledge have made it impossible to speak of reality in a naive way.

It is hard to explain why there is a long tradition of fiction, if it does not have a clear function in our personal lives or for the survival of our culture. Various attempts to define the function of fictional literature focus on the aesthetic function. Jakobson and Mukařovský have convincingly argued that a text may have an aesthetic function in combination with other functions, with the possibility that certain recipients may conclude that the aesthetic function predominates. A combination of the aesthetic or poetic function with the referential function, however, was excluded by Frege's dichotomy. This can be concluded on the basis of Frege's view, in 'Über Sinn und Bedeutung' that the question whether a particular utterance is true or false is incompatible with aesthetic pleasure: 'Mit der Frage nach der Wahrheit würden wir den Kunstgenuss verlassen und uns einer wissenschaftlichen Betrachtung zuwenden' (Frege 1892, 48). Frege's later pragmatic considerations qualify this view to the extent that it is up to the hearer to decide whether the truth question applies. However, I understand that, according to Frege, the recipient too is confronted with a binary choice: either the truth question is posed or it is not posed. And if a recipient wishes to interpret a text as literature, the truth question cannot be asked (cf. Frege 1918–19, 36). The functionalist approach as developed by Mukařovský has proven to be more viable than Frege's classification on the basis of static definitions.

Fiction may be considered pertinent to the world we live in, if we can argue that our ways of dealing with the world through communication need texts with an aesthetic function; in other words, if we can argue that the possibility, presence, and sometimes predominance of the aesthetic function increases – in an indirect way – our communicative competence. That argument can probably be made, but it will require more research to test this view.

The high esteem for literary, including fictional, texts in occidental culture has led several theoreticians to conclude that fiction is truthful in a general, but not in a literal, sense. Fictional texts maintain a claim to truth while defying a direct comparison with reality. This is the position of Špet (1922–3), of Mukařovský (1934), and of Ingarden (1960, 325).

Umberto Eco does not deny that fictional texts pertain to the world we live in, but in his *A Theory of Semiotics* (1976) he insists on excluding truth-values from his field of inquiry. Eco rejects Frege's concept of meaning and wants to investigate the *content* of an utterance, not the referent (the entity in the world to which the utterance refers). Semiotics cannot handle the distinction between true and false, which, according to Eco, is a pre- or post-semiotic problem. We are bound to conclude that semiotics must abstain also from the problem of fictionality, unless it is studied in connection with cultural conventions (which in our multicultural society may be unequally maintained between the inhabitants of one and the same city, between the students of one and the same university, between the members of one and the same family). Eco views semantic content as a cultural unit. This leaves room for interpreting *The Satanic Verses* both as fiction (in one culture) and as libel offensive to Islam (in another culture).

For Eco, the question of truth-valuation was bracketed. In his view, the judgment that a text should be read as a fictional one depends on a cultural convention. In this context, a certain degree of cultural relativism makes sense, and even opens new ways for research.

If the acknowledgment of the fictional character of a text is based on convention, the convention must be known to the author, or to the readers (or listeners), or to both. In practice, knowledge of the convention that certain texts can be attributed fictional status is unequally divided over the world of readers and listeners, and also unequally spread even within one culture. First, one must learn the indicators of fictionality from early childhood onward, beginning with 'once upon a time' or 'it was so, it was not' (Rushdie

1988, 143), and arriving later at a stage of sophisticated knowledge of textual – and contextual – signs that point at the plausibility of a fictional interpretation. There is no veto on reading a text as a fictional one, even if its author never intended to write a fictional text. Indeed, various medieval hagiographic works are now being read as fictional texts. Or, the other way round, a book that an author announced to be fiction can sometimes be interpreted as (partly) autobiographic. *To the Lighthouse* may serve as an example. At times, critics are divided over the question whether a particular text should be read as a predominantly fictional or referential text. In cases of possible offence, the answer to the question is a crucial one, as appears from the upheaval around *The Satanic Verses*.

Siegfried J. Schmidt has discussed the matter in terms of the 'aesthetic convention' and the 'fact convention' ('tatsachenbezügliche Konvention'), but deliberately he has left open the possibility that one and the same text may be read by some people in conformity with the aesthetic convention, attributing a fictional interpretation to it, whereas others, in accordance with the fact convention, will look for truth-values (cf. Fokkema 1989). Knowledge and the disposition of the recipients play a crucial role. Look at the bronze mirror of a story: it will vaguely reflect your own intentions and interest, your own restricted cultural knowledge, and your own mood.

If we now turn to the question of fictionality in Chinese literature, one thing will have become clear: fictionality is not a textual feature. On the basis of the text alone, we can never be sure that it was meant to be fiction, and that under all circumstances it has been read and will be read as fiction. However, we may acquire conventional knowledge that enables us to recognize the fictional intention of an author, or to project contemporary reading habits on texts from a distant past.

We also may have been taught to distinguish between a significant hypothesis and correspondence to reality, between a general insight and particular veracity. It is conventional knowledge in the West that this distinction is useful and adds to our communicative competence. In order to gain a general insight, we must be able to abstract from references to certain particulars. The capacity to do so is not unlike the processing of a metaphor, which also implies that we ignore certain aspects of meaning and focus on others.

The decision whether an utterance should be considered fictional is taken by someone participating in a particular communication situation. In the process of taking this decision, the cultural knowledge of such a person is as important a factor as the possible indicators of fictionality he or she believes to see.

The more time that has passed since a text was produced and the less knowledge we have of the original historical context, the more chance there is that we will attribute a fictional interpretation to that text. In fact, since history has erased part of the referential relations to a setting we can no longer reconstruct, we will focus inevitably on general aspects, on internal coherence, on the 'autonomous sign' (Mukařovský 1934). Older texts are often handled in the same way as old paintings hanging in museums that have titles such as 'Portrait of an Unknown Man' or 'Portrait of an Unknown Woman,' which definitely were portraits of real human beings whose names have been lost. These paintings are not referring (anymore) to a particular member of a distinguished family or to a famous patrician. They simply represent, for instance, an old man suffering with dignity or a rich woman staring at you with eyes that convey both satisfaction and curiosity. These paintings, which were portraits, have become fictions about the human condition.

The fate of these paintings, which are so numerous in our museums, is also the fate of many traditional Chinese texts. Occasional poetry, once meant to express a farewell to a particular friend, is now interpreted as a general complaint about separation. Tu Fu's lines 'Human parting is not new; / We understand now why the ancients were sad' (Hung 1969, 153) in a poem that describes the departure of a friend receive probably more emphasis now than at the time the poem was written.

The evolution of fiction to postmodernist extremes in the work of Borges, Calvino, and Fuentes and the evolution of metaphor to surrealist proportions show a striking parallelism. Postmodernist fictions and surrealist metaphors result from highly selective procedures. This sort of text production is based on the assumption that parts of our knowledge of language and of the world can temporarily be suppressed. Borrowing a term that Poggioli (1968) used to describe the avant-garde, the notion of non-correspondence to reality in the modern occidental concepts of fictionality and metaphor can be said to be motivated by an 'agonistic' impulse. Reading, too, in particular modern texts, can be seen as a struggle, into which we must be initiated. Indeed, in the case of postmodernist or surrealist texts, educated occidental readers have learned to screen the semantic content and to separate features that should be ignored from features that should be maintained.

My thesis is that the lack of this agonistic impulse in Chinese poetics has created a completely different condition for the notion of fictionality. James Liu has argued that the unitary principle of the universe or Dao does not 'exist in the individual mind as a distinct concept or image; rather it absorbs the individual mind' (Liu 1975, 48). The imagination, then, is considered not a subjective force, as opposed to reality or factuality, but rather a vehicle that mediates between universe and the individual mind. Here Liu Xie (circa AD 500) can be quoted; he writes, in a non-antagonistic way, that 'through the subtlety of imagination, the spirit comes into contact with external things' (in Liu Hsieh 1959, 154).

In discussions about fictionality in Chinese traditional poetics, two basic assumptions may serve as points of departure. First, the notion of reality or factuality differs from occidental conceptions. Reality never is empirical reality; the Chinese traditional concept of reality is pervaded by metaphysical principles. Wilt Idema reminds us that, for instance, Feng Menglong (circa 1600) in his stories 'tried to retell facts, but he bent them to his will when the expediency of Truth required him to do so' (1974, 55).

Second, the antagonistic opposition of imagination (fiction) versus reality (framed by metaphysical principles) is avoided. Fiction, of course, is possible, but good fiction will not contradict veracity. Fiction in Chinese traditional poetics should conform to a combination of (empirical) truth and (metaphysical) Truth, whereas in occidental poetics fiction may contradict empirical truth, only if it respects Truth. The Chinese traditional reader has no need for shading off certain aspects of a story in order to see its metaphysical value. Occidental readers do exactly that; they split up their various conceptions of a modern text and select the one conception that offers most.

These considerations made Andrew Plaks observe that in the Chinese tradition there is a 'narrative continuum from history to fiction' (1977, R319). He notices an extensive overlapping of historical and fictional writings and refers to Zhang Xuecheng's discussion of the 7:3 proportion of historical fact and fictional arrangement in *Sanguo yanyi* (Romance of the three kingdoms) as 'indicating not so much an epistemological issue as a relative aesthetic variable ranging from the more concrete to the more abstract perception of reality, what we might call representational and non-representational mimetic positions' (1977, 317). Plaks goes as far as to suggest that the distinction between historical and fictional narrative is mainly validated by a division of labour. It is content rather than form or epistemological view that decides. On the one hand, there is historiography and historical fiction that deal with the affairs of state and public life, and, on the other hand, there is narrative dealing with the individualized and intimate details of the private lives of characters of various backgrounds. Such a distinction will hold as long as the narrative about private life does not deviate too much from patterns that can be framed by metaphysical principles.

The latter condition depends, of course, on interpretation. The seventeenth-century critic Zhang Zhupo, however, had no difficulty in postulating that even *Jin Ping Mei* (Golden lotus), the well-known erotic novel, 'is the result of a comprehensive understanding of the Way' (in Doleželová-Velingerová 1989, 142). Or consider the *incipit* of the last chapter of *Jou p'u t'uan* (The prayer mat of flesh), that other erotic novel from the seventeenth century, which claims that the narration of erotic episodes is not an end in itself, but rather it serves to gain a hearing for the voice of reason (Li Yü 1963, 343). Here the connection with metaphysical principles is a strained one, and probably only an excuse for allowing the reader to read a piece of pornography.

The misuse of the metaphysical connection as a pretext does not invalidate the theoretical principle of seeing a connection between story and Truth. However, the strained pretence of the metaphysical connection also makes us aware of the fact that this metaphysical theory of fiction is merely a convention, and that readers may wish to forget about that convention while reading. This also seems to be the argument of Anthony Yu, who, with reference to *Hongloumeng* (Dream of the red chamber), asks the rhetorical questions: 'How should the reader regard those pages full of idle words, which not only pretend to be lived experience, but also render it irresistibly attractive? If life is illusory like fiction, why is fiction about life such an engaging illusion?' (1988, 18).

Conventions of reading are restricted to a particular group of people, at a particular place and time. To read a text as fiction is such a convention. My conventional way of reading a text may go against the grain of other, perhaps traditional, ways of reading, but that does not make my way of reading incorrect. This is just a simple way of saying that the restricted validity of conventions is a semiotic fact. The traditional Chinese way of reading narrative texts certainly differs from fictional reading in the West. However, if we, or a new generation of Chinese readers, would prefer to attribute fictionality – in the occidental sense of the word – to *Sanguo yanyi* or *Jin Ping Mei*, this would be no mistake. To the contrary: subscribing to the traditional Chinese reading of these texts would imply subscribing at the same time to traditional assumptions about history as cyclical recurrence and about human life as being just a dream. Are we obliged to embrace traditional metaphysics and beliefs if we wish to read these classical novels? The bronze mirrors of the Tang dynasty hardly reflect anything. More than a thousand years have turned them dark. One may scratch their surface, one may try to polish them – usually in vain. But if their original shine is partly restored, they reflect the observer, with his or her own inclinations, restricted knowledge, and mood. There is no fictionality in Chinese narrative, nor in occidental stories, but readers may choose from among the conventional ways of reading they know of (including a fictional reading) and attribute that way of reading to the text at hand that suits their present interest and disposition best.

22

Formalist and Structuralist Activity in Poland: Tradition and Progress

EDWARD MOŻEJKO

The first attempts at critical literary writing in Poland can be traced back to the late Middle Ages and early Renaissance; they were tied to the rise and development of modern literature. Originally prevalent religious content was gradually superseded by secular themes which began to grow stronger at the end of the fifteenth century and, as in other western European literatures, reached their full bloom during the Renaissance. During this long cultural period, the Polish language formed its present grammatical structure and lexical framework.

The greatest contribution to this development belongs to Jan Kochanowski (1530–84), considered by some European critics to be one of the most prominent poets of the Renaissance. Kochanowski was a bilingual author who wrote in both Polish and Latin, but the Polish part of his writing, by far the largest, laid the foundations for the evolution of the Polish literary language and established its modern canon. Like A. Pushkin in Russia at the beginning of the nineteenth century, Kochanowski became, in the mid-sixteenth century, the father-figure of Polish national literature. His texts remain as readable for an average educated Pole today as they were for his or her ancestors four centuries ago.

Parallel to the rapid growth and enrichment of literary life, one can discern the first serious attempts to assess its aesthetic, as well as its religious, social, or even political values. We find, for example, in Kochanowski's poetry scattered comments about the place of the writer in society and remarks about the significance of literature in general.

The strongest impulse to set up and develop a separate branch of knowledge that would focus on verbal art came with the establishment of the first Polish university in Kraków, Jagellonian University, in 1364. Here the disciplines of poetry and rhetoric were fostered in the faculty of artium (liberal arts) and were taught in the lower (undergraduate) level of university education. However, in 1406 a separate department of grammar and rhetoric was established, and in 1449 the first department of poetics was added to the existing disciplines in the humanities. Specialists in these areas of research worked in Latin as well, but it was not long before Polish texts began to attract their attention. Comments on Polish authors and the variety of their styles gradually became a part of textbooks devoted to rhetoric. As a rule, these early treatments were concerned with three major components of the subject: *inventio* (creation of poetic fiction), *dispositio* (division of poetry into genres and larger literary categories), and *elocutio* (stylistic shape or form).[1]

It is clear that the beginnings of literary critical thought in Poland are unquestionably dominated by the treatment of literature as art, and that early critical attention focuses almost exclusively on the formal aspects of imaginative writing. It is impossible to trace all the characteristics of this approach and their evolution in a short paper, but I would like to mention the name of one important critic and theoretician of literature, Maciej Kazimierz Sarbiewski (1595–1640) and his treatise of 1627, *De Acuto et Arguto* (About the sharp-pointed and the distinct). Sarbiewski was a Jesuit, well versed in the classics, and an author of Baroque poetry; Pope Urban VIII bestowed the title of *poeta laureatus* on Sarbiewski and appointed him to revise the Latin hymns in the Roman Breviary. Although during his life he was known all over Europe as the Christian Horace, the most lasting contribution he left behind remained in the field of poetics. Sarbiewski defined the subject of his research as a theory of *acumen*, a word which we should translate as 'shrewdness,' 'ingenuity,' or even 'trickery,' but which is related directly to the language (*oratio*) of imaginative literature, as distinct from conversational speech. Of course, the very existence of rhetoric and its boisterous revival during the Renaissance point to the fact that those who cultivated this branch of the humanities assumed the difference between spoken language and the language of literature. Sarbiewski's contribution, however, seems to be unique in a twofold manner: first, he clearly formulated the distinction between the two modes of communication; secondly, he brought to our attention the question of the recipient, the reader, or – as he called it – the audience. According to Sarbiewski, the effects and proprieties of the pointed (*acutus*) speech must please the 'audience's soul' and evoke admiration and delight. In other words, Sarbiewski touched upon the question of both the initial and the final stages of literary productions in suggesting that reception constitutes an important part of the creative process (Ulčinaite 1984; see also Kroll 1974, 99–100).

The predominance of formalist critical tendency in Polish literary tradition came to an end during the gradual decline of Polish statehood in the second half of the eighteenth century. The loss of independence coincided more or less with the rise of Romanticism. Its writers and critics alike propounded a completely different literary model and assigned new tasks to literature. Literature was perceived as an expression of national spirit, and its mission was to preserve the integrity and identity of the nation. Ironically, it was during the period of Romanticism that literary criticism separated and established itself as a professional activity, distinct from other forms of literary endeavours. Polish Romantic criticism treated writers not only as artists but first of all as political leaders and impellers of moral resistance.

This state of affairs, with a few deviations, remained unchanged throughout the nineteenth century. The two most prominent historians of Polish literature during this period, Piotr Chmielowski (1848–1904) and Bronislaw Chlebowski (1846–1916), were motivated by French positivist philosophy to discuss literature as a tool expressing either a writer's individual frame of mind or the external social, political, historical events that were thought to be of national importance. Hence, an acute interest developed in writers' biographical data and in gathering material which had little to do with the literary work of art itself (Gorski 1960).

A gradual elimination of this critical school, or rather an intense polemics with it, began on the eve of the First World War and coincided chronologically with the rise of Russian formalism. We cannot speak of any dominant theoretical school in Poland at that time. Polish literary scholars who undertook the task of transcending the positivist cultural legacy represented a greater variety of aesthetic approaches, and undertook by far a stronger and richer multidirectional theoretical quest than, for example, their Russian counterparts who were marked by the formalist obsession. In Poland, the frontal attack against the positivist tradition and the derived symbolist practice of impressionistic criticism took almost simultaneously three parallel theoretical paths: neo-Kantian formalism, phenomenological objectiveness, and stylistic-structural expediency born out of linguistic inspiration.

Four scholars ought to be credited for their role in bringing about new possibilities and opening new perspectives in literary studies: Juliusz Kleiner (1886–1957), Zygmunt Łempicki (1886–1943), Manfred Kridl (1882–1957), and Kazimierz Wóycicki (1876–1938) (Markiewicz 1985a, 148–52; see also Markiewicz 1985b). If, in the history of modern Polish literary criticism, their contribution can be defined as a 'formalist bent' then it should be added that 'the bent' implied, in fact, a return to the aesthetic values that were cultivated prior to the decline of the Polish state in the eighteenth century.

In 1913 Kleiner, in his article 'Character i przedmiot badań literackich' (The nature and subject of literary studies), used for the first time the formulation 'science of literature' ('nauka o literaturze' or 'wiedza o literaturze'). Following Dilthey and Rickert, Kleiner suggested that, unlike natural sciences, the historico-literary cognition does not so much generalize as it does individualize the phenomena of its examination. It evaluates more than it explains. Inspired by Bergsonian philosophy, Kleiner also recommended that at the initial stage of critical investigation one should develop the closest possible direct psychic rapport with a literary work of art, to strive for its intuitive cognition as a whole. According to Kleiner, the subject of literary scholarship is the content of texts themselves, understood in the broad sense of the word. He defined it as a 'distinct sphere of human reality' and insisted that it ought to be approached from an aesthetic point of view. Kleiner grasps the analysis of literary work as a process composed of three stages: an intuitive embrace of the whole; an investigation of details based on the understanding of the whole; a construction and sense of the richest possible psychic entity which is most closely connected with the text and which is closest to the work in the writer's own consciousness. Later Kleiner considerably modified the importance of the psychic factor in his theoretical considerations and stressed the need for pursuing an artistic and aesthetic analysis of literature. It should be emphasized that, in the early years of this century, he was among the first to reject the didactic function of literature, questioning its role as a means of cognition of reality and most forcefully advocating the concept of the literary text as an act of creativity.

New ideas about literary scholarship, which led beyond those that Kleiner postulated, were developed by Zygmunt Łempicki. Łempicki's contribution seems to be even more sophisticated, valuable, and advanced than that of his other Polish contemporaries. In this respect, two of his early articles, both published in 1920, deserve special attention: 'W sprawie uzasadnienia poetyki czystej' (Concerning the justification of a pure poetics) and 'Idea a osobowosc w historii literatury' (Idea and individuality in the history of literature).[2]

In the first article, Łempicki makes it clear that his prime task is the rejection of genetic-psychological methods of literary investigation. Implicit in Łempicki's point of departure is the assumption that there exist two opposite poles of the creative process: the author of the text and its recipient. He defines the artistic object (produced by an author) as an individual relation of factors capable of producing effects thanks to which, under appropriate apperception, an aesthetic object comes into being. The artistic object is different from other objects in that it is created by an artist for the sole purpose of enabling a receiving individual to realize the aesthetic object or, in other words, to evoke aesthetic impression. It's worth noticing that Łempicki does not share the Russian formalists' claim that poetic devices are oriented towards themselves or are, in short, self-centred. Thus, Łempicki differentiates between artistic object

– the creation of an artist – and aesthetic object – the result of a recipient's mental operations in assimilating what has been created.

The task of pure poetics is to describe the manifold structure of literary creativity with the help of what Husserl called *Beschreibungsbegriffe* (descriptive concepts). This does not, however, exhaust the task of poetics. Each work of art is a psycho-physical creation (*twór*, a word that can also mean 'composition'). Poetics is a science about such creations. The psycho-physical creation expresses certain psychic products. Therefore, in Łempicki's view, on the one hand, poetics becomes a part of a general theory of signs, or semiotics, and, on the other, it ought to be included in hermeneutics, or the science of understanding signs and expressions. The terms 'semiotics' and 'hermeneutics' are not ushered in here from today's theoretical vocabulary to conceptualize or indicate, so to speak, the modernity of Łempicki's thought. They were used by him and seem to suggest that, in developing his ideas of literary science, he came close to formulating a semiotic theory of literature and art.[3]

In the second article, Łempicki developed a more coherent and comprehensive theoretical view, one that later became the corner-stone of modern literary theory and poetics, namely, the basic scheme of the communicative channel: author–text–receiver. In this chain of interdependencies, the most important link, according to the Polish theoretician, remains the author. The individual effort of the artist occupies a central place in Łempicki's theoretical speculations, yet at the same time he stresses that the individual life of the creative person takes place within a social milieu. Even the effort of a genius requires strengthening by the accompanying movements of the masses. 'History of literature,' writes Łempicki, 'is in equal degree a history of creative genius as it is a history of public taste' (my translation). The initial and direct object of literary scholarship is, of course, the text. Critics who subject texts to analysis act as intermediaries between the writer and the reading audience. Critical activity is not a passive function but has multiple consequences and, first of all, sends new creative stimuli back to the writer. It is, therefore, important to investigate literary criticism itself. Out of the relationship between the writer, the readership (the relationship between the writer and the readership creates historical ideas which are nothing else but a response to the thoughts and deeds of individuals), and the critic evolves literary life or what, ten years later, Eikhenbaum defined as *literaturnyi byt*.[4] In the concluding remarks of the section dealing with these issues, Łempicki postulates that the history of literature, as a subject, encompasses the whole literary life, not just literary texts.

Łempicki's theoretical stand, particularly his remarks about the literary work of art as a psycho-physical creation, and his references to Husserl lead us to believe that he can be perceived as an immediate predecessor of Roman

Ingarden.[5] Since Ingarden's work is available today to Western literary scholars in English translations and is relatively well known,[6] I shall omit a discussion of his work in favour of a less-known yet important Polish theoretician, Manfred Kridl. Kridl was a professor of Polish literature at the University of Wilno, then for a period of four years (1929–32) he lectured at the University of Brussels. During the war he emigrated to the United States where he became a professor of Polish literature at Columbia University. He occupied this position until his death in 1957.

Kridl was, first of all, a historian of literature, but in the early thirties he suddenly showed interest in theoretical problems and produced three publications: 'Przelom w metodyce badań literackich' (The breakthrough in the methodology of literary studies [1933]); 'Podstawy nauki o literaturze' (Foundations of literary studies [1935]); *Wstęp do badań nad dziełem literackim* (Introduction to the study of the literary work of art [1936]; see Kridl 1978).

Although the initial inspiration for Kridl's theoretical interests came from his Polish and some Western colleagues,[7] his enthusiastic reception of the Russian formalists attests to his desire to cross national boundaries and perhaps find his own understanding of literature. Whatever the case, it can be said that the decline and eventual suppression of Russian formalism in the late twenties had an almost immediate Polish reaction and eventually led to the revival of this theoretical current of literary theory in Wilno under the guidance of Manfred Kridl. He managed to gather a few capable young scholars around himself, and this circle formed a group referred to at times as the Wilno School of Formalists.[8]

Although the time span of the group's activity was short, covering roughly the period from 1934 to the outbreak of the Second World War in 1939, its members managed to publish quite a few important theoretical and analytical studies, the most important being Kridl's *Wstęp do badań nad dziełem literackim*. The book is comprised of a preface and eight chapters: (1) introductory explanations; (2) the nature of literary studies; (3) the subject of literary studies; (4) the literary work of art; (5) the scope and classification of literary studies; (6) the problems of methodology, which is subdivided further into general comments and classification of methods, extra-literary methods, and ergocentric methods; (7) principles of the integral literary method; (8) doubts and perils.

Kridl concentrates his attention on the literary work of art and rejects the traditional treatment of literary texts as products of practical human activity oriented towards the satisfaction of social, political, or psychological needs of the reader. Literary works of art must contain characteristics that do not occur or exist in other products of the human mind. Referring to Ingarden's *The*

Literary Work of Art, Kridl acknowledges its importance but expresses doubts as to whether the four strata enumerated by him as determinants of literature are sufficient to define its specificity and distinctness. All these four layers can also be found in scientific and philosophical treatises, essays, journalistic articles, and so on. Kridl sharply opposes all attempts made by some Polish literary historians to include as literature some political works written by, for example, Roman Dmowski (leader of the National Democratic Party) or by Marshall J. Pilsudski, who led Poland to independence in 1918. According to Kridl, the task of the literary theoretician is to defend the 'autonomy' of the literary work of art by discovering such elements as will prove and determine its 'otherness' from non-literary texts. Scientific works may please the reader but various strata serve a different purpose than they do in literature. Kridl emphasizes the fact that non-literary texts fulfil practical functions, which is not the case with fictional literature. For Kridl, fictionality, or the fictional world, seems to be the first criterion that should be considered in any discussion of literature as a distinct object of study. Literature represents fiction which has little to do with 'truth,' in the scientific sense of the word, or with life. Consequently, what Kridl looks for is literariness.

What then makes the literary work of art distinct from other texts? It is in this answer that we can perceive how Kridl was influenced by Russian formalists. First, he introduces the distinction between poetic language and language of information. The latter is divided into two subcategories, colloquial and scientific language, both of which have 'communication' as their primary goal. As for poetic language, its function consists of creating fictional reality, and it is devoid of any practical ends. Second, Kridl argues that structure or composition is the important element contributing to the existence of a literary text. In relation to external reality, structure is even more distinctly pronounced than the poetic language, because one cannot find its equivalence (parallels) in reality. Structuring, or composing, is a strictly literary activity, independent from external factors.

Finally, Kridl suggests that literariness is determined by a third category of characteristics which include elements such as themes, plots, motifs, and so on. Although in themselves they constitute indispensable features of literary texts, together they contribute to the deformation of an emerging structural whole, and thus set it apart from external reality.

In his search to define the ontological status of the literary work of art, Kridl also touches upon the question of authorship and differentiates between the real author and the one who gradually becomes known from the text itself. In stressing this point, Kridl targets those still inclined to treat a novel, drama, or poem as a manifestation of a writer's 'soul.' He argues against the Ingardian notion of a literary work of art as an intentional object and refers to the formulation given by the famous Polish logician K. Twardowski of the Warsaw School of Logic, who defined the work of art as a psychological creation. Kridl is inclined to accept such a definition, but suggests at the same time that the work could be more adequately termed an 'artefact.'

As for the methods of literary investigation, Kridl divides them into extra-literary methods and ergocentric methods. He gives a lengthy survey of the former and leaves no doubt that the only way to approach and to understand literature is through the medium of methods which he calls 'ergocentric' or 'integral.'

On the whole, it should be pointed out that Kridl's effort did not find many followers. On the contrary, his theoretical postulates were subjected to severe criticism at times, if only because they showed a clear affinity with something that came from Soviet Russia. Indeed, considering the general hostility that Poles nourished towards everything that came from the Soviet Union, Kridl's theoretical preferences ought to be seen as an act of intellectual honesty and moral courage.

It should be mentioned, however, that yet another factor may have played a role in limiting the appeal of Kridl's Wilno group as a source of theoretical inspiration. It is related to the theoretical writings and activity of Kazimierz Wóycicki, a contemporary of Kridl, Łempicki, and Kleiner. Wóycicki's impact on the whole generation of young scholars of literature, particularly those who studied at the University of Warsaw in the thirties, cannot be overestimated. The origins of Polish structuralism are indissolubly linked with his name. It seems that, in the course of later developments, his branch of theoretical discourse attracted more attention than that elicited by Kridl.

In the early years of this century, Wóycicki initiated in Poland (partly under German influence) a branch of studies that could be defined as literary stylistics but that eventually led him far beyond the initial purpose.[9] In 1914 Wóycicki published two important studies: 'Historia literatury i poetyka' (History of literature and poetics) and 'Jednosc stylowa utworu poetyckiego' (Stylistic unity of the literary work of art). In the first, he proposed to divide the history of literature into the external history of literature (which would explore the relation of *belles-lettres* and poetic works to reality) and the internal literary history. The task of the latter is to supplement the former by analysing the aesthetic value of literature or, in other words, to create a history of poetic art (in today's terminology we would say 'historical poetics'). In addition, Wóycicki proposed that poetics should also include two subcategories: psychological poetics (that is, poetics which would discover the laws of the creative process and of the reading experience) and aesthetic or 'objective' poetics, the goal of which is to explore the structure of the poetic work as a 'verbal (lexical) aesthetic location.' Wóycicki's most significant theoretical contribution is to be found, however, in the second article which focuses on the stylistic unity of the literary work of art, where he states that the work of art is a separate, self-contained entity composed of some elements that are connected by certain relationships:

The work of art is a separate, closed-in-itself entity composed of certain elements which are cemented by certain relationships. In the work of art each element acquires a proper sense and significance; it lives in an appropriate manner, and acts only in relationship with other elements, and thanks to this interdependence all parts are united in a common aim, tend towards an aggregate goal ... There, where all factors act in harmony, condition themselves, [and] have the same impress, the same measure and proportions, where they perfectly fit together and are tied into one whole, there comes into existence a stylistic unity of a work of art, a stylish work of art. (1961, 272; my translation)

In Wóycicki's view, a literary work of art is not the sum total of static formal devices, but an entity of dynamically correlated elements. It is worth noting that Wóycicki's article appeared almost fifteen years before the publication of Tynianov's and Jakobson's 'Problems in the Study of Literature and Language,' considered to be the 'manifesto' of structuralist poetics. Although Wóycicki did not go as far as to view theoretical principles of analysis on the plane of interrelated systems as Tynianov and Jakobson did, he certainly introduced the notion of literature as a dynamically evolving phenomenon. It should be remembered, however, that in the same article Wóycicki raised a number of other theoretical questions and formulated, for example, the idea of the 'artistic dominant.' Among various structural (or stylistic) constituents of the literary work of art, there exists always one 'leading' component which Wóycicki proposes to call 'dominant.' This 'governing' or dominant constituent lends to a given literary text a dimension of depth; it determines its principal point of view and prevents the literary work of art from being interpreted at will or misinterpreted. The importance of the dominant does not depend on the number of words, pages, or fragments, but on the role it plays and the emotional tension it creates within the literary work of art (Markiewicz 1985a, 250–2).[10]

Out of Wóycicki's early theoretical inquiries emerged a centre of literary studies known as Kolo Polonistow Uniwersytetu Warszawskiego, The University of Warsaw Students' Circle of Polish Literature or, in short, the Warsaw Circle. The initial members of the group were Dawid Hopensztand (1904–43), Franciszek Siedlecki (1906–42), Kazimierz Budzyk (1911–64), and Stefan

Żółkiewski (1911–91). They closely co-operated with the Wilno group but, at the same time, established working relations with the Prague school. It is the Warsaw Circle that proved to be the most prolific source for the unprecedented bloom of structuralism in Poland after the Second World War.

The early stage of its development is marked by the publication in 1937 of a collection of articles under the title *Prace ofiarowane Kazimierzowi Wóycickiemu* (Essays in honour of Kazimierz Wóycicki). The participation of Jakobson and Trubetzkoy in this volume was not only a sign of Polish literary scholarship leaving the confines of traditional interests, but also a proof of the existing ties with both Russian formalism and the Prague school.

The outbreak of the Second World War brought these developments in Polish structuralism to a standstill. Some of its representatives died (a few perished in concentration camps).

The immediate postwar period did not foster the structuralist revival either. The imposition of Marxism as an official doctrine and theoretical direction in all spheres of cultural life also affected literary structuralism in a negative manner. Still, in 1946 under the editorship of Kazimierz Budzyk, a volume was published which was entitled *Stylistyka teoretyczna w Polsce* (Theoretical stylistics in Poland). It contained a few essays which can be considered as written from a structuralist theoretical position or as being inspired by it.

Generally speaking, Budzyk was the scholar who revived literary structuralism in Poland, though he did so under the banners of the stylistics.[11] This reflected Budzyk's strong interest in the discipline, although in postwar reality the use of the term 'stylistics' was needed in order to placate the watch-dogs of Marxist ideological 'purity,' to whom the word 'structuralism'·was an anathema. In his early studies such as 'Z zagadnién stylistyki' (The problems of stylistics), 'Gwara a utwór literacki' (Dialect and the literary work of art), 'Sprawa neologizmow w literaturze' (The question of neologisms in literature), Budzyk stressed the fact that literature is first of all a linguistic phenomenon, but it is additionally governed by specific laws of composition (today we would say 'structure'). He was aware that narrative prose is characterized by more complex structural units that cannot be reduced to purely linguistic analysis, and he consequently differentiated narrative prose into four major structural segments: narration, description, dialogue, and monologue.

In the late fifties, structuralism began its spectacular recovery, reaching its full bloom in the second half of the sixties and throughout the seventies. In Poland, this development brought about a gradual rejection of so-called Marxist literary scholarship. This happened mainly thanks to the theoretical activities of two scholars, Janusz Sławiński (b. 1934) and Michal Głowiński (b. 1934), both students and followers of Budzyk.[12]

By and large, one can distinguish three currents in Polish structuralism: one that concentrates its attention primarily on the structure of literary texts and poetics, as found in the works of M.R. Mayenowa, L. Pszczołowska, A. Wierzbicka, and J. Faryno; a trend represented by S. Żółkiewski, J. Lalewicz, W. Grajewski, and K. Rudzińska which situates the literary work of art within a wider integrating context of anthropological, semiological, and social perspective, all of which can be understood as components of a general knowledge about literary culture; and a stream represented by J. Sławiński, M. Głowiński, K. Bartoszynski, E. Balcerzan, and A. Okopien-Sławińska who, unlike the other scholars mentioned, seem to be more interested in what can be called literary entities of a higher and more complex order (for example, the 'group code' or the notion of 'compound poetics') than in the questions of text or of the pragmatics of the socio-anthropological, semiological approach advocated by S. Zółkiewski. Thus the range of theoretical inquiries of this third group extends over such problems as tradition, literary periods, literary process, historical poetics, the narrative creative process itself within social ambiance (for example, reception), and so on. In the final analysis, their interests led them to the development of a comprehensive theory of literary communication understood both as a communication between structural constituents of imaginative literature itself and as communication on the author–text–receiver axis, located in the external (that is, outside strictly literary matters) reality. This division of Polish structuralism into three groupings does not mean that inflexible barriers exist between them. These boundaries are rather fluid, and members of one group often encroach on the 'territory' of another. Such movement is particularly true of what one may call Sławiński–Głowiński's line of theoretical reflection. Diversity of interests is evident in Sławiński's important book *Dzieło. Język. Tradycja* (The literary work. Language. Tradition), published in 1974. It can be treated as a programmatic statement in which he delineated his areas of theoretical investigation: historical poetics, sociology of literature (or literary communication), and linguistic poetics. The latter aspect of his research manifested itself earlier in the book *Koncepcja języka poetyckiego awangardy Krakówskiej* (The concept of poetic language in Kraków's avant-garde), published in 1965, in which Sławiński formulated poetic language as 'language within the language.' However, his most significant theoretical statements are to be found in 'Synchronia i diachronia w procesie historycznoliterackim' (Synchrony and diachrony in historico-literary process), 'Socjologia literatury i poetyka historyczna' (Sociology of literature and historical poetics), 'Semantyka wypowiedzi narracyjnej' (The semantics of narrative discourse), and 'Funkcje krytyki literackiej' (Functions of literary criticism) – all of which are found in *Dzieło. Język. Tradycja*. Sławiński's methodological point of departure is based on three fundamental premises: one should not confuse the consideration of the structure of the literary work of art with the analysis of the literary process; one should not confound the structure of the literary work of art with the analysis of literature's communicative situation; the characterization of the literary work's structure requires an application of a twofold terminology in order to describe both its linguistic stratum and its 'represented objects.'

The totality of this theoretical approach is clearly at work in the article on the semantics of narrative discourse (1967), in which Sławiński addresses the question of differentiation between poetry and prose. According to this work, the existing distinction between poetry and prose is wrong because it is founded on inconsistent criteria. While poetry is viewed as intra-lexical reality in which the 'content' is generated by verbal relationships and operations (syntax, intonation, metaphors, similes, and so on), the ontological status of prose is usually determined by its referential value, by what is (re)presented in it as an extra-lexical reality. It is quite a common claim that in poetry the cognitive (or referential) function of the word is weaker than in prose. Sławiński does not question this view. What he objects to is the treatment of prose as the exclusive result of extra-literary conditions. Like poetry, the novel, or any sub-genre of literary prose, is comprised of words but they are used differently than in a poetic utterance. Still, both are built of lexical fabric. It is exactly the commonness of this main feature that compels us to treat prose in terms of poetics. At the same time, through the mediation of prose's specificity (the word has stronger cognitive value than in poetry) arises the opportunity to enrich the discipline of poetics by the inclusion of the semantic aspect of literature – or, in short, literary semantics – in its range of issues.

In 'Synchronia i diachronia w procesie historycznoliterackim' (Synchrony and diachrony in historico-literary process), an essay published in 1967 which one can consider to be Sławiński's theoretical *credo*, the author raises two major issues: that the relationship between the structure of an individual literary work of art and literature as a system is subject to continuous evolution; and that the existence of the literary work of art is only possible within a literary tradition. The author aims to overcome a strictly synchronic approach, which treats the literary work of art as a correlate of a certain aggregate of literary norms, and to reconcile this approach with a dychronic analysis; the latter makes us aware that the 'structure' of each literary work is at the same time part and parcel of the historico-literary process. Hence the interest in historical poetics. In short, he points out the necessity of reconciling the category of structure with the category of evolutionary process. In accordance with Saussurean structuralism, the former was perceived as static and the latter as dynamic. It is imperative to understand, claims Sławiński, that the literary process takes place on the level of langue, in other words, it evolves as a system through the sum total of individual literary realizations. Thus, the concept of the evolutionary process assumes an inevitably correlative understanding of structure thanks to the participation of individual literary works in the historico-literary process. This means that they cannot be treated as 'illustrative' material only, but as active participants in what can be defined as a system. As for the literary work of art and its relation to tradition, Sławiński defines literary utterance (or discourse) as the 'application (or "use") of tradition.' The relation between the supra-individual (general) system and its individual use (or application) is always of a functional nature. To make this functional relationship clearer, Sławiński uses the concepts of 'phenotype' and 'genotype,' concepts imported from the vocabulary of genetics, and also known to other disciplines of humanities. The term 'phenotype' refers to an explicit structure of a given literary work of art, while 'genotype' is to be understood as the implicit structure of literary norms which remain at work in shaping an individual work of art. Tradition enters, as it were, into each literary work of art. At the same time, however, a simple work of literature becomes part of the tradition in the degree to which it is able to interiorize literary heritage. Sławiński's formulation of literary tradition is similar to that of intertextuality, made popular a few years later by Kristeva and known in Doležel's terminology as literary transduction (see his *Occidental Poetics*, 1990). The concept as such has its roots in Czech structuralism.

Głowiński's theoretical contribution intersects at many points with that of Sławiński's studies, with one essential difference. Głowiński tends to combine theoretical reflection with a more pragmatic attitude and a concrete literary analysis. In his work one can isolate three or four areas to which he devotes particular attention: narratology (particularly the question of the narrator), the theory of reception, tradition and literary periods, and genres (first of all the novel). The extent of Głowiński's versatile theoretical and critical interests is only partly revealed in the following studies: 'Wirtualny odbiorca w strukturze utworu poetyckiego' (Virtual receiver in the structure of poetry), published in 1967; 'O konkretyzacji' (On concretization), published in 1973; 'O powieści w pierwszej osobie' (On the first-person novel), published in 1968; 'Narracja jako monolog wypowiedziany' (Narration as uttered monologue), published in 1963; 'Grupa literacka a model poezji' (Literary group and the model of poetry), published in 1965. Some of these titles reflect Głowiński's intense preoccupation with the problems of literary communication. He differentiates between 'internal' and 'external' literary communication. The literary work of art constitutes a communicative act which is always addressed to unknown readers (external communication). The reader, however, constitutes part and parcel of the signifying structure and yet he or she cannot be identified with a real person, existing outside the text and actually reading the text. According to Głowiński, each literary text contains an 'embedded' or implied reader whom he calls 'virtual receiver' (internal communication). The existence of 'the virtual reader' (*wirtualny czytelnik*), who is determined by the structure of the text, prompts the latter to be read in a particular way. A writer can opt for a variety of strategies to address a virtual reader (for example, directly or indirectly) who is delineated not only by the structure of the individual work (the text), but also by the nature of a given literary convention.

Thanks to Sławiński's and Głowiński's theoretical contributions, Polish structuralism experienced its most triumphant results in the realm of literary communication and historical poetics. Less visible were its achievements in the theory of literary texts. This is understandable if one takes into account the legacy of Ingarden's phenomenological definition of the literary text as a dynamic stratified formation compounded of sounds, meaning units, represented objects, and schematized features. With its early presence in Polish literary scholarship, dating from the early thirties, Ingarden's theory seems to have exercised everlasting pressure on the way structuralism, and literary theory in general, evolved in Poland. This influence also explains to a degree why Polish structuralists displayed a greater interest in dealing with what we earlier termed 'literary entities of higher/larger order.' They simply filled spaces left 'empty,' or insufficiently developed by Ingarden's theory. Still, one cannot brush aside the remarkable inroads made by M.R. Mayenowa (1910–88) into the theory of literary texts in her book *Poetyka teoretyczna. Zagadnienia języka* (Theoretical poetics. Problems of language), published in 1974. Instead of stratifying the artistic text, Mayenowa speaks of its cohesion (*spójność*). A cohesive text has to fulfil three indispensable conditions. By and large, such a text must have a single sender, the same receiver, and the same theme. It should be noted that Mayenowa does not subscribe to the Tartu School's view that poetic language, being a secondary modelling system, grew primarily out of and above natural language. This leads to a further tightening of the understanding of the artistic text. First of all, one should not overlook the fact that artistic texts are creations of the language *stricto sensu*, and in this case we are not obliged to take their specificity into account; secondly, each poetic text contains some additional transformational rules which impose on it new limitations because they enter into different relations with other systems and structures (for example, versification system); thirdly, there exists yet another, non-linguistic sign system which also transmits essential meanings contained in the text. To discover secondary modelling systems which function in various texts is, according to Mayenowa, the most difficult and least formalized task of literary scholarship.

From among the above-mentioned representatives of Polish structuralism, only E. Balcerzan lived outside Warsaw. All the others were from Warsaw where they were employed either as researchers at the Instytut Badań Literackich (Institute of Literary Studies), a branch of the Polish Academy of Sciences, or as professors at the University of Warsaw. Combined with the existence of the prewar Warsaw Students' Circle of Polish Literature, this concentration of 'structuralist activity' in postwar Warsaw gave some scholars (for example, W. Kroll from Germany) the inducement to speak of the Warsaw school of structuralism. If, indeed, such a school ever existed, it should be realized that it never achieved theoretical consistency; rather, in addressing literary issues it was characterized by subtle methodological diversity and quite an impressive richness of analytical approaches to literature. This range of concerns remains very much in agreement with the tradition of Polish literary scholarship. Unlike in Russia and Czechoslovakia, where formalism and structuralism, respectively, strongly dominated intrinsic approaches to literary studies, modern literary theoretical thought in Poland was characterized from its inception by theoretical polarization and an almost simultaneous rise of three major tendencies: structuralism (Wóycicki in Warsaw); phenomenology (Ingarden in Lwow); and formalism (Kridl in Wilno). Although Warsaw structuralism gained the upper hand in the sixties and seventies, it reflected to some extent the diversity of theoretical attitudes. In other words, it assimilated quite a few concepts and ideas of both formalism and phenomenology.

It should be also kept in mind that Warsaw is not the only centre of modern theoretical thought in Poland. Two scholars seem to have made particularly significant contributions to the development of Polish literary scholarship: Stefania Skwarczyńska (1902–88) and Henryk Markiewicz (b. 1922) from Kraków. In the general field of literary inquiry, Markiewicz should be credited with the clarification of many theoretical viewpoints by providing a comprehensive analysis of several theoretical schools and of specific problems, such as those of literary period, character, etc. In undertaking this task, he played an extremely inspirational role in paving the way for a new understanding of literary scholarship in Poland.

Thanks to its dynamic evolution in the sixties and seventies, Polish structuralism provided a kind of intellectual shelter for those who could not accept the imposition of Marxist philosophy. This was possible due to the somewhat milder political conditions in Poland, especially when compared with those existing, for example, in the Soviet Union or East Germany. At the same time

Polish structuralism managed to exercise considerable impact on theoretical discussions in Central Europe, particularly in Slovakia, Yugoslavia, and West Germany, and in Israel. Comprehensive anthologies of Polish structuralism were published in Slovakia (Popovič 1972), West Germany (Fieguth 1975), and Yugoslavia (Kroll 1974).[13] Translations of Polish structuralist texts appeared in many other languages, including English, French, Russian, Italian, Spanish, Japanese, and Hebrew.

In conclusion, I would like to raise a question which is sometimes addressed in Western scholarship: How could it happen that such a long, rich, and versatile tradition of literary scholarship in Poland remained practically unknown in the West? If not in essence, then at least in chronology it preceded, in some respects, both the discoveries of Russian formalism and even those of the Prague school of structuralism.[14]

There exist, I believe, a number of reasons. First of all, none of the prominent representatives of these schools ever settled in the West. True, Kridl emigrated to the United States, but while there, he resumed interest in his first love – the history of Polish literature – and completely abandoned theoretical pursuits. To his credit, it should be recalled here that he was the first scholar ever on this continent to introduce (in a short article) Russian formalism to an American audience.

Secondly, many scholars of the prewar generation who participated in theoretical literary debates lost their lives during the war, killed either by Germans or Russians. Those who survived (like Ingarden) were silenced by the communist regime which imposed strict Marxist control over the humanities; they were also effectively cut off from any serious contacts with the West.

Finally, there are those scholars (among whom I count myself) who managed to emigrate after the political thaw of the mid-fifties. Why didn't they undertake the task of popularizing the Polish theoretical experience in literary scholarship? Probably for a variety of reasons. Some perhaps for a lack of interest in the subject, others because of difficulties in finding the necessary material. Czeslaw Miłosz, for example, the Nobel Prize winner for 1980, who was a close friend of some of the Polish formalists and attended Kridl's lectures in Wilno, does not even mention their existence or activities in his textbook *The History of Polish Literature* (1969). I can only suggest an answer. Most of those who found themselves in the West after the fifties wanted to explain the mechanism of intellectual subjugation practised by the Polish communists and, if I may use the well-known title of Miłosz's book, to describe the phenomenon of 'the captive mind.' Thus, most of them embarked on a sort of ideological thematic criticism, addressing the most painful issues related to literature and art in the countries of Central and Eastern Europe.

NOTES

1 For a detailed discussion of the beginnings and evolution of Polish literary scholarship (criticism and theory), see Markiewicz 1985a, esp. 5–34.

2 Both articles have been reprinted in Łempicki 1966, 121–36 and 105–20, respectively. The article 'W sprawie uzasadnienia poetyki czystej' has been translated into German by Peter Lachmann and is followed by the translator's lengthy commentary 'Zygmunt Łempicki's Ausdruckskritizistischer Entwurf' in Łempicki 1971.

3 For a detailed discussion of semiotics in Poland, see Pelc 1974.

4 The Polish term is *zycie literackie*.

5 Indeed, Ingarden makes numerous references to Łempicki, and after the Second World War he wrote a lengthy introduction to Łempicki's works, collected in two volumes.

6 In the Translator's Introduction to Ingarden 1973, especially li–lxx, George G. Grabowicz gives quite a detailed account of Ingarden's reception in Poland.

7 It is interesting to note that in his inaugural lecture for the academic year 1932–3 (later published as an article) 'Przelom w metodyce badań literackich,' Kridl does not mention Russian formalists at all. See H. Markiewicz, 'Recepcja formalizmu rosyjskiego w Polsce' in 1985b, 344. M. Rzeuska claimed that Kridl did not consider himself to be a formalist, and she suggested that German and English theoretical sources played a greater role in his evolution as a scholar of literature than Russian formalists; see Wyka 1960, 283.

8 A discussion of M. Kridl's views as a theoretician of literature can be found in Zgorzelski 1957 and in Subotin 1958. For a useful characterization of modern Polish historians and theoreticians of literature, see Zgorzelski 1983.

9 On the question of stylistics in Poland, see Mayenowa 1968.

10 Thus the commonly held view that the concept of the dominant was introduced to modern literary scholarship by Tynianov and Jakobson ought to be corrected. Wóycicki's article appeared, as indicated earlier, in 1914.

11 For a detailed discussion of Budzyk's theoretical views, see Sławiński 1966, 199–219.

12 A short and very sparse discussion of Polish structuralism can be found in Głowiński 1975.

13 The entire issue of this periodical is devoted to the question of literary communication as developed by Polish theoreticians.

14 Some additional information on Polish theoretical thought can be found in Erlich 1969, 164–6. See also Bojtar 1973, 205–24.

PART 6
DOLEŽEL AND HIS WORLDS

An Improbable Side by Side:
Doležel and Borges in Prague

HANS-GEORGE RUPRECHT

It is common knowledge that the 'improbable,' considered as a faint likelihood, cannot be 'verified,' in spite of the fact that there may be 'serious' arguments *ab incredibili* that either put into question or endorse its presumptive philosophical status. Hence from the outset a few cautionary words. The urban space that will be evoked here is not an actual one; it is fictitious. Making a return to Prague with Borges and Doležel, in two different periods (1939, 1968), requires a distinction between the persons (Jorge Luis Borges, Lubomír Doležel) and the characters (the writer and the academic).[1] What is the purpose of this distinction? It will permit me, within the necessarily minimalist perspective of this study, to focus upon the imaginary conditions that pervade the literary domain, especially those forms that engender in us a process of virtualization. Here this process is meant to be parabolic and metafictional. A rereading of one of Borges's *ficciones* offers an entry into this problematic. I am thinking of 'El milagro secreto,' whose spatio-temporal specifications evoke Malá Strana, that is, the 'Lesser Town' of the old Prague at a tragic moment in its history (1939). This context raises questions concerning what Lubomír Doležel terms 'fictional time' (1973a, 121). In fact, this interrogation will take on a distinctly *meta*fictional quality, namely, in the original Greek sense of *meta*, expressing succession, change, and participation.

The approach aims to be intentionally fictive. Arbitrary and mimetic, it will outline the 'factual' space of a simulacrum where the simulator – this enunciative instance that manifests itself as a first-person plural (we) – will propose the bringing together of two affective consciences: those of the writer and the academic. This coming together will be effected not within the uninhabitable space of the logos of a textual science but more exactly (in fact, inexactly) by means of a return to the habitable space of Prague, the city. It is chiefly by suggesting certain architectural analogies that the central problem of this study will emerge: How can we participate on the imaginary level in the referential spatialization of the reversibility of time in fictional texts? One could object that this is to mistreat the problem of reference and claim, along with François Rastier, that the irrefutable evidence is rather that 'the referential effect produced by a text depends on the referential value of the utterances which constitute it' (Rastier 1973, 108; trans. L. Marks). Agreed, but does this solve in any definitive way the questions we can ask about an adequate understanding (in the Kantian sense) of the notion of referential value? Likewise, what of the categorical problem of quality, of quantity, and of relation, for example, insofar as they concern the effort of the semiotician seeking to establish, by theoretical differentiation, what Rastier calls 'the principal levels of semantic description' (1973, 108; trans. L Marks)? Could not such a judgment, reconsidered from the basis of Kant's First Critique, circumvent as well the modal tension that exists between the assertoric, the problematic, and the apodeictic (Kant 1934, 69)? Whence from our perspective a preoccupying question: How can a semiotics of the text, when it is grappling with the problems of *référenciation* and *référencialisation discursive* – to recall an important distinction introduced by Denis Bertrand, (1985, 29–54) – effectively guard its premises against drifting into the 'world of fiction'? Some would advise a reading of Thomas Pavel (1986). But a good deal of the knowledge that we claim to possess about this world has in itself something of a certain fictionality about it. It is as though we were in search of the 'unattainable' which appears both as perennial in relation to 'seasonal' intellectual fashions and as altogether volatile in its very substance. We might even say, somewhat facetiously, that knowledge about the fictional – insofar as it can be known intersubjectively – is like that knowledge filmed in the manner of Woody Allen who, as actor, director, and producer, asks himself in one of his films: If knowledge is knowable, how do I know? We would answer that it is by means of fiction as a mode of knowledge.

In this connection Doležel's theoretical position is unequivocal. He writes: 'if the fictional text has a referential function then this function aims at possible *fictional* worlds rather than the real world,' adding that 'fictional worlds do not pre-exist texts' (1985a, 1: 8). This position is of course linked with his reflections concerning the 'fabrication' and 'modelisation' of possible worlds according to those strategies at literature's disposal. As a whole, these strategies produce what has been called the form of expression and the form of content of a fictional world. If such is the case, a possible convergence of our ideas – in respect to the work ('El milagro secreto'), the author (Borges), and the scholar (Doležel) – on the 'exotopic/endotopic dimensions' of Prague might lead us to founder in a chaos of impressions, thereby causing innumerable confusions. Furthermore, what becomes of the 'referential function' when the category of the 'improbable' subsumes both the 'possible' and the 'real'? One of Friedrich Schlegel's *Ideas* may answer this question: 'Nur diejenige Verworrenheit ist ein Chaos, aus der eine Welt entspringen kann' (1964, 97).[2] And what, for example, if this world belonged indeed to the realm of the metafictional and was comprised, in the final analysis, of all the dimensions of the literary? Let us leave this question open and return to Prague.

For Borges, Prague seems predestined to symbolize the irruption of the ineffable into the heterotopic field of all possible fabulations, believable or unbelievable, whether these be already realized or existing only as potentialities. Of course, this also includes the ficta of history. As the historian Eduardo Zimmermann (a character in another of Borges's works) remarks, a lot of things can happen in Prague because, he says, thinking of Gustave Meyerink's novel *Der Golem* (1915): 'Todo es extraño en Praga o, si usted prefiere, nada es extraño. Cualquier cosa puede ocurrir' (Borges 1974, 1, 1066). Admitting the possibility, certainly debatable (and doubtlessly inadmissible within a 'science of literature'), that Borges's intuition also invites us to consider the unlikely, let us then imagine an encounter between Borges and Doležel, keeping in mind what has been mentioned before about the other (character) of the same (person). Finally, let us suppose that they met in Prague during the so-called Spring of Hope of 1968.

It is from this period that we recall – among the least important events – certain 'aventures de la différe/a/nce' (Vattimo 1985) experienced by Western intellectuals. In a few Parisian salons, for example, the martial artists of abstraction – the 'samourais' (Kristeva 1990) – discussed the anagrams of Saussure, the undecidable, the concept of game, and the temporalization of the *differend*. Elsewhere, in the context of certain seminars, one came to discover the legacy of Russian formalism and Czech structuralism. Across the Channel, the demure *British Journal of Aesthetics* (1968, 8: 319–34) published an article about Frege's philosophy of language and its importance for the analysis of literature. In the United States, M.I.T. Press had just published Bakhtin's *Rabelais and His World*. Also in 1968 came the publication of Jean Piaget's *Le Structuralisme*, a work which better than most thematizes one of the major currents of intellectual life during that period. And it goes without saying that Doležel was perfectly aware of all this at the time of his rendezvous with the famous writer.

But, curiously, on the eve of their encounter the scholar felt himself transported, as in a daydream, into an earlier period. It was after the war. Or was it a little later, towards the end of the fifties, that he had read Borges's 'El milagro secreto' for the first time? Rereading the text, Doležel suddenly became aware again of two auditory signs which signal, punctiliously, the moments of reversible time. The first was, in effect, the 'clangor of the terrible clocks' mentioned at the beginning of the story (Borges 1962, 143). How could one not recognize at this moment the terrible harbinger announcing the coming of the Shoah in central Europe? In any case, the protagonist Jaromír Hladík, 'author of the unfinished drama entitled *The Enemies, or Vindication of Eternity*' (143) and a few other learned texts, was awoken immediately because of this dreadful noise – and perhaps because of a premonitory dream about the infinite and also because of his being a Jew threatened with execution. All this took place at his home in the Zeltnergasse (today, Celetná ulice, also known as the street where Kafka was born) during the 'dawn' of the fifteenth of March 1939. In fact, it took place at the moment when 'the armored vanguards of the Third Reich were entering Prague' (143), according to the narrator, who sounds as though he is reading from a BBC International information bulletin. Did this background noise sound an angel's preparation for battle? Once again Doležel asked himself a few distressing questions about the meaning and the role of history in Borges's text. Yet, if there was a battle, it would certainly not have been led by the 'Engel' of Saint Ludmila's statue, precisely because this angel, whom the young Kafka so admired during the period of his 'Beschreibung eines Kampfes' (1904), this angel with hands so delicate, could never have taken arms against the Nazis. But the battle for truth during a period of many crimes – crimes committed from March 1939 onwards against the humanity of Prague – could well have been led by another angel, bearer of the ensigns of law, justice, and protection. Yes, led by the angel, the *bon génie* of Prague, who is stationed on an allegorical dial underneath the central wall clock of the Hôtel de Ville (1490). From there she is pointing towards a 'temporal asymmetry,' as the physicists say (Doležel had read this somewhere), a dissymmetry of the temporal relations between a reversible mobility, which can be measured, and the absolute inertia, which in reality does not exist.

The second auditory sign is the result of the same clock-work and is subject to, in both a strict and a figurative sense, the measurability of reversible time. This sign is to be found at the very end of the story following the central events of the narration, such as Jaromír Hladík's accusation, arrest, and interrogation by the Gestapo. It takes place after the Jewish writer's death sentence, which has been fixed for 'the twenty-ninth of March at nine in the morning' (144). In fact, it is in the 'barracks' where he is awaiting 'the strike of nine' (145) that he is freed from his feeling of existential fatality, and that enables him, finally, to accomplish in his own memory – the only 'document' at his disposition – the tragedy that had hitherto remained unfinished. It was a question only of seconds, long enough however to recompose, to carry out his project 'within the time of his great invisible labyrinth' (148). The rest is literature, as the someone else said. Everything is brought to an end without lament. Doležel, on the other hand, replays the multiple echo of sorrowful words in another possible world, reflecting late into the night upon Liszt's variations of Bach's 'Weinen, Klagen, Sorgen.'

The next day, at their very first meeting, the writer and the scholar become fast friends. It remains for us to see what followed this first encounter (an outcome having to do not only with another miracle but with, in a word, the improbable). Thus we at last find ourselves witness to an intersubjective dynamics, a simulacrum of metafictionality.

During a stroll, side by side, through the streets of the Malá Strana, the writer and the professor suddenly marvel at the sight before them, illuminated by the summer sun: one discovering, despite his poor vision, the other rediscovering, after many years of exile, a beautiful fountain dating from the Renaissance. Found on the Small Square (Malostranské Námestí), the fountain appears as if crowned with the finest metal grill-work, whose uppermost part bears the likenesses of eight angels above whom stand proudly, as on a semicircular vault, the Hapsburg lion. A symbol of omnipotence, the lion sits atop a globe of brass fashioned in the image of the earth. Within the octagonal space of the fountain, as Doležel explains to his guest, is a jet of water, itself encircled by a trellis fence. This trellis, thus surrounded, differs from the surrounding fencing in a very subtle way; the former displays a kind of figurative supplement whose unique charm blends quite elegantly with the more decorative splendour of the exterior fence. Borges stands fascinated by these details – the strapwork, the braids, the little rosettes – which he can hardly recognize or can see, only thanks to his friend, through a more profound vision. The writer is suddenly reminded of Jurgis Baltrušaitis's *Études sur l'art médiéval en Géorgie et en Arménie*, a work he consulted often as a librarian in Buenos Aires. He recalls a long, well-documented footnote where the author draws a rather curious parallel between this precise genre of architectural ornamentation and Romanesque interlacing and the knots of intrigue joined and linked at many different levels of signification, such as one finds, for example, in the panegyric writings of the eleventh-century Georgians. In fact, Borges has always had a great passion for this type of erudite comparison. But out of consideration for the internationally renowned Slavist in his company, Borges remains silent. As for Doležel – who has just published an important study in *To Honor Roman Jakobson* (1967), devoted to the typology of the narrator – he is meditating upon the problem of point of view. He is as though in the grip of an emotion that is at once sensory and cognitive, facing this fountain drenched in sunlight whose strangely lined shadow, full of the flourishes of style characteristic of Prague's best wrought-iron craftsmen, stretches out under the midday sun on the cobblestones whitened by the passing seasons. The shadow is like a transparent texture, an aesthetic thought of white topped with black, which spreads out over the public square. Yet it is but a fleeting impression quickly withdrawn by a cloud, and Doležel instead becomes more deeply intrigued by the fountain's octagonal forms which fit together and intersect just like the stories one still tells today about the lives and work of the master iron craftsmen. Who is the storyteller, who represents, controls, and interprets these stories? Could it be, Doležel asks himself, this 'symposium' of eight angels who secretly direct one side of the city's artistic activity, and in so doing represent and interpret the absolute will of the Hapsburg lion? Even while contemplating this possibility, the professor reveals nothing of the innermost reaches of his thought, thus showing, like Borges, a great deal of tact and politeness.

However, something inside him, perhaps the vague recollection of readings in Canada, made Doležel want to break the silence of these two solitudes. Suddenly, he takes his friend by the arm, turns to him, and says casually: 'Sabes que, Jorge, tengo para mi que esta fuente es como un milagro secreto.' Borges, having grasped the allusion immediately, replies in his own unique accent: 'Nu – Lubomire, jak to vite?'[3] Then the writer, as though he were trying to recall some small detail that he had long ago associated implicitly with the fact that Hladík's mysterious story transpired in March 1939, calmly suggests that a miracle in any case is always relative. From this reflection a detail – but is it really important? – a date, the fourth of March 1939, the day that Einstein had chosen, as Borges explained, to announce in New York that he was ready to offer 'a new explication of the mystery of gravity. De veras no cabe duda.' He remembers having read this phrase in the *Action Française* of March the fourth, 1939, a paper that Drieu La Rochelle used to send to him from time to time. It is true, he thought, the miracle of this fountain consists of a secret emanation, which flows from profound sources and emerges from a nozzle of gold, itself the symbol of absolute determination, to be discovered at the apex of the fountain's spray. Somewhat perplexed, Doležel, not quite sure what the writer is attempting to express, remarks nevertheless that the fountain also serves as a water fountain to be drunk from. To this end, it is fitted with two intermittently operating pumps as well as double pipes which run through the fountain's enclosure in two directions so that the underground reservoir, for reasons of economy, may discharge its water into the marble basins at two distinct intervals. These basins are solidly fixed to the fountain's periphery and accessible from the Small Square. As Doležel explains, these basins are positioned upon a slightly elevated stone border such that the two basins are diametrically opposed one to the other. Borges is delighted. In fact, the writer and the professor both reach the conclusion – with a smile of complicity no less philosophic than poetic – that the flow of water has always been an image of Time.

And if by chance, as the writer and the scholar observe, there is any concomitance between the states of before and after, as there was for Jaromír Hladík, then apparently the water that flows into these two complementary basins would make a lovely metaphor of reversible time. And what goes for Hladík who feels, facing a Nazi firing squad in the lugubrious barracks courtyard, 'between the command to fire and its execution' (149), that the inevitable movement of his being towards death is suddenly reversed, also goes for those hydrological catastrophes occurring, in a measurable way, within a well-delimited space such as the fountain's. Moved by the impulse of a fortuitous intuition, Borges looks upward to the globe on which sits the immobile emblem of state power and asks himself, wondering all the while about the 'mystery of gravitation,' whether it is not the fountain that gravitates around the royal lion. Perhaps it is even this very power that causes the water to flow in two directions. Yet what seems obvious turns out to be more complex because, just like Hladík, who in a dream state had submitted himself to the grace of God, Borges found the idea of an *omnipotencia* to be fanciful and illusory. What finally is so mysterious about this 'milagro secreto'? In order to understand, the author notes, there is no need to draw arms against someone and fire a salvo of 'German lead' (149);[4] it should suffice, in effect, to draw water from the pump. That's the way! Then: 'Déjame de joder!' Maybe the kid would only shut up, Borges shouts in mock gauchesco anger as he notices some little street urchin, clever Cartesian devil, making fun of him just as he is giving himself up to, under Doležel's analytical eye, the beautiful sensory-motor experience of reversible time. The more he pumps, drawing water into the basins, the better he senses how the 'substancia fugitiva del tempo,' an expression used in his narrative, flows through the pipes stretching across the fountain's octagonal space whose slightly elevated base covers, hides more precisely, the unfathomable depth of its well. Immersed in the imaginary space of his narrator, Borges now deduces – how could it possibly be otherwise in 1968, twenty years before anyone would speak to him of Stephen Hawking's famous book *A Brief History of Time*? – that 'time had stopped' (148); for Jaromír Hladík, this was neither true in the world of facts nor false in the world of dream. Maybe, he conjectures, a more appropriate image of irreversible time would be the following: if the surface of the water at the bottom of the well remains forever tranquil, it is no less true that the water level rises and falls according to predictable seasonal variations which continually alter the amount of water contained by the subterranean space surrounding the well. All this seems to him all the more obvious now that he feels, somewhat tired from his working of the pump, truly outside the octagonal space of the fountain.

Doležel, observing his friend with a certain gentleness, comes to understand the so-called physicalism of the objective narrator in Borges's text. To this quality Doležel adds a few observations of a more logical nature. Given the octagonal space of the fountain as the writer perceives it – more precisely, imagines it – under the aspect of reversible time, one could thus say that this conception of time is articulated according to the logical octagon of *de dicto* modal relations. For Doležel, more theoretically inclined than Borges, the central question is to know whether it is necessary, possible, contingent, or impossible that every flow of water in opposition say to some currents could be considered in relation to the generally accepted idea of the *panta rein*. Borges, hardly interested in such a proposition, merely nods his head. Conscious of his embarrassment, Doležel says to him cheerfully: 'Pues, vámonos ... no tenemos mucho tiempo! At this late hour, it would be nice to drink a *plezenské*.'

After leaving, and thanks to the secret miracle of a sudden and perfect convergence of thought, they finally ask themselves: What does it really mean when we say we do not have any time? How long have we been in this deficient state? What is to become of us in these circumstances? And what is the nature of this time that we both agree may be taken from us? What do we answer should it prove impossible to know the truth about these things within the span of a life, be it a real or imaginary one? While contemplating these problems, Doležel already has the plan for a typology of fictional worlds in mind; for him, there could be nothing more appropriate for the understanding of time than the study of the novelistic and the fictional. More precisely, what is the nature of this temporality Doležel attempts to analyse (1973a, 152)? His analysis focuses not only on the natural or human dimensions of temporality but also on the temporal structures of narration, that is, the multiple relations between the person who narrates and what is narrated with its own particular temporal configuration. Taking into account some of the quintessential phenomena of fictional discourse, Doležel is already inclined to devote particular attention, as he will later write, to certain macrosemantic problems, problems whose particular constraints – of a logical-modal nature – would have distinctive, demarcating, even cumulative functions with respect to the genesis of the fictional and would eventually enable a classification into different types of 'possible worlds' (1989a). This represents a research project that is informed by a theoretical rationality that is partially founded on and anticipates the relevance of some of the fundamental work of his contemporaries such as N. Goodman's *Fact, Fiction and Forecast* (1955), A.J. Greimas's *Sémantique Structurale* (1966), J. Hintikka's *Knowledge and Belief* (1962), G.H. von Wright's *Norm and Action* (1963), etc. For Doležel, one of the principal attractions of these works is that they encompass and exemplify what used to be called in Prague 'the scientific study of literature.' Was it

Mukařovský, Bém, or Bogatyrev who talked in these terms? Whatever the case, it was undeniably one of the central notions motivating the structuralist debates about literature to which Doležel contributed as a member of the Prague School.

Reflecting anew on all this, Doležel is attentive to an inner voice which suggests to him a troubling question: Nu …? Borges's question is indeed unsettling: How can I really know what I claim to know, for example, about the subject of time and space in 'El milagro secreto'? It is as though some doubt suddenly arose in his mind about the scientificity of his endeavours. Fortunately the doubt disappears just as quickly during the course of the afternoon, spent happily with Borges drinking slivovice in a restaurant on Mostecká ulice.

In the possible continuation of this story the last drink taken in the restaurant could well have been, by virtue of the reversibility of time, the first: a friendly toast to a long correspondence. These letters would probably have been reminiscent of imagined labyrinths; and this in part because, while still in the restaurant, the professor probably spoke of his current research on Jan A. Komensky's famous novel, a study that was to appear for the first time in 1969 (see Doležel 1973a, 55–77). Under this pretext – if it really is one, given the the interest generated by the idea of 'negative symmetry' in Komensky – their epistolary exchanges might very well have been the occasion for an original interpretation of the symbolism of the labyrinth in 'The Secret Miracle,' particularly as it informs Jaromír Hladík's ultimate trial. 'He dressed. Two soldiers entered his cell and ordered him to follow them. From behind the door, Hladík had visualised a labyrinth of passageways, stairs, and connecting blocks. Reality was less rewarding: the party descended to an inner courtyard by a single iron stairway' (148).

Some would say, and quite justly, that this is really tilting things towards the improbable, but in another sense, it seems, because one must remember that we transported ourselves back, fictitiously, to the beginning of the summer of 1968. It was at this time that tanks and other 'armoured vanguards' were preparing their march towards Prague. And under these circumstances, the writer's and the professor's preoccupations would doubtless have been quite different from those we have just imagined here. His hopes somewhat dashed, Borges himself probably wished, upon saying farewell to Doležel in Prague's Old Town, that his 'concepción de ciclos similares, no idénticos' (1974, 1: 394), as far as it concerns history, be just as improbable.

Why did we tell this story? Why did we believe it profitable to imagine this *adequatio rei et intellectus*: this strange correspondence between the fountain (the thing) and fictional time (the idea)? Our representation and interpretation of the fountain is partly inspired by a picture taken by Karel Plicka (1953), which has been 'touched up' – quite artificially – by a heterogeneous play of references, as much historical as literary, and as much narratological as theoretical. This rearrangement of the architectural symbolic through the literary imaginary – because of the effect of all transpositions, including those of place – constitutes, of course, a distanciation in relation to the fictional time of 1939 Prague. Moreover, it is through a process of semiotic mediation – like the principle of extensionality in Frege's sense or again, according to the operation of hypostatic abstraction in Peirce (see Parmentier 1985, 9) – that one becomes conscious of the complexity of what Ricoeur calls 'narrated time': 'à savoir que le travail de pensée à l'oeuvre en toute configuration narrative s'achève dans une refiguration de l'expérience temporelle' (1985, 9). Yet our observations thus far seem to indicate that at diverse levels of narratological reflection there is, in Ricoeur's sense, a 'triple mimetic relation' at play. We would add, however, that these three different relations or orders tend to conflate with each other once we attempt to 'transcribe' a fictional entity into the form, however modest it may be, of a new fiction. It is along these lines that a broadening of the schematic framework of the 'triple relation' proposed by Ricoeur might be conceived: the concretization of the ordre du récit, for example, the one of the 'Milagro secreto,' presupposes the actualization of the ordre de l'action, such as, for example, the one of interpretive practices which themselves presuppose an ordre de la vie, an order which is reducible neither to the probability nor to the improbability of an encounter between a professor and a writer. However disconcerting this might seem, it is from this basis that a new reflection on metafictionality must begin.

(Translated by Larry Marks.)

NOTES

1 Following Michel Zéraffa, we could say that 'la personne correspond à une société constituée, ayant tel ordre, telle hiérarchie et surtout tels valeurs ou idéaux propres à les garantir,' whereas 'le personnage littéraire représentera cette société et ses niveaux' (1976, 36, 97). In fact, as in the world of the novel, the character of the scholar and that of the writer are also 'symbolic individuals' in Zéraffa's sense.
2 A translation of this fragment might read: 'Only this kind of confusion may be a chaos out of which a world can emerge.'
3 Cf. Doležel 1973a, 21, 129.
4 Consider the context: 'For his sake, God projected a secret miracle: German lead would kill him, at the determined hour, but in his mind a year would elapse between the command to fire and its execution.'

Lubomír Doležel's Contribution to Contemporary Literary Studies

THOMAS G. PAVEL

Lubomír Doležel's personal and intellectual destiny is highly emblematic of the cross-currents – political and philosophical – of our time. Born in the young Republic of Czechoslovakia in 1922, Lubomír grew up at a time when the new states of Central Europe placed their hopes in the values of the Enlightenment: democracy, science, truth, and education. The 1930s was a period of rich cultural and scientific blossoming in Prague. The record of the meetings of the Linguistic Circle (republished a few years ago) is revealing: Czech and Slovak scholars freely interacted with Russian emigrés and with German and Austrian philosophers. It was a place in which one could meet and hear people such as Mukařovský, Vodicka, Troubetzkoy, Roman Jakobson, Husserl, and Carnap. It encouraged its members to harmonize humanistic and scientific ideals, to look beyond the borders of disciplines, and to modernize knowledge without resorting to fanatical ideologies. As we know, twentieth-century history showed no clemency for Central Europe: the growth of the most successful liberal democracy in the region was thwarted by National Socialist Germany, the Second World War, and the Communist take-over. The war delayed Lubomír's university studies. He finished his BA in 1949 at Charles University in Prague, one of the oldest and finest in Europe. He joined the Institute for Czech Language of the Academy of Sciences, an institution modelled after the Soviet Academy of Sciences, and taught at the University as assistant, and later associate, professor in the Department of Czech Language. Like many other young humanists who had little attraction for the compulsory ideology in power, Lubomír found a haven in the application of mathematical models to language and literature, and became the head of the Department of Mathematical Linguistics. He published numerous articles on stylistics, poetics, cybernetics, linguistics, and philosophy of language. In 1960, his book *On the Style of Modern Czech Prose*, originally his PhD dissertation, was published by the Academia press in Prague. It soon became internationally known.

The years 1959–65 witnessed the intellectuals' struggle against dogmatic Marxism, which was soon forced into a defensive stance. Literary structuralism was gradually reorganizing itself into an influential trend. In 1960, Roman Jakobson and Thomas Sebeok called a major conference on poetics in Warsaw, whose proceedings, published soon afterwards as *Poetics–Poetika–Poetyka* signalled the rebirth of formalist literary criticism in Central Europe. Lubomír, one of the key participants, contributed with an influential article on the relationship between poetics and stylistics.

In 1965, Lubomír, who by then was recognized as an authority in Slavic languages, mathematical linguistics, and structuralist poetics, was invited to spend three years at the University of Michigan. During his stay in Michigan, he edited the influential series 'Prague Studies in Mathematical Linguistics' and coedited the volume *Statistics and Style*. In 1968, the year of the Spring of Prague, and of the Soviet invasion of Czechoslovakia, Lubomír, like many other Czech and Eastern European intellectuals, chose the path of exile. The University of Toronto offered him a position, and Canada a new home.

His book *Narrative Modes in Czech Literature* (1973), together with a series of articles published between 1970 and 1974, signal a shift in Lubomír's scholarly interests. From stylistics and mathematical linguistics, he turned now to the rapidly developing field of narratology, to which he brought essential contributions. At first, as a stylistician, Lubomír was attracted by the narratology of discourse. In a memorable article published in *To Honor Roman Jakobson* (1967), he was the first narratologist to propose a complete and systematic typology of point of view in fiction. At the same time, as someone versed in the formal techniques of mathematical linguistics, Lubomír felt a strong affinity with the growing body of work in text theory and began, in the early 1970s, to construct a narrative semantics. His three articles published in 1976, 'Narrative Worlds,' 'Narrative Modalities,' and 'Narrative Semantics,' laid the foundation for what in the last decade was to become a comprehensive theory of literary meaning based on the results of modal logic. This theory, Lubomír Doležel's literary system, if I may call it so, not only addresses a vast array of critical issues, such as the nature of fictionality, the typology of fictional universes, mimesis, and thematics, but also demonstrates its hermeneutic productivity when applied to major modern writers, in particular Franz Kafka, Andrej Belyj, and Karel Čapek.

Finally, as one the founders of contemporary theoretical poetics, Lubomír decided to elucidate the antecedents of the discipline. His most recent volume, *Occidental Poetics: Tradition and Progress* (1990), is the first comprehensive history of poetics, from Aristotle to our time.

These achievements are momentous, and although, given Lubomír's legendary energy, we expect – and request – yet more seminal work from him, in particular the much awaited synthesis of his views on fictional semantics, it is perhaps already possible to sum up the main thrust of his influence on contemporary literary studies. In every major scholar's work, one can detect an explicit or implicit polemical stance, which gives shape to the central message of his work. In Lubomír's case, given the limpid, objective, and understated nature of his critical writings, it is not easy to find their common polemical message. This difficulty is compounded by the fact that quite often those trends in contemporary literary theory that Lubomír criticizes (speech-act theory, Russian formalism, and sociological approaches to literature) are, in more than one sense, quite close to his own project. And yet, in a short commentary in a special issue of *New Literary History* (1975), an allusion to impressionist literary criticism makes it clear that Lubomír's dislike for this variety of criticism is so profound that he virtually never bothers to refute it. Lubomír calls 'meaningless' an impressionistic piece of criticism about Samuel Beckett, whose author describes Beckett's 'fulcrum' as 'a vanishing point, an open unregulated intersection in which ontological and epistemological realms constantly collide in search for their pivot point' (467). From a study by Geoffrey Hartman, Lubomír quotes a similar passage: 'in Goethe's ballad, voice is ghostly because overdefined – so essentialized, so voice-like, it does not require localization.' Such critical intuitions are by nature artistic; they imitate the semantics of the object they describe, namely, literature, and, Lubomír concludes, 'cannot raise above the level of paraphrase or parody' (467). Impressionistic criticism does not qualify for a proper refutation; the decision to ignore and transcend impressionism is the main impulse in Lubomír's system. But this does not mean that every kind of theoretically explicit criticism finds favour with Lubomír. He opposes radically idealist views of literature which situate it 'beyond language,' in the realm of the inexpressible, as well as reductive materialist views, which assume that language is nothing but the form expressing an ideological or emotional content (Doležel 1979b).

It is therefore natural that Lubomír's preference goes towards those critical approaches that blend a preference for explicit theory with an interest in the empirical embodiment of literature in natural language. The forerunners of this mixture are the Russian and Czech formalists, together with their immediate ancestry, the tradition of German poetics, and, in the distant background, the poetics of Aristotle.

Doležel's Aristotle is presented as a forefather of modern science, who, unable to reach the axiomatic-deductive level of modern knowledge, at least made a lasting contribution to the description of the taxonomic level (Doležel 1984a).

Being a legitimate taxonomic project, Aristotle's poetics qualifies as scientific, Lubomír tells us: in particular, it develops abstract knowledge about literature and a whole-and-parts model, whose theoretical relevance is far from being superseded. The model survived vigorously through the centuries, in spite of inept neo-Aristotelian normative criticism, resurfacing in the eighteenth century in the work of German and Swiss critics who, under the influence of Leibniz's philosophy, developed the powerful notion of literary world, and in the late nineteenth century in the German 'compositional analysis,' a lesser-known trend which, as Lubomír demonstrates, was the immediate predecessor of Russian formalism (Doležel 1973b). The difference between German and Russian formalists is that, while the former identified form with traditional rhetoric, the latter, because of their involvement in twentieth-century avant-garde art, were particularly sensitive to formal innovation. Lubomír's own preference, however, does not go to the extreme formalism of Shklovsky and Eichenbaum, whose view of literature as incessant production of novel formal devices is geared towards the explanation of modern prose and poetry, rather than towards a comprehensive theory of literature as verbal art.

Closer to Lubomír's own search, Mukařovský and Vodicka's poetics aims higher. Instead of opposing form to content, Czech poeticians distinguish between material and formal elements of an artistic product. In literature, the material elements involve both purely linguistic devices and the thematic material. Form refers to organizational principles, which affect as well the verbal level as the thematic load of the work. Vodicka's ideas on thematics significantly helped Lubomír shape his own. Formally, thematics is structured into motifs, thematic planes, and worlds. The literary meaning of a text emerges at the intersection of the reference to the 'human setting' it represents and the formal principles of its aesthetic organization (Doležel 1982).

Faithful to this tradition, Lubomír conceives literary theory as an empirical discipline, based on a rigorous framework of concepts. He avoids purely intuitive hermeneutic statements, striving instead to construct explanatory models refined enough to explicate the meaning of individual literary texts. Stylistic analysis and the theory of narrative discourse are among his major contributions to the study of prose fiction. They belong to a harmoniously built poetics, whose centre-piece is a strikingly original and powerful narrative semantics.

In his articles on the history of Czech poetics, Lubomír noticed that Mukařovský failed to provide an adequate answer to the question of the reference of literature: the tensions between the aesthetic and the referential functions of the literary text remained without solution in Mukařovský's work. In Lubomír's system, in contrast, literary texts obey several layers of local and global constraints. Among the latter, the most important are those that govern the referential modality of the text. Modalities can be alethic (referring to possibility and necessity), deontic (related to permission and prohibition), axiological (that is, expressing value statements), and epistemic (referring to knowledge and belief). Global constraints on modality lead to projection of narrative worlds. To be sure, such worlds have no genuine ontological weight; they are only textual constructs. Yet, the notion of world allows Lubomír to make dazzling generalizations about the nature of fictional literature.

In a Leibnizian mode, a narrative world is defined as a set of compossible narrative agents (Doležel 1979a). Each text contains a primary narrative world, a world of fictional facts. Compossibility is understood here as a *de facto* relation of presence within the borders of a given text. Thus, Emma Bovary is compossible with Charles Bovary in, and only in, Flaubert's novel and with the adventurous narrator in, and only in, Woody Allen's story.

Narrative worlds can be extensional or intensional, according to which semantic functions they are a projection of. In other words, they can be seen as sets of objects, or as sets of meanings. The world of Robinson Crusoe, to take up Lubomír's own example, can be visualized either as a set of objects and properties (Crusoe, Friday, the island, etc.) or as a set of descriptions (the lonely Englishman, the noble savage, etc.).

Since to every extensional world there corresponds a variety of intensional worlds, Lubomír's narrative semantics generously accommodates the diversity of interpretations at the intensional level. It vindicates, therefore, modern hermeneutic pluralism. Yet it rejects postmodern hermeneutic anarchism. For, Lubomír notices, 'interpretation requires paraphrasing the original text'; and he adds, in the best empiricist vein, 'it is possible to devise specific evaluation procedures whereby the correspondence of the paraphrase to the original text will be assessed' (Doležel 1985b). An interpretation is valid only when the inspection of a text, and in particular of its semantic organization, supports its claims. In other words, support for an interpretive statement requires not only the inspection of the material text, but also detailed knowledge of the worlds projected by the text. Narrative semantics is thus more than a logical game: it is part and parcel of any serious literary inquiry.

A particularly forceful move on Lubomír's part consists in linking narrative semantics with the rhetoric of fiction. He distinguishes between the introduction (or construction) of narrative worlds and their authentication. To introduce a narrative world, the text redistributes the actual and the possible as it is found in the natural world. It does so by using small details in realist works, or massively when the purpose is the construction of supernatural worlds. The authentication is the textual function that gives weight to the worlds introduced in the text. In classical third-person narratives, the worlds introduced by the narrator have maximal authority. Motifs introduced by the narrative agents, however, enjoy lesser authority. Sometimes literary texts strongly contrast authentic and non-authentic motifs (the giants versus the windmills in *Don Quixote*). On other occasions, the system includes various degrees of authenticity, from the most authoritative statements of the narrator, to the least reliable motifs introduced by him, as it happens in Dostoevsky's *The Possessed*. Some literary worlds completely lack authentication, for example, the worlds of the Russian *skaz*, in which the narrator has little or no credibility.

This battery of notions is put to use to elucidate the narrative meaning of several modern texts, notably those of Franz Kafka. Lubomír notices that fictional texts often juxtapose more than one imaginary world. He describes three varieties of such junctions: (1) In the mythological worlds, in which the supernatural and the natural domains are clearly separated but interact frequently, power and accessibility are asymmetrical, exercised from the supernatural towards the natural domain. (2) From the basic dual structure of mythological worlds, one can form hybrid worlds by removing the boundaries that separate the everyday world from the beyond. Strange phenomena happen in a 'matter-of-fact' fashion in the midst of what appears to be a normal world, but it is crossed by an alien strand. Some of Kafka's stories, *The Metamorphosis*, for instance, exploit this vein. (3) If both realms of the mythological world become natural but the dividing line is kept, the resulting structure is a visible/invisible world. Again, Kafka's works are the best examples: in *The Castle*, the invisible world of the governing nobility is carefully segregated from the village. The same structure is present in *The Trial*, which opposes the world of the bank, efficient, rational, predictable, to the world of the court, mysterious, random, oneiric. The invisible worlds of these two novels are infinite in their depths, therefore impossible to explore, or even describe. They are inaccessible to the inhabitants of the visible world, yet these live with the obsessive desire to see the invisible. Equally asymmetric, the relation of power is overwhelmingly tilted in favour of the invisible realm. The force of the latter derives from the fact that while rebellion against it comes only from isolated individuals, the invisible is organized as an institution. But paradoxically, the infinite institution becomes, like nature itself, or like life in Borges's 'The Lottery at Babylon,' entirely random. Implicit in Kafka's novels and Lubomír's analyses is a reflection on the power of modern totalitarian states, whose countless levers annihilate the isolated individual. Yet, as Lubomír's reading of Kafka suggests, the infinite power and depth of the invisible bureaucracy are in the end the mark of its fragility: at first a sign of majesty, in the end randomness fosters decay, indifference, and dissolution.

We are fortunate enough to have witnessed the end of the Kafkian world in Czechoslovakia and the rest of Central Europe. The place Lubomír had to leave twenty-four years ago belongs again to the normal world. It is wonderful that he found a new home in Canada, and a warm and responsive intellectual milieu, in which he developed his powerful literary system. At the crossroads between continents and disciplines, Lubomír stands as a symbol of contemporary intellectual life: eager to understand the visible and the invisible, to achieve the impossible, and to firmly stand on the side of rationality and freedom.

Bibliography

Abish, Walter. 1983. *How German Is It?* London: Faber.

Adam, Jean-Michel. 1985. *Le texte narratif.* Paris: Nathan.

Adler, Mortimer. 1937. *Art and Prudence*. New York: Longman, Green.

Allen, Woody. 1981. *Side Effects*. New York: Ballantine Books.

Aquinas, Thomas. 1913–42. *Summa Theologica*. Translated by the Fathers of the English Dominican Province. London: Burns and Oates.

– 1955–7. *Summa Contra Gentiles*. Translated by A.C. Pegis et al. 5 vols. Garden City, N.Y.: Image Books.

Aristotle. 1984a. *The Nicomachean Ethics*. Translated by W.D. Ross. In *The Basic Works of Aristotle*, edited by Richard McKeon, 927–1112. New York: Random.

– 1984b. *Metaphysics*. Translated by W.D. Ross. In *The Basic Works of Aristotle*, edited by Richard McKeon, 681–926. New York: Random.

– 1984c. *The Politics*. Translated by Carnes Lord. Chicago: University of Chicago Press.

– 1987. *The Poetics of Aristotle*. Translated by Stephen Halliwell. London: Duckworth.

– 1991. *The Art of Rhetoric*. Translated by H.C. Lawson-Tancred. London: Penguin.

Armstrong, D.M., ed. 1989. *A Combinatorial Theory of Possibility*. Cambridge: Cambridge University Press.

Auerbach, Erich. 1953. *Mimesis: The Representation of Reality in Western Literature*. Translated by W. Trask. Princeton: Princeton University Press.

Augustine. 1912. *Confessions*. Translated by W. Watts. 1637. Cambridge: Harvard University Press.

Austin, John L. 1962. *Sense and Sensibilia*. Edited by G.J. Warnock. London: Oxford University Press.

Bakhtin, M.M. 1929. *Problemy tvorčestva Dostoevskogo*. Leningrad: Priboj.

– 1963. *Problemy poètiki Dostoevskogo*. (Revised and expanded version of Bakhtin 1929). Moscow: Sovetskij pisatel.

- 1965. *Tvorčestvo Fransua Rable i narodnaia kul'tura srednevekov'ia i renessansa.* Moscow: Khudozhestvennaia Literatura.
- 1973. *Problems of Dostoevsky's Poetics.* Translated by R.W. Roetsel. Ann Arbor: Ardis.
- 1974. 'K éstetike slova.' *Kontekst, 1973.* Moscow: Nauka, 258–81. Translated as 'Towards an Aesthetics of the Word' by Kenneth N. Brostrom. *Dispositio* 4 (1979), 11–12, 299–315.
- 1975. *Voprosy literatury i éstetiki: Issledovaniia raznykh let.* Moscow: Khudozhestvennaia Literatura.
- 1981. *The Dialogic Imagination.* Edited by Michael Holquist; translated by Caryl Emerson and M. Holquist. Austin: University of Texas Press.
- 1984. *Problems of Dostoevsky's Poetics.* 1929. Translated by C. Emerson. Theory and History of Literature, vol. 8. Minneapolis: University of Minnesota Press.
- 1990. 'The Problem of Content, Material, and Form in Verbal Art.' Translated by Kenneth Brostrom. In *Art and Answerability: Early Philosophical Essays by M.M. Bakhtin,* edited by M. Holquist and V. Liapunov. Slavic Series, vol. 9: 257–325. Austin: University of Texas Press.
- Barfield, A.O. 1947. 'Poetic Diction and Legal Fiction.' In *Essays Presented to Charles Williams,* by Dorothy Sayers et al., 106–27. Grand Rapids, Mich.: Eerdmans.
- Barthes, Roland. 1970. *S/Z.* Paris: Seuil.
- 1977. 'Introduction to the Structural Analysis of Narratives.' 1966. In *Image–Music–Text,* edited and translated by Stephen Heath. New York: Hill and Wang.
- 1984. 'De l'oeuvre au texte.' In *Le Bruissement de la langue,* 67–76. Paris: Seuil.
- Baudrillard, Jean. 1985. 'The Masses: The Implosion of the Social in the Media.' *New Literary History* 16, no. 3: 577–89.
- Benn Michaels, Walter, and Steven Knapp. 1982. 'Against Theory.' *Critical Inquiry* 8, no. 4 (summer): 723–42.
- Bentham, Jeremy. 1932. *Theory of Fictions.* c. 1814. Edited by Ch. K. Ogden. London: Kegan Paul, Trench, Trubner.
- Bertrand, Denis. 1985. *L'espace et le sens*: Germinal *d'Émile Zola.* Paris/Amsterdam: Hadès-Benjamins.
- Bhabha, Homi. 1984. 'Of Mimicry and Man: The Ambivalence of Colonial Discourse.' *October* 28: 125–33.
- 1985. 'Signs Taken for Wonders: Questions of Ambivalence and Authority Under a Tree Outside Delhi, May 1817.' *Critical Inquiry* 12, no. 1: 144–65.
- Bigazzi, R. 1978. 'Narrativa e teatro nell'età del romanzo.' *Filologia e critica.* N.p.: Sperno Editrice.
- Bojtar, E., 1973. 'Poljska "integralisticka skola."' *Umjetnost rijeci* 17, no. 3: 205–24.
- Borges, Jorge Luis. 1962. *Ficciones.* Translated by Anthony Kerrigan. New York: Grove Press.

- 1974. *Obras completas*. 4 vols. Buenos Aires: Emecé Editores.

Bouveresse, Jacques. 1976. *Le mythe de l'intériorité; Expérience, signification et langage privé chez Wittgenstein*. Paris: Minuit.

Brady, R.T. 1989. 'The Non-triviality of Dialectical Set Theory.' In *Paraconsistent Logic*, edited by Graham Priest, Richard Sylvan, and Jean Norman. Munich: Philosophia Verlag.

Bremond, Claude. 1973. *Logique du récit*. Paris: Seuil.

Brink, C.O. 1971. *Horace on Poetry. The 'Ars Poetica'*. Cambridge: Cambridge University Press.

Budzyk, Kazimierz, ed. 1946. *Stylistyka teoretyczna w Polsce*. Warsaw: n.p.

Buleau, Frédéric. 1861. *Personnages Enigmatiques: Histoires Mystérieuses, Evénements Peu ou Mal Connus*. Translated from German by W. Duckett. Paris: Poulet-Malassis et De Broise.

Burke, Kenneth. 1966. *Language as Symbolic Action*. Berkeley: University of California Press.

Butor, Michel. 1972. 'Le Voyage et l'écriture.' *Romantisme* 4: 4–19.

Bya, Joseph. 1990. *Le Traitement du sujet*. Calaceite: Noesis.

Carnap, Rudolf. 1959. 'The Elimination of Metaphysics through Logical Analysis of Language.' 1931. In *Logical Positivism*, edited by A.J. Ayer. Glencoe: Free Press.

Casanova. 1988. *Icosameron ou Histoire d'Édouard et d'Élisabeth qui passèrent quatre-vingt-un ans chez les Mégamicres, habitants aborigènes du protocosme dans l'intérieur de notre globe*. 1788. Paris: François Bourin.

Casteñeda, Hector-Neri. 1979. 'Fiction and Reality: Their Fundamental Connections.' *Poetics* 8: 31–62.

Černý, Václav. 1977. *Plác koruny ceské*. Toronto: Sixty-Eight Publishers.

Christiansen, Broder. 1909. *Philosophie der Kunst*. Hanau: Claus & Feddersen.

Clark, Katerina, and Michael Holquist. 1984. *Mikhail Bakhtin*. Cambridge: Harvard University Press.

Coetzee, J.M. 1986. *Foe*. Toronto: Stoddart.

Collins, Wilkie. 1978. *No Name*. 1873. New York: Dover.

Costa Lima, Luiz. 1988. *Control of the Imaginary: Reason and Imagination in Modern Times*. Translated by Ronald W. Sousa. Minneapolis: University of Minnesota Press.

Coste, Didier. 1989. *Narrative as Communication*. Minneapolis: University of Minnesota Press.

Crapanzano, Vincent. 1989. 'Self Characterization.' In *Cultural Psychology: Essays in Comparative Human Development*, edited by James W. Stigler, Richard A. Schweder, and Gilbert H. Herdt, 401–23. Cambridge: Cambridge University Press.

Cunliffe, Richard John. 1963. *A Lexicon of the Homeric Dialect*. Norman: Oklahoma University Press.

Defoe, Daniel. 1975. *The Life and Adventures of Robinson Crusoe*, edited by Michael Shinagel. New York: Norton.

Delillo, Don. 1985. *White Noise*. New York: Viking/Penguin.

de Man, Paul. 1969. 'The Rhetoric of Temporality.' In *Interpretation: Theory and Practice*, edited by Charles S. Singleton, 173–209. Baltimore: Johns Hopkins University Press.

– 1979. *Allegories of Reading: Figural Language in Rousseau, Nietzsche, Rilke, and Proust*. New Haven: Yale University Press.

– 1988. *Wartime Journalism, 1939–1943*. Lincoln: Nebraska University Press.

Derrida, Jacques. 1967. *De la grammatologie*. Paris: Minuit.

– 1976. *On Grammatology*. Translated by Gayatri Chakravorti Spivak. Baltimore: Johns Hopkins University Press.

– 1984. 'Living On.' In *Deconstruction and Criticism*, edited by Harold Bloom. New York: Continuum.

– 1988. *Limited Inc*. Edited and translated by Gerald Graff. Evanston: University of Illinois Press.

Detienne, Marcel. 1986. *The Creation of Mythology*. Translated by M. Cook. Chicago: University of Chicago Press.

D'haen, Theo, Rainer Grübel, and Helmut Lethen, eds. 1989. *Convention and Innovation in Literature*. Amsterdam: Benjamins.

Diels, Hermann, and Walther Kranz. 1971. *Die Fragmente der Vorsokratiker*. 1903. 3 vols. Berlin: Weidmannsche Verlagsbuchhandlung.

Diengott, Nilli. 1988. 'Narratology and Feminism.' *Style* 22: 42–51.

Dimock, George E. 1956. 'The Name of Odysseus.' *Hudson Review* 9: 52–70.

– 1989. *The Unity of the Odyssey*. Amherst: University of Massachusetts Press.

Doherty, Lillian. 1992. 'Gender and Internal Audiences in the *Odyssey*.' *American Journal of Philology* 113, no. 2: 161–77.

Doležel, Lubomír. 1973a. *Narrative Modes in Czech Literature*. Toronto: University of Toronto Press.

– 1973b. 'A Scheme of Narrative Time.' In *Slavic Poetics: Essays in Honor of Kiril Taranovsky*, edited by Roman Jakobson et al., 91–8. The Hague: Mouton.

– 1976a. 'Narrative Semantics.' *PTL: A Journal for Descriptive Poetics and Theory of Literature* 1: 129–51.

– 1976b. 'Narrative Modalities.' *Journal of Literary Semantics* 5: 5–14.

– 1977. 'A Pragmatic Typology of Dialogue.' In *Papers in Slavic Philology I*, edited by Benjamin A. Stolz, 62–8. Ann Arbor: University of Michigan Press.

– 1979a. 'Extensional and Intensional Narrative Worlds.' *Poetics* 8: 193–211.

– 1979b. 'In Defence of Structural Poetics.' *Poetics* 8: 521–30.

– 1979c. 'Narrative Worlds.' In *Sound, Sign and Meaning*, edited by L. Matejka, 542–52. Ann Arbor: University of Michigan Press.

– 1980. 'Truth and Authenticity in Narrative.' *Poetics Today* 1, no. 3: 7–25.

– 1982. 'The Conceptual System of Prague School Poetics: Mukařovský and Vodicka.' In *The Structure of the Literary Process: Studies Devoted to the Memory of Felix Vodicka*, edited by Peter Steiner, M. Cervenka, and R. Vroon, 109–26. Amsterdam: Benjamins.

– 1983. 'Proper Names, Definite Descriptions and the Intensional Structure of Kafka's *The Trial.*' *Poetics* 12: 511–26.

– 1984a. 'Aristotelian Poetics as a Science of Literature.' In *Semiosis: Semiotics and the History of Culture, In Honorem Georgii Lotman*, edited by Morris Halle et al., 125–38. Ann Arbor: Michigan Slavic Contributions.

– 1984b. 'Kafka's Fictional World.' *Canadian Review of Comparative Literature* 11, no. 1: 61–83.

– 1985a. 'Pour une typologie des mondes fictionnels.' In *Exigences et Perspectives de la Sémiotique/Aims and Prospects of Semiotics*, edited by H. Parret and H.-G. Ruprecht, 1: 7–23. Amsterdam: Benjamins.

– 1985b. 'Literary Text, Its World, and Its Style.' In *Identity of the Literary Text*, edited by Mario J. Valdés and O.J. Miller, 189–205. Toronto: University of Toronto Press.

– 1985c. 'Towards a Typology of Fictional Worlds.' *Tamkang Review* 14: 262–74.

– 1988. 'Mimesis and Possible Worlds.' *Poetics Today* 9, no. 3: 475–96.

– 1989a. 'Possible Worlds in Humanities, Arts and Sciences.' In *Proceedings of Nobel Symposium 65*, edited by Sture Allén, 221–42. Berlin: de Gruyter.

– 1989b. 'Mimesis and Contemporary Criticism.' *Comparative Criticism* 11: 253–61.

– 1990a. *Occidental Poetics: Tradition and Progress.* Lincoln: University of Nebraska Press.

– 1990b. 'Fictional Reference: Mimesis and Possible Worlds.' In *Towards a Theory of Comparative Literature, Proceedings of the XIth International Comparative Literature Congress*, edited by M. Valdés, 3: 120–1. Bern: Peter Lang.

Doleželová-Velingerová, Milena, ed. 1989. *Poetics East and West.* Monograph Series, no. 4. Toronto: Toronto Semiotic Circle.

Dovey, Teresa. 1988. *The Novels of J.M. Coetzee: Lacanian Allegories.* Cape Town: Ad. Donker.

Eco, Umberto. 1976. *A Theory of Semiotics.* Bloomington: Indiana University Press.

– 1979. *The Role of the Reader: Explorations in the Semiotics of Texts.* Bloomington: Indiana University Press.

– 1984. *Semiotics and the Philosophy of Language.* Bloomington: Indiana University Press.

Elgrably, Jordan. 1987. 'Conversations with Milan Kundera.' *Salmagundi* 13 (winter): 3–24.

Else, Gerald Frank. 1957. *Aristotle's Poetics: The Argument.* Cambridge: Harvard University Press.

Erlich, Victor. 1969. *Russian Formalism, History, Doctrine*. New Haven: Yale University Press.

Felson-Rubin, Nancy. 1987. 'Penelope's Perspective: Character from Plot.' In *Homer: Beyond Oral Poetry, Recent Trends in Homeric Interpretation*, edited by J.M. Bremer, I.J.F. de Jong, and J. Kalff, 61–83. Amsterdam: B.R. Gruner.

– 1990. 'Behind the Poet's Back: Characters Who Spin.' In *Textual Fidelity and Textual Disregard*, edited by Bernard P. Dauenhauser, 121–38. New York: Peter Lang.

– 1994. *Regarding Penelope: From Character to Poetics*. Princeton: Princeton University Press.

Fergusson, Francis. 1949. *The Idea of a Theater: A Study of Ten Plays*. Princeton: Princeton University Press.

Fieguth, Rolf. 1975. 'Semantik und literarische Tradition. Ein struckturalistisches Gesamtkonzept der Literaturwissenschaft.' Introduction to his translation of *Literatur als System und Prozess* by J. Sławiński, 11–39. Munich: Nymphenburger Verlagshandlung.

Fink, Eugen. 1966. *Studien zur Phänomenologie 1930–1939*. The Hague: Martinus Nijhoff.

Finkielkraut, Alain. 1982. 'Interview with Milan Kundera.' *Cross Currents*, 15–29.

Flaubert, Gustave. 1950. *Madame Bovary*. 1857. Translated by Alan Russell. Harmondsworth: Penguin.

– 1983. *Madame Bovary*. 1857. Edited by Béatrice Didier. Paris: Livre de Poche.

Fokkema, Douwe. 1989. 'The Concept of Convention in Literary Theory and Empirical Research.' In *Convention and Innovation in Literature*, edited by Theo D'haen, Rainer Grübel, and Helmut Lethen, 1–16. Amsterdam: Benjamins.

Foley, Barbara. 1986. *Telling the Truth: The Theory and Practice of Documentary Fiction*. Ithaca: Cornell University Press.

Forbes, Graeme. 1986. 'In Defense of Absolute Essentialism.' *Midwest Studies in Philosophy*, edited by Peter French et al., 11: 3–31. Minneapolis: University of Minnesota Press.

Foucault, Michel. 1977. *Discipline and Punish*. 1975. Translated by Alan Sheridan. New York: Random/Vintage.

Frege, Gottlob. 1966a. 'Über Sinn und Bedeutung.' 1892. In *Funktion, Begriff, Bedeutung: Fünf logische Studien*, edited by Günther Patzig. Göttingen: Vandenhoeck & Ruprecht.

– 1966b. 'Die Gedanke: eine logische Untersuchung.' 1918–19. In *Logische Untersuchungen*, edited by Günther Patzig. Göttingen: Vandenhoeck & Ruprecht.

Freud, Sigmund. 1938. *Wit and Its Relation to the Unconscious*. 1905. In *The Basic Writings of Sigmund Freud*, translated and edited by A.A. Brill, 631–803. New York: Modern Library.

Fry, W.R.F. 1963. *Sweet Madness: A Study of Humor*. Palo Alto: Pacific Books.

Frye, Northrop. 1957. *Anatomy of Criticism*. Princeton: Princeton University Press.

Fučík, Julius. 1947. *Reportáž psaná na oprátce*, edited by Gusta Fučíková and Ladislav Štoll. Prague: Svoboda. English translation: *Notes from the Gallows*. New York: New Century, 1948.

Fučíková, Gusta. 1961. *Vzpomínky na Julia Fučíka: Okupace*. Prague: SNPL.

Genette, Gérard. 1966. 'Frontières du récit.' *Communications* 8: 152–63.

– 1972. *Figures III*. Paris: Seuil.

– 1980. *Narrative Discourse: An Essay in Method*. Translated by Jane Lewin. Ithaca: Cornell University Press.

– 1982. *Palimpsestes: la littérature au second degré*. Paris: Seuil.

– 1983. *Nouveau discours du récit*. Paris: Seuil.

– 1987. *Seuils*. Paris: Seuil.

– 1989. 'Le statut pragmatique de la fiction narrative.' *Poétique* 78: 237–49.

– 1990. 'The Pragmatic Status of Narrative Fiction.' Translated by William Nelles and Corinne Bonnet. *Style* 24: 59–72.

Gilbert, Sandra M., and Susan Gubar. 1979. *The Madwoman in the Attic: The Woman Writer and the Nineteenth-Century Literary Imagination*. New Haven: Yale University Press.

Głowiński, Michal. 1975. 'Polish Structuralism.' *Books Abroad* 49, no. 2: 238–43.

Godzich, Wlad. 1987. 'Religion, the State, and Post(al) Modernism.' Afterword to *Institution and Interpretation* by Samuel Weber. Theory and History of Literature, vol. 31: 153–64. Minneapolis: University of Minnesota Press.

Goodman, Nelson. 1978. *Ways of Worldmaking*. Indianapolis: Hackett.

Gordimer, Nadine. 1984. 'The Idea of Gardening.' *New York Review of Books*, 2 February: 3–4.

Górski, K. 1960. 'Przeglad stanowisk metodologicznych w polskiej historii literatury do 1933 rokn.' In *Zjazd naukowy polonistów 10–13 grudnia 1958*, edited by K. Vyka, 89–123. Wroclaw: Zaklad Narodowy im. Ossolińskich.

Grayling, A.C. 1988. *Wittgenstein*. Oxford: Oxford University Press.

Groos, K. 1899. *Die Spiele der Menschen*. Jena: G. Fischer.

Hamburger, Käte. 1973. *The Logic of Literature*. 1959. Translated by Marilyn J. Rose. Bloomington: Indiana University Press.

Harris, Wilson. 1981a. 'The Frontier on which *Heart of Darkness* Stands.' In his *Explorations*, edited by Hena Maes-Jelinek, 134–41. Mundelstrup: Dangaroo.

– 1981b. 'The Complexity of Freedom.' In his *Explorations*, edited by Hena Maes-Jelinek, 113–24. Mundelstrup: Dangaroo.

Hart, Jonathan. 1988. 'A Comparative Pluralism: The Heterogeneity of Methods and the Case of Fictional Worlds.' *Canadian Review of Comparative Literature* 15, no. 3–4: 320–45.

Hawking, Stephen. 1988. *A Brief History of Time*. New York: Bantam Books.

Heidegger, Martin. 1977. 'The Age of the World Picture.' 1938. In his *The Question Concerning Technology and Other Essays*, 115–54. Translated by William Lovitt. New York: Harper.

Heintz, John. 1979. 'Reference and Inference in Fiction.' *Poetics* 8, 85–99.

Herington, John. 1985. *Poetry into Drama: Early Greek Tragedy and the Greek Poetic Tradition*. Berkeley: University of California Press.

Hintikka, Jaakko. 1981. 'Semantics: A Revolt against Frege.' In *Contemporary Philosophy*, edited by Guttorm Floistad, vol. 1: 57–82. The Hague: Martinus Nijhoff.

Hintikka, Jaakko, and Merrill B. Hintikka. 1982. 'Towards a General Theory of Individuation and Identification.' In *Language and Ontology: Proceedings of the Sixth International Wittgenstein Symposium, 1981*, edited by Werner Leinfellner et al. Vienna: Hölder Pichler Tempsky.

Hölscher, Uvo. 1989. *Die Odyssee. Epos zwischen Märchen und Roman*. Munich: Beck.

Howell, Robert. 1979. 'Fictional Objects: How They Are and How They Aren't.' *Poetics* 8: 129–77.

Hung, William. 1969. *Tu Fu, China's Greatest Poet*. New York: Russell and Russell.

Husserl, Edmund. 1950. *Idées directrices pour une phénoménologie*. 1928. Translated by P. Ricoeur. Paris: Gallimard, coll. Bibliothèque de philosophie.

Idema, W.L. 1974. *Chinese Vernacular Fiction: The Formative Period*. Leiden: Brill.

Ingarden, Roman. 1960. *Das literarische Kunstwerk*. 2nd ed. Tübingen: Niemeyer.

– 1973. *The Literary Work of Art*. Evanston: Northwestern University Press.

Ivanov, V.V. 1957. 'Kod i soobscenie.' *Bjuleten' ob'edinenija po problemam masinnogo perevoda* 5: 48–50.

– 1973. 'Značenie idej M.M. Bakhtina o znake, vyskazyvanii i dialoge dlja sovremennoj semiotiki.' In *Trudy po znakovym sistemam*. Učenye zapiski tartuskogo gosudarstvennogo universiteta, vol. 6: 5–44. Tartu: Tartu University.

Jakobson, Roman. 1958. 'Medieval Mock Mystery: The Old Czech Unguentarius.' In *Studia philologica et litteraria in honorem L. Spitzer*, edited by Anna Granville Hatcher and Karl Ludwig Selig, 245–65. Bern: Francke.

Jamblichus. 1991. *On the Pythagorean Way of Life*. Text, translation, and notes by John Dillon and Jackson Hershbell. Atlanta: Scholars Press.

Jameson, Fredric. 1987. 'On Islands and Trenches: Neutralization and the Production of Utopian Discourse.' 1977. In his *The Ideologies of Theory: Essays 1971–1986*. Theory and History of Literature, vol. 48: 75–101. Minneapolis: University of Minnesota Press.

JanMohamed, Abdul R. 1985. 'The Economy of Manichean Allegory: The Function of Racial Difference in Colonialist Literature.' *Critical Inquiry* 12, no. 1: 59–87.

Joyce, James. 1957. *Letters of James Joyce*. Vol. 1. Edited by Stuart Gilbert. London: Faber and Faber.

– 1963. *Ulysses*. 1922. Harmondsworth: Penguin.

– 1966. *Letters of James Joyce*. Vol. 2, edited by Richard Ellmann. New York: Viking.

– 1977. *Portrait of the Artist as a Young Man*. 1916. New York: Penguin.

– 1979. 'Paris Notebook, 1903.' In *Selections*, edited by Hans Walter Gabler. New York: Garland.

Kant, Immanuel. 1934. *Immanuel Kant's Critique of Pure Reason*. 1781. Translated by Norman Kemp Smith. London: Macmillan.

Kermode, Frank. 1967. *The Sense of an Ending: Studies in the Theory of Fiction*. New York: Oxford University Press.

Koestler, Arthur. 1989. *The Act of Creation*. 1964. London: Arkana.

Kridl, Manfred. 1978. *Wstęp do badań nad dziełem literackim*. 1936. Würzburg: Jal-Reprint.

Kripke, Saul. 1963. 'Semantical Considerations on Modal Logic.' *Acta Philosophica Fennica* 16: 83–94.

– 1971. 'Identity and Necessity.' In *Identity and Individuation*, edited by M.K. Munitz. New York: New York University Press.

– 1980. *Naming and Necessity*. 1972. Cambridge: Harvard University Press.

Krippendorff, K. 1990. 'Models and Metaphors of Communication.' In *Funkkolleg Medien und Kommunikation. Konstruktionen von Wirklichkeit*. Studienbrief 3, 11–50. Weinheim and Basel: Beltz.

Kristeva, Julia. 1968. 'La sémiologie: Science critique et/ou critique de la science.' In *Théorie d'ensemble*, by Michel Foucault et al. Paris: Seuil.

– 1990. *Les Samourais*. Paris: Fayard.

Kroll, W. 1974. 'Poljska znanost o književnosti u kontekstu novije književnoteorijske diskusije.' Special triple issue of *Umjetnost riječi* 18, nos. 2–4: 99–100.

– ed. 1974. 'Književna komunikacija. Antologija poljske znanosti o književnosti.' *Umjetnost riječi* 18: nos. 2–4.

Kundera, Milan. 1953. *Člověk zahrada širá*. Prague: Čs. spisovatel.

– 1955. *Poslední máj* (The last May). Prague: Čs. spisovatel.

– 1969. *The Joke*. Translation of *Žert* (1967) by D. Hamblyn and D. Stallybrass. London: Macdonald.

– 1979. *Život je jinde*. Toronto: Sixty-Eight Publishers.

– 1980a. *Life Is Elsewhere*. Translated by P. Kussi. Harmondsworth: Penguin.

– 1980b. *The Book of Laughter and Forgetting*. Translation of *Kniha smíchu a zapomnění* by M.H. Heim. Harmondsworth: Penguin.

Kushner, Eva. 1988. 'Les Colloques et l'inscription de l'autre dans le discours.' In *Dix conférences sur Erasme, Éloge de la folie – Colloques*, edited by Claude Blum, 33–47. Paris and Geneva: Champion; Slatkine.

LaCapra, Dominick. 1983. *Rethinking Intellectual History: Texts, Contexts, Language.* Ithaca: Cornell University Press.

Lakoff, George. 1987. *Women, Fire and Dangerous Things.* Chicago: University of Chicago Press.

Lakoff, George, and Mark Johnson. 1980. *Metaphors We Live By.* Chicago: University of Chicago Press.

Lane-Mercier, Gillian. 1990. *La parole romanesque.* Ottawa: Presses de l'Université d'Ottawa.

Langbaum, Robert. 1956. 'Aristotle and Modern Literature.' *Journal of Aesthetics and Art Criticism* 15, no. 1: 74–84.

Lanser, Susan Sniader. 1981. *The Narrative Act: Point of View in Fiction.* Princeton: Princeton University Press.

– 1986. 'Toward a Feminist Narratology.' *Style* 20: 341–63.

– 1988. 'Shifting the Paradigm: Feminism and Narratology.' *Style* 22: 52–60.

Lattimore, Richmond, trans. 1967. *The Odyssey of Homer.* New York: Harper & Row.

Łempicki, Zygmunt. 1966. *Studia z teorii literatury. Wybór pism. II.* Warsaw: Państwowe Wydawnictwo Naukowe.

– 1971. 'Zum Problem der Begründung einer reinen Poetik.' German translation by Peter Lachmann. *Poetica* 4, no. 3: 378–408.

Levin, Samuel. 1976. 'What Kind of Speech Act a Poem Is?' In *Pragmatics of Language and Literature,* edited by T.A. van Dijk. Amsterdam: North-Holland.

Lewis, David K. 1973. *Counterfactuals.* Oxford: Blackwell.

Li Yü. 1963. *Jou p'u t'uan* (The prayer mat of flesh). Translated by Richard Martin. New York: Grove.

Liddell, Henry George, R. Scott, and H.S. Jones. 1968. *A Greek-English Lexicon (with Supplement).* Oxford: Clarendon Press.

Liehm, Antonin J. 1980. 'Milan Kundera: A Czech Writer.' In *Czech Literature since 1956: A Symposium,* edited by William E. Harkins and Paul I. Trensky, 40–4. New York: Bohemica.

– 1988. 'Milan Kundera.' *Generace,* 47–56. Cologne: Index.

Liu, James J.Y. 1975. *Chinese Theories of Literature.* Chicago: University of Chicago Press.

Liu Hsieh. 1959. *The Literary Mind and the Carving of Dragons.* Translated by Vincent Yu-chung Shih. New York: Columbia University Press.

Lodge, David. 1989. *Nice Work.* London: Penguin.

Lotman, Juri. 1977. *The Structure of the Artistic Text.* Ann Arbor: University of Michigan Press.

Loux, M., ed. 1979. *Universals and Particulars.* Notre Dame: Notre Dame University Press.

Maitre, Doreen. 1983. *Literature and Possible Worlds.* Middlesex: Polytechnic Press.

Mallarmé, Stéphane. 1943. *Divagations*. Paris: Fasquelle Editeurs.

Mannheim, Karl. 1936. *Ideology and Utopia: An Introduction to the Sociology of Knowledge*. 1929. Translated by L. Wirth and E. Shils. New York: Harcourt Brace Jovanovich.

Markiewicz, Henryk. 1985a. *Polska nauka o literaturze*. Warsaw: Państwowe Wydawnictwo Naukowe.

– 1985b. *Swiadomość literatury*. Warsaw: Państwowy Instytut Wysawniczy.

– ed. 1961. *Teoria badań literackich w Polsce*. 2 vols. Cracow: Wydawnictwo Literackie.

Martínez-Bonati, Félix. 1980. 'The Act of Writing Fiction.' *New Literary History* 11: 425–34.

– 1981. *Fictive Discourse and the Structures of Literature*. Ithaca: Cornell University Press.

– 1983. 'Towards a Formal Ontology of Fictional Worlds.' *Philosophy and Literature* 7, no. 2: 182–95.

Matejka, Ladislav. 1978. 'The Roots of Russian Semiotics of Art.' In *The Sign: Semiotics around the World*, edited by R.W. Bailey et al., 146–72. Ann Arbor: Michigan Slavic Publications.

Mathesius, Vilém. 1947. 'Jazykozpytné poznámky k řečnické výstaubě souvislého výkladu.' *Čestina a obecný jazykozpyt: Soubor stati*, 380–414. Prague: Melantrich.

Mayenowa, M.R. 1968. 'Stylistics in Poland.' *Style* 2, no. 2: 159–73.

McCormick, Peter. 1988. *Fictions, Philosophies, and the Problems of Poetics*. Ithaca: Cornell University Press.

McHale, Brian. 1978. 'Free Indirect Discourse: a Survey of Recent Accounts.' *Poetics and Theory of Literature* 3: 249–87.

– 1987. *Postmodernist Fiction*. New York: Methuen.

Medvedev, P.N., and M.M. Bakhtin. 1978. *The Formal Method in Literary Scholarship: A Critical Introduction to Sociological Poetics*. Translated by A.J. Wehrle. Baltimore: Johns Hopkins University Press.

Merrel, Floyd. 1983. *Pararealities: The Nature of Our Fictions and How We Know Them*. Amsterdam: Benjamins.

Michaels, Walter Benn, and Steven Knapp. 1982. 'Against Theory.' *Critical Inquiry* 8, no. 4: 723–42.

Mitterand, Henri. 1990. 'Chrontopies romanesques: *Germinal*.' *Poétique* 81: 89–104.

Modiano, Patrick. 1968. *La Place de l'Étoile*. Paris: Gallimard.

Morselli, Guido. 1974. *Roma senza papa*. Milano: Adelphi.

– 1975. *Contro-passato prossimo*. Milano: Adelphi.

Morson, Gary Saul, and Caryl Emerson. 1990. *Mikhail Bakhtin: Creation of a Prosaics*. Stanford: Stanford University Press.

Mukařovský, Jan. 1970. 'Die Kunst als semiologisches Faktum.' 1934. In his *Kapitel aus der Ästhetik*, 138–46. Translated by Walter Schamschula. Frankfurt: Suhrkamp.

Nagy, Gregory. 1974. *Comparative Studies in Greek and Indic Meter.* Cambridge: Harvard University Press.

– 1979. *The Best of the Achaians: Concepts of the Hero in Archaic Greek Poetry.* Baltimore: Johns Hopkins University Press.

Nicole, Eugène. 1983. 'L'onomastique littéraire.' *Poétique* 54: 239–53.

Nietzsche, Friedrich. 1954. 'On Truth and Lie in an Extra-Moral Sense.' In *The Portable Nietzsche.* Translated by Walter Kaufmann. Princeton: Princeton University Press.

– 1967. *The Birth of Tragedy.* 1872, 1878. Translated by Walter Kaufmann. New York: Random/Vintage.

Olson, Douglas. 1989. 'The Stories of Helen and Menelaus (*Odyssey* 4.240–89) and the Return of Odysseus.' *American Journal of Philology* 110: 387–94.

Oppenheim, Lois. 1989. 'Clarifications, Elucidations: An Interview with Milan Kundera.' *The Review of Contemporary Fiction* 2: 8–9.

Ouellet, Pierre. 1988. 'Énonciation et perception: La représentation sémiolinguistique des événements perceptifs.' *Recherches Sémiotiques/Semiotic Inquiry* 8, nos. 1–2: 109–30.

– 1990. 'Représentation et perception; Sémiotique des événements esthésiques.' *Protée* 18, no. 2: 55–66.

Parmentier, Richard J. 1985. 'Signs' Place *in Medias Res*: Peirce's Concept of Semiotic Mediation.' In *Semiotic Mediation: Semiotic and Sociocultural Perspectives*, edited by E. Mertz and R.J. Parmentier. New York: Academic Press.

Parsons, Terence. 1980. *Non-Existent Objects.* New Haven: Yale University Press.

Pavel, Thomas G. 1980. 'Narrative Domains.' *Poetics Today* 1, no. 4: 105–14.

– 1986. *Fictional Worlds.* Cambridge: Harvard University Press.

– 1989. 'Fictional Worlds and the Economy of the Imaginary.' In *Possible Worlds in Humanities, Arts and Sciences*, edited by Sture Allén, 251–9. Berlin: de Gruyter.

Pears, D. 1987. *The False Prison: A Study of the Development of Wittgenstein's Philosophy.* Vol. 1. Oxford: Oxford University Press.

Peirce, Charles Sanders. 1932. *Collected Papers.* Vol. 2, edited by Charles Hartshorne and Paul Weiss. Cambridge: Harvard University Press.

Pelc, J. 1974. 'The Development of Polish Semiotics in the Post-War Years.' *Semiotica* 10, no. 4: 369–81.

– 1986. 'On Fictional Entities and Fictional Texts.' *Recherches Sémiotiques/Semiotic Inquiry* 6: 1–35

Peradotto, John. 1990. *Man in the Middle Voice: Name and Narration in the* Odyssey. Princeton: Princeton University Press.

Pirandello, Luigi. 1958. *Maschere nude.* Milan: Mondadori.

Plaks, Andrew H., ed. 1977. *Chinese Narrative: Critical and Theoretical Essays.* Princeton: Princeton University Press.

Plato. *Cratylus*. Translated by Benjamin Jowett. In *The Collected Works of Plato*, edited by Edith Hamilton and Huntington Cairns. Bollingen Series, 71: 421–74. Princeton: Princeton University Press.

Plicka, Karel. 1953. *Prag. Ein fotographisches Bilderbuch*. Prague: Arcia.

Plutarch. 1956. *Moralia*. 15 vols. With an English translation by Frank Cole Babbitt. Cambridge: Harvard University Press.

Poe, Edgar Allan. 1965. 'The Philosophy of Composition.' In *Literary Criticism of Edgar Allan Poe*, edited by Robert L. Hough, 19–32. Lincoln: University of Nebraska Press.

Poggioli, Renato. 1968. *The Theory of the Avant-garde*. Translated by Gerald Fitzgerald. Cambridge: Harvard University Press.

Popovič, A., ed. 1972. *Slovo. Vyznam. Dielo. Antologia pol'skej literarnej vedy*. Bratislava: Slovenský Spisovatel'.

Prévert, Jacques. 1949. *Paroles*. Paris: NRF/Folio.

Priest, Graham. 1987. *In Contradiction*. Boston: Martinus Nijhoff.

Priest, Graham, and Richard Routley. 1984. *On Paraconsistency*. Canberra: Australian National University.

Prince, Gerald. 1983. 'Narrative Pragmatics, Message, and Point.' *Poetics* 12: 527–36.

– 1986. 'Re–Membering Modiano, or Something Happened.' *Substance* 49: 35–43.

– 1989. 'Introduction to the Study of the Narratee.' Translated by Francis Mariner. In *Reader-Response Criticism*, edited by Jane P. Tompkins, 7–25. Baltimore: Johns Hopkins University Press.

Proust, Marcel. 1956. *A la Recherche du temps perdu*, edited by Pierre Clarac and André Ferré. Paris: Bibliothèque de la Pléiade.

– 1987. *Remembrance of Things Past*. 3 vols. Translated by C.K. Scott Moncriel and Terence Kilmartin. Harmondsworth: Penguin.

Pseudo-Longinus. 1985. *On the Sublime*. Translated by G.M. Grube. New York: Mellen Press.

Putnam, Hilary. 1983. *Realism and Reason: Philosophical Papers*. Vol. 3. Cambridge: Cambridge University Press.

Raczymow, Henri. 1988. *Maurice Sachs*. Paris: Gallimard.

Rastier, François. 1983. 'Isotopies et impressions référentielles ou: le soleil et la bergère.' *Fabula* 2 (October): 107–20.

Rescher, Nicholas. 1975. *A Theory of Possibility*. Oxford: Blackwell.

Rich, Paul. 1982. 'Tradition and Revolt in South African Fiction: The Novels of André Brink, Nadine Gordimer and J.M. Coetzee.' *Journal of Southern African Studies* 9, no. 1: 54–73.

Richards, I.A. 1924. *Principles of Literary Criticism*. London: Kegan Paul, Trench Trubner.

Ricoeur, Paul. 1975. *La métaphore vive*. Paris: Seuil.

– 1983. *Temps et récit.* Paris: Seuil.
– 1984. *Time and Narrative.* Vol. 1. Chicago: University of Chicago Press.
– 1985. *Le Temps raconté* (*Temps et récit* III). Paris: Seuil.
Riffaterre, Michael. 1990. *Fictional Truth.* Baltimore: Johns Hopkins University Press.
Rimmon Kenan, Shlomith. 1983. *Narrative Fiction: Contemporary Poetics.* London: Methuen.
Ronen, Ruth. 1988. 'Completing the Incompleteness of Fictional Entities.' *Poetics Today* 9: 497–514.
Rorty, Richard. 1982. 'Is There a Problem about Fictional Discourse?' In his *Consequences of Pragmatism (Essays, 1972–1980)*, 110–38. Minneapolis: University of Minnesota Press.
Roth, Gerhard. 1987a. 'Erkenntnis und Realität: Das reale Gehirn und seine Wirklichkeit.' In *Der Diskurs des Radikalen Konstruktivismus*, edited by S.J. Schmidt, 229–55. Frankfurt: Suhrkamp.
– 1987b. 'Autopoiese und Kognition: Die Theorie H.R. Maturanas und die Notwendigkeit ihrer Weiterentwicklung.' In *Der Diskurs des Radikalen Konstruktivismus*, edited by S.J. Schmidt, 256–86. Frankfurt: Suhrkamp.
Routley, Richard. 1979. 'The Semantic Structure of Fictional Discourse.' *Poetics* 8: 3–30.
– 1980. *Exploring Meinong's Jungle and Beyond.* Canberra: Philosophy Department, Australian National University.
Routley, Richard, and Robert K. Meyer. 1975. 'Dialectical Logic and the Consistency of the World.' *Studies in Soviet Thought* 16: 1–25.
Rushdie, Salman. 1988. *The Satanic Verses.* New York: Viking.
Ryan, Marie-Laure. 1980. 'Fiction, Non-factuals and the Principle of Minimal Departure.' *Poetics* 8: 403–22.
– 1984. 'Fiction as a Logical, Ontological, and Illocutionary Issue.' *Style* 18, no. 2: 122–39.
– 1985. 'The Modal Structure of Narrative Universes.' *Poetics Today* 6, no. 4: 717–55.
– 1991. *Possible Worlds, Artificial Intelligence, and Narrative Theory.* Bloomington: Indiana University Press.
Salmon, Christian. 1987. 'Conversations with Milan Kundera on the Art of the Novel.' Translated by Lidia Asher. *Salmagundi* (winter): 119–35.
Schlegel, Friedrich. 1964. *Kritische Schriften*, edited by W. Rasch. Munich: Carl Hanser.
Schmidt, S.J. 1976. 'Towards the Pragmatic Interpretation of "Fictionality."' In *Pragmatics of Language and Literature*, edited by T.A. van Dijk, 161–78. Amsterdam: North-Holland.
– 1980. 'Fictionality in Literary and Non-Literary Discourse.' *Poetics* 9, no. 5–6: 525–46.

- 1982. *Foundations for the Empirical Study of Literature: The Components of a Basic Theory*. Translated by Robert de Beaugrande. Hamburg: Buske.
- 1988. 'Kreativität aus der Beobachterperspektive.' In *Kreativität – ein verbrauchter Begriff?*, edited by H.U. Gumbrecht, 33–51. Munich: Fink.
- 1989. *Die Selbstorganisation des Sozialsystems Literatur im 18. Jahrhundert*. Frankfurt: Suhrkamp.
- 1990a. 'Literary Systems as Self-organizing Systems.' In *Selforganization: Portrait of a Scientific Revolution. Sociology of the Sciences, Yearbook 1990*, edited by W. Krohn, G. Küppers, and H. Nowotny, 153–63. Dordrecht: Kluwer.
- 1990b. 'What Advertising Can Tell Scholars of Empirical Aesthetics.' *Poetics* 19: 389–404.
- ed. 1987a. *Der Diskurs des Radikalen Konstruktivismus*. Frankfurt: Suhrkamp.
- ed. 1987b. *Media genre*. Special issue of *Poetics* 16, no. 5.
Schmidt, S.J., D. Sinofzik, and B. Spieß. 1990. 'Wo lassen Sie leben? Kulturfaktor Werbung – Entwicklungen und Trends der 80er Jahre.' In *Die 80er Jahre*, edited by Christian Thomsen. Cologne: DuMont.
Schmitt, Rüdiger. 1967. *Dichtung und Dichtersprache in indogermanischer Zeit*. Wiesbaden: Otto Harassowitz.
Scott, William C. 1989. 'Oral Verse-Making in Homer's *Odyssey*.' *Oral Tradition* 4, no. 3: 382–412.
Scully, Stephen P. 1981. 'The Bard as the Custodian of Homeric Society: *Odyssey* 3.263–72.' *Quaderni Urbinati di Cultura Classica* 8: 67–83.
Searle, John R. 1975. 'The Logical Status of Fictional Discourse.' *New Literary History* 6: 319–32.
- 1979. *Expression and Meaning: Studies in the Theory of Speech Acts*. Cambridge: Cambridge University Press.
Sextus Empiricus. 1949. *Against the Grammarians*. In *Against the Professors*, 4: 25–187. Cambridge: Harvard University Press.
Siegle, Robert. 1989. *Suburban Ambush: Downtown Writing and the Fiction of Insurgency*. Baltimore: Johns Hopkins University Press.
Skyrms, B. 1981. 'Tractarian Nominalism.' *Philosophical Studies* 40: 199–20
Sławiński, Janusz. 1966. 'Zainteresowania teoretycznoliterackie Kazimierza Budzyka.' Afterword to *Stylistyka. Poetyka. Teoria literatury* by Kazimierz Budzyk, 199–219. Breslau: Zakład Narodowy im. Ossolińskich.
- 1974. *Dzieło. Język. Tradycja*. Warsaw: Państwowe Wydawnictwo Naukowe.
Slemon, Stephen. 1988. 'Post-Colonial Allegory and the Transformation of History.' *Journal of Commonwealth Literature* 23, no. 1: 157–68.
Sollers, Philippe. 1983. *Femmes*. Paris: Gallimard.
Šor, R. 1929. 'V.N. Volosinov. Marxism i filosofija jazyka.' *Russkij jazyk v skole* 3: 149v54.

Špet, Gustav. 1922–3. *Estetičeskie fragmenty*. 3 vols. Petersburg: Knigoizdatel'stvo 'Kolos.'

Spinoza, Benedict. 1985. *Ethics*. In *The Collected Works of Spinoza*, vol. 1, edited by Edwin Curley, 408–617. Princeton: Princeton University Press.

Stalnaker, R.J. 1987. *Inquiry*. Cambridge: MIT Press.

Stanford, W.B., ed. and trans. 1958. *The Odyssey of Homer*. 2nd ed. 2 vols. New York: St. Martin's Press.

Stewart, Susan. 1986. 'Shouts on the Street: Bakhtin's Anti-Linguistics.' In *Bakhtin: Essays and Dialogues on His Work*, edited by G.S. Morson. Chicago: University of Chicago Press.

Subotin, S. 1958. 'Knjieževno-teoretska shvatanja Manfreda Kridla.' *Umjetnost riječi* 2, no. 2: 171–83.

Svenbro, Jesper. 1976. *La Parole et le marbre: Aux origines de la poëtique grecque*. Lund: Studentlitteratur.

Thalmann, William G. 1984. *Conventions of Form and Thought in Early Greek Poetry*. Baltimore: Johns Hopkins University Press.

Thorlby, A., ed. 1969. *Penguin Companion to European Literature*. New York: McGraw-Hill.

Titunik, I.R. 1984. 'Bakhtin &/or Voloshinov &/or Medvedev: Dialogue &/or Doubletalk?' In *Language and Literary Theory*, edited by B.A. Stolz et al., 535–64. Ann Arbor: Michigan Slavic Publications.

Todorov, Tzvetan. 1969. *Grammaire du Décameron*. The Hague: Mouton.

– 1981. *Mikhaïl Baktine: Le principe dialogique*. Paris: Seuil.

Trahman, Carl R. 1952. 'Odysseus' Lies (*Odyssey*, Books 13–19).' *Phoenix* 6: 31–43.

Tynianov, Iurii N. 1975. *Death and Diplomacy in Persia*. Translation of *Smert Vazir-Mukhtara* (1938) by Alec Brown. Westport: Hyperion Press.

Tynianov, Iurii N., and Roman Jakobson. 1978. 'Problems in the Study of Literature and Language.' In *Readings in Russian Poetics: Formalist and Structuralist Views*, edited by L. Matejka and K. Pomorska, 79–81. Ann Arbor: Michigan Slavic Publications.

Ulčinaite, E. 1984. *Teoria retoryczna w Polsce i na Litwie w XVII wieku*. Breslau: Zaklad Narodowy im. Ossolińskich.

Vattimo, Giani. 1985. *Les aventures de la différence*. Paris: Minuit.

Vaughan, Michael. 1982. 'Literature and Politics: Currents in South African Writing in the Seventies.' *Journal of Southern African Studies* 9, no. 1: 118–38.

Veltrusky, Jiri. 1984. 'Semiotic Notes on Dialogue in Literature.' In *Language and Literary Theory: In Honour of Ladislav Matejka*, edited by Benjamin A. Stolz, I.R. Titunik, and Lubomír Doležel, 595–607. Ann Arbor: University of Michigan Press.

Verga, Giovanni. 1969. *Documenti e prefazioni del romanzo italiano dell'800*, edited by R. Bertacchini. Rome: Studium Editrice.

Voloshinov, V.N. 1973. *Marxism and Philosophy of Language.* Translated by L. Matejka and I.R. Titunik. Cambridge: Seminar Press; 2nd ed. Harvard University Press, 1986.

– 1976. *Freudianism: A Marxist Critique.* Translated by I.R. Titunik. New York: Academic Press.

von Glassersfeld, Ernst. 1985a. 'Einführung in den radikalen Konstruktivismus.' In *Die erfundene Wirklichkeit,* edited by P. Watzlawick, 16–38. Munich: Piper.

– 1985b. 'Konstruktion der Wirklichkeit und der Begriffs Objektivität.' In *Einführung der Konstruktivismus,* edited by H. Gumin and A. Mohler, 1–26. Munich: Oldenbourg.

Walton, Kendall. 1978. 'How Remote Are Fictional Worlds from the Real World?' *Journal of Aesthetics and Art Criticism* 37: 11–23.

– 1984. 'Do We Need Fictional Entities? Notes toward a Theory.' *Aesthetics: Proceedings of the Eighth International Wittgenstein Symposium.* Vienna: Holder-Pichler-Temsky.

– 1990. *Mimesis as Make-Believe: On the Foundations of Representational Arts.* Cambridge: Harvard University Press.

Warhol, Robyn. 1989. *Gendered Interventions: Narrative Discourse in the Victorian Novel.* New Brunswick: Rutgers University Press.

Wellek, Rene, 1970. 'Leo Spitzer (1887–1960).' In *Discriminations,* 187–224. New Haven: Yale University Press.

Wellek, Rene., and Austin Warren. 1949. *Theory of Literature.* New York: Harcourt Brace Jovanovich.

Wilson, K.J. 1984. *The Incomplete Fiction.* Washington: Catholic University of America Press.

Wittgenstein, Ludwig. 1974. *Philosophical Grammar,* edited by Rush Rhees; translated by Anthony Kenny. Berkeley: University of California Press.

Wolterstorff, Nicholas. 1980. *Works and Worlds of Art.* Oxford: Clarendon.

Woods, John. 1974. *The Logic of Fiction: A Philosophical Sounding of Deviant Logic.* The Hague: Mouton.

Woolf, Virginia. 1953. *Mrs. Dalloway.* New York: Harcourt Brace Jovanovich/Harvest Books.

Wóycicki, K. 1961. 'Jedność stylowa utworu poetyckiego.' In *Teoria badań literackich w Polsce,* edited by Henryk Markiewicz, 1: 245–74. Cracow: Wydawnictwo Literackie.

Wyka, K., ed. 1960. *Zjazd naukowy polonistow 10–13 grudnia 1958.* Breslau: Zaklad Narodowy im. Ossolińskich.

Yu, Anthony C. 1988. 'History, Fiction and the Reading of Chinese Narrative.' *CLEAR* 10: 1–19.

Zéraffa, Michel. 1976. *Roman et société.* Paris: Presses Universitaires de France.

Zgorzelski, Czeslaw. 1957. 'Manfred Kridl, jego dziela i osobowość.' *Przegład Humanistyczny* 1, no. 1: 66–72.

– 1983. *Mistrzowie i ich dziela.* Cracow: Znak.